THE WISC-R COMPANION

Steve Truch, PhD

SPECIAL CHILD PUBLICATIONS / SEATTLE

**A Desk Reference
for the Wechsler Scales**

Copyright © 1989, by Steve Truch. All rights reserved. Printed in the United States of America. This book, or parts thereof, may not be reproduced, stored in a retrieval system, or transmitted, in any form or by any means, electronic, mechanical, photocopying, recording, or otherwise, without the prior written permission of the publisher.

Special Child Publications
J. B. Preston, Editor & Publisher
P.O. Box 33548
Seattle, Washington 98133

International Standard Book Number: 0-87562-100-7

98	97	96	95	94	93	92	91	90	89
10	9	8	7	6	5	4	3	2	1

Library of Congress Cataloging-in-Publication Data

Truch, Stephen
    The WISC-R companion.

    Bibliography: p.
    Includes index.
    1. Wechsler Intelligence Scale for Children
I. Title.
BF432.5.W42T78   1989   155.4'13'0287   88-35570
ISBN 0-87562-100-7

Contents

Introduction	7
Chapter 1	
Questions Frequently Asked about the WISC-R	9
Chapter 2	
Intelligence and the WISC-R: Some Considerations	21
What Is Intelligence?	21
Is Intelligence Fixed?	24
How Much Can Intelligence Scores Change?	25
Importance of the Home	31
Intelligence—More Definitions	32
What Is Potential, Anyway?	32
Interpreting a WISC-R Score: Some Initial Considerations	39
Diagnosing Learning Disabilities in North America	48
Chapter 3	
Affective Considerations in WISC-R Testing and Reading Success	57
Success, Promise, Confidence: Breaking the Stress Cycle	59
Chapter 4	
Two Reading Models and Some Links to WISC-R Testing	71
What Is Reading?	71
The Psycholinguistic Model of Reading	73
Beginning Reading—Another Look	76
The Bilateral Cooperative Reading Model	82
Remedial Teaching Strategies	88
Chapter 5	
WISC-R Interpretation: Levels I and II	97
Level I—The Full Scale IQ Score	99
Level II—Verbal and Performance IQs; Three-Factor Splits	108
Three-Factor Splits	123
Gifted Students and the WISC-R	132
Chapter 6	
Level III and IV Interpretation of the WISC-R	145
Level III Interpretation	145
The WISC-R and Learning Styles	146
Level III Interpretation: Subtest-Specific Strengths and Weaknesses	168
Level IV Interpretation: Patterns within a Subtest	171
Chapter 7	
Level V WISC-R Interpretation	173
Verbal Subtests	173
Performance Subtests	180
Temporal Plotting	186
Afterword	191
Sources and Annotations	193

Appendices

2-1.	The "Language-Immersion" Environment	203
2-2.	Using Imagery to Improve Story Recall and Comprehension	213
2-3.	Teaching Sequencing	215
2-4.	Distractibility	217
2-5.	Assisting Sight-Word Acquisition	221
3-1.	Self-Rating Scales for Teacher Effectiveness	223
3-2.	Potential Reinforcers	229
3-3.	Hints for Successful Study at Home	231
3-4.	Changing "Learned Helplessness"	233
3-5.	Relaxation Procedures for Teachers and Students	237
5-1.	Word Banks and Word Sorts	241
5-2.	Written Expression	247
5-3.	Self-Instructional Training for Arithmetic Operations	257
6-1.	Reciprocal Teaching: A Strategy for "Word-Callers"	259
Index		263
The Author		269

Index of Figures

1.1.	Jason's WISC-R profile	13
2.1.	Vernon's model	22
2.2.	Guilford's model	23
2.3.	A WISC-R profile showing a three-factor split	36
2.4.	The normal curve	39
2.5.	A completed WISC-R profile, graphing strengths and weaknesses	44
2.6.	A completed WISC-R profile, strengths and weaknesses within the average range	45
4.1.	Schematic diagram of the psycholinguistic model of reading	73
4.2.	Jason's WISC-R profile	81
4.3.	The bilateral cooperative model of reading	84
4.4.	Functions of tracks in the bilateral cooperative model	85
4.5.	Individual education plan	88
4.6.	Michael's second-grade WISC-R profile	95
5.1.	Hierarchical factor structure of the WISC-R	98
5.2.	Characteristics of educable mentally handicapped students	103
5.3.	Reading comprehension development strategies for educable mentally handicapped students	105
5.4.	Index of specific outcomes (ISOs) for basic skills, cognitive skills, and affective measures	107
5.5.	Verbal-Performance relationships	109
5.6.	Semantic mapping of the seasons of the year	115
5.7.	Refined semantic map of one of the seasons of the year	116
5.8.	Using a keyword (1)	117

5.9.	Using a keyword (2)	118
5.10.	Basic list of 99 multiple-meaning words	122
5.11.	Semantic map of a multiple-meaning word	122
5.12.	The effect of individual differences in the development of selective attention at various age levels	126
5.13.	The enrichment triad model	134
5.14.	Michael's WISC-R profile	136
5.15.	Jonathan's WISC-R profile	137
5.16.	Thomas' first-grade WISC-R profile	139
5.17.	Thomas' fourth-grade WISC-R profile	141
6.1.	Example of profile of strengths and weaknesses	147
6.2.	Diagnosing learning styles	148
6.3.	A WISC-R profile which suggests a field-dependent orientation	152
6.4.	Simultaneous/successive split, favoring simultaneous processing	157
6.5.	Picture Completion / Object Assembly split in WISC-R profile	164
6.6.	A prediction map	165
7.1.	An attributional model of achievement motivation	181
7.2.	Field sensitive and field independent teaching strategies	182
7.3.	A traditional graph of "Emma's" WISC-R performance	187
7.4.	A temporal plot of "Emma's" WISC-R performance	188
7.5.	WISC-R subtests arranged temporally	189

Index of Tables

1.1.	Shared abilities and influences	14
2.1.	Estimated WISC-R deviation IQs for Factors I, II, and III	51
2.2.	WISC-R scores and percentile ranks	53
2.3.	WISC-R IQ scores and percentile ranks (abbreviated version)	56
5.1.	Mean IQ of different professional and occupational groups	101
5.2.	AAMD classifications of mental retardation, with descriptions of developmental characteristics	102
5.3.	Comparison of methods with achievement in terms of percent-correct	121
5.4.	Error types: comparison of percentage total error for regular, mentally handicapped, and learning-disabled student groups	128

Acknowledgments

I would like to credit some of the very knowledgeable and experienced educators I've had the privilege of working with over the years. Their ideas, in one fashion or another, have found their way into this book.

In particular, Karen Clark, reading specialist and author, has been most helpful. I have woven her materials into some of the Appendices, and I would like to thank her for her kind permission to do so. I would also like to thank Marilyn Znider, Jo-Ann Koch, and Linda Nosbush for their assistance and suggestions over the years. Thank you all, for what you've taught me!

I would like to thank my family for their continued encouragement and support.

The publisher of this volume, J. B. Preston, joins me in expressing thanks to the Psychological Corporation for extending permission to reproduce the face sheet of the WISC-R record form.

Finally, I would like to thank the many students and teachers I have met over the years who have motivated me to forever "keep digging" for new ideas that might prove helpful to them.

ST
Calgary
December 1988

Introduction

This book is intended primarily for practicing school psychologists and those who are in training for this field. Clinical and counseling psychologists who use the WISC-R should also find it of value. It will also be of interest to reading specialists, special educators, and those involved in the more general educational enterprise, such as regular class teachers, principals, supervisors and other administrators—all of whom must deal with the particular needs of the special child (that is, the child with one or another learning deficit) at some time or another.

This book is an aid to hypothesis generation concerning a particular child's learning patterns. Those educators who read this book, but who do not have specific training courses in psychology normally required for individualized test administration *cannot* and *should not* use this book as a substitute for interpretation of the WISC-R by a qualified psychologist. Readers without proper training cannot assume that they are in a position to interpret WISC-R profiles, just because they read this book.

By the same token, school psychologists are not reading specialists. They cannot presume to prescribe reading programs or strategies exclusively based on WISC-R patterns. School psychologists need to have a deeper understanding of the reading process. They must understand sound teaching philosophies and reading methods, and be able to go considerably beyond using a reading test for screening and placement purposes only. This book will only scratch the surface of that area.

So, the school psychologist must know more about reading, and the reading specialist must know more about intelligence testing and other psychological interventions. That obviously implies that the two professions are very complementary, and that a team approach will best serve the disabled student. That is certainly my experience. When all the parties who are involved with a student—including parents—work in concert, they generate a most sound academic and behavioral set of strategies on behalf of that student.

Throughout this book, I use phrases like, ". . . suggested by the WISC-R." That is what I mean. These are suggestions only. And the person in the best position to determine what applies in a particular child's case, and what doesn't, is the qualified examiner: usually, the school psychologist, who in turn must act as a team member, rather than an ultimate authority. The school psychologist must interpret hypotheses in light of teacher and parent observations about the student, as well as his own. Before suggestions become written recommendations, the school psychologist must consult with many of the "significant others" involved with the student.

I am sensitive to the fact that a book of this nature (one which, I have been told many times, is "impossible," to begin with), could be abused. I will, therefore, state again: *Only qualified, well-trained personnel* should be interpreting the WISC-R. And, *only qualified, well-trained personnel*, reading specialists, should be interpreting reading tests. But there is a great deal of room for overlap, and this book is intended as a true *companion* to those efforts.

I have been a consulting psychologist to several school districts for more than a decade. During that time, I have seen thousands of students on an individual basis, and have consulted with as many teachers on a variety of psychological/learning problems. Questions of cognitive ability and individual strengths and weaknesses frequently arise, particularly in the case of students with learning disabilities or other handicapping conditions. Like many of my colleagues, I use the WISC-R frequently to help answer pertinent questions. Despite the development of new intelligence tests, such as the *Kaufman Assessment Battery for Children* (K-ABC), the WISC-R is still the most widely used intelligence test; and, in my opinion, it is likely to remain so for some time to come.

I am always impressed by what the WISC-R does and does not tell me. Being a practical person, I'm also always on the look-out for teaching implications that can legitimately be teased out of WISC-R profiles on individual students, especially in terms of remedial reading. And that presents another problem. I am well aware of the dangers of extrapolating directly from WISC-R profiles to individual reading programs. This book doesn't do that. It's only an attempt to help bridge the gap that does exist. The WISC-R is *not* a reading test. Nor is it a complete test. It does not tell us everything about a child. No test possibly could. To ignore what *does* lie in the WISC-R profile in terms of the various academic implications it suggests, however, is to ignore a wealth of potentially invaluable information. But the WISC-R is only *part* of a battery of formal and informal tests and observations about a student. And that fact should not be forgotten.

There is always the danger that psychologists who read this book will go directly to scores and numbers and ignore the individual student. This is *not* a cookbook. The behaviors and intentions and feelings of the student that come across as he or she is being tested, are vital, and are as much a part of the student as any score. It is a great disservice to ignore such behaviors. They are, in fact, part of the diagnostic process. All score interpretations must be complemented by what we know about and observe about the student in a variety of environments across time. That means input from teachers, parents, and other professionals is extremely valuable. It has taken me over fifteen years to accumulate the background knowledge and professional experience just to attempt this project. In those fifteen years, I have never stopped my professional reading. And yet, I still feel *inadequate* in many ways to interpret WISC-R profiles. I am humbled by the astonishing background needed to interpret the WISC-R. An equally astonishing background is needed to track down all the educational implications suggested by what are seemingly simple scores. This book can only be a *beginning*, then, for the sensitive psychologist.

The published material now available on educational implications of the WISC-R is often offered with no rationale at all, or giving only splintered suggestions for teaching to individual WISC-R subtests—a conceptually and psychometrically very unsound practice. The suggestions that are made in this book—particularly in the appendices—are meant primarily for the school psychologist who is looking for something practical to share with a teacher. Exercises are to be modified by the team approach. One cannot, however, ignore the theoretical underpinnings of various teaching strategies and how they might relate to a particular student with a particular WISC-R profile. Without the rationale, we risk reverting to the cookbook or shotgun approach, with our energies scattered in all directions except "on target." So, please bear with me as I provide some of the background information and theory that supports a particular technique that I'm advocating. I think you will find it interesting anyway. I think you'll also quickly realize that interpreting the WISC-R is a something of an artistic endeavor, requiring much skill and ability to synthesize conclusions from the information before you.

I truly hope that those who read this book will find it a useful resource for developing some practical teaching implications and strategies as they particularly arise from using the WISC-R. These are to be then artfully implemented in the remedial programs of those wonderful, special students who *need* our very best expertise as they grapple with their sometimes overwhelming educational challenges.

Chapter 1

Questions Frequently Asked about the WISC-R

School psychologists are frequently asked very basic questions about the WISC-R and intelligence testing in general by teachers and parents. Here are 30 of the more common ones. The questions and their answers should provide the reader with a good overview and serve as background information for some of the remaining chapters.

1. *What is the WISC-R? Is it an intelligence test?*

The *Wechsler Intelligence Scale for Children–Revised* (WISC-R), is one of a class of individual intelligence (or IQ, for intelligence quotient) tests. It is an individual test because it must be administered by a qualified examiner on a one-to-one basis with a student. There are also *group* IQ tests which can be administered, often by classroom teachers themselves, to a whole class. Scores on the two kinds of tests are related, but the individual test obviously provides more reliable data and more information about how a student responds to a formal, problem-solving situation.

2. *What is the history of the WISC-R? How was it developed?*

Alfred Binet is considered the real father of intelligence tests. The Binet-Simon "1905 Scale" was the first IQ test. It was designed to help separate mentally handicapped students from non-mentally-handicapped students in the Paris public school system. The test was readily accepted all over the world, and was first introduced in the U.S. by Henry Goddard in 1908. Since then, a number of revisions were made and are still being made to the Binet test.

David Wechsler, an American, conceptualized intelligence as the "overall capacity of an individual to understand and cope with the world around him." He developed the Wechsler-Bellevue test in the 1930s to measure adult intelligence. The *Wechsler Intelligence Scale for Children* (WISC) was developed in 1949 as a downward extension of the Wechsler-Bellevue.

Unlike the Stanford-Binet, the WISC did not employ the *mental age* concept for measuring IQ. (Using this concept, the IQ score is calculated by taking the student's tested mental age, dividing it by the chronological age, and multiplying by 100.) Rather, it uses a *deviation IQ* method which determines how far a student's score deviates (if at all) from the scores of a representative sample of his or her peers. In 1974, the WISC was extensively revised and became the WISC-R.

3. *Why do you administer an IQ test?*

An IQ test is administered when one wants information about a student's cognitive profile—how the student thinks and reasons. The WISC-R is often used to obtain such information because it samples both verbal and nonverbal aspects of intelligence. Such information is particularly valuable when a student is experiencing difficulty with school-related work. In the hands of an experienced tester, the WISC-R can help to generate a number of hypotheses (which can lead to further, more precise diagnosis), and lead to recommendations designed to help a student perform or feel better about school.

4. *What are some of the pros and cons of IQ testing?*

Probably the most serious criticism against IQ tests is that they are culturally biased, particularly against blacks. Another criticism that has been raised is that of the "self-fulfilling prophesy" (i.e., knowing that a student has a "low IQ" could lead to negative consequences, even a withdrawal of educational services). This kind of thinking is typified by the rhetorical question, "After all, why bother, if the student is just really slow?" Or, perhaps a more subtle kind of behavior change on the teacher's part takes place, so that the student receives less attention, less praise, and so on. This leads to less learning, and perpetuates the vicious circle. Other criticisms are that a single IQ score does not do justice to the many aspects of thinking, does not get at the underlying thought processes, and serves only to stereotype students.

An advantage of IQ testing (at least for individual IQ tests) is that a profile of strengths and weaknesses can be obtained. This *can* lead to improved educational planning. It has also been my experience that, when a teacher discovers that a student has a "low IQ" score, the tendency is to respond to the challenge that that score represents, rather than using it as an excuse not to bother. It would be naive, however, to think that "not bothering" *never* happens. Sometimes, students with undiscovered or unrecognized abilities are "discovered" via IQ testing. This has happened many times in my experience. Furthermore, IQ tests are useful tools to see how students *do* differ and compare with each other on a number of standardized tasks. IQ scores are good predictors of academic achievement and success in other areas, as well.

An IQ test in the right hands is a proper diagnostic tool. It is not, however, a be-all and end-all. An IQ score is only the *start* for better educational planning and prescription via the team approach. The IQ score should *never* be interpreted in a rigid fashion, or as being indicative of "innate, unchanging, genetic ability." IQ tests measure learning across a wide spectrum of tasks. They tell us how students compare with each other in our culture.

5. *What is intelligence, anyway?*

An excellent question. Much of the next chapter is devoted to answering it. For me, intelligence is a kind of purposeful "mental energy" that we use to guide our actions in virtually everything we do. It is guided by the self, or ego—the inner, most personal core of our being.

6. How much training do you need to administer the WISC-R?

The administration and interpretation of individual IQ tests such as the WISC-R, the Stanford-Binet, the McCarthy Scales, and K-ABC, is generally taught at the graduate level over a full year's time or more, and is usually part of a program leading to the MA or PhD degree in psychology or educational psychology. Close supervision is required, to ensure that the novice examiner is trained in some of the "finer points" of administration and interpretation. Considerable practice is required before a person is ready to administer and interpret test results for school purposes. (Some training departments, and even state laws, have added an element of "secretiveness" to the WISC-R which, I think, only contributes to the unfounded beliefs that people have about intelligence tests.)

The point is, *extensive* training is required to administer and interpret the WISC-R. In fact, the school psychologist should *never stop* reading in this area, in order to keep fine-tuning his or her interpretation skills.

7. *Can a classroom teacher administer the WISC-R?*

Because of the extensive training required, the answer is definitely *no*. More unfortunately, classroom teachers generally do not receive *any* training in the interpretation of IQ scores. Frequently, teachers are completely misinformed, or not informed at all, or hold a number of unfounded beliefs about IQ testing and what it represents. As a result, they too fall victim to the many myths that abound about the IQ and what it may mean for any one student. So, school psychologists who inform teachers about the results of an IQ test cannot take anything for granted. Simply telling a teacher an IQ score is certainly not good enough. Information needs to be passed on carefully and followed with a written report of the results. Follow-up of educational recommendations is terribly important. As a member of the educational team, the school psychologist's job is to interpret the WISC-R in terms of the educational implications it has, to consult with the reading specialist about how the hypotheses which are generated can be put into practical reading and other academic strategies, to discuss and help implement these recommendations with the remedial or classroom teacher, and, of course, to convey all this to the parents.

8. *Is the WISC-R highly regarded by psychologists? What about educators? Do principals know about it? Do reading specialists know about it?*

The WISC-R and the Stanford-Binet (which has recently undergone extensive revision) are generally highly regarded by psychologists. This is so for a number of reasons. These tests provide valid and reliable IQ scores when properly administered. Vast sums of money are spent by test publishers to ensure that the tests are well-standardized (i.e., have representative children from different socioeconomic levels, equal numbers of boys and girls, proportionately the same number of urban and rural children as are found in the population at large, and proportionate numbers of minority groups). The scores themselves have reasonably small measurement error and the items are rigorously analyzed to see that they discriminate properly.

Because of the high regard for the WISC-R held by psychologists, this attitude is generally passed on to educators. Again, though, most of this group—principals, resource teachers, reading specialists, other administrators, and supervisors—generally know very little about the WISC-R unless they received this information in their training or sought it out themselves. For the majority of educators, however, such knowledge is lacking.

9. *What ages does the WISC-R cover?*

The WISC-R can be administered to students who have just turned six, or are as old as 16 years, 11 months: virtually the entire school-age years, in other words.

10. *How subjective is the scoring on the WISC-R?*

Subjectivity *can* enter into scoring some responses on the WISC-R, and it is a factor that every examiner must remain conscious of. The WISC-R manual provides guidelines for scoring all the subtests. Those on the Verbal Scale, however, are more likely to have scoring errors, resulting from the wide range of possible responses. Simple errors in addition can also occur, resulting in mistakes on the reported IQ score. Examiners need to double-check their scoring and adding to help minimize such errors.

Despite the element of subjectivity, there is still a very high degree of test-retest reliability on the WISC-R (i.e., the IQ score will be very consistent from one testing to the next). Though gross errors can and do occur, their frequency can be minimized.

11. *How does the student's mood on the day of testing affect the test scores? For example, does lack of sleep or breakfast affect it? Would you get better results under more favorable conditions?*

The WISC-R examiner always tries to make sure a student is tested under optimal conditions. If there is evidence that the student has experienced some untoward stress prior to testing, it would remain at the examiner's discretion to determine whether testing should even proceed. Lack of sleep and/or breakfast is common among some students. Again, the examiner has to determine whether such conditions affected the test results to any appreciable degree. Any major or minor stress that the student has recently experienced should be noted in the examiner's report, as well as the examiner's opinion on how it may have affected the results.

12. *If a student is really afraid, does this affect his performance? Does the student get an explanation of what's happening, and would it matter? What about self-concept? Does it affect results?*

Sometimes, it looks to a teacher as if an examiner just takes the student into a room and does something to him or her—"tests" the student. Of course, the WISC-R is a formal and important test; but examiners are trained to first establish rapport with the student, including some explanation of what is happening, and why. This is generally quite easy to do with experience. *Some* degree of anxiety is not necessarily a bad thing, as it can actually facilitate test performance, so an initial degree of fear or anxiety is common among students. Usually, it disappears quickly as testing proceeds. If it doesn't, again, it needs to be noted, or testing needs to be discontinued. Some of the WISC-R subtests are more affected by anxiety than others, particularly the timed ones. In my personal experience, however, I have rarely encountered a student who was so afraid that he or she could not be tested.

"Self-concept" is a very general term. If a student lacks confidence in himself, and fails to take risks or make guesses on the WISC-R, then, yes, the score will be lower than it might otherwise have been.

For all of the reasons we have been discussing, a WISC-R score should never be stated without its "error band." There is built-in measurement error on every test, because what we are measuring cannot be done with the precision that lies in, say, a yardstick or a thermometer. A score should therefore be reported as, for example, 100 ± 6. The "± 6" is the "confidence band" of the Full Scale IQ score on the WISC-R. It means that, if the student were tested 100 times, then 95 times out of the 100 (a 95 percent confidence level), the Full Scale IQ score would fall between 94 and 106.

So, if a student seemed overly anxious, or did not have a full breakfast, the Full Scale IQ score probably lies closer to the upper level of the confidence band. The Full Scale IQ is *not* a precise score, cast in concrete.

13. *If a student is on medication, how does this affect the test score?*

It would depend on the medication. If it were a major tranquilizer, it might have more of an effect than, say, Ritalin.™ Ritalin™ or Cylert™ are, unfortunately, fairly commonly administered to hyperactive students, who in turn are often referred for individual intellectual testing. The chances of having a student who is on Ritalin™ come for WISC-R testing is therefore quite high. This drug does have some effect on some of the WISC-R subtests, particularly Digit Span and Coding, raising performance by a few points. Digit Span is an optional subtest, so it is not used in calculating the Full Scale IQ anyway. Coding, however, is part of the Performance Scale, so it *is* used to calculate the Full Scale IQ. Some students will do paper-and-pencil tasks better on Ritalin,™ and Coding is such a task. Again, if it is known that the student is on Ritalin™ when the WISC-R is administered, then its possible effect on the score needs to be stated in the report.

14. *You keep mentioning "Full Scale IQ." What is that?*

The WISC-R consists of 12 subtests, six on the "Verbal Scale," and six on the "Performance Scale." The raw score the student receives on each subtest is converted to a standard score, called a "scale score," by using a set of tables provided in the manual. There is a different table for every three-month age band from 6 years, zero months (6-0), to 16 years, 11 months (16-11). The student is therefore compared to others his own age within a very narrow age band. The examiner adds up the scale-score totals for each Verbal and Performance subtest, and then adds these sums. The total scale score is then converted to a single score, the "Full Scale IQ" score, by using yet another table in the WISC-R manual.

A Verbal and a Performance IQ score are calculated. This gives three IQ scores for every WISC-R profile: the Verbal IQ, the Performance IQ, and the Full Scale IQ. A profile of the subtest scores can also be graphed on the face sheet of the WISC-R test protocol, which looks like the one shown in Figure 1.1.

Note the Verbal IQ, Performance IQ, and Full Scale IQ scores in the lower right corner. The scale scores on the profile are also graphed in. A Verbal and a Performance scale score average is also calculated, and significant strengths (S) and weaknesses (W) are noted. These form the basis for further hypotheses and interpretation.

15. *What does each WISC-R subtest measure?*

Every WISC-R subtest has something in common with one or more of the other subtests. This cannot be forgotten when it comes to interpretation. In fact, when two or more subtests share something in common, that result is more reliable than the results of one subtest alone. The following, Table 1.1, shows some shared abilities and influences on the WISC-R.

When interpreting WISC-R subtest results, this table should be consulted first, before making any subtest-specific interpretations.

With that said, following Figure 1.1 and Table 1.1 is a list of the WISC-R subtests and the unique ability each subtest measures.

FIGURE 1.1. Jason's WISC-R profile.

TABLE 1.1. Shared abilities and influences.

Abilities and Influences	Verbal Scale I S A V C DS	Performance Scale PC PA BD OA Co M
Abilities:		
Verbal Comprehension	• • •	
Acquired Knowledge	• • •	
Memory	• • •	
Abstract Thinking	• • •	
Long-Term Memory	• • •	
Verbal Expression	• • •	
Perceptual Organization		• • • • •
Spatial Reasoning		• • • •
Right-Brain Processing		• • •
Integrated Brain Functioning		• • • •
Paper and Pencil Skill		• •
Planning Ability		• •
Visual Memory		• •
Freedom from Distractibility	• • •	•
Sequencing	• • •	(•) •
Facility with Numbers	• • •	•
Social Judgment	• •	•
Influences:		
Anxiety	• • •	•
Field Dependent/Independent		• •
Extent of Outside Reading	• • •	
Richness of Early Environment	• •	
Working under Time Pressure	•	• • • • •
Simultaneous/Successive Proc.		Si Su Si Si Su Su

Adapted from: Kaufman, A. 1979. *Intelligent testing with the WISC-R*. New York: John Wiley.

Verbal Subtests

- Information—general factual knowledge
- Similarities—logical abstract thinking with verbal categories
- Arithmetic—mental computational skill
- Vocabulary—lexical knowledge and language development
- Comprehension—verbalizing practical information; evaluating and using past experience
- Digit Span—auditory short-term memory for random numbers

Performance Subtests

- Picture Completion—visual long-term memory and visual alertness
- Picture Arrangement—sequencing and anticipating consequences
- Block Design—nonverbal reasoning; spatial visualization; analysis of an abstract design into its component parts
- Object Assembly—flexibility; anticipating part-whole relationships
- Coding—psychomotor speed; ability to follow directions
- Mazes—foresight; following a visual pattern

Everything measured on the WISC-R has been learned, usually incidentally, in the course of growing up in our culture. The test therefore measures how well students have learned these processes compared to each other.

16. *How much reading is involved in administering the WISC-R?*

On the part of the student, virtually none. All items are read by the examiner, and the student responds either verbally or manually. The last three items of the Arithmetic subtest are to be read by the student; but, even here, the examiner may read the items if the student has difficulty.

This is yet another reason to favor an individually administered test over a group IQ test. In a group test, students must read the questions themselves. If they have reading difficulties, then you will not obtain a fair sample of their reasoning ability.

17. *What are the effects of a handicap like hearing or vision impairment on intelligence? What about an undiagnosed hearing problem?*

If the student has a known hearing handicap but is wearing a hearing aid which corrects or partly corrects it, the WISC-R can be administered, although the Performance Scale is likely to be more valid than the Verbal Scale in such cases. If the student has a visual handicap, then the Verbal Scale of the WISC-R is the more useful measure. There is also a special adaptation of the Stanford-Binet test, called the Hayes-Binet, that can be used specifically for blind children.

Undiagnosed hearing problems could possibly show up on the WISC-R in the form of a low Verbal, higher Performance IQ split. I do know of some cases where a hearing problem was discovered through WISC-R testing in this way. It is not just a pattern of scores that does this, however; it is keen observation on the part of the examiner.

All students, particularly those in special education classes, should have at least a routine audiometric and vision screening. This is frequently done, particularly in Canada, by public health nurses, for all school-age children.

As far as these handicaps and their effect on intelligence are concerned, blind children tend to score in the average range as a group, but their distribution of scores is not "normal." There are more blind children who score in the superior as well as inferior ranges. This distribution is called a *bi-modal* one. Deaf children seem to obtain lower Verbal IQ scores, while the results on Performance kinds of tests are mixed. Some studies show them doing worse than normally-hearing students on Performance items, while others show them doing as well, or even better.

When testing such handicapped students with the WISC-R, the examiner must be particularly alert to how the handicap is affecting the responses of *this* particular child. The examiner must also be extremely cautious in interpreting the results themselves as being a fair measure of the child's potential.

18. *How much does language affect the WISC-R? Could a foreign student, for example, take it?*

The student's knowledge of his own language is an important component of intelligence. Such knowledge constitutes a very important part of the WISC-R—the Verbal Scale. Language is also involved in giving instructions to the student in all the other WISC-R subtests. The only truly culture-fair test, therefore, would be one where the items came from the child's culture, were asked in the child's native tongue by examiners from the same culture, and, most importantly, where the scores were *normed* in that culture. Whenever we administer an IQ test like the WISC-R to a minority-group child, then the element of fairness must always be considered.

The examiner must therefore be extremely cautious and sensitive to language differences in our own culture, particularly black dialect and Mexican-American language differences. Minority students may do better on the WISC-R for examiners of their own culture; but the key to any student's responding is the initial positive rapport and understanding that must be established right at the beginning of testing. The examiner must be knowledgeable enough about cultural and language differences that could affect WISC-R performance. Students should not be penalized for use of language that is "different" from the dominant culture, especially where such language is perfectly acceptable in the student's own community. The examiner should therefore first become acquainted with any regional differences that might exist in a particular geographic area.

It should be obvious, then, that a student has to have a solid exposure to the English language before the WISC-R can be considered a fair measure of reasoning ability. If a student is bilingual, the examiner should be aware of it and remain cautious when it comes to interpretation of the IQ score.

Students who have recently learned English, or who are just learning English, cannot be tested with valid results. The only purpose a WISC-R would serve in such cases would be as an informal assessment of a student's *current* language functioning. In no way would it be a measure of "intelligence."

Sometimes, useful information can come out of specific subtests. The Block Design subtest is considered the most culture-fair of the WISC-R subtests. I recall assessing one Vietnamese student using the Performance Scale only. The child could not speak a word of English. She displayed extraordinary flexibility and reasoning skill on the Block Design subtest, however; and, in fact, she obtained the highest possible scale score. I felt her academic prognosis was excellent, even though it was not possible to calculate a single WISC-R IQ score. Had a portion of the WISC-R not been administered, her facility in some reasoning areas would not have come to light.

19. *Is the WISC-R used in other countries?*

The WISC-R has been translated into a number of different languages, including Chinese. The difficulty with direct translations is that we cannot expect students in other cultures very different from ours to ever have been exposed to some of the content. Since the WISC-R measures what students have learned, once exposed to a "common" environment, then we cannot expect it, or any other test, to be universally applicable. The WISC-R is best used in the English-speaking Western world, and *is* widely used, as is the Stanford-Binet, in those nations.

20. *How does the WISC-R compare with the Stanford-Binet?*

The two tests measure intelligence, but from different perspectives. For Binet and Simon, intelligence was the ability to "judge, comprehend, and reason well." They were very interested in individual differences in such ability in a number of areas, such as memory, imagination, attention, comprehension, and esthetic appreciation. Despite this, their test yielded only one global IQ score, based on the mental-age construct.

For Wechsler, intelligence was the global capacity of the individual to deal effectively with his environment. Neither Binet nor Wechsler had particularly well-delineated definitions of intelligence. Despite this, their tests have more than stood the tests of time.

The two tests do correlate with each other. The correlation between the Stanford-Binet and the Full Scale WISC-R IQ is about .73 on the average. This shows that they both measure something very similar; but, at the same time, there is enough difference in the tests so that the constructs are not identical.

IQ scores from the two tests are roughly similar. When students are measured on the Stanford-Binet and then the WISC-R, they score only about two points higher on the Binet at ages six, nine, and twelve. At age 16, they score about two points higher on the WISC-R.

The Stanford-Binet is still widely used today, though probably not as much as the WISC-R. It is more difficult to administer, being more cumbersome, especially for very young children;

and it is difficult to interpret scores beyond the global IQ score, since it is not composed of two major scales like the WISC-R. Current revisions of the Stanford-Binet, however, attempt to take such criticisms into account. The new version (1986, 4th ed.) might become a very useable test for practitioners, even though at the moment it is meeting with rather severe criticisms.

The Binet's strength lies in the fact that it can be administered to children as young as age two. In addition, the IQ scores go well below and well above the limits of the WISC-R. On the WISC-R, no student can score an IQ below 40 or above 160. Some students have functional IQ levels below and above these limits, so the Binet is often a better test to use to assess students who may be profoundly mentally handicapped or exceptionally talented in intelligence.

21. *Does the WISC-R take into account cultural differences, environmental deprivation, varying socioeconomic levels, and so on?*

The WISC-R was standardized on a wide cross-section of children from various ethnic groups and varying socioeconomic backgrounds. The standardization sample conforms very closely to the 1970 United States census (this poses a slight problem for Canadian children). You can say, then in that sense the test itself takes into account such differences insofar as relative ranking goes. But it does not eliminate the *advantage* that a particular group (such as students from highly educated parents) might have on the WISC-R.

As well, the results achieved by one *particular* child is a different matter. Children who have experienced extreme deprivation, for example, may be functioning very low at one point in time, but could be much brighter and score higher on the WISC-R, once placed in a more intensive, stimulating environment.

The question of environmental deprivation is a very interesting one, which I will discuss in more depth in the next chapter. Meanwhile, examiners must be very cautious in interpreting a score as a measure of "potential."

22. *Is creativity measured by the WISC-R? What about special talents?*

Creativity is difficult both to define and to measure. It is *not* measured by the WISC-R. Neither are any of a class of special talents such as musical or athletic aptitude, leadership skills, social skills, and so on. Intelligence is only one part of the whole child. Other measures and behavioral observations about a child are needed to provide a better picture of the student as a total person.

23. *Does the WISC-R indicate mental illness or other states of mental instability or emotional disturbance?*

The WISC-R cannot be used to *diagnose* such conditions. If a child is extremely unstable, however, it is quite likely that his responses, particularly to the more open-ended Verbal subtests, will be bizarre. The examiner needs to determine just how unconventional any response or behavior is, and do some further diagnostic work, to help determine to what degree any student is mentally ill or disturbed. If a student is psychotic, for example, his behavior will usually be so bizarre that the student is institutionalized long before any referral for intelligence testing is made.

Sometimes, there are some patterns which appear on the WISC-R which *suggest* emotional disturbance; but such a pattern *by itself* is *not* a diagnosis, and should never be interpreted as such.

24. *Does the WISC-R diagnose brain damage?*

Again, there are some patterns and responses that the student may make which could be associated with organic brain damage. Brain damage can be very localized or very diffuse (i.e., spread over various areas of the brain). No one type of test or pattern, therefore, could possibly diagnose these. The examiner who suspects neurological difficulties needs to refer the student for a complete neuropsychological battery of tests to help pinpoint any damage which might be there.

25. *Can students "cheat" on the WISC-R? Can an examiner recognize that? Can a student "fake good" or "fake bad"? Can a student lie?*

Students can try to do all these things, of course. It is impossible to "fake good," but it is certainly possible to "fake bad" on the test. For example, some students who may want to go to a special educational program such as vocational school, may not try hard on the test, deliberately trying to get a lower score which is sometimes a prerequisite to entrance into some programs. If a student is particularly clever about it, he may be able to fool an examiner some of the time. Most experienced examiners, however, can quickly recognize how much effort a student is making.

26. *How often would you administer a WISC-R to a student?*

The WISC-R, like most tests, is subject to a practice effect. This is especially true for the Performance Scale. The WISC-R should therefore be administered infrequently to the same student. Schools wishing to have IQ scores on students should sample ability with a group IQ test three or four times in the course of the twelve years of schooling.

The WISC-R is most often administered to students in special education, or who are eligible for special education classes. "Intelligence" is one factor which should be monitored for such students. IQ scores should be reviewed about every two years. If there is reason to believe that the score has changed, then the WISC-R or an alternative test could be administered.

Should the examiner need to readminister a WISC-R on one particular student, then six months is the minimum time that should be allowed to elapse between test administrations.

27. *Are kids labeled because of an IQ test score? Is this damaging?*

It certainly can be damaging. Group IQ scores are generally entered on a student's cumulative folder, which follows the student from teacher to teacher throughout his school years. If a teacher puts too much credence in a group IQ score given years before, than that might have a negative effect, depending on what the teacher *does* with such information. That is why intelligence should periodically be measured for more up-to-date results.

An IQ score, if valid, represents a picture of a student's functioning *at that time*. However, that picture can and does change in the course of the student's development.

WISC-R and other individual intelligence scores are not generally entered on a student's cumulative file. Such scores are confidential. Written parental approval is required in order to even administer the WISC-R. Furthermore, the results cannot be released to any agency or other professional without the parent's written permission.

28. *Should a student be informed of the results of the WISC-R? How about parents?*

There is a widespread belief that providing IQ results to people could be damaging. There is, however, little evidence to support that belief. Nevertheless, WISC-R results are normally not given to students. I have frequently discussed results with older students when they are eager for feedback, and have always had good results. Time and care must be taken to explain the results and their meaning. Students' questions usually reveal a number of mistaken beliefs about "IQ" scores.

Results of the WISC-R are almost always discussed with the student's parents in a face-to-face interview. Sometimes the examiners give only vague information to parents. Knowing their child has "average intelligence," for example, tells them nothing of the child's cognitive strengths and weaknesses. Parents should be given a full explanation of the results. This should include some definition of what intelligence is, how the normal curve works, and the error of measurement. It should also be stressed that the score represents a picture of the student's functioning at the present time, and is not to be construed as forever cast in concrete. The actual scores can also be given, but are probably best explained by using percentiles. Finally, the importance of the score in terms of the educational strategies that the testing and test results suggest, should be explained. In other words, parents need to know how the test directly helps their child in school.

29. *Does the WISC-R measure dyslexia?*

"Dyslexia" is a term generally reserved for certain severe cases of reading disability. Some specialists do not like the term at all because it represents a kind of medical term for what they say is essentially an educational problem.

In any case, the WISC-R does not diagnose dyslexia or any other kind of reading problem because it is not a reading test.

There are, however, certain WISC-R patterns which seem to accompany reading and other academic problems; but the presence of the WISC-R pattern cannot be used to *diagnose* the problem, since some students who have such patterns do not have *any* academic problems. The WISC-R is used to give some indication of a student's ability, and is only part of the picture of the whole child.

If a certain pattern *is* present on the WISC-R which suggests academic difficulties, these must be confirmed or denied with individual academic testing, teacher observations, other tests, etc.

30. *What will I, as a classroom or special education teacher, get out of it, once the WISC-R is administered? Does it pinpoint problems? Will I understand the student better? Will my expectations change? What recommendations might I expect?*

The WISC-R results should be explained by the examiner as carefully to a teacher as to a parent. The educational implications should be emphasized as much as possible. In most cases, that is what the teacher wants anyway. There is no question that the student will be understood much better and in greater depth as a result of WISC-R testing. Teacher and parent expectations might change, depending on what they were beforehand. One of the most important things to understand is that a student who has "average ability" may not be "average" in all areas. Therefore, expectations may have to be modified for certain skills as a result.

The recommendations that you as a teacher receive will depend on the student, of course, since we are dealing with individuals, and also upon the expertise of the examiner. They will also depend on how much time the examiner has to think about the results, and draw out all the educational implications possible. Most examiners have limited time because of long referral lists.

Chapter 2

Intelligence and the WISC-R: Some Considerations

What Is Intelligence?

The WISC-R measures intelligence. But what is intelligence? Many psychologists, from Alfred Binet to modern information-processing theorists, have offered their particular definition of this elusive word.

For Binet, the original developer of the IQ test, "intelligence" meant to comprehend, judge, and reason well. For Sir Cyril Burt, "intelligence" was primarily an innate (inherited) general ability. (Burt was obviously very committed to this view, since it was recently discovered that he falsified much of his "heritability" data.) David Wechsler defined "intelligence" as the global capacity of the individual to act purposefully, to think rationally, and to deal effectively with the environment. For Jean Piaget, adaptation to the environment via the processes of assimilation and accommodation expressed "intelligence" best. Piaget's thinking is the basis of much of modern information-processing descriptions of "intelligence." Certainly no one today views "intelligence" as a fixed, innate ability; but, like Piaget, more as a fluid, ever-changing "thing."

Spearman was the first to propose that "intelligence" was a kind of "mental energy." Although there are conceptual problems with this definition (there are, with all the definitions), I find it appealing. If we compare "mental energy" to electricity, for example, we find some similarities. Both are in the real world, although both are very subtle forms of energy. Both can be measured, stored, used in different ways, and transformed. Both depend on "wiring" to carry them. For electricity, this "wiring" may be copper or aluminum. For "intelligence," it is the type and complexity of the organism's brain and nervous system. Both are also subject to great fluctuations at any given time. There may be sudden "bursts" of energy, followed by periodic lows. This ebb and flow of energy continues throughout the life cycle of a person or, indeed, any living thing. "Intelligence," then, is certainly not fixed, but continually "more" or "less"—flowing and ever-changing in evanescence.

To me, intelligence is expressed and observed as the orderly, purposeful flow of this energy. It is governed by the individual's "will" (if I may be permitted to use such an old-fashioned term), and the person's decision-making abilities. Information processors call these decision-making abilities "executive functions"—a term, I suppose, that many readers will find more palpable than "will." "Intelligent behavior" is the channeling of this energy for a purposeful act. The act itself may promote the welfare of the person and/or a social group, in which case it could be called "life-supporting." An example would be the devoting of time and energy, one's "intelligence," to a worthy cause such as cancer research or making sure the kids get to school on time. Conversely, "intelligence" can be directed to "life-destroying" acts of various kinds, too, such as unwarranted acts of aggression. These are relative terms, however, since in some instances it may be very difficult to determine what is "life-supporting" and what is not.

Intelligence is also very akin to what "factor analysts" call g. Spearman noticed that most tests of ability, such as memory, reasoning, social judgment, and so on, "correlated" with each other. That means that people who did well on one test tended to do well on others. When one performs a complex statistical procedure called "factor analysis" on all these different tasks, then a "common factor" emerges. This is called g. It represents what is common to all of the tasks. What is "left over" after taking g into account, Spearman called s, because it was specific to the particular task. Spearman's "two-factor" theory was too simple to last long, and underwent considerable modifications by Sir Cyril Burt and Dr. Philip Vernon. David Pyle, in his book, *Intelligence, An Introduction*, gives us us a good description of this more complex model, which is outlined in Figure 2.1.[1]

FIGURE 2.1. Vernon's model: Diagram of the hierarchical group-factor theory, showing the main general and group factors underlying tests relevant to educational and vocational achievements.

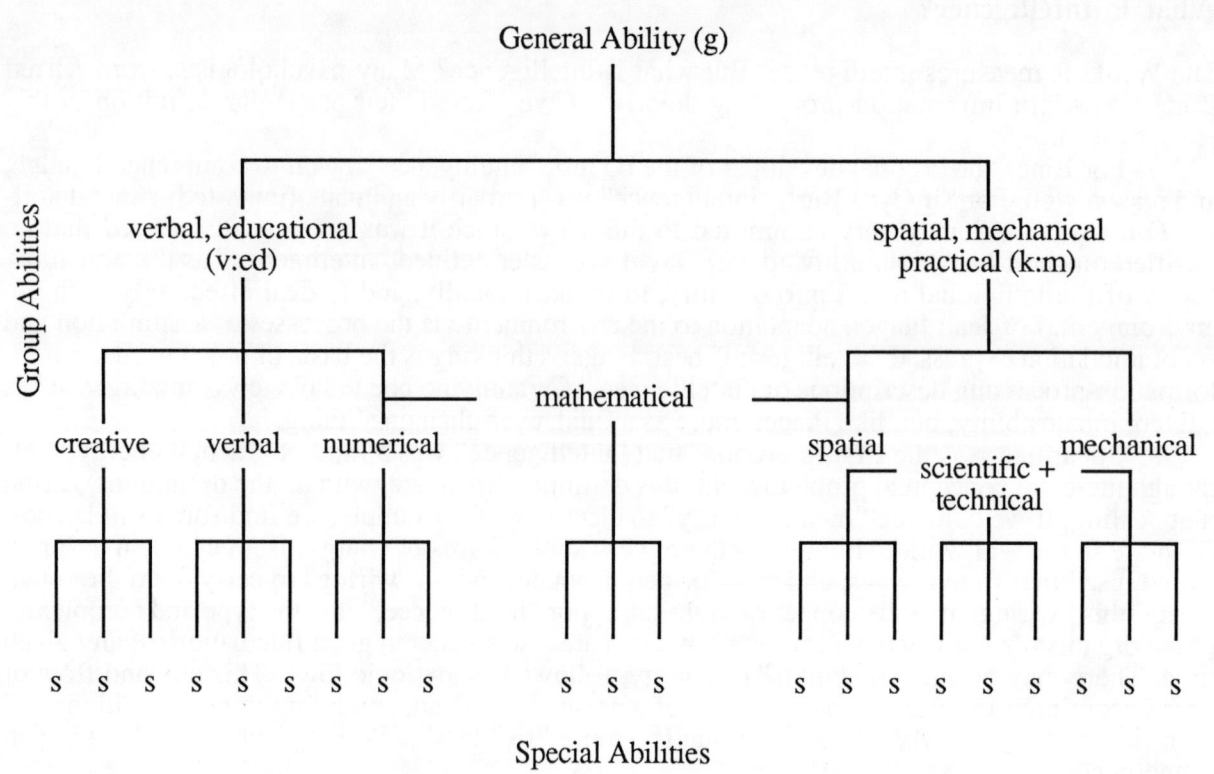

Adapted from: Vernon, P. E. 1969. *Intelligence and cultural environment*, p. 22. London: Methuen.

This model is primarily "top-down." (I will discuss this definition later.) Mental energy, or *g*, "flows" into different tasks from the "top-down." It may be transformed, depending on the nature of the task. It follows from this model that we should find evidence of *g* in animals, too, since I do not see any inherent reason why humans should have the exclusive market on "intelligence." Evidence of *g* in higher-order mammals is indeed supported by some experimental evidence.[2]

The reader interested in pursuing these definitions of "intelligence" in more depth, and some of their corresponding educational implications, is invited to consult Pyle's book.

There are other models and definitions of intelligence, such as Guilford's three-dimensional model of human intellect, which posits the existence of at least 120 unique human abilities, each of which (in theory, anyway) can be taught. Figure 2.2 offers a diagram of this model.[3]

Many school psychologists are aware of the work done by Mary Meeker of the SOI Institute, using Guilford's model as the base.[4] She has developed remedial tasks which can be used to help students who have identified weaknesses in many of the 120 abilities. The SOI Institute has developed its own cognitive tests to measure these abilities, but the WISC-R can also be subjected to an SOI analysis, and remedial suggestions of an educational nature may be teased out. I have found some of the material quite useful in certain individual cases. School psychologists and remedial teachers owe it to themselves to read some of the SOI literature and use what they find useful from it. I personally find it too "bottom-up" an approach to recommend widespread adoption; but it does have its place.

FIGURE 2.2. Guilford's model: The structure of intellect.

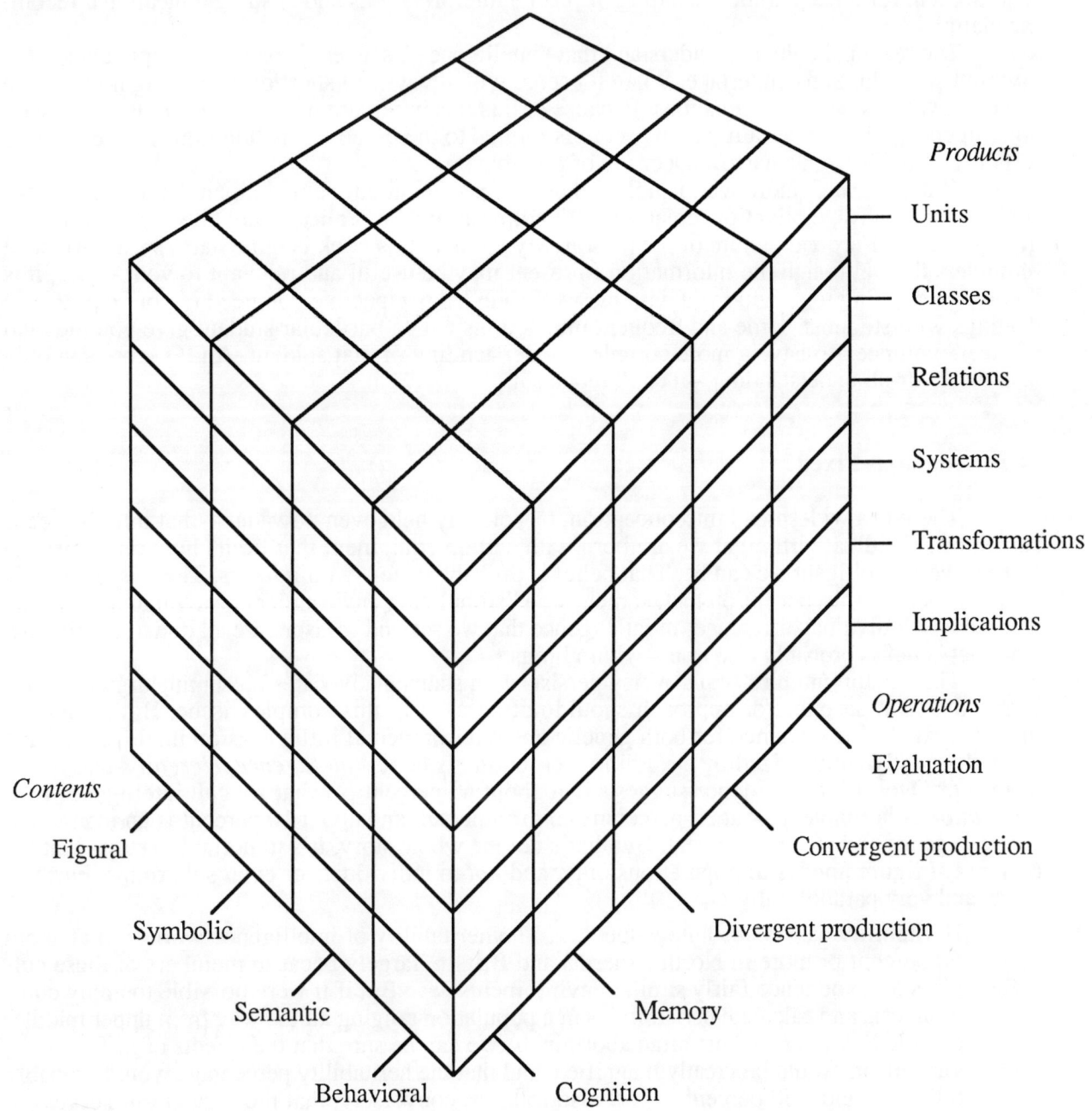

Adapted from: Guilford, J. P., and Hoepfner, R. 1971. *The analysis of intelligence*, p. 19. New York: McGraw-Hill.

Not all the theoretical approaches to intelligence that we've mentioned so far have accompanying IQ tests. And, some IQ tests, like the WISC-R, are developed without benefit of a theoretical framework. Certainly, David Wechsler had a strong *rationale*, but he did not develop the WISC from a theoretical perspective, as such. On the other hand, newer tests like the K-ABC, which *does* have an underlying theoretical basis, I find not nearly so useful as the WISC-R. Perhaps the theoretical base I find too narrow, though again, the K-ABC is useful at times.

In any case, as Alan Kaufman has so ably pointed out, the WISC-R needs to be understood and interpreted from a number of different theoretical perspectives.[5] I will introduce these as we require them for a deeper understanding of profile interpretations and ensuing educational recommendations.

The reader should also understand that "intelligence" is a *very* broad term, applicable to everything we as humans undertake. So an IQ score will always fall short of measuring how people can do in various tasks and situations. Because of this it is important not to *equate* an IQ score with "intelligence," though certainly an IQ score is *related* to the broad term, "intelligence." But an IQ test only samples from a narrow spectrum of possible tasks.

"Intelligence," moreover, is not all that is important about being human. Other qualities—such as personality, motivation, creativity, friendliness, and "morality"—are all very important in giving us the all-around picture of the person. My focus in this book is quite narrow; and we need reminders that, although the information I present may be useful and relevant to your needs, it is by no means going to provide you with the well-rounded perspective you need in your day-to-day dealings with students. Time and frequent interactions with a particular student give you the kind of "feel" you need to have a more complete understanding of that student. An IQ score can only *help* that over-all understanding—it can't replace it.

Is Intelligence Fixed?

There is a widespread misconception, tenaciously held even nowadays, that intelligence is somehow "fixed" at birth, that we are born with certain equipment that limits how much we can learn or how intelligent we can be. That belief is probably true—within limits. There is an equally tenaciously held misconception that, somehow, a "stimulating environment" is all that counts, and that the vast individual differences in intelligence that we see and measure are all due to upbringing. And that belief is probably also true—within limits.

This "nature/nurture" controversy persists with staunch advocates presenting arguments for both sides. But an either/or approach should not be used in this complex issue. Both sides are probably right. The evidence for both genetic and environmental influences on intelligence have been eloquently summarized by Dr. Philip Vernon in his book, *Intelligence, Heredity, and Environment*.[6] Over-all, the evidence suggests that about 60 percent of what we call intelligence *in a population* is heritable. About 30 percent is environmental, and about 10 percent is an interaction between genes and the environment. But that's not the whole story. It's important to stress that the 60 percent figure applies to populations only, and *not* to individuals or even subgroups. Furthermore, and very paradoxically:[7]

> Heritability has no absolute value.... The heritability of intelligence works out at about 60 percent or more in North America and Britain, largely because members of these cultures do experience fairly similar environments.... But if it were possible to apply common tests and calculate heritabilities in a population ranging all the way from upper middle-class U.S. whites to Australian aboriginals, we can be sure that the effects of different environments would be greatly magnified, and that the heritability percentage would probably fall well below 50 percent.... It also follows, conversely, that the greater our success in equalizing environments through social and educational reform, the more will any remaining differences in ability depend on the genes; in other words, heritability will be raised.

All this says that "intelligence" is *not* a fixed entity. The opposite seems true, which makes sense if we see intelligence as "mental energy."

It is also important to understand that, just because something is "genetically determined," it does not mean that it cannot change. (Some of our physical features, such as eye color, cannot change; but, even so, we could cheat a little and use colored contact lenses.) But let us look at height. Height is about 90 percent heritable. Yet, the average height in the population has been rising steadily over the years! A visit to a medieval castle, for example, confirms how short the inhabitants were then. Visitors from the twentieth century always have to duck under the low doors! Height in the population keeps rising. Why is this so? Probably, for two major reasons: First, a female is not likely to have a mate who is shorter than she is (a genetic influence); and second, we have much better nutrition today compared to yesterday (an environmental influence). So, genetics does not "fix" intelligence in the population at large. The same is true for individuals. It is not possible to determine, for any single person, how much of his or her intelligence is heritable, and how much is environmental. Even if it were possible to calculate such figures for a person, we know that intelligence is *modifiable* by environmental conditions, including good teaching. Learning and teaching will *always* play critical roles in maximizing opportunities for people to use and develop their intelligence.

And partly because of the good efforts of millions of teachers in all countries of the world, it seems that populations and countries, by and large, *are* becoming more intelligent. Again, Vernon says:[8]

> ... There is good reason to believe that the average intelligence level of the human race will continue to rise as education improves in underdeveloped countries; and that, in Western countries, further gains may occur as developments in our knowledge of child psychology and in educational technology increase what Bruner calls human amplifying systems.

Ultimately, even if intelligence were 100 percent inherited, we just couldn't have the same level of it expressed in our culture or in any one person *without* the stimulation that education and other positive environments provide. A seed may contain all the growth potential and other features of the plant. But it does not grow well, or at all, in the wrong environment where water and sunlight are lacking. The same is true for us as humans. We need love, nurturance, and stimulation from birth (and maybe even before that).

Intelligence does not "fix" or determine school achievement, either. There is a correlation between how "smart" you are and your achievement levels in academic skills, but the relationship is by no means perfect. We will discuss the importance of this imperfect relationship shortly, especially in the diagnosis of "learning disabilities." In terms of the main idea of this section, however, school achievement has even *less* heritability than intelligence. So, do not let any parent tell you that "Johnny's just like his father when it comes to spelling." Certainly, some of Johnny's spelling ability may be genetically influenced, and that is always interesting to discover; but there is a great deal of room for change via teaching. Teaching in the classroom, and what we do with students, is very important. Says Vernon:[9]

> ... Now that the findings of heritability researches and of environmental modifications are beginning to confirm or complement one another, we surely do not need to bother about which is the most important—genes or the environment. Both are essential, and neither can be neglected if we are to plan children's upbringing and education wisely.

"Good" school environments are like "good" home environments. *Both* nurture the development of intelligence. I do not want to leave you with the impression that it's all uphill from here, however. Just how difficult it is to make lasting changes in IQ scores (and presumably, in "intelligence") will become apparent in the next section.

How Much Can Intelligence Scores Change?

Intelligence scores can and do change, on their own, from one testing to another just because of the imprecise nature of our instruments and the underlying dimension of "energy" they measure. This practice effect can be very large on the WISC-R, especially on the Performance Scale. For this reason alone, no student should be reassessed on the WISC-R unless there is a *minimum* six-month interval between first and second evaluations. There is also the effect of measurement error itself, which we will discuss later. But aside from these testing considerations themselves, can we actually raise intelligence levels in people? From my own perspective of seeing intelligence as "mental energy," I believe the answer is "yes." But there are at least two issues to discuss in answering that question. The first is the issue of "teaching to the test," since this is a common and often desireable educational practice. The second issue is "stimulation." Can we stimulate children and raise their intelligence levels? What does research tell us about that, and what is the latest thinking on this important topic?

In terms of the first issue, IQ scores are not quite like reading or other achievement scores when it comes to remediation. As every teacher knows, the closer the test comes to testing what the teacher has taught, the better that test is in terms of validity. If a teacher knows a student is weak in reading comprehension, for example, then the student can be assessed using an appropriate test, a remedial program can begin, and the student can then be retested. Some of the test items can be close approximations of what the teacher taught. Therefore, "teaching to the test" is an appropriate educational strategy when it comes to all academic subjects.

Not so for IQ tests. We *could* teach to the WISC-R or the Stanford-Binet, and set up IEPs with improvement of certain subtests as the objective. We could use materials geared to each of the WISC-R subtests, for example, and spend a lot of remedial time "teaching" the presumed underlying process. But the result of that kind of remedial effort would only waste time and *not* raise "intelligence" as such. It might raise the IQ score on the WISC-R, but that score would then be spurious! That is because "intelligence"—as opposed to, say, "reading"—is a much more abstract entity. When we measure a student's IQ, we are sampling from a very broad base of learned behaviors. The learned behaviors in reading, by contrast, are much more specific. So, raising IQ scores cannot be *legitimately* done in any "canned" way. As Barbara Holmes puts it:[10]

> ... The use of remedial prescriptions (and the *WISC-R Compilation* [Whitworth and Sutton 1978] is a good case in point) tends to result in "teaching to the test." In the *Compilation*, the long-term goal stated for each WISC-R subtest task is to do that particular task itself. All that it does, then, is train "block designers" and "picture completers": that is, WISC-R–competent test takers. Since we have no proof that the academic correlations of the Full Scale IQ will benefit from excellence in block design, the most we can count on is uselessness of the test scores for predictive purposes.

And:[11]

The arguments presented in this paper are uniformly critical of programmed remediation based on WISC-R profiles. It will be recognized, of course, that the fault is not in the technology but in the erroneous conceptual and theoretical bases underlying the approach. Most damning is the lack of validation for the relationship implied between the test and ability, and ability and academic program. It cannot be overemphasized that, in the absence of empirical support, WISC-R remedial programs can be considered no more than arbitrary exercises, and therefore contrary to ethical practice and professional intent. The real solution to appropriate test usage is to continue to recognize the need for the mediating, interactive role of the artisan-professionals, school psychologists and teachers, in maintaining the ideal of individually meaningful educational intervention.

The approach I am advocating in this book is anything but "canned," and, I believe, a step toward the ideal Holmes advances. I want the reader to know more about reading and intelligence theory. Only then can school psychologists and remedial specialists work together to program appropriate remediation for the individual student. Being knowledgeable makes one more sensitive to what is appropriate for any given student. I hope it is clear, then, that this book is not a "canned" approach. Many suggestions will certainly be provided; but it is the school psychologist who works with the student, and the teacher who knows the student, who must decide together what is ultimately useful and what is not. And those decisions are as much "art" as they are "science."

However, despite the fact that the *WISC-R Compilation* has been much maligned, I am not prepared to say it has no place in the school psychologist's list of useful references. It does. Once the school psychologist has pinpointed some of the student's needs using theoretically sound approaches (many of which are discussed in depth in this book), the psychologist will find some of the very specific suggestions in the *Compilation* will be useful. For example, if there is a need for expressive language development as evidenced by, say, a low score on the Verbal Scale, then some of the suggestions in the Vocabulary section of the *Compilation* could be helpful to the student.

So, in respect to the first issue, teaching specifically to WISC-R subtests in order to raise intelligence, it is both spurious and a waste of precious time. The second issue, that of environmental stimulation, is a much deeper one. And there are several kinds of studies bearing on this important area of concern.

One of the more common methods, usually done at the early childhood level, is to pretest the student with an IQ test, and then introduce some *general* program of stimulation, designed to enhance some broad areas of cognitive development. We then might posttest, even using the same IQ test (provided that the time interval is adequate), and see if our intervention had any effect on the student's general ability or other areas. We could also follow-up the student in later years, to see what effect the early intervention had on other variables such as academic achievement, self-concept, social adjustment, career choices, time spent in special education classes, and so on.

Several studies have been done at an early intervention or Head Start level. Some of them have reported very dramatic increases in intelligence test scores. The most widely publicized was the Milwaukee Project, which claimed to produce increases of about 30 points overall.[12]

Unfortunately, these results have never been replicated and are now considered very suspect.

So, on the side of the heritability issue, is the fact that Sir Cyril Burt falsified information; and on the environmental side, the Milwaukee Project is very suspect! This shows what can happen when even the most reputable scientists are bent on proving a point, one way or another.

It does leave us out in the cold, though, because the issues are very complex, and the results often not clear-cut. It is my personal belief that early stimulation can and does produce positive effects on children. Some problems can be, and are, prevented this way; and efforts at early stimulation should be continued vigorously.

Sometimes, confusion arises over *what* to stimulate, and for *what purpose*. Later on, I will discuss what I consider to be a very exciting possibility in the field of early intervention in terms of increasing reading ability and preventing reading problems via the stimulation of phonemic awareness.

We should also look beyond just gains in IQ scores as the measure of success for these programs. Some studies have shown that, although IQ scores drop steadily once intervention ceases, achievement scores do not. And fewer students from such stimulated preschool groups are assigned to special education classes later on.[13] This is certainly an important and noteworthy finding, one with great social significance. Students do seem to function better in the school environment as a result of Head Start–type programs, and there is a resulting positive chain of events—even though we might not see much advantage in IQ scores alone.

There is another line of research showing that a *total and long-term change in environment*, such as occurs when children are adopted, can reverse the damage of even extreme early deprivation.[14] These changes are manifested in many aspects of the individual's life and are, in my opinion, far more important than changes in IQ scores alone, though these too change for the better. There are a few studies now which show such long-term and lasting positive changes when children are placed in appropriate long-term care. Even long-term institutional care is better than a severely deprived environment. This speaks also for the resiliency and plasticity of human beings, and demonstrates that long-term care at any age is more important than early experiences or a "head start."

The time, money, and resources available for some projects are also obviously not those available to the vast majority of school psychologists or teachers. However, at a more practical level, some early childhood mother-child programs, which are far less costly, have been quite successful, too (bringing about a 15-point IQ gain over a two-year period). Although this book is not geared to the early childhood level, I would like to point out some of the essential elements of success in these programs, since many school psychologists do get involved with children in the early years. Some of those elements seem to be:

1. That the program aims primarily at showing the mother how to be a better interactor with the child.
2. That the program aims primarily at developing language skills both for awareness training and information processing.
3. That the mother be shown how to participate in her child's play and speech, and how to accompany this with verbal interactions. Furthermore, the mother needs to be shown how to do this incidentally, while at home with the child—not just during the tutoring or training sessions. Merely counseling or advising the mother is *not* enough. Demonstrations must be given.
4. That the program be carried out for at least two years, beginning at about age two.

The interested reader should consult Levenstein's Mother-Child Home Program, as this is quite a successful one which has been in use since 1965, and which has replicated results.[15]

Direct Teaching of Intelligence: Recent Formulations

Robert Sternberg, a professor of psychology at Yale University, has provided what I consider to be some important distinctions about the teaching of intellectual processes.[16] He says there are three types of mental processes: (1) metacomponents, (2) performance components, and (3) knowledge-acquisition components. We can intervene and teach at any one or more of these levels. Let's have a look at each of them.

Metacomponents are higher-order, "executive decisions" and processes used to plan and monitor what we are going to do when we are faced with a problem. For example, when we see an arithmetic problem, we have to be aware of and decide what operation(s) we will use to solve it. These are the metacomponent decisions and strategies. Sternberg says that the Instrumental Enrichment (IE) program of Reuven Feuerstein is an example of a program designed mainly to teach metacomponent strategies. The IE program is as content-free as possible, and consists of 13 process-type exercises repeated throughout the program.

Sternberg says that IE training can be recommended for a number of cultural and subcultural groups, but it is limited in the breadth of skills taught, and in its potential for generalization. Nevertheless, his over-all judgment is that "... IE is an attractive package in many respects. It is among the best of available programs emphasizing thinking-skill training."[17]

Performance components are processing skills used to actually carry out the task. In our example, they are the actual steps used in performing the arithmetic operations, be they adding, multiplying, etc. The Philosophy for Children (PC) program is an example of a largely performance-based program, he says—though of course, metacomponents are also included. The goals of PC are to try to teach 30 thinking skills in children in the range of grades five through eight. The major advantage of PC over IE is that PC maximizes a knowledge-based content, whereas IE minimizes it. "PC stories are exciting and highly motivating . . . . The thinking skills taught are clearly the right ones to teach for both academic and everyday information processing." "No program I am aware of," writes Sternberg, "is more likely to teach durable, transferable thinking skills than PC."[18] Unfortunately for special educators, PC is also heavily reading- and reasoning-based. Additionally, the story characters are middle- and upper middle-class in value orientation. Therefore, the application of PC in special education may be somewhat limited. Nevertheless, it is a program worthy of perusal, and could be suitable for some students.

Knowledge-acquisition components are the reasoning components used to first learn new materials, such as the multiplication tables. The Chicago Mastery Learning Reading Program

(CMLR) is an example of such a program. So is most of what happens every day in a classroom, I might add. The CMLR, like PC, was written for grades five to eight. There is a strong emphasis on learning to learn. There are two units at each grade level; these consist of comprehension and study skills. The units are concrete, simple, literal, and familiar, to begin with; and gradually, they become more abstract, inexplicit, and unfamiliar. This program seems to have several features suitable for the special educator:

1. The material easily incorporates into any reading program, whereas PC would best fit into an enrichment or philosophy curriculum (certainly, very few schools have this); and IE does not easily fit into any curriculum at all.
2. It emphasizes learning strategies.
3. It can be used with a wide variety of students, including those above and below grade level.
4. It can be used with a wide range of socioeconomic groups.
5. It has immediate applicability to school and life situations.
6. It seems developed for the heart of where many handicapped students have difficulty in the first place—acquiring knowledge.

Its weaknesses are the limited range of skills it covers (reading and verbal comprehension only) and its weaker theoretical foundation.

Overall, these new programs are exciting developments in education. I would caution against jumping on any bandwagons, however. Remember, the teacher ultimately creates the program. To date, only a few school districts have actually made the direct teaching of thinking skills one of their stated objectives. As more and more districts do so, however, programs such as IE, PC, and CMLR will gain more attention. Educators need to be in a better position to evaluate such programs; and Sternberg's metacomponent, performance component, and knowledge-acquisition component distinctions should be very useful as a framework for such evaluations. Educators can then choose or develop what is best for their own goals.

These distinctions can also be useful for an informal "process analysis" of many academic and cognitive tasks, including the WISC-R. For example, if a student does poorly on one of the Arithmetic subtest questions, is it because he or she doesn't know what operations and procedures to use in the first place (indicating a lack of *metacomponent* awareness); because the student broke down in the *performance* of the task (perhaps the student subtracted as was called for, but obtained an incorrect answer), or did not *acquire the knowledge* in the first place (such as the multiplication tables), so it would be impossible to get the right answer? Careful observation and error analysis, as well as "testing the limits" afterwards, can help answer some of these questions and provide a direction and theoretical framework for some remedial strategies.

Top-Down and Bottom-Up Information Processing

"Top-down" information processing is primarily conceptually-driven processing—processing which begins with meaning and demands meaning. For example, in the sentence, "The pig was in the _____," there are several possibilities as to what "fits" in the empty space. Some likely candidates are "yard" and "barn" and even "garden." Our top-down processes or conceptual knowledge allows us to make those guesses, but the guesses or predictions have to fit the context or over-all *meaning* of the sentence.

"Bottom-up" processing is data-driven. The information is sequentially pieced together to form a whole, so meaning is *derived from* the data. "Sounding out a word" in isolation would be an example of a primarily bottom-up process in reading. The reader is urged to rely primarily on phonics, finally acquiring meaning from the knowledge of sound-symbol relationships in our language.

The distinction between top-down and bottom-up processing can be applied to reading. Mature readers use a combination of top-down (meaning and syntax cues) and bottom-up (phonics cues) processing when reading. Flesch recognized this, when in 1949 he said:[19]

> And that's the way we read: We race along, making quick guesses at the meanings of little bunches of words, and quick corrections of these first guesses afterwards.

The business of "meaning-acquisition" in reading is very important, and should be woven into the remedial activities that special education teachers provide for their students. Appendix 2-1 contains several practical strategies for emphasizing the act of "predicting" and meaning-acquisition in reading, using primarily a "whole language" approach.

Top-down and bottom-up processing can be applied in a number of areas besides reading. For example, John Naisbitt in *Megatrends* (1982) observes that trends always start bottom-up.[20] Trend-setting ideas or products are most often observed locally first, and usually in a few states (mainly California, Florida, Washington, Colorado, or Connecticut) before being adopted nationwide. Fads, on the other hand, are always top-down.

Darwin's theory of evolution, as another example, is primarily a bottom-up explanation. But as Buckminster Fuller once commented, all the evidence is just as consistent with a top-down interpretation as well. In my mind, the universe *is* conceptually driven. Orderliness seems to be an inherent part of its makeup. Once started, however, the evolutionary process is both top-down and bottom-up interacting together.

It is important to note that neither top-down nor bottom-up processing is inherently superior or inferior to the other. Frequently, we see that *both* are needed in concert for the best results. And that should be the basic principle in providing instruction to students.

Now, let us use this distinction to evaluate further the current thinking-skills packages. It seems to me that IE is far too top-down. Students engaged in learning in school must still work with some sort of basic content. If the content is too far removed from their ordinary experience, as it seems to be in IE, the chance of transfer to those everyday tasks is limited. CMLR, on the other hand, uses knowledge-acquisition, which is bottom-up, as the basis for training the metacognitive, or top-down, skills. PC also uses this combined approach; but, as we have already stated, this has some other drawbacks for special educators.

Special education students, who usually have so much difficulty acquiring knowledge, need programs which make the transfer as easy as possible. So, when the day comes—as it already has in some states and provinces—when remedial teachers must also teach thinking skills, then the CMLR program will have to be looked at carefully. I am using "program" in the broad sense of "that which is designed by the teacher." I'll say again that I do not advocate the canned use of canned programs in the school system. Such programs can be used, but always need to be modified in light of the teacher's objectives for a particular student or class. They can be part of a good over-all teacher's program.

The broad goal of special educators, at least until now, has been to improve *achievement*, not intelligence. Intelligence tests sample from a broader range of life and learning experiences than do achievement tests. Achievement tests depend heavily on formal learning, and the skills that achievement tests measure are far more specific. Of course, there is some overlap between the two, and IQ tests can predict achievement scores to some extent. Roughly, the correlation between the two kinds of tests is around .60 on the average. (A correlation coefficient [r] is a measure of how two variables are related. If A and B are perfectly related inversely [i.e., as A is increased, then B is decreased by the same amount], then the correlation coefficient would be −1.00. If A and B were perfectly related in a positive way, then A and B would increase proportionately; and the calculated r would be 1.00. Correlation does *not* imply causation. If A and B are correlated, then [1] A might be the cause of B, or [2] B might be the cause of A, or [3] A and B could be both related to some *other* cause that is common to both.)

The correlation between IQ scores and achievement scores is statistically very significant, but in no way is it perfect. So when we are comparing "intelligence' to "achievement" and are making judgments about where a child *should* be achieving because of an IQ score, we need to be very cautious indeed. This point will be discussed in greater depth in another section of this chapter.

It is important for educators and psychologists not to hold unrealistic expectations for the students or make rash promises to parents. As we have seen, the business of "raising intelligence" is complex and difficult. It is, furthermore, a life-long process involving many factors outside the control of the school.

Psychologists and educators need always to keep in mind the importance of the child's home background in their efforts to educate the child. Just how important the home is, in terms of cognitive development, is what we turn to now.

Importance of the Home

Every teacher, remedial or otherwise, intuitively knows that there is no substitute for a good home. We know there are home environments which are very incompatible with normal cognitive and emotional growth—indeed, destructive to both. Fortunately, the effects of extreme deprivation in such homes seems to be reversible. However, we know less about what stimulates "normal" growth, although we do know a few correlates.

The Berkeley Growth Study, for example, found that higher IQ scores in children are associated with (not, necessarily, caused by):[21]

1. Higher socioeconomic status of the parents
2. Superior play facilities
3. Parental concern that children get a good education
4. Parental harmony, and
5. Mothers who appear worrisome, tense, highly active and energetic.

Another group of researchers found that, of a group of children who showed increases or decreases in IQ scores as they grew older, the *increase group* had families that encouraged their children in a clear way by providing structure and enforcement of consequences. This does *not* mean severe punishment. *In fact, severe punishment was clearly associated with the largest decreases* in IQ scores. Children who made the biggest gains had parents who adopted a middle-of-the-road discipline policy—not too severe, not too lax. Being lax, however, was better than being too severe.[22]

Very high correlations were found in another study between total ratings of the home environment on:

1. Quality of language models available to the child
2. Opportunities for enlarging vocabulary
3. Feedback about appropriate language usage, and
4. Opportunities for language practice

... and general intelligence ($r = .69$), as well as academic achievement ($r = .80$).[23] Does that mean that the child's capacity for learning is already largely fixed before the child even enters school? Certainly some eminent authorities, like Philip Vernon, believe so. However, more recent evidence seems to suggest that the type of schooling the child receives *does* make a difference.

A good portion of this book is devoted to remedial teaching strategies as they arise or are suggested by the WISC-R profiles (and supplemented by additional testing as needed, of course). I personally firmly believe in the *big* difference teachers can make in the lives of their students. However, I would like to temper my enthusiasm by pointing out that we need to enter the educational enterprise with our eyes open. The importance of other factors, such as the home and genetics, should not be underplayed, either. Our admirable goals of improving IQ scores and academic achievement through well thought-out interventions may still fall short, despite our best efforts, because of such factors. The evidence clearly supports the notion that some environmental factors which influence the development of intelligence—such as low birth weight, early poor nutrition, parental harmony, socioeconomic status, certain personality characteristics of the mother, father absence, father nurturing, discipline models in the home, and the child's own temperament—are well beyond the school's control.

We must do what we can, then, with what we have, to our best ability, every day. Remember that we cannot control all those factors. But the kind of school environment the teacher creates has, I believe, a very profound effect on the child—for better or worse. For students who are "at risk" in terms of their family backgrounds, the quality of *your* classroom and relationship with that student may be *all* that student has.

Intelligence—More Definitions

We are now in a position to make more definitional distinctions of the term "intelligence." Following Vernon, we'll call them Intelligence *A*, *B*, and *C*. I find these distinctions very useful in explaining the results of IQ scores to both parents and teachers.

Intelligence *A* refers to innate genetic potential. It is that portion of intelligence which is heritable for an individual. It is the genotype. There is simply no way of measuring Intelligence *A*.

Intelligence *B* refers to the interaction between *A* and the environment. It is affected by culture, home environment, birth weight, birth trauma, malnutrition, and a host of other factors. It is the phenotype.

Intelligence *C* is the score on an individual test of intelligence. Intelligence C_2 is the score on a group test of intelligence. The two *C*s are correlated, but by no means identical. The score on an individual test of intelligence is a better indicator of the child's "potential," and gives considerable information on individual strengths and weaknesses not available from group tests. Intelligence *C* is used to *infer* Intelligence *B*. Vernon claims, however, that the Verbal Scale of the WISC-R (and the verbal portions of the Binet) are direct measures of Intelligence *B* in our culture (though, of course, not all aspects of *B*).

Because of the fluid nature of intelligence, any score from any IQ test, group or individual, should only be interpreted like a snapshot. It gives a picture of a child's cognitive development at a particular point in time. If a film was properly loaded, the camera held steady, and other conditions were right, then the picture will be clear. Likewise, if an IQ test was administered properly and the child made to feel comfortable and do his or her best, the IQ score will be a valid and reliable estimate of the child's development *at that point in time*.

The score is fluid, however. It can change over short or long periods of time, so such "snapshots" need to be taken reasonably frequently to get a better long-range picture.

The younger the child, the less reliable the IQ score is of the same child's IQ score at a later age. Scores obtained on elementary children, as opposed to preschool children, are much more stable. These are the age ranges covered by the WISC-R.

Brighter children show greater changes from one test time to another than do lower IQ children.[24] This research finding has been confirmed in my own experience with students. For some reason, brighter children do show greater variations on IQ testings over time. One year, the student may qualify for the district's Gifted program; and two years later, the student will score lower and perhaps no longer technically qualify, only to score higher again at a third testing.

Because of such fluctuations in Intelligence *C*, all scores from all IQ tests must be treated with a healthy caution. It is paramount that parents and educators understand this, so that no wild generalizations about a student's potential are made on the basis of an IQ score.

What Is Potential, Anyway?

IQ scores are often interpreted as an estimate of the student's "learning potential." Though I find this interpretation useful in my day-to-day work as a school psychologist, it must be used very cautiously. The IQ score, if valid and reliable, may be a good indicator of the student's academic potential *at that point in time*, but it cannot be rigidly adhered to. The IQ score is not necessarily an indication of a fixed potential for more learning. As far as I can tell, that potential is infinite for everyone—within lifetime limits.

To illustrate this point, I like to use the Russian psychologist Vygotsky's concept of the "zone of potential difference." The idea is quite simple. First, you measure a student's performance in a certain area. Then, you see how well the child performs, once you add certain external prompts, cues, or strategies (psychologists call this "testing the limits"). The improvement noted may be small or large. Whatever it is, is the "zone of potential difference" for that child on that particular task. But remember, we are not talking about teaching to a subtest. The "zone of potential difference" indicates what might be possible with good, general remediation.

Reading specialists employ a similar concept when they want to find out what the "reading potential" is of a student who has a reading problem. If the student is a poor reader and can function only at, say, the 10th percentile for his age group when he himself is asked to read a story, but is able to answer questions displaying good comprehension of the story *when it is read to him* (say, to the 75th percentile for his age group), then his score on the "listening comprehension" task is a good indicator of the "reading potential" for that student. The assumption is that, with proper instruction, the student should eventually be able to read independently as well as he can when the story is read to him. The "zone of potential difference" for this student on this task, then, is a whopping 65 percentile points.

Similar reasoning can be applied to the concept of intelligence. When we measure a child's current performance, we are not measuring the "zone of potential difference" most of the time. We are only getting a measure of current functioning within an "error" limit. Does this mean that intelligence tests like the WISC-R should not be used to place students in special programs? My experience says that IQ tests are very useful in placement decisions, but the placement decision should not be based on an IQ score alone.

Suppose a student has been having great difficulty with reading and other subjects, despite modifications by the teacher and remedial help. If a WISC-R assessment shows an IQ of, say, 70 ± 6 (percentile 2), then we could say that the child's "learning potential" was nowhere near average at the time of testing (provided, of course, that we were confident the student did his or her best). That being the case, the student might better be placed in a program geared to his or her current level, such as an Educable Mentally Handicapped class. Such situations occur frequently in all school systems. It has been my experience that we really do a great deal of good for the child when we place him or her in a special class. Our so-called labeling is very helpful, provided the label is not seen as something that is forever fixed. If the child is placed in a special class and forgotten; if teachers and parents don't work to "stretch" the student as far as possible; then, of course, the placement will be harmful. But the alternative of letting the student sink-or-swim in the "mainstream" is even more unpalatable. There is only so far a regular classroom teacher can go in trying to meet the needs of handicapped students. Their needs are usually far better met in special programs. But "mainstreaming" should occur whenever and to whatever extent possible. Should a student make enormous gains in the special program, most schools would only be too happy to fully reintegrate the student.

Let's take another example, one where the Full Scale IQ score by itself may not be a good predictor of a student's academic "potential." Suppose the student's Full Scale WISC-R score came out at 100 ± 6 (percentile 50 ± 15). This student's score on the surface can be interpreted as indicating average learning potential.

But "mental energy" does not seem to flow evenly between individuals, nor does it flow evenly *within* the same individual at times. Therefore, "learning potential" might be too misleading a term, because "average IQ" implies, to most people, that the student should be at least "average" in all he does. This is simply contrary to fact and quite unreasonable. Yet we mistakenly do this all the time in school systems (I'll have much more to say on this point when I discuss the diagnosis of learning disabilities).

What we really need to ask is, "What kind of learning?" and, "To what type of task will this student respond best?" and, "When can we expect 'average' performance, and when do we have to modify our expectations?" The WISC-R can help us in answering these questions.

As I mentioned in Chapter 1, the WISC-R provides a number of different scores. Each of them has educational implications. The Full Scale IQ is the most stable score, and corresponds to general ability, or *g*. Next, we can calculate both a Verbal and a Performance IQ. If you reread Figure 2.1, you will see that these two scores are next down on Vernon's hierarchy, being more akin to group abilities.

It's also possible that the WISC-R subtest scores "split off" into three distinct factors on some profiles. Factor analysis is a statistical procedure which shows what subtests "go together," because they "load" on some underlying common "factor." The factor is then given a name. The WISC-R has been factor-analyzed numerous times. Three distinct factors emerge. These factors, their names, and the subtests which load on each factor are as follows:

Factor I (Verbal Comprehension)	*Factor II* (Perceptual Organization)	*Factor III* (Freedom from Distractibility)
Information	Picture Completion	Arithmetic
Similarities	Picture Arrangement	Digit Span
Vocabulary	Block Design	Coding
Comprehension	Object Assembly	
	Mazes	

You can see that Factors I and II correspond very closely to the Verbal and Performance IQs, respectively. Factor II contains two subtests from the Verbal scale and one from the Performance scale. Not every child tested on the WISC-R shows this kind of split, but many students who have learning difficulties do show such a split when the WISC-R is administered.

An example of this three-way split is shown in Figure 2.3.

It is possible to calculate an IQ score and percentiles for each of the three factors. Table 2.1, at the close of this chapter, allows you to do that. These scores are primarily for professional use to enhance understanding of the student's profile. As such, they are not usually included in formal written reports of assessment results.

To calculate the IQs on the three factors, add up the scale scores on each of the subtests for that factor. Then use Table 2.1 to determine an IQ and corresponding percentile for each of the three factors.

You can also calculate your own scale score average for each factor. Simply add up the scale scores that load on each factors and divide by the number of subtests. Round off the answer to the nearest whole number. When the scale score averages for each of the factors differs by three or more points, then the three-factor split can be legitimately interpreted. (See A. Kaufman, *Intelligent Testing with the WISC-R*, New York, John Wiley, 1979, for a full treatment of this issue).

In this student's case, we have the following:

Factor I (Verbal Comprehension)		*Factor II* (Perceptual Organization)		*Factor III* (Freedom from Distractibility)	
Information	12	Picture Completion	12	Arithmetic	8
Similarities	10	Picture Arrangement	12	Digit Span	6
Vocabulary	10	Block Design	10	Coding	6
Comprehension	10	Object Assembly	10		
		Mazes*	12		

Avg. (42 ÷ 4) = 10.2 ≈ 10 (percentile 50)

Avg. (56 ÷ 5) = 11.2 ≈ 11 (percentile 63)

Avg. (20 ÷ 3) = 6.6 ≈ 7 (percentile 16)

Using Table 2.1:

VC IQ = 103　　　　　　　PO IQ = 106　　　　　　　FD IQ = 78
(percentile 56)　　　　　　(percentile 65)　　　　　　(percentile 8)

(Note the discrepancy in percentiles. This is because of the rounding-off procedure. Mazes [*] is not included in the Perceptual Organization IQ in Table 2.1.)

You will note that, for this student, the very large discrepancy among the three factors becomes apparent in both the IQ scores and the percentiles. Using Kaufman's rule-of-thumb interpretation of a significant difference, we see that the Factor III average of 7 is significantly lower than *both* the Factor I and II averages. The "third factor" can therefore legitimately be interpreted. When the Factor III average is 3 points (or more) lower than *either* the Factor I or II averages, then, says Kaufman, such interpretations are psychometrically valid.

So, for this student, the Full Scale IQ is exactly 100 ± 6; but look at the difference in factor abilities! Many educators and parents will base their expectation of the child's potential on the Full Scale IQ and miss the important implications of the three-factor split. In this case, expectations for all academic tasks based solely on the Full Scale IQ would be a great disservice to the student because his factor abilities are unevenly developed—significantly so. His Verbal and Performance abilities are about evenly developed, but the Freedom from Distractibility factor is not, and seems to preclude academic success in certain areas at the present time. That means that some modifications of expectations is necessary, as is the likelihood of some type of remedial help.

What educational implications are there for this student? There are many, actually; but the WISC-R scores only *suggest* certain hypotheses. Like a good detective, the school psychologist and remedial teacher must track down the clues, do further testing if necessary, and develop a program based on the student's individual needs.

To make matters more complicated, the three-factor split of scores *by itself* cannot be used to *diagnose* learning problems, since there are students who show such splits on their WISC-R profiles, but who display no academic difficulties.

With those cautions in mind, let's make a few attempts at hypothesizing about this student. Since both the Verbal Comprehension and Perceptual Organization factors are developed to an average extent, we might expect this student to display good skills in many areas of his life, including some aspects of academics. For example, this student might be a good reader. His facility for language is solidly average, and he can show this when asked. Sometimes, though, students with low scores on Factor III have not "cracked the code" in reading, and are not good readers. Therefore, more detective work is necessary to address that hypothesis. If the student is not overly shy, we would also expect him to be able to express himself verbally, at least to an average extent. Therefore, his answers to oral questions in class would show him as having the ability to do the work. And this is very important, because most classroom teachers (and, of course, parents) base their academic expectations for a student on how well they see him performing in oral situations. Once the expectation is set, then if the student is not performing at least to this average extent in *all* areas, they begin to ask themselves why. And a vicious cycle can begin. Because the teacher expects average work in all areas, he may become very upset when the student does not produce. Labels such as "lazy" are then applied, and a negative set of expectations is introduced. The teacher might put pressure on the student to perform at the same level as the rest of the class; and, when he cannot, he is perhaps kept in after school until all his work is completed. This extra pressure might cause undue stress for the student, but maybe he doesn't like to show it. So he bottles it up inside until he gets home, and then lets his parents know how much he hates school or a particular teacher. And so on. This is all speculation from a few scores, of course; and all of these guesses must be followed up. Interviews with the student's teacher and parents will serve to confirm or deny many of them, and thereby suggest appropriate courses of action. Let's not forget that some students *are* truly lazy. This makes accurate diagnosis even more important in such situations. But, as a rule-of-thumb, *never* assume that the student is lazy. It's often a cover-up.

FIGURE 2.3. A WISC-R profile showing a three-factor split.

[WISC-R Record Form]

Age: 9 years, 5 months, 5 days

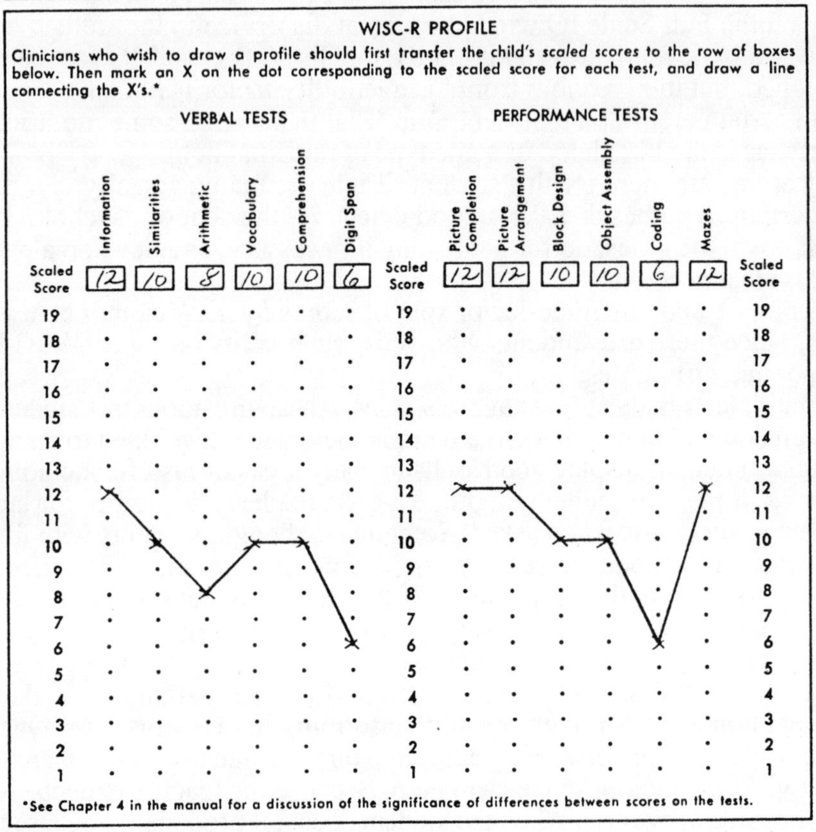

Verbal Tests (Raw Score / Scaled Score)
- Information: 14 / 12
- Similarities: 11 / 10
- Arithmetic: 9 / 8
- Vocabulary: 27 / 10
- Comprehension: 15 / 10
- (Digit Span): 7 / 6
- Verbal Score: 50

Performance Tests (Raw Score / Scaled Score)
- Picture Completion: 19 / 12
- Picture Arrangement: 28 / 12
- Block Design: 22 / 10
- Object Assembly: 20 / 10
- Coding: 25 / 6
- (Mazes): 22 / 12
- Performance Score: 50

	Scaled Score	IQ
Verbal Score	50	100
Performance Score	50	100
Full Scale Score	100	100

Factor I = 103 (Percentile 56)
Factor II = 106 (Percentile 65)
Factor III = 78 (Percentile 8)

The concept of the "zone of potential difference" should also be employed here. The student is functioning to an average level in Factors I and II. His "zone of potential difference," here, may not be very large (depending on his age and other factors). For Factor III, the zone may also be large or small, depending on the nature of the problem and its severity. The type and frequency of remediation, the attitude of the student and the parents, and so on, are all important considerations when it comes to a prognosis. Actually, what little research there is on the prognosis for various types of WISC-R profiles, shows that this particular pattern—provided that the home environment is not chaotic—is quite amenable to remediation.[25] By "remediation," I don't mean the WISC-R profile itself; I mean the accompanying reading difficulty, if there is one.

Moreover, even though the name for Factor III on the WISC-R is Freedom from Distractibility, distractibility itself may not be the underlying problem. There are many possible reasons why the student scores low on this factor. Perhaps it *is* distractibility. But it may also be because of poor facility with numbers, because of poor auditory short-term memory, because of difficulties with simultaneous or sequential information processing, difficulties with phonemic manipulation, or a combination of these. Or something else. The educator and school psychologist must track down these various hypotheses.

In this case, the student actually was a good reader but a very poor writer. His facility for numbers was excellent. Much of his academic performance was consistent with results on Factors I and II, but his written output was very weak. The student had to make speed/accuracy trade-offs all the time because of his poor psychomotor speed (the low score on Coding especially reflects this). If he wrote quickly, he became very sloppy. If he slowed down, he was able to be neat, but his output was low. And indeed, a very vicious cycle had been set up with a very negative home/school interaction, each side blaming the other for the boy's problem. It is important to realize in this case that the problem was genuine. The student *could* not, without modification, match his verbal potential with his written output. The results of my testing and the educational implications were discussed with the student's teachers and with his parents. A short-term remedial program was set up with the goal of increasing his written output. In the meantime, his teachers decreased the amount of written work he had to do, thus easing some of the pressure caused by unrealistic expectations. Within six months, the student had made significant gains in written output. This was documented, because charts were used as a means of keeping track of his gains. He still couldn't produce as much as his classmates, but he was certainly producing much more. The parents, and of course both the student and his teachers, were much happier.

This example illustrates how important it is to go beyond the scores themselves. The scores are only suggestive. The rest is energy and creativity—intelligence in motion on the part of educators concerned about the student.

Because of the frequency of their occurrence, I will have much more to say about interpreting three-factor splits in a later chapter.

Bannatyne's Recategorizations

Alexander Bannatyne regrouped the WISC subtests in the following way:[26]

Conceptual	*Spatial*	*Sequencing*	*Acquired Knowledge*
Similarities	Picture Completion	Arithmetic	Information
Vocabulary	Block Design	Digit Span	Arithmetic
Comprehension	Object Assembly	Coding	Vocabulary

These groupings are based on a logical interpretation and are therefore not as vigorously supported or researched as the factor-analytic groupings. Bannatyne did his work on the WISC originally, but the regroupings apply equally well to the WISC-R. Note that Picture Arrangement and Mazes are not used at all, whereas Vocabulary and Arithmetic are used twice under different headings.

I have found the fact that Vocabulary falls on both the Acquired Knowledge and Conceptual categories so often as to be a hindrance to interpretation. For example, suppose a student obtains the following scale scores on the Verbal Scale:

Information	5
Similarities	7
Arithmetic	6
Vocabulary	5
Comprehension	10

Using the regroupings, we find a significant difference between the Conceptual (scaled score average = 5, or percentile 25) and Acquired Knowledge categories (scale score average = 5, or percentile 5). But the fact that Vocabulary is one of the subtests in *both* categories is puzzling.

But Bannatyne's regroupings are very useful at other times in interpreting some profiles. There is evidence that students with learning disabilities, for example, obtain a pattern of scores on Bannatyne's categories which goes: Spatial > Conceptual > Sequencing > Acquired Knowledge (Sequencing and Acquired Knowledge may be equally low, however). This pattern was found for learning-disabled students *as a group*, so the presence of the pattern in a specific student's profile *cannot* be used to diagnose a learning disability. The pattern is merely suggestive, and should be followed up by other tests. This pattern is also *not found* in the WISC-R scores of learning-disabled students from minority groups. The pattern in those groups is generally Spatial > Sequential > Conceptual.

Though the pattern is present on the WISC-R, it is *not* a predictor of learning difficulties on the *Wechsler Preschool and Primary Scale of Intelligence* (WPPSI), the downward extension of the WISC-R. Interestingly, no boys who showed this pattern on the WPPSI at age five developed reading problems when followed-up three years later, but about half the girls who had the pattern, did.[27]

Also useful is the so-called "ACID" profile. You will frequently find that Arithmetic, Coding, Information, and Digit Span are significantly lower than other subtest scores. These subtests seem to share "memory" in common, and again are suggestive of learning problems. Information and Arithmetic, from the Acquired Knowledge cluster, also fall into the ACID group. If we go back to Sternberg's distinctions, it seems that students with good conceptual abilities have internalized the metacomponents, performance components, and learning components required to perform well on verbal-conceptual areas as tapped by subtests like Similarities, Vocabulary, and Comprehension, and on the perceptual-performance areas as tapped by most of the Performance scale of the WISC-R. But they have not acquired or developed the same strategies for the ACID or Freedom from Distractibility group. Sometimes, the metacomponent awareness is definitely there. For example, the student knows *what* to do on the Arithmetic or Coding subtest, but cannot *perform* (or performs incorrectly), or has not *learned* the critical subskills necessary. So the ACID group taps into some areas that appear to be very important for school-based learning. This can be useful to know in some ways; but again, in an of itself, it is not *diagnostic*, only suggestive.

Note also, that Bannatyne's Sequencing category is identical to the Freedom from Distractibility factor. It is important to remember, then, that "sequencing," as such, may not be why the student scores low on the Arithmetic, Digit Span, and Coding cluster of subtests. Sequencing difficulties may be part of the reason; but that hypothesis must now complete or complement the other possible explanations for the low scores. Interpreting a WISC-R profile is never easy or clear-cut!

Perhaps, based on the input you receive from the teacher, your own observations, and those of the reading specialist, you decide that sequencing *is* a difficulty for the student. How can that be linked to a reading program? Appendix 2-3 could be useful in terms of providing some reading strategies taking the sequencing problem into account. But perhaps you decided that distractibility is also involved. Then, perhaps, some of the behavioral strategies and principles for classroom management found in Chapters 3 and 5, and in Appendix 2-4, will be helpful.

Interpreting a WISC-R Score: Some Initial Considerations

The raw scores on the WISC-R are converted, through the use of tables provided in the WISC-R manual, to a number of *standard scores*. It is the standard scores which are interpretable. Raw scores, by themselves, don't tell you very much.

Whenever one samples scores on a large number of people, the scores themselves fall into a "normal" (Gaussian) distribution. This simply means that some of the scores will be very low, some are very high, and a majority cluster around a central point. One can develop a *frequency distribution* of these scores; and when the distribution is graphed, it looks like this:

FIGURE 2.4. The normal curve.

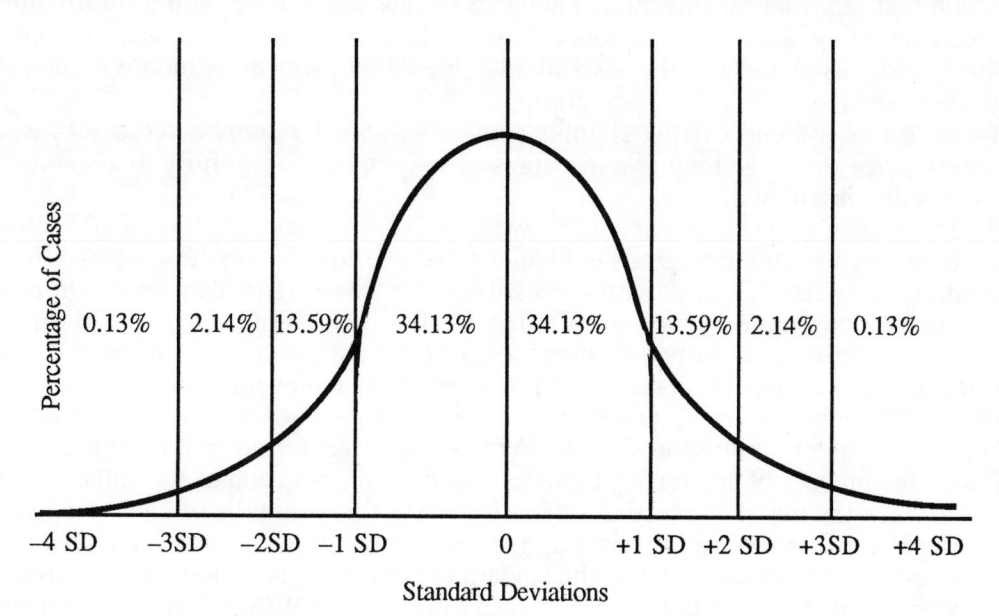

Percentage of Cases: 0.13% | 2.14% | 13.59% | 34.13% | 34.13% | 13.59% | 2.14% | 0.13%

Standard Deviations: −4 SD, −3SD, −2SD, −1 SD, 0, +1 SD, +2 SD, +3SD, +4 SD

WISC-R:
Scores	69−	70-79	80-89	90-109	110-119	120-129	130+
Scaled Scores	1-3	4-5	6-7	8-11	12-13	14-15	16-19
Percentile	2−	3-8	9-24	25-74	75-90	91-97	98+

This curve (also known as a "bell curve" because of its shape) is a mathematical representation of what exists "out there" in the real world of scores.

Let's take the Information subtest of the WISC-R as an example. This subtest has 30 items; the subtest itself can be administered to a child as young as age six or as old as 16 years, 11 months. Let's suppose a student who is eight years and two months old answers 15 of the 30 items correctly. The raw score represents only a 50-percent-correct rate. Does this mean that the student did poorly on this subtest? From the raw score alone, it is not possible to answer that question. Maybe it's a good score, and maybe it isn't. It would really depend on how other students in the same age group did. If his peers, on the average, only get eight items correct of the 30, then this student will be scoring much higher than his peers. If, on the other hand, his peers score correctly on 20 of the 30 items on the average, then this student will be below his peers.

How can we know? This is where "norming" the test comes in. We can know how any age group of students does on the WISC-R by going out and selecting "representative samples" of students in each of the age groups. We will obtain a normal distribution of scores for each of the WISC-R subtests and the test as a whole. From the raw scores, we can calculate standard scores applicable to each age group. In this way, we can see how the standard score that the student obtains compares to a representative sample of other students of the same age. As it turns out, in the sample I am using, the raw score of 15 for a student who is eight years, two months of age, also converts to a scaled score of 15. Now, what does *that* mean?

Every distribution of scores has a midpoint. We can assign any number to represent the midpoint. In the case of the IQ score, the midpoint is usually represented by 100. In the case of each of the WISC-R subtests, *their* midpoint is represented by the number 10. So, if 10 is the midpoint, we know that 50 percent of the students will score above 10, and 50 percent will score below 10. In fact, we know exactly how many students will score above and below any given point on the distribution. We can therefore convert the standard score of 10 to a *percentile*, and see where the student stands, compared to his peers. In this example, a standard score (called a scaled score on the WISC-R) of 15 is very high, falling at the 95th percentile, compared to the student's peers. By contrast, if a 14-year-old student achieved a raw score of 15 on the Information subtest, then the corresponding scaled score is only 7, which is only at the 16th percentile, compared to other 14-year-olds. By the use of these standard scores, then, we can compare eight-year-olds to other eight-year-olds, or to any other age group.

Table 2.2 at the end of this chapter provides some IQ scores, scale scores, and their corresponding percentiles and their classifications. Study the table carefully to get some "feel" for how the scores are distributed.

Besides scaled scores and percentiles, we can also calculate other standard scores from the same raw score, such as stanines, grade equivalents, or age equivalents (test ages). On the WISC-R, the standard score itself, and perhaps percentiles, are most frequently used. On achievement tests, other conversions, mainly grade equivalents, are frequently used. These are all manipulations of the same raw score data. For my own purposes, I prefer the use of percentiles to explain results to both teachers and parents. This preference also extends to achievement tests where I continually see the abuse of "grade-equivalent" scores.

Once the student's raw scores on the WISC-R are transferred to the front page of the test protocol, then the process of converting them to scaled scores for each of the subtests begins. This is quite easy, since the manual provides a table for every three months of chronological age. The examiner simply looks up the appropriate age table, and the conversion is there. Since there is a new table for every three months of age, the student is being compared to a very narrow age range, thus increasing the accuracy of the comparison. (However, the WISC-R was standardized on the 1970 U.S. Census. So it is already outdated. Is it time for a WISC-R-2?)

The examiner then adds up the scale score totals for the five main Verbal and five Performance subtests, and adds those two numbers together. By using another table in the manual, a Verbal IQ, a Performance IQ, and a Full Scale IQ are calculated on the test protocol for that student.

Both Digit Span and Mazes are "optional" subtests. That means, they can be used to calculate an IQ if one of the main subtests is spoiled for some reason. This does not happen very often, so I always administer them anyway, because of the additional and very valuable information they provide. Digit Span is almost essential to administer since, without it, one cannot calculate the Factor III score.

The Digit Span Subtest

The Digit Span subtest consists of a "digits-forward" and a "digits-backward" series. The student is presented with random numbers and is asked to repeat them. The student is first presented with three digits forward, then four, five, and so on, up to nine digits. There are two trials for each series. When the student fails both trials, then the backward series is introduced. The student is given some trial examples and then asked to repeat two digits backwards, then three, four, and so on, up to eight digits. Again, if the student fails both trials of a given series, testing is discontinued. Raw scores for the two tasks are then summed, and a *single* scale score is determined from the raw score total.

A "memory span" of 7 ± 2 digits is normal for adults. This span gradually increases between the ages of two to 16, presumably because the child gradually acquires mnemonic strategies such as "chunking" and "rehearsal" with age. Such strategies are very important in many academic subjects, including reading. In Appendix 2-5, I have outlined a rehearsal strategy to be used in assisting a student to acquire sight words.

Sometimes, students perform markedly differently on the digits-forward or -backward series; but this information is lost when the scores are combined and averaged. As a rule-of-thumb, if a student's digit *span* is greater or lesser by three numbers on either task, then that difference has some diagnostic significance. For example, if a student is able correctly to recall 7 digits in the forward series (even on just one trial), but only 4 digits in the backward series, then the *span* is significantly different for the two types of tasks. The information-processing requirements for these tasks is quite different, and different explanations are possible. Some authorities regard the digits-forward series as a sequential task, because the information is to be remembered in its correct sequence. Digits-backward is seen as a simultaneous task, because the numbers must be remembered as a group and then broken down into their constituent parts.[28] The distinction between sequential and simultaneous information-processing also has a number of educational implications; but these will be dealt with in the chapter on learning styles.

Cooper calls digits-forward a serial task involving mostly auditory sequential memory; while digits-backward involves more complex mental operations.[29] The student may rely primarily on an auditory strategy to begin with, he says, by subvocalizing the digits, then saying them aloud. If the digits go beyond 3 or 4 in number, however, this strategy will be inadequate. The student would be better off trying to visualize the digits mentally, and then "pick them off" from this visual array. The examiner needs to be alert to whether or not the student is able to "switch" strategies appropriately.

Brighter students simply may find digits-forward boring, while digits-backward is seen as more challenging. Again, the examiner must determine which of many possibilities has the most explanatory power for the student's performance on any one subtest.

There is evidence that learning-disabled students have difficulty employing mnemonic strategies for many types of memory and academic tasks. The Digit Span subtest of the WISC-R is no exception. There are a number of studies which show that students with learning disabilities perform particularly poorly on this subtest.[30] However, we cannot, at this point, generalize this deficiency to reading or other academic tasks per se. Further, there is a learning-disabled group that does poorly on Digit Span, and another that does not. Nevertheless, the alert examiner can glean some hypotheses by careful observation of the student during this deceptively simple subtest; and these may suggest useful remedial strategies. The student who finds it difficult to visualize digits, for example, may also not visualize when reading. Yet there is evidence that encouraging students to visualize can improve reading ability.[31] In Appendix 2-2, you will find some concrete steps for encouraging visualization in the task of reading.

Finally, because memory span develops with age, it is sometimes useful for the remedial teacher and the WISC-R examiner to have some idea of where the student stands developmentally. The scaled score provides this, but only for the combined tasks. Sometimes it is useful to have separate norms for the digits-forward and digits-backward series when there is a discrepancy.

Fortunately, these have been researched.[32] The tables provided in the article cited can be used to obtain separate norms.

By way of summary, here are some recommendations from Mishra, Ferguson, and King, who undertook a review of the Digit Span literature:[33]

> First, in light of the research, the forward and backward components can be analyzed separately. Second, digit span should be considered a measure, not only of memory, but of attention, sequencing ability, symbolic or numerical skills, mnemonic strategies, and speed of item identification. Better interpretations will be made when the psychologist weighs a number of hypotheses before arriving at a conclusion. Third, the psychologist should be well acquainted with the score patterns, of which Digit Span is a part, that are typical of certain impairments. Finally, even in view of all the research, the practicing psychologist needs to recognize the strengths and limitations of the subtest. Despite a century-long history, indicating the importance of digit span in memory research and in mental ability assessment, it should be noted that the task, at best, provides only a glimpse into the cognitive make-up of the examinee. A sound understanding of the sources of variance accounting for differences in digit span performance is still far from attained. The recent research on the cognitive basis of digit span performance, however, has begun to reveal the nature of the association between memory, learning, and thinking. The presence of such association should help clinicians feel confident that digit span tasks are an integral part of ability assessment procedures.

The relationship between auditory short-term memory, which the Digit Span subtest partly measures, and reading, is important to understand. I will discuss this relationship in more detail in a later chapter.

Calculating and Interpreting Individual Subtest Strengths and Weaknesses

Once the scaled scores are entered on the front page of the WISC-R protocol, the examiner should calculate a Verbal and Performance scaled score average. Add up the scaled scores of the six Verbal subtests and divide by six. Round your answer to the nearest whole number. Do the same for the Performance Scale. Draw the averages in on the profile and determine the corresponding percentiles. Now you are in a position to determine the student's own individual strengths and weaknesses. The rule-of-thumb is that any subtest which deviates from the student's own Verbal and Performance average by ± 3 points, should be regarded as an individual strength or weakness, depending on the direction of the difference.

Figure 2.5 presents a profile which illustrates this.

You will note that each subtest that deviates by three or more points from its corresponding Verbal or Performance mean is marked with an S or W respectively. (In this particular case, there is a very large Verbal/Performance IQ discrepancy of 33 points. More on this in a later chapter.)

At this juncture, many examiners begin a bottom-up interpretation, giving subtest-specific interpretations to parents and teachers. This is not a psychometrically preferred practice. If you turn back to Table 1.1, you will see that the subtests are grouped according to certain "abilities" and "influences" that two or more subtests share. These abilities and influences should take preference over the subtest-specific interpretations. The subtest-specific interpretation should be used only after other hypotheses are exhausted. This makes sense. Any test with, say, 30 items, will not be as reliable as a test with, say, 60 items. So, if one can combine subtests and arrive at a more stable measure of a presumed underlying strength or weakness, one has a stronger base for educational intervention. The Freedom from Distractibility factor is a good case in point. There are many possible reasons why a student scores poorly on this cluster, as already mentioned. It is up to the examiner to track these down. For example, if the student scores poorly on the Digit Span subtest, then many examiners immediately invoke an explanation of "poor auditory short-term memory," which is what is specifically measured by this subtest. Now, perhaps "poor auditory short-term memory," as evidenced by a low score on Digit Span, *does* enter the picture; but this hypothesis should be examined first in conjunction with the scores on Arithmetic and Coding. If auditory short-term memory was an observed factor on the other two subtests and is also upheld by teacher observations, then that interpretation is far more reliable than one based on the Digit Span subtest *alone*, and becomes the primary explanation for the low score on Factor III. Again, I would urge the reader to look to Kaufman for more information on these subtleties.

The Average Range

Figure 2.6 shows one student's completed profile on the WISC-R.

Now, let's give a brief interpretation to the scores so you understand how they function. (Just for practice, you should calculate the scores on the three factors for this particular profile.)

The Full Scale IQ is 96 ± 6. That score falls at the 39th percentile. Is this average, or not?

Many people, parents and teachers included, have the mistaken idea that an IQ of 100 is "average." A score of 100 is in the average range, all right, because it is the midpoint of the distribution of scores. But not all IQ scores will be exactly 100, even though it is the single most frequently occurring score. In fact, *50 percent of all IQ scores will fall below 100*. Many people are amazed when I tell them that; but it couldn't be any other way. Have another look at the bell curve illustration to verify this.

Once we set a number for a midpoint, then half the scores will fall below this number, and the other half will be above the midpoint. In the case of the IQ, half the IQs of all children in North America will be below 100, and half will be above 100. If we set the midpoint at 10, as is done for the individual WISC-R subtests, then half the scores will be below 10; the other half, above 10. If we use grade-equivalent scores, then *half the students will score below "grade level,"* and the other half will score *above* "grade level." This does *not* mean that half the students are "underachieving," however.

So, then, what is "average"? We can see that there could be disagreement over this (and there is), because "average" has to be a *range* of scores, not just a single score. Some people like to set the average range as any score falling between 85 and 115 on an IQ test. About 68 percent of all children will score between those two numbers. Since this is a majority, then, so the argument goes, that range should be considered "average."

I find that range is too generous, however. A score of 85 falls at the 16th percentile. My experience has been that students whose IQs consistently fall in the 80s have considerable difficulty with mainstream academics, especially in the upper grades. To call such students "average" is to set an unreasonably high expectation for them, one they most often cannot attain, at least in the mainstream academic programs.

The range I prefer is 90 to 109. This includes 50 percent of all students, and is—in my experience—a more realistic standard. Even 90 is only at the 25th percentile and is, therefore, a minimum-standard average, if you will. By contrast, an IQ score of 109 falls at the 73rd percentile.

Different states and provinces may set different criteria and cut-off scores for average and other classifications—thereby affecting who goes into what special classes. This can be confusing to parents and professionals alike, but there is nothing that can be done about it from a theoretical perspective. "Average" is an arbitrary range; and, as long as it is so, people will argue over it. Many diagnostic problems therefore ensue. To use an uncomplicated example, a student whose IQ falls at 85 and who shows a two-year lag in reading might be labeled "learning disabled" in one state or province, and a "slow learner" in another.

WISC-R COMPANION

FIGURE 2.5. A completed WISC-R profile, graphing strengths and weaknesses.

WISC-R RECORD FORM

Wechsler Intelligence Scale for Children—Revised

NAME _____ AGE ___ SEX ___
ADDRESS _____
PARENT'S NAME _____
SCHOOL _____ GRADE __2__
PLACE OF TESTING _____ TESTED BY ___
REFERRED BY _____

WISC-R PROFILE

Clinicians who wish to draw a profile should first transfer the child's *scaled* scores to the row of boxes below. Then mark an X on the dot corresponding to the scaled score for each test, and draw a line connecting the X's.*

VERBAL TESTS (S, W, W annotations above): Information, Similarities, Arithmetic, Vocabulary, Comprehension, Digit Span

Scaled Score: 16 | 18 | 10 | 16 | 17 | 11

$\bar{x} = 15$ (%95)

PERFORMANCE TESTS (W, W, S annotations): Picture Completion, Picture Arrangement, Block Design, Object Assembly, Coding, Mazes

Scaled Score: 12 | 7 | 13 | 12 | 8 | 19

$\bar{x} = 12$ (%75)

*See Chapter 4 in the manual for a discussion of the significance of differences between scores on the tests.

NOTES

	Year	Month	Day
Date Tested			
Date of Birth			
Age	8	0	1

	Raw Score	Scaled Score
VERBAL TESTS		
Information	17	16
Similarities	19	18
Arithmetic	9	10
Vocabulary	32	16
Comprehension	22	17
(Digit Span)	(10)	(11)
Verbal Score		77
PERFORMANCE TESTS		
Picture Completion	17	12
Picture Arrangement	12	7
Block Design	28	13
Object Assembly	20	12
Coding	26	8
(Mazes)	(29)	(19)
Performance Score		52

	Scaled Score	IQ
Verbal Score	77	135
Performance Score	52	102
Full Scale Score	129	121±6

*Prorated from 4 tests, if necessary.

Copyright © 1971, 1974 by The Psychological Corporation. All rights reserved. No part of this record form may be reproduced in any form of printing or by any other means, electronic or mechanical, including, but not limited to, photocopying, audiovisual recording and transmission, and portrayal or duplication in any information storage and retrieval system, without permission in writing from the publisher. See Catalog for further information.

The Psychological Corporation, New York, N.Y. 10017

Printed in U.S.A.

74-103AS 9-990334

WISC-R COMPANION

FIGURE 2.6. A completed WISC-R profile, strengths and weaknesses within the average range.

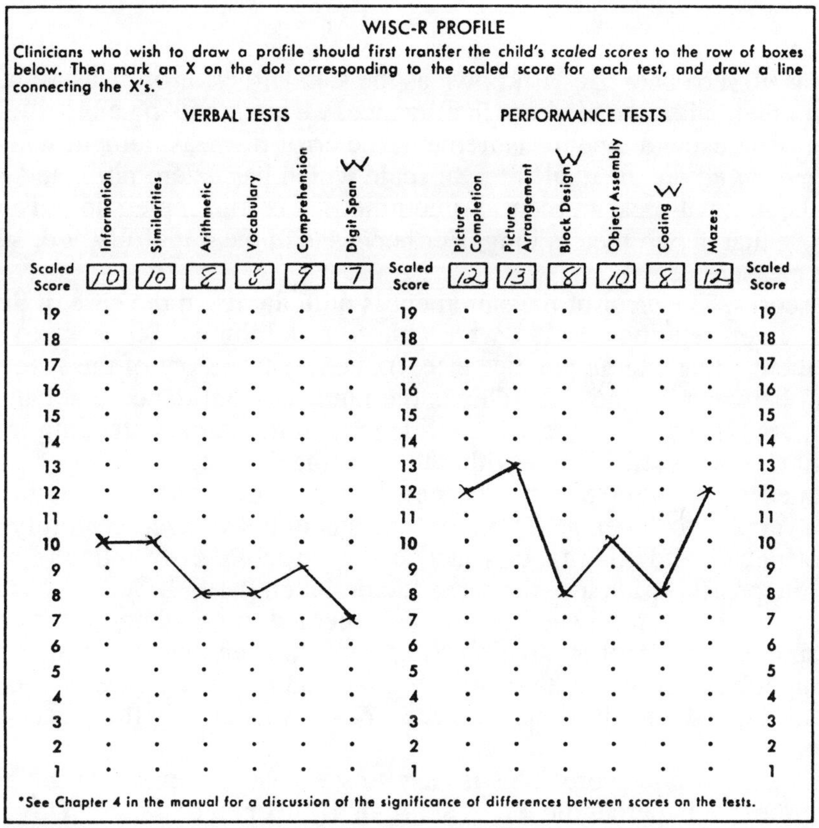

In the elementary grades, this may not cause serious placement problems, since resource room teachers frequently serve a heterogeneous group in terms of IQ scores, and are usually more interested in helping a student with difficulty than with any diagnostic label. But many placement (and therefore, funding) problems are created by the often arbitrary nature of these classifications. Later on, in junior high school, for example, a prevocational program, rather than a learning disabilities program, might be more suitable for the student. If the law says that the student is "average," however, because of an 85 IQ, then the student could be placed in yet another learning disabilities class with more attempts to "catch him up." This unnecessarily frustrating situation is discouraging to the parent, the student, and teacher alike. The student's practical needs are not likely to be met, and the end result could be more frustration and dismal academic progress. Such is the "stuff" of endless educational lawsuits.

Standard Error of Measurement

Another very complicating factor must now be discussed. You will note that I have reported the Full Scale IQ score as 96 ± 6. The "± 6" is known as the standard error of measurement (SEM); it is an acknowledgment that, when we measure intelligence, we are not using a precise instrument. When we measure a table using a tape measurement, the error of measurement will be very small, because length is measured on an equal-interval scale which has a zero point and exactly equal portions between the units of measurement. Something that is four meters long is exactly twice as long as something that is two meters long. Further, we can meaningfully add, subtract, multiply, or divide those measurements.

This is *not* true for IQ scores. The error of measurement is quite large. In the case of 96 ± 6, what we can say by way of interpretation is: "If I were able to test Johnny 100 times today (without him getting tired, or there being a large practice effect), then 95 times out of the 100, his Full Scale IQ score would fall between 90 and 102. This is the range of confidence that can be placed in the obtained score of 96. Notice: The range of confidence is quite large, extending from percentile 25 to 54. However, this score is still clearly within the "average" range.

But suppose the obtained score was 88 ± 6. The range of confidence is now 82 to 94 (percentile 12 to 34), or "low average" to "average." So, does the student have average ability, or not? At this point, it is a judgment call; and other factors such as the particular distribution of subtest scores (remember that, if the profile splits into the three factors, then the Full Scale IQ is regarded as an *underestimate*), or how well motivated the student seemed to be when he took the test, enter the picture. The examiner might feel that the obtained score was an underestimate for a variety of reasons. Or, there might be a school or state policy on the matter. In any case, the judgments are not easy to make at times, and must be done with great care—particularly if a placement in a special program is at stake.

An IQ score is *not* an equal-interval score. This is easy to see, just by looking at the percentiles in Table 2. An IQ score of 95 is percentile 37. A score of 100 is percentile 50. This is a difference of 13 percentile points on an IQ difference of 5 points. Now, look at an IQ score of 125. The score falls at the 95th percentile. But an IQ score of 130, which is also 5 points higher, falls at the 98th percentile. This is a difference of only 3 percentile points at this upper end of the distribution. At both the higher and lower ends of the distribution, the percentile differences are much smaller. That is why it isn't possible to say that a student whose IQ score is 120 is "twice as bright" as someone whose IQ score is 60. In a mathematical sense, a standard *score* of 100 is twice as great as 50 (and that is why standard scores are used in the first place: we *can* add, subtract, multiply, or divide them meaningfully); but the *underlying dimension* of intelligence is not, so far as we can tell, "equal-interval." What we *can* meaningfully say is that the one whose IQ is 120 is at the 91st percentile compared to students his own age, while the one who scores 60 is only at the 2nd percentile for his age. The first student obviously ranks higher than the second (even taking the SEM into account); but we cannot meaningfully say that he ranks "twice as high," because the underlying mental energy is simply not equally distributed, nor does it have a zero point.

If what I've said about IQ scores makes their measurement seem "fuzzy" and imprecise, the situation is even *worse* for so-called "grade-equivalent" scores.

Grade-Equivalent Scores

Grade-equivalent standard scores are not used in interpreting IQ scores; but they are used in almost all standardized achievement tests, so it is worthwhile spending a little time discussing them. Let's use the *Peabody Individual Achievement Test* (PIAT) as an example. The PIAT is a well standardized achievement test. That means that many students from a variety of age, sex, and socioeconomic groups from across the United States (but not Canada) were used in the standardization sample. Different norms for different age groups are to be found in the PIAT manual. Unfortunately, grade-equivalent norms are most frequently reported, but almost *never* with the accompanying SEM, even though they should be. This is not the fault of the test-makers; it is the responsibility of the examiner.

For example, let's say that Mary achieves a raw score of 33 on the PIAT Reading Comprehension subtest; and let's assume she is eight years old when tested in February of the school year. The manual provides tables that allow the examiner to report grade-equivalent scores, age scores, percentiles, and/or standard scores. In Mary's case, a raw score of 33 is converted to a grade-equivalent score of 3.5, or mid-grade-3, which is where the student is actually placed. The corresponding percentile score is 50, which means her score falls above 50 percent of the students her own age; also, it is the mid-way mark in terms of ranking.

Most likely, the examiner will choose to report Mary's results using the grade-equivalent scores, and Mary will be reported to be reading "at the mid-grade-3 level." This statement is misleading in a number of ways. The SEM, for instance, is almost never reported. In the case of the PIAT and most achievement tests, this is very significant. The PIAT manual provides the SEM for *raw scores* for each of the subtests at different grade levels. In this case, the SEM for the raw score is ± 5. That means there is 68 percent confidence that the raw score from 29 to 39 contains Mary's "true" raw score. This means the score on Reading Comprehension could be anywhere from the 39th to the 65th percentile. That's quite a range. In terms of grade-equivalent scores, the range of confidence is from 3.1 to 4.2—over a full grade level! And the 68 percent confidence level is regarded as quite low! To increase the confidence *level*, we have to increase the confidence *range*. So, to achieve the 95 percent confidence level, we have to *double* the ± 5. This changes the range of confidence to 33 ± 10 for the raw score; and the range of confidence in the equivalent percentiles is now 15 to 77! For the grade-equivalent scores, the range of confidence is now 2.4 to 5.0. One cannot be very confident in such a range! I suppose the lesson to be learned, is that our scores are not very precise, after all, even though we work under the illusion that they are. (You can see, though, that the WISC-R does have a "tighter" confidence range than the PIAT at the 95 percent level.)

Additionally, the PIAT items, like the WISC-R items, are chosen for their "discrimination power," not their match to any particular third-grade curriculum. This student may or may not be reading third-grade material at her school. It depends on what is being taught, and where. Canadian students, for example, typically score higher than their U.S. counterparts on achievement tests. And the difference can be substantial. To illustrate, the PIAT was administered to randomly selected students in the province of Alberta. Percentile equivalents were then determined from the raw scores the students obtained. These percentiles are recommended for use whenever possible for Alberta students. If we take Mary's raw score of 33 on the Reading Comprehension subtest, the equivalent percentile score in Alberta is only 28, as opposed to the American percentile of 50. The range of confidence is from percentile 10 to 46. So, Mary would be functioning a *lot* lower, according to Alberta standards. I am not sure that American test makers (and Canadian examiners continually use their products) ever take this cultural difference into account. Very few tests produced in the U.S. have any type of Canadian norms or appreciation of the "bias" to U.S. content. This is most unfortunate; and efforts should be made to correct it, as it adds yet another complication to the already complicated business of measurement.

So, is Mary functioning at grade level, or not? You can see that the question is not easy to answer because the test results have such a large error band, and the test content doesn't necessarily match the curriculum. So a score of 3.5 on the PIAT does not necessarily mean that Mary comprehends third-grade reading material. To get a more accurate picture of where she does comprehend, requires a more in-depth reading assessment. Usually, an informal reading inventory is used for this purpose. But, no matter what reading test is used, formal or informal, someone has made a judgment of where the student stands, relative to some standard or criterion. A criterion-referenced test is one that specifies how a student performance against that criterion, whereas a norm-referenced test, such as the PIAT, compares the student's scores against a norm. *Both* kinds of achievement tests are useful, despite these interpretation problems. However, the results of norm-referenced tests should be reported with the same care and caution that IQ tests should be. "One-shot tests"—either IQ or achievement—can be terribly abused, and so can the results.

I think it's very important to get some idea of what we can expect children to be doing by way of reading and mathematics at different grade levels. Check your local, state, or provincial curriculum guides for assistance. I have also found the Barbe Reading Check Lists (Barbe, Walter B., 1961, *Educator's Guide to Personalized Reading Instruction*, Englewood Cliffs, New Jersey, Prentice-Hall) to be very useful.

The last point worth mentioning is that a grade score of 3.5 on the PIAT is a midpoint if the student is tested in the middle of the school year. That means that 50 percent of all students in the middle of the third-grade year will score *below* grade 3.5 on the PIAT when administered in the middle of the school year. This fact has unfortunately often been misinterpreted to mean that any student who scores below "grade level" must be "underachieving," perhaps even "learning disabled." However, as we will see in the next section of this chapter, notions of underachievement and the diagnosis of learning disabilities are complex issues. In the meantime, remember that 50 percent of all students will score between the 25th percentile and the 74th percentile on an achievement test. This is the average range on the achievement test; and, in this case, it would correspond to grade-equivalent scores from 2.7 to 4.7.

Despite their own drawbacks, I strongly urge the use of percentile scores on achievement tests, rather than grade-equivalent scores, whenever results are being discussed with parents or teachers. However, the practice of using grade-equivalent scores is very entrenched. So, if you do use them in your feedback to teachers and parents, be sure your audience has some understanding of the large standard errors of measurement that are involved.

Many kinds of achievement tests are used in both Canada and the U.S. Reading and achievement tests, like IQ tests, should never be used *alone* for major decisions such as placement in special classes. They can be helpful to the classroom teacher for screening pupils who may have greater remedial needs, and to assist in flexible grouping for classroom instructions. Results can also be entered into regression equations (see the next section of this chapter) and, again, prove helpful in placement decisions; but they should not be used *by themselves* for such decisions. Readers might find the article by Ysseldyke and Marston in *School Psychology Review* (Summer [1982] 11:3) useful for better understanding of the underlying skills measured by different standardized reading tests.

**Diagnosing Learning Disabilities
in North America**

The issue of whether or not a student is learning disabled is one which school psychologists must continually answer. The issue is complex, and it is extremely important that the school psychologist be *very* sophisticated in understanding the major issues in this field. A thorough discussion of the matter could be the subject of another book entirely, and would take us too far off our main topic, so, here, I will deal with only a few of the most relevant issues.

First, we need a definition. There are four key components found in almost every definition of learning disabilities. Here, for example, is the definition currently used by the Canadian Association for Children and Adults with Learning Disabilities:

- Learning disabilities is a generic term that refers to a heterogeneous group of disorders due to identifiable or inferred central nervous system dysfunction. Such disorders may be manifested by delays in early development and/or difficulties in any of the following areas: attention, memory, reasoning, coordination, communicating, reading, writing, spelling, calculations, social competence, and emotional maturation.

- Learning disabilities are intrinsic to the individual, and may affect learning and behavior in any individual, including those with potentially average, average, or above-average intelligence.

- Learning disabilities are not due primarily to visual, hearing, or motor handicaps; to mental retardation, emotional disturbance, or environmental disadvantage; although they may occur concurrently with any of these.

The key concepts found in this definition and the many others of learning disabilities are: (1) Learning disabilities involve a *discrepancy* between the student's (average) ability and achievement in one or more academic areas or (2) thinking (processing) skills. *Difficulties in information processing* or other psychological processes such as attention, perception, memory, reasoning, and conceptualization, are also part of the problem. (3) This definition also contains an *exclusionary clause* stating that learning disabilities are not to be confused with mental handicap, emotional disturbance, or other handicapping conditions. Finally, (4) a presumed *central nervous system dysfunction* is specified.

Every one of the four key concepts contained in the definition has at one time or another posed tremendous difficulty to legislators, school administrators, school psychologists, special educators, and parents.

The second major issue in this area, and an even more difficult one, has been the ability to meaningfully *operationalize* and *measure* learning disabilities. An extremely helpful article on the complexity of the measurement issues is one by Cone and Wilson. In it, they identify eight variables which must be considered in using any *expectancy formula*, which is the usual method whereby a "diagnosis" of learning disabilities is made.[34] Also very helpful is the article by Dr. Cecil Reynolds in the *Journal of Special Education*.[35] His state-of-the-art [as of 1988] computer software program for severe discrepancy analysis is available from Trainware (Neshaminy Plaza II, Suite 101, Bristol Pike and Street Road, Bensalem, Pennsylvania 19020). I have found it quite helpful in some cases.

Until there is some consensus regarding a standardized format for the diagnosis of learning disabilities (and there may never be), school psychologists involved in this tricky business can only follow their own existing state or provincial guidelines. Some of these guidelines are more sophisticated than others. The Iowa Department of Public Instruction, for example, has gone a very long way in the right direction for their own school population. School psychologists in North America should support any efforts made in their own areas for adoption of similar procedures. But the way it stands right now, the diagnosis of a "learning disability" is almost whimsical in many places. Almost *everyone* who is assessed could be labeled "learning disabled," just because of the broadness of the definition. It also depends on who does the assessment, what tests are used, and how the results are interpreted in light of local guidelines. Most often, only one or two of the eight critical variables identified by Cone and Wilson are ever incorporated into the diagnosis. This makes the task of the school psychologist even more arduous, aside from all the "political" ramifications of making such a diagnosis. The process is complex and can be extremely frustrating to professionals and parents alike. Therefore, when discussing your results with parents, be sure to tell them which definition of learning disabilities and which guidelines you are using to make your judgment. As well, become very familiar with the intricacies of discrepancy assessments. The diagnosis of learning disabilities is *not* like a medical diagnosis of, say, appendicitis, where the "patient" presents certain "symptoms," which then require a specific course of action, such as an operation. That kind of precision simply doesn't exist in the field of learning disabilities, because the *underlying construct* is *not*, in my opinion, primarily a medical one. It is an *educational* one. Try not to become too embroiled in the political issues, or "take sides." Your primary role is to *assist the child*.

TABLE 2.1. Estimated WISC-R deviation IQs for Factors I, II, and III.

Sum of Scaled Scores	Factor I IQ	Percentile Rank	Factor II IQ	Percentile Rank	Factor III IQ	Percentile Rank
3	—	—	—	—	41	.01
4	47	.02	42	.01	43	.01
5	49	.03	44	.01	45	.01
6	50	.04	46	.02	47	.02
7	51	.05	47	.02	49	.03
8	53	.09	49	.03	52	.07
9	54	.11	50	.04	54	.11
10	56	.17	52	.07	56	.17
11	57	.21	54	.11	58	.26
12	59	.31	55	.13	60	.38
13	60	.38	57	.21	63	1
14	62	1	58	.26	65	1
15	63	1	60	.38	67	1
16	65	1	62	1	69	2
17	66	1	63	1	71	3
18	68	2	65	1	74	4
19	69	2	66	1	76	5
20	71	3	68	2	78	7
21	72	3	70	2	80	9
22	74	4	71	3	82	12
23	75	5	73	4	85	16
24	76	5	74	4	87	19
25	78	7	76	5	89	23
26	79	8	78	7	91	27
27	81	10	79	8	93	32
28	82	12	81	10	96	39
29	84	14	82	12	98	45
30	85	16	84	14	100	50
31	87	19	86	18	102	55
32	88	21	87	19	104	61
33	90	25	88	21	107	68
34	91	27	90	25	109	73
35	93	32	92	30	111	77
36	94	34	94	34	113	81
37	96	39	95	37	115	84
38	97	42	97	42	118	88
39	99	47	98	45	120	91
40	100	50	100	50	122	93
41	101	53	102	55	124	95
42	103	58	103	58	126	96
43	104	61	105	63	129	97
44	106	66	106	66	131	98
45	107	68	108	70	133	99
46	109	73	110	75	135	99
47	110	75	111	77	137	99

Sum of Scaled Scores	Factor I IQ	Percentile Rank	Factor II IQ	Percentile Rank	Factor III IQ	Percentile Rank
48	112	79	113	81	140	99.6
49	113	81	114	82	142	99.7
50	115	84	116	86	144	99.8
51	116	86	118	88	146	99.9
52	118	88	119	90	148	99.9
53	119	90	121	92	151	99.97
54	121	92	122	93	153	99.98
55	122	93	124	95	155	99.99
56	124	95	126	96	157	99.99
57	125	95	127	96	159	99.99
58	126	96	129	97	—	—
59	128	97	130	98	—	—
60	129	97	132	98	—	—
61	131	98	134	99	—	—
62	132	98	135	99	—	—
63	134	99	137	99	—	—
64	135	99	138	99	—	—
65	137	99	140	99.6	—	—
66	138	99	142	99.7	—	—
67	140	99.6	143	99.8	—	—
68	141	99.7	145	99.9	—	—
69	143	99.8	146	99.9	—	—
70	144	99.8	148	99.9	—	—
71	146	99.9	150	99.96	—	—
72	147	99.9	151	99.97	—	—
73	149	99.95	153	99.98	—	—
74	150	99.96	154	99.98	—	—
75	151	99.97	156	99.99	—	—
76	153	99.98	158	99.99	—	—

Verbal Comprehension (Factor I):
 Information, Similarities, Vocabulary, Comprehension
Perceptual Organization (Factor II):
 Picture Completion, Picture Arrangement, Block Design, Object Assembly
Freedom from Distractibility (Factore III):
 Arithmetic, Digit Span, Coding

Add up the scaled scores for each factor, then enter the table under the appropriate column for each factor, and note the IQ and corresponding percentile rank.

Adapted from: Sattler, J. 1982. *Assessment of children's intelligence and special abilities*, 2nd ed. Boston: Allyn and Bacon.

TABLE 2.2. WISC-R scores and percentile ranks.

IQ	Scaled Score	Percentile Rank	Approx. Class.*
155	—	99.99	VS
154	—	99.98	VS
153	—	99.98	VS
152	—	99.97	VS
151	—	99.97	VS
150	—	99.96	VS
149	—	99.95	VS
148	—	99.93	VS
147	—	99.91	VS
146	—	99.89	VS
145	19	99.75	VS
144	—	99.83	VS
143	—	99.79	VS
142	—	99.74	VS
141	—	99.69	VS
140	18	99.62	VS
139	—	99.53	VS
138	—	99	VS
137	—	99	VS
136	—	99	VS
135	17	99	VS
134	—	99	VS
133	—	99	VS
132	—	98	VS
131	—	98	VS
130	16	98	VS
129	—	97	VS
128	—	97	VS
127	—	96	VS
126	—	96	VS
125	15	95	S
124	—	95	S
123	—	94	S
122	—	93	S
121	—	92	S
120	14	91	S
119	—	90	HA
118	—	88	HA
117	—	87	HA
116	—	86	HA
115	13	84	HA
114	—	82	HA
113	—	81	HA
112	—	79	HA
111	—	77	HA
110	12	75	HA

IQ	Scaled Score	Percentile Rank	Approx. Class.*
109	—	73	A
108	—	70	A
107	—	68	A
106	—	66	A
105	11	63	A
104	—	61	A
103	—	58	A
102	—	55	A
101	—	53	A
100	10	50	A
99	—	47	A
98	—	45	A
97	—	42	A
96	—	39	A
95	9	37	A
94	—	34	A
93	—	32	A
92	—	30	A
91	—	27	A
90	8	25	A
89	—	23	LA
88	—	21	LA
87	—	19	LA
86	—	18	LA
85	7	16	LA
84	—	14	LA
83	—	13	LA
82	—	12	LA
81	—	10	LA
80	6	9	LA
79	—	8	MH
78	—	7	MH
77	—	6	MH
76	—	5	MH
75	5	5	MH
74	—	4	MH
73	—	4	MH
72	—	3	MH
71	—	3	MH
70	4	2	MH
69	—	2	MH
68	—	2	MH
67	—	1	MH
66	—	1	MH
65	3	1	MH
64	—	1	MH
63	—	1	MH
62	—	1	MH
61	—	.47	MH

IQ	Scaled Score	Percentile Rank	Approx. Class.*
60	2	.38	MH
59	—	.31	MH
58	—	.26	MH
57	—	.21	MH
56	—	.17	MH
55	1	.13	MH
54	—	.11	MH
53	—	.09	MH
52	—	.07	MH
51	—	.05	MH
50	—	.04	MH
49	—	.03	MH
48	—	.03	MH
47	—	.02	MH
46	—	.02	MH
45	—	.01	MH

*Classification abbreviations:
   VS = Very Superior
   S = Superior
   HA = High Average
   A = Average
   LA = Low Average
   MH = Mentally Handicapped

Note: Scores 79 and below were chosen to represent the Mentally Handicapped category. There could be some disagreement over this, but such a wide variety of cut-off scores are used from state to state and province to province to classify varying degrees of mental handicaps such as the Educable and Trainable groups, that the generic term was chosen for scores of 79 and below. Consult your own state or provincial guidelines for scores to be used in your area.

Adapted from: Sattler, J. 1982. *Assessment of children's intelligence and special abilities*, 2nd ed. Boston: Allyn and Bacon.

An abbreviated version of this table is shown in Table 2.3.

TABLE 2.3. WISC-R IQ scores and percentile ranks (abbreviated version).

IQ	Scaled Score	Percentile Rank	Approx. Class.*
145	19	99.9	VS
140	18	99.6	VS
135	17	99	VS
130	16	98	VS
125	15	95	S
120	14	91	S
115	13	84	HA
110	12	75	HA
105	11	63	A
100	10	50	A
95	9	37	A
90	8	25	A
85	7	16	LA
80	6	9	LA
75	5	5	MH
70	4	2	MH
65	3	1	MH
60	2	.4	MH
55	1	.1	MH

*Classification abbreviations:
  VS = Very Superior
  S = Superior
  HA = High Average
  A = Average
  LA = Low Average
  MH = Mentally Handicapped

Note: Scores 79 and below were chosen to represent the Mentally Handicapped category. There could be some disagreement over this, but such a wide variety of cut-off scores are used from state to state and province to province to classify varying degrees of mental handicaps such as the Educable and Trainable groups, that the generic term was chosen for scores of 79 and below. Consult your own state or provincial guidelines for scores to be used in your area.

Adapted from: Sattler, J. 1982. *Assessment of children's intelligence and special abilities*, 2nd ed. Boston: Allyn and Bacon.

Chapter 3

Affective Considerations in WISC-R Testing and Reading Success

As a school psychologist, you constantly receive referrals on students who exhibit behavioral and academic problems. As part of the process, a WISC-R is often administered. This basic test provides extremely valuable information about a student's cognitive functioning in relation to his or her peers. But just as important is how the student reacts to the structure of testing itself. Students' disposition, attitudes, and reactions during the testing are all as much clues to remediation as the test scores themselves. In addition, the student's teachers and parents will often provide extremely valuable observations about the individual's behavior and reactions to academic tasks.

It is very important for the school psychologist and special educator to have some grasp of how the student's cognitive and affective states interrelate. For this purpose, I have organized our discussion using "stress" as the umbrella term. Other theoretical frameworks for discussing a student's behavior may be equally valid, but stress is an area in which I have some expertise, and am comfortable with. I will digress into a number of areas that are only indirectly related to WISC-R testing per se, but which certainly belong to the broader category of the "psychology of reading." The school psychologist should be aware of these areas since, directly or indirectly, they come into play when making recommendations about a specific student.

In Chapter 2, I suggested that intelligence is a kind of mental energy, a sort of primary substance which guides actions in orderly and purposeful ways. This energy is fueled by the emotions. So intelligence and emotion are closely intertwined, giving rise to observed behavior. From the behavior, we infer the "valence" of the emotion and purpose of the action. This valence may be positive or negative. Every time a student sits in front of an examiner to be tested on the WISC-R, both intelligence and emotions are being tapped.

In this respect, mental energy is closely akin to Hans Selye's concept of "adaptation energy."[1] Selye was a pioneer in the area of human stress research. He suggested that we are all born with a finite amount of such energy, which we could squander quickly, or use appropriately to prolong our lives. He also discovered that, in response to stress, human beings go through three distinct stages:[2]

1. Alarm reaction
2. Resistance
3. Exhaustion

These stages constitute the General Adaptation Syndrome, or GAS. We all have a level of homeostasis, or balance, which we try, at all times, to maintain. When homeostasis is threatened, the stress response is triggered automatically. The body mobilizes its resources to "fight, flight, or freeze"—whatever is the appropriate response to the situation. Continued triggering of the stress response uses up more adaptation energy.

Stress, itself, is the amount of adaptation energy it takes to adjust to change. Stressors trigger stress. Stressors may be strictly environmental in nature, such as excessive noise. Excessive noise automatically triggers the stress response. Such stressors, though present in our environment, are limited in number. By far the largest class of stressors are those that are *psychological* in nature. The stress response is triggered primarily when the environment is *perceived* as threatening. The key word is "perceived," because, of course, people perceive and interpret their environments very differently. In a classroom situation, a teacher or student may feel comfortable and at ease, or very uncomfortable and "stressed." Because of these individual differences in interpretation of environmental stressors, Selye said that stress, like beauty, is in the eye of the beholder.

Because stress is self-perceived, Selye's work can be linked to phenomenologists like Carl Rogers (and, more recently, James Battle), who view behavior as the result of the person's perception of reality.[3,4] This point of view is helpful when it comes to trying to understand what at times seems to be very irrational behavior on the part of the student. Try to remember that there is always a *purpose* for that behavior, even though the student is unable to express it himself. As a school psychologist, your task will frequently be to make sense of a host of behavioral concerns that the teacher or parent has about the child. Two additional sources that will be most helpful to you for this role include the STEP and STET programs (*Systematic Training for Effective Parenting*, and *Systematic Training for Effective Teaching*) from American Guidance Service (in Canada, this material is available from Psycan), and the book, *You Can Handle Them All*.[5,6] I find the latter helpful, even though it is quite a cook-bookish format. The model used in the book's introduction is very helpful and is really an extension of Rudolph Dreikurs' work.

In my experience, it is better if teachers have the opportunity to actually practice some of the techniques that arise from any theoretical viewpoint, rather than simply reading about them. I teach an accredited inservice course at the University of Calgary for practicing teachers, called "Self-Esteem and Discipline." The approach I use is largely phenomenological, and I have structured it in such a way that teachers must implement and keep track of strategies they learn in the course over a period of time in their classrooms. The positive results that the teachers experience are very encouraging to myself and to them. When implementing some of the ideas you might get from this book, then, remember that you are going through a *process*. If an idea is not working out, try to fine-tune it in some way before abandoning it. Also, try to talk to colleagues about it, since this feedback often helps immensely.

Everyone requires some stimulation to function. Because the environment constantly makes demands on us, even when we are sleeping, some degree of adaptation energy is always required. Therefore, we are always under some degree of stress. Too much stress on a continual basis could lead to "burnout," while too little stress leads to "rustout." In my book, *Teacher Burnout and What to Do about It*, I discuss the effects of stress on teachers and students.[7]

The concept of stress is one I find useful in discussing students with learning difficulties. Anxiety is, of course, related to stress—a close cousin, one might say. Some people, including children, can be described as high-anxious or low-anxious. We would expect that too much anxiety would interfere with good performance in school, but only when the situation is perceived as threatening, such as during a test. Some anxiety is helpful, as long as it isn't too much. Of course, test anxiety can affect performance on the WISC-R as much as on other, more academic tests. It is important that students be made to feel as comfortable as possible during the WISC-R administration, to optimize performance. Keep in mind, however, that too little in the way of anxiety may be equally debilitating. The examiner should note any instances where anxiety obviously affects performance. This is more likely to be true on all the timed subtests of the WISC-R than on the untimed ones. If anxiety *is* a factor, then the Full Scale IQ is likely an *underestimate* of the student's ability; and this should be strongly stated in the report.

We might also expect that excessive stress would reduce students' ability to concentrate, therefore affecting their learning and academic performance. The result becomes a vicious circle. A lack of success in reading, for example, would automatically lead to the perception of threat on the part of the student. When the stress response is triggered, then the student is "alarmed," and energy is required to resist the stressor. This will require much expenditure of energy (both intellectual and emotional) to "fight" or "run away from" or "freeze" ("block") the reading task. Such students spend vast amounts of energy avoiding the task. Their concentration is impaired. They may become excessively active in the threatening situation, or they may withdraw and "play dead." Abrams and Smolen, two researchers who have related the GAS to reading failure, state:[8]

> ... The child who experiences initial reading failure ... is ultimately subjected to emotional stress. If the reading failure persists, it is almost inevitable that frustration, reduced attention, anxiety, and a real sense of helplessness will be involved.

Reading-disabled students may take flight or play dead (regarding the reading task), as already mentioned. Psychologically, this can be measured through arousal levels. Reichurdt found that the running-away group was the less seriously handicapped in reading.[9] The most disabled readers were the playing-dead group, who showed a sharp drop in arousal as they progressed into a reading task. So, what develops, is what Downing and Leong call the "failure → threat → anxiety syndrome" or "emotional blocking," a phenomenon which every school psychologist and special educator has witnessed.[10] This syndrome leads to four major categories of emotional reaction.[11]

1. Overt fear reactions—these include anxiety, depression, the fear of making mistakes, of failure, and of people discovering how poorly the student has read.

2. Nonspecific emotional behaviors—these reactions include submissiveness, indifference, inattentiveness, laziness, daydreaming, and evasive actions such as joining gangs or playing truant from school.

3. Escape behaviors—these include withdrawal, psychosomatic disorders, rigidity, and various avoidance strategies. The student who makes an irrelevant remark (showing that he or she was not paying attention to the task) fits in here. Another escape behavior is to "play stupid."

4. Attack behaviors—these reactions include restlessness, antisocial behavior, and a rebellious attitude, as well as aggressiveness.

These categories are all-encompassing. School psychologists need to be *very* cautious about attributing *every* negative emotion/behavior that a student has to reading failure. Not every case of reading failure is accompanied by such reactions, for one thing. For another, sometimes, antisocial behavior runs quite independently of reading failure. Finally, home factors may be just as important, if not more so, than the reading failure per se. There are many students who model aggressiveness or daydreaming or any of the reactions just listed on what they see at home. And the intense disappointment and anxiety that a parent feels in reaction to a slower-reading child is almost always conveyed to the child, and aggravates the situation immensely.

Lansdown, for example, mentions three negative parenting styles. These are:[12]

1. Expecting too much of a child and . . . communicating this to the child. Children faced with this attitude see themselves as constantly failing to meet parental demands.

2. . . . Being actively hostile towards a child . . . . Given this situation, the child is likely to fail at everything, except possibly crime, since [he or] she has so firmly received the message of [his or] her worthlessness.

3. . . . Being indifferent.

I have met all these kinds of parents over and over in my consulting work. In one interview, recently called to discuss WISC-R results, the father began by berating his daughter to me, and giving a long list of things she couldn't do at home, in contrast to her brother, who was the "apple of Dad's eye." It's obvious that such attitudes are very powerful. I quickly steered the conversation away from the test results as such (which might have served only to confirm many of the father's comments), and more into how I found his daughter behaving and performing. She had, like all students, a number of strengths. In particular, this student had a quiet sense of humor and a remarkably persistent sense of effort. As I began listing these for the father, I could see him softening somewhat. By the end of the interview, he asked me for more suggestions for what he could do to help his daughter at home. Now this father was receptive. Such parental attitudes are critical in understanding an individual child's reaction to academic stress, and go well beyond just an IQ score.

Success → Promise → Confidence: Breaking the Stress Cycle

The opposite of the failure → threat → anxiety syndrome, state Downing and Leong, is the success → promise → confidence one. I feel that this syndrome is very aptly stated.

There is no doubt that reading or arithmetic failure *can* cause untoward stress for many students. In some cases, this can be extreme. Many times, the emotional factors are primary, and sometimes they are secondary in reading failure. In either case, more use of the student's adaptation energy is required. Such failure almost always destroys self-confidence, as it would for anyone, and cannot be ignored when developing IEPs.

There are a number of ways of breaking into the vicious stress cycle and making it a more "virtuous" one. The focus of these interventions can be on the student or on the teacher. I will discuss the following general categories which school psychologist needs to be aware of:

1. Classroom atmosphere
2. Success
3. Setting goals (purposes) for reading
4. Attitudes
5. Self-efficacy
6. Deep relaxation

In addition, the reader should be aware of an excellent publication from the International Reading Association called *Stress and Reading Difficulties*.[13] In it, the authors succinctly describe the effects of stress from students' reading failure (primarily in terms of fight-or-flight), provide an informal means of assessing such behaviors, and then provide a detailed lesson plan for reading intervention with appropriate guidelines for the flight- and fight-type student.

Classroom Atmosphere

Any classroom, particularly a special education one, needs to convey a sense of security to the student. This responsibility rests primarily with the teacher, but may be tied in to the general atmosphere of the whole school. Not only should the atmosphere be comfortable, it should also convey a sense of purpose and mutual respect where learning can and does take place. Of course, "atmosphere" is also related to "effectiveness." What is effective teaching? It can be described, thus:[14]

> Effective teaching involves "direct instruction," which refers to academically focused, teacher-directed instruction using structured materials. Teaching goals are clear to pupils, time allocated for instruction is sufficient and continuous, coverage of content is extensive, performance of pupils is monitored, feedback to them is immediate, and questions are easy enough that they can produce many correct responses. High-achieving classrooms tend to be convivial, democratic, and warm.

Effectiveness is very difficult to measure, but one way of doing it is simply to rate one's teaching behaviors. In Appendix 3-1, you will find three self-rating scales which break the larger concept of effectiveness into three smaller components: classroom management, instructional organization, and teaching presentation. All the variables listed in the scales have been shown in research studies to relate to teacher effectiveness. The scale itself is not standardized, so there are no cut-off scores established for the various categories. However, any teacher wishing to use the scale will find the majority of it self-explanatory. Low scores on any one variable suggest that it is an area where improvement can take place. I have found that even very excellent, experienced teachers have found it useful to go through the rating exercises.

You will note that all of the variables are behaviorally oriented. If a teacher practiced all of them faithfully, but did not like students, then you would be observing an effective technician. Nothing substitutes for human sensitivity when it comes to reducing stress for a student. The variables listed are all under a teacher's direct control, but the motivation to change one's teaching practices must come from a genuine desire to help the student.

Success

Another cornerstone of reading rejuvenation is success in reading. *The threat of failure must be reduced for the student experiencing difficulty.* This is vitally important in those few precious weeks when beginning reading instruction occurs. Most remedial teachers and school psychologists, however, have the student *after* two or three years or more of the failure → threat → anxiety syndrome, when it is well established. The student's sense of self-efficacy (the feeling of I-can-do-it) is sometimes severely disrupted at this point.

There are several key ingredients to success with such a student:

1. Material must be used which the student can handle. This is important both in the remedial and regular classroom. A number of approaches to teaching reading may be successful, including radical, mainly bottom-up departures such as *Distar*. In general, I prefer a language-immersion approach, as is described in Appendix 2-1. This approach immediately taps into the student's interests and, frequently, his direct experiences. There is a place for a variety of approaches, however. Proponents of a particular approach can always find research to support it, it seems.

2. No approach will work if it is done without regard for the student's delicate feelings. Therefore, feedback, and the correction of false self-attributions, are very important. The student should have some visual form of feedback, like a chart which focuses in on the success he is achieving. Students and teachers live in a day-to-day world. It is therefore difficult to keep a broader perspective and appreciate gains being made unless some form of feedback is implemented. The teacher should also stress the student's strengths, his "new interest in reading," and how "different" he is in terms of personality and behavior whenever the opportunity arises. Such feedback is vital in terms of strengthening or rebuilding a weak self-concept. One researcher found that students who charted their progress in word recognition and comprehension performed as well as students who received money as a reinforcer, and *better* than those who received reinforcement in the form of teacher praise and free time.[15] Using reinforcers may be necessary for some students in the short term. School psychologists and teachers will need to keep looking for new reinforcers, as they tend to lose their potency with time. One system that can help is to develop a "reinforcement menu" for each student. In Appendix 3-2, you will find a list of potential reinforcing activities. For students you have referred, you can ask whether they find the activity to be something they "don't like," something that's "OK," or something they "really like." In this way, it's possible to find several activities, usually, which students "really like," and would work for. The general aim is to have students enjoy reading for its own sake, not for anything else. The first step, however, sometimes cannot be taken unless the vicious stress cycle is first broken.

3. Communication with parents about success is also very important. All too often, parents of special students hear only negative reports about their child. Some parents will no longer even come to the school; and many who do, when called, don't want to. They, too, are caught in the failure → threat → anxiety syndrome. Remember that positive feedback takes time. A student or parent will not change overnight. Relapses into old thinking, feeling, and behavior patterns will occur.

A weekly or even daily report card sometimes provides the home and school communication that is vital in some situations. Here is an example of one which I have recommended from time to time:

Daily Report Card

Name _____

	Academic		Social / Behavioral	
Period	OK	Not OK	OK	Not OK
1	___	___	___	___
2	___	___	___	___
3	___	___	___	___
4	___	___	___	___
5	___	___	___	___
6	___	___	___	___
7	___	___	___	___
8	___	___	___	___

Comments:

Happy faces or check marks can accompany the columns. Also, sometimes contracts or contingencies are attached. For example, if the student achieves, say, 6 of 12 possible marks, he receives a hug and 15 minutes of "private time" with Mom and/or Dad in the evenings. Three "good days" out of the week might mean a special treat, like breakfast at a fast-food restaurant on Saturday. These numbers are arbitrary, of course, and depend on the student's baseline behavior.

Such feedback systems can work well, provided the participants are all willing to make it happen. Success should almost be guaranteed initially. The standards have to be set low enough initially so that the student can achieve; but the standards should not be so low as to be without challenge. The standards can gradually be increased as the weeks go on. Reinforcers can also be varied.

One thing that frequently goes wrong with such systems, however, is that the student "forgets" the report card when a "bad day" has occurred. A quick call to the parents (or vice versa, from home to school) is all it takes. Such incidents should be dealt with in a matter-of-fact way, such as, "Well, yesterday wasn't such a good day; but today is a new day. Let's try again." Unfortunately, I have seen many teachers and parents abandon these systems after one or two bad days. Persistence is the key to success, and so are expectations. By abandoning a workable system at the first hitch, participants are showing that they expect instant and permanent results. There is no such thing.

Of course, if the system is obviously not working, something else is needed.

This "something else" can sometimes be accomplished by focusing on the class as a whole, rather than an individual student. Teachers often complain that setting up a reward system for one student is unfair to the rest of the class. The "Good Behavior Game Plus Merit" bypasses this objection because it *does* involve the whole class. This approach has been shown to be effective in:[16]

1. Reducing disruptive behaviors
2. Increasing academic output

Implementing it is reasonably easy. The class is divided into two or three teams, with approximately equal numbers on each team. If there are two or three disruptive students in the class, they can be distributed equally among the teams. One teacher who used this had three teams in the class. The teams were called W, I, and N. The students are then told that they will be playing the game for a special treat at the end of each week. Usually, 15 minutes of free time is an excellent reinforcer, which most students will gladly work toward. They are told that, each time one of the classroom rules is broken, a mark is made on the chalkboard *against that team*. The majority of classrooms I've ever seen always have a list of classroom rules. The list should be short, and it is better if the students were involved in making them up initially. As a rule of thumb, every team should strive for five marks or less per day. This criterion approach is very important. *Do not turn this game into a competition to see "who gets the least marks."* Every team should be able to win by getting five marks or less each day. In fact, all teams can win, some might win, or all may not reach the daily criterion.

What saves this approach from being strictly a demerit system is the introduction of "merit cards." The teacher simply runs off about 200 cards, each of which says "One Merit" on it. The merit cards are handed out by the teacher any time during the day for *academic or academically related work*. For example, the teacher could hand out a merit card to a student who raises his hand to answer a question (especially if the student rarely does so), or to anyone who completes the math assignment, or for achieving some other relevant academic task in the classroom. Merit cards are kept by each student and are exchanged at the end of each day. They can be collected by a team captain (students can take turns being captain). For every five merit cards earned by a team, one mark made against the team for violating a classroom rule can be erased. So, even if a team has more than five marks against them in a day, the team still has a chance to win by earning merit cards.

This system covers the two major components of every classroom—behavior and academics.

I have recommended its use in a number of situations where one student in a classroom was particularly disruptive. Because the system treats that student as a member of the whole class (indeed, doesn't even focus on that student, particularly), it can work well and has done so in my experience. Many teachers in my self-esteem course have used this game (or variations of it); the majority have had very good results. In the classroom research study from which the game was developed, the effects were dramatic and very positive in terms of improving on-task and limiting disruptive behavior for the "target" students, and for the class as a whole. Results were equally dramatic in terms of improving assignments completed. Everyone wins!

Again, though, this system can break down and may need "fine tuning" from time to time, especially if there is a "bad day" for everyone, or if the teacher is insensitive, or if a disruptive student continues to be disruptive. Remember not to throw out the baby with the bath water.

Setting a Purpose for Reading

Downing and Leong state:[17]

... In order to become flexible readers, students must know the purposes of reading and must learn to adjust their skilled acts to different purposes.... The reading process actually changes with the purpose of the reading act. Hence, children need to practice reading for different purposes, and they need to practice changing from one type of purpose to another if they are to develop that flexibility of timing that is such a noteworthy feature of superior skill performance in reading.

Mature, adult reading serves various purposes such as diversion and escape, information-getting, and self-development, but that is not the same as setting a purpose for a student in a classroom. Often, these purposes are told to a student ahead of time. Students are told to:

1. See how fast they can read a passage,
2. Look for the specific sequence of events,
3. Look for specific details or content,
4. Read for "general comprehension,"
5. Look for specific wording,
6. Read for spelling errors.

I'm sure you can add to this list. You need to be aware, however, that setting a purpose also influences what a student will remember from a text. If a student is asked to read a passage for the sequence of events, he will remember those better than any other aspect of the story, and will forget other aspects. Asking questions in advance does focus a student on getting just that information.

Smith gives five very general suggestions for training students to be purposeful readers:[18]

1. Pupils should be fully aware of the purposes of materials they have been asked to read. They should know what they are expected to obtain from their reading.

2. Pupils need to learn how to set their own purposes. For some pupils, this will be a gradual process. Teachers will need to continue setting purposes for such pupils and guiding them in setting their own goals. Help the student verbalize the purpose if he has difficulty.

3. Pupils should be given a wide variety of purposes for reading, both in their reading periods and in their content-area subjects.

4. The kinds of questions should be asked in harmony with the purposes for which students have been asked to read.

5. Students should be taught how to read for different purposes. In this respect, students could be asked to read a passage several times, each time for a different specific purpose such as:

    a. To grasp the main idea,
    b. To note the important details,
    c. To answer specific questions which are posed in advance,
    d. To evaluate what is read, etc.

Helping students set goals and listen for certain details has shown to be very helpful for learning-disabled students' listening comprehension.[19] Thirty-two (32) learning-disabled students between the ages of 8 and 12 showed a significant improvement in their ability to recall a story with higher-level understanding (a folk tale was used), over another group of learning-disabled students who were simply asked to listen to the story. The procedure was simple. Each child was asked to focus on three things:

1. The problem,
2. How it was solved, and
3. The lesson to be learned from the story.

Th reading of the story was broken into three parts, each part being introduced by the comment, "Now, in this part, watch for . . . ."

This simple procedure is an excellent way for the teacher to help build meaningful cognitive structures and sustain attention for a group of learning-disabled students. It is an example of a highly structured, teacher-directed strategy. As with many such procedures, students need to eventually learn to internalize the process for themselves.

In summary, then, setting a purpose for reading reduces stress because it reduces the uncertainty which accompanies reading. In the long term, mature readers need to be able to read for a variety of different purposes, depending on the text. The strategies for this need to be directly taught for students who have difficulty. Reading *purpose* and reading *comprehension* are closely related, because purpose affects what is remembered and comprehended. John McNeil, in his book, *Reading Comprehension, New Directions for Classroom Practice* (Scott, Foresman; Glenview, Illinois, 1984) provides excellent reading comprehension strategies for the classroom or remedial teacher. These strategies are all "language-immersion" oriented (see Appendix 2-1). McNeil divides the strategies into those for the prereading phase of reading; those which can be used during reading; and those which can be used after reading a passage. Different strategies are suggested for narrative and expository texts.

Attitudes

Attitudes on the part of students, parents, and teachers alike, are very important in trying to establish a success → promise → confidence syndrome. Attitudes of hostility, passivity, attitudes toward task persistence, toward certain social situations, toward authority, and so on, frequently surface during administration of the WISC-R. The examiner needs to follow up on any noted, important attitudes by discussing them with the teacher or parents. In particular, I am mainly concerned in this section with attitude (defined by Downing and Leong as "a tendency to behave in a particular manner toward a certain object or situation") toward books and reading. There is a surprising dearth of research on the topic, despite the fact that every teacher and parent mentions its importance. What has been done has focused on sex differences, home background, and school experiences, all of which tend to shape attitudes in some way.

In North America, girls typically have more positive attitudes toward reading than boys, and typically score higher on attitude scales. This fits in with clinical experience in terms of the greater ratio of boys to girls with reading problems. That is not true in all cultures, however. In England, one researcher found no differences in attitudes toward reading in ten- or eleven-year-old boys and girls.[20] I feel it is important, especially in the beginning stages of reading, for teachers to try to select materials that are interesting to each child. Therefore, a wide range of classroom materials, with both boy and girl protagonists and subjects, covering a wide range of interests, should be present in the classroom and supplemented by the school's library. Even physical surroundings convey attitudes. Surroundings should encourage reading with reading corners, reading lofts, pillows, couches, paperback racks, and so on, available. This is just as true, if not more so, for remedial classes as for regular classes.

One factor that may be more important than all others in developing attitudes toward reading, is the home environment. One researcher provides some detail as to *which* home environment variables make a difference:[21]

> ... The one factor that stands out from all the others is the role of the parent in being involved with his child's reading activities. Working with homework; encouraging, helping select, and discussing his reading; reading to him; assistance in looking things up in dictionaries and encyclopedias; and setting reading goals were more important than the mere provision of materials.

Also, very surprisingly, the researcher found that parents themselves did *not* have to be avid readers to have children who were. *It was the active interactions with the child's reading that made the difference.*

Teachers and school psychologists are continually asked by parents what they can do to help at home with a student who has a reading problem. I have taken some of the research findings

I've discussed and composed a letter to parents that you might find useful for parents of elementary-age students. (See Appendix 3-3.)

Of course, the school is a vital factor in the development of good reading and positive reading attitudes. There is a host of studies done on teacher attitudes, methods, materials, school characteristics, etc., and reading achievement and attitudes. An excellent discussion and summary of the findings can be found in Downing and Leong's Chapter 13.[22]

I will simply list here some of the more important considerations. Details and the supportive research studies can be found in Downing and Leong.

1. Physical features of the school:
   a. There is a significant correlation between good reading attainment and better physical facilities themselves, such as size of classroom, type of furniture, presence of a sink, storage space, type of lighting, playground equipment, general appearance, noise pollution, and so on.
   b. Urban schools and large schools were found, surprisingly, to have better reading attainment.
   c. Poor reading is associated with poor provision of books.

2. School system characteristics:
   a. Despite popular belief, there is evidence that people learn languages better when they are *older*, rather than younger. Children do better on almost all aspects of language acquisition when they are older. "Reading readiness," then, is the gap between the child's level of development and task difficulty, and has little to do with "mental age" per se. Children can be prepared for the reading task, and the task can be modified so that the reading readiness "gap" can be narrowed at any time. After all, we can teach chimpanzees some elementary reading. Very young children can be taught to "read," provided that the task is sufficiently modified. On this point, Taylor and Taylor make a very interesting observation. Since reading is a receptive language task, they say, then it should be easier for a child to learn to "read" than to speak!

      In any case, there is no "optimal age," it seems, for learning to read. Public law in North America demands that all children enter school by the age of six. Some of these children will already be reading; many will learn to read at age six; and some will have difficulty. Nothing would change if the entrance age were to be raised or lowered. No matter what the age, the child has to be prepared and/or the task modified so success can be experienced and stress reduced.
   b. Class size *can* make a difference to reading attainment, so long as teachers individualize instruction and actually spend more time interacting with pupils. Reducing class size, even to as low as 15 to 1, *by itself*, makes no difference to reading achievement and attitudes. It makes a difference *if* teachers take advantage of it.
   c. The lock-step grade system seems to be damaging to pupils who lag behind. Multi-age groupings of various kinds, along with individualized instruction, are better alternatives.

3. Teacher characteristics:
   a. Teachers need to be aware that their own beliefs regarding gender of the pupil (the "boys versus girls" problem), desirability of the language spoken by pupils, and how "bright" or "dull" they seem to be, might have an influence on actual reading attainment. This is the so-called "Pygmalion Effect." How it operates is explained by Downing and Leong:[23]

      > Under normal conditions, teachers' perceptions of their pupils may be in some way signaled to the children as feedback about their behavior, progress, and so

on. In this way, pupils may be guided (or misguided) about the effectiveness of their responses in the tasks of reading instruction.

So the message seems to be: "Watch your expectations. Your students will live up to them."

Despite contradictory research about this, my experience has taught me that expectations are indeed very important—if not in reading or cognitive scores, then certainly in behavior. Some temperamental students who may be difficult to begin with, most assuredly act much worse when the message, overt or covert, is: "I don't like you!" I have repeatedly had pupils referred to me where the teacher is quite prepared to describe the student in *very* negative terms. This is a signal to me that at least part of the problem lies in negative expectations and beliefs the teacher has about the student, as in actual behavior. Somehow, this vicious circle must be interrupted. The teacher must be involved in a corroborative way in the planning and implementation of a program designed to change such attitudes. A sure sign of frustration is when the teacher says: "I've tried everything. Nothing works!" In these situations, try to get the ball rolling in a more positive way.

b. "Teachers teach best when they are teaching by what they believe to be the best method," Downing and Leong write. They also say:[24]

> ... There is no real concensus of research conclusions on the comparative advantages of the various alternative [reading] methods described.... Usually, research evidence is selected to support the current fashion when its latest method comes into vogue. Then, a new series of researches tends to develop to "prove" the value of the "new" trend. The reader will find little help from research quoted in support of current methods from one country to another.

So, whether a teacher emphasizes a "meaning-based" or "code-based" approach to reading depends on whether she feels that reading is "taught" or "caught." At this moment, there seems to be no research to support a particular superiority for either one. My own bias is more toward an appropriate blending of the two, but with more emphasis on a "meaning-base."

At any rate, the important message from this section is that teacher *beliefs* about how reading should be taught are more important than any *theories* about how it should be taught, or any administrator's or consultant's beliefs or edicts or policies or government laws about how it should be taught. There is no way to change a teacher's methods, then, unless the teacher is herself receptive to the changes suggested, and is directly involved in planning and implementing such changes. Many reading consultants and school psychologists are frustrated when their best planned prescriptions are ignored or bypassed. Part of this problem comes from the fact that the teacher is not the initiator. Follow-up of all referrals is one way to help ensure recommendations are followed. The other way is to have an administrator in the school take charge and see that recommendations are carried out in the absence of the consultant. Schools where such a mechanism is in place, do, in my experience, initiate more positive individual change for students than those which have no such mechanism. Such schools are more positive places for consultants, also, since they know their work is taken seriously. This helps to shape a more positive attitude to the school for the consultant, and better service to the school. The "Pygmalion Effect" operates at all levels! However, the best method is when the consultant works *with* a teacher. The school psychologist must be prepared to make a variety of suggestions from different theoretical perspectives. Together, the consultant and teacher arrive at a plan of action. If teachers are involved in the planning, they will more likely implement change.

An effective approach which incorporates this principle is the concept of having a *school-based* intervention team whose purpose is to work in consultation with the teacher who makes the referral. The team (comprised of appropriate people from the school) brainstorms a variety of alternative intervention strategies designed to offer a solution to the problem. The strategies are arranged according to priority, the resources needed to implement it are identified, and the teacher attempts to carry them out. The intervention plan is written out, and a date is set for reviewing its effectiveness. Only when all school-based alternatives have been exhausted, is a referral made for in-depth assessment and intervention from resource personnel outside the school. This concept is very exciting in terms of professional development for the teacher, and assures that school psychologists will receive referrals only after a number of "pre-referral" strategies have been attempted. Readers interested in pursuing this idea in depth are urged to consult the document, *Intervention Assistance Teams: A Model for Building-Level Instructional Problem Solving*.[25]

c. Personality has some bearing on both "effectiveness" and reading achievement. Enthusiasm is a very important ingredient, as is the ability to develop a sympathetic, friendly, and understanding relationship with pupils. In one extensive review of the literature on this topic, Hamachek concluded:[26]

> Effective teachers appear to be those who are, shall we say, "human" in the fullest sense of the word. They have a sense of humor, are fair, empathetic, friendly, enthusiastic, more democratic than autocratic, and apparently more able to relate easily and naturally to students on either a one-to-one or group basis. Their classrooms are something akin to miniature enterprise operations in the sense that they are more open, spontaneous, and adaptable to change. Teachers who are less effective apparently lack a sense of humor, grow impatient easily, use cutting, reducing comments in class, are less well integrated, are inclined to be somewhat authoritarian, and are generally less sensitive to the needs of their students.

Additionally, students who have reading difficulties make better progress in classes where teachers:[27]

> ... more frequently displayed behaviors allowing for student freedom of expression use of pupils' ideas, and praise.

In other words, less stress makes for better learning.

Self-Efficacy

Self-efficacy is the personal judgment a student has about how well he can perform in certain situations that might be ambiguous or stressful.

The student who lacks a good sense of self-efficacy usually displays it sometime during WISC-R administration. This is the student who says, "I don't know," *too* quickly, or the one who says, "I can't do this," after making a feeble effort on Block Design or Object Assembly. Observe how the student reacts when task difficulty increases.

Many students give up before they ever start a task. You will often get students described by teachers that way. Such students are, of course, "blocking." *It is more comfortable for such students to fail a task by never making an effort, than it is to make the effort and fail.*

The perception that "I can't do it" may or may not be accurate, depending on task difficulty. These students, however, have a poor sense of judgment in terms of matching their perceptions of their ability to do the task with the task itself.

It is possible to "realign" such faulty perceptions, so to speak.

Since the student says, "I can't do it," immediately upon seeing a task, it is this perception which is the focus of change.

First, devise an "I Can Do It" scale of some type, with a 10 to 100 grading, perhaps like the one following:

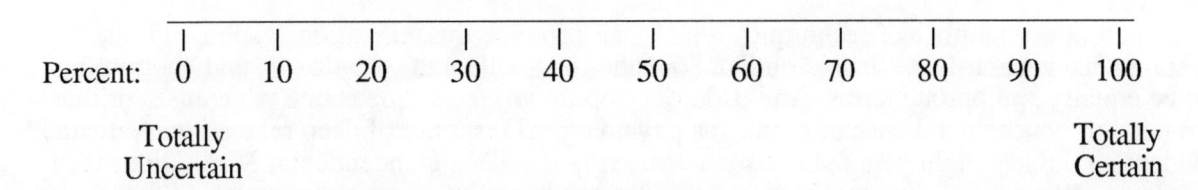

```
Percent:  0   10   20   30   40   50   60   70   80   90   100
```
       Totally   Totally
       Uncertain   Certain

Next, teach the student how to use the scale. It is best to do so with a nonacademic task initially. I have the student try to jump a real or imagined line in front of him. Make sure the first jump is so easy that the student is certain to jump it. Then, have him make a guess on the "I Can Do It" scale. Of course, he should circle the 100 percent certain line. Then have him jump the line. If he does so, *praise his correct perception*. We are not interested in whether he actually can or cannot broad-jump. We are far more interested in "aligning" his perception with his efforts. Keep moving the line back so it becomes more difficult for the student to jump it. But each time before he jumps, have him take a guess and commit himself to paper on the scale. If this is all done in the context of a fun game, then its novelty alone is sure to attract the interest of any student.

Once you are certain that the student can use the scale correctly, then the next step is to apply it to his academic tasks. Arithmetic problems may be easier, initially, than others; but there is no reason why it cannot be used with basically any short task. If the task is very long, such as a research project, then the student may be overwhelmed. In that case, break the task down into smaller steps, and have the student apply the scale to each sequence of steps.

Prior to the student doing the task, have him make a prediction, as with the jumping, on how certain he is he can or cannot do the work. In each case, praise him whenever he is consistent with his appraisal, and reward him with a point. Let him accumulate points toward a self-selected reinforcer. In most cases, students go from about 40 percent certain to 70 to 80 percent certain. It is also appropriate to introduce goal-setting and rewards (the combination of the two works better than either one alone) into this program. The important point is that the student must begin to feel some degree of self-competence and confidence in his own predictions.[28]

Closely allied to self-efficacy are self-attributions. What kind of "self-talk" is the student using when he feels he cannot do a task? In more severe cases, the student simply puts his head down and "refuses" to do it. The "self-talk" is probably very simple—"I can't do it"—though the message to the teacher might be, "I won't do it" (it's very important that the student not be labeled as lazy because of this).

Such students may begin to respond more appropriately through modeling. A fairly detailed procedure is given in Appendix 3-4 which I have found to be quite helpful. Using this procedure twice a week (half-hour sessions) for three weeks, researchers found that it made a very significant difference in helping learning-disabled students persist in the face of difficult reading tasks.[29] By changing the student's self-attributions (internal "self-talk"), it is possible to change his persistence on given tasks. The work becomes less stressful, and the vicious circle is broken.

Deep Relaxation

Deep relaxation is an important component of an anxiety/stress-reduction program for students. Physiologically, deep relaxation is the exact opposite of the stress response.[30] During stress, the body's natural response is to prepare to fight or run. Heart rate and blood pressure rise, oxygen consumption increases, as does breathing rate. Even brain-wave changes occur, with high-frequency beta waves predominating. This response, or parts of it, can be activated many times in the course of a day; and each time, of course, some use of "adaptation energy" is made.

Unfortunately for us, there is no built-in relaxation response, the way there is a stress response. The relaxation response must be taught, learned, and practised frequently in order for it to become natural for a person. The relaxation response is the exact opposite of the stress response;

and it is measured physiologically by lowered breathing rate, lowered heart rate, and "de-excited" brain waves.

There are a number of techniques which can produce the relaxation response. I classify them somewhat arbitrarily as "inside-out" or "outside-in"—although "top-down" and "bottom-up" might be equally appropriate terms. An inside-out (top-down) technique is one which uses primarily a mental or conceptual device to produce a physiological response of deep relaxation. A mental or conceptual device might be a mantra such as used in the TM (Trancendental Meditation) technique (an excellent technique, by the way); or, it might be an imagined scene, such as those employed in various visualization techniques. The primary reason I call such techniques inside-out or top-down is because the major focus is on the mental side. The physiological aspect of deep relaxation is a byproduct of the process.

An outside in (or bottom-up) technique, on the other hand, focuses primarily on the physiological process to eventually produce a state of deep relaxation. A good example is Edmund Jacobson's progressive relaxation.[31] In this technique, the person learns to tighten and relax various major muscle groups in the body in a progressive, systematic way. In so doing, the relaxation response is elicited.

Of course, many techniques are a combination of inside-out or outside-in procedures, but usually one or the other predominates. All the techniques have the potential to bring a host of positive changes. The choice of *which* technique is an individual one. There is evidence to show that the effectiveness of a technique is enhanced when a person has the choice of which one to use when several options are offered. My own preference is for the TM technique.

A number of studies have been done showing the effectiveness of such techniques for a variety of student problems. Of special interest here is a study from Germany which showed reading improvement was better when a deep relaxation technique was added to a remedial program, than when the remedial program was used alone.[32]

In Appendix 3-5, I have included two deep relaxing scripts which originally appeared in my book, *Teacher Burnout and What to Do about It*. One script is for adults. No teacher who hopes to use deep relaxation with students or classes should do so without having some personal experience. So that script is basically for teachers themselves and for older students. The other script is very useful for younger students.

If a teacher decides to use it, deep relaxation should be incorporated on a regular basis into the daily routine of the classroom. Several teachers with whom I have worked in the setting-up of such procedures with their classes, found that first thing after opening exercises in the morning, and first thing in the afternoon after lunch break, were good times to use deep relaxation with the whole class. All the teachers reported good to excellent results, particularly with more restless students. The calming influence in the class as a whole was very positive, they found.

A number of programs introducing deep relaxation to students have now been packaged and are available commercially. One of the better ones, I think, is *Kiddie QR* (Quieting Response).[33]

From my own experience, I have found deep relaxation to be an excellent therapeutic tool, one which every school psychologist and every special educator should be using in some form or another to help break the stress cycle and introduce success → promise → confidence.

Finally, I would like to mention the program, *Coping for Kids* (Center for Applied Research in Education, West Nyack, New York 10994) as another valuable resource, particularly for counselors. Deep relaxation and numerous other topics related to stress reduction are covered in a very practical format.

Chapter 4

Two Reading Models and Some Links to WISC-R Testing

Reading is the magic key that unlocks the door to the wonderland of stories and information.

—*Taylor and Taylor*

In this chapter, I will digress somewhat from direct WISC-R interpretation with a discussion of the reading process. It is important for school psychologists to be aware of the reading process for obvious reasons. However, I will stress again that the WISC-R is *not* a reading test. Nor is the school psychologist necessarily in the best position to say anything about a student's reading. That is usually the province of the reading specialist, though not all school districts have reading specialists (or even school psychologists, for that matter). So if information regarding the student's reading is required, then an informal reading inventory (together with miscue analysis) will reveal much about how the student actually reads. At best, the WISC-R can complement such testing, so WISC-R results and observations should, when possible, be combined with the reading specialist's test results and observations to provide the most creative, useful recommendations and programming for a particular student. In reality, the knowledgeable school psychologist sometimes makes recommendations about reading. And in reality, the knowledgeable reading specialist sometimes makes recommendations that are more the province of the psychologist. Teamwork always brings better results for the student.

When a WISC-R is administered, some underlying cognitive processes are being tapped. To the extent that these processes also underlie the act of reading, then there may be some direct overlap between reading and the WISC-R. I will try to make some of these "links" in this chapter and in the remaining chapters of this book. Forging such links, however, is an art, not a science. All attempts to directly diagnose particular kinds of reading problems from particular profiles have not been very fruitful. But that does not mean that individual profiles should not be carefully examined to see what fruits may be there.

What Is Reading?

Reading is an act of "languaging." It *is* language, the language of reading, specially coded via our particular alphabet. The purpose of reading is to derive meaning from print. Whether we read for leisure or for information, *meaning* is paramount. The same is true of oral language. It is not the sounds of a language that we listen for. We listen for *meaning*. But—and this is a very important point—we do have to learn the *sounds* of our language prior to speaking it.

Unlike the learning of language, which is acquired and developmental, and which seems to *unfold* in an incidental way, reading is more directly taught. It is true that, for some children, reading seems to unfold in a process similar to the learning of oral language. But these children definitely form a small minority. Various studies have shown that only about 1 to 4 percent of a school population reads prior to school entry. On the average, such students have measured IQs of around 120 (percentile 90), though a very few children with IQs in the 80s also may read prior to school entry.

Taylor and Taylor point out that reading is an act of receptive language. Because receptivity precedes production, it should be possible to teach children to read before they speak. To further support this claim, remember that congenitally deaf children are taught to "sign" their first words at six months. This is months before normal children utter their first words. And indeed, there are recorded cases where parents have taught their children some sight words before they spoke. The desirability of learning to read at such an early age for children may be another matter. Where the parent is extremely motivated, and the child quite bright, then perhaps no harm is done. But, for the vast majority of children, reading must be directly taught. In North America, this happens at age six, though there is nothing magical about that age. For some students, perhaps waiting until they are eight or even nine might be better.

Learning to read, then, is learning to extend oral language through the special "code" of the written language. Taylor and Taylor describe four "levels" of learning to read:[1]

1. The Letter and Word Recognition Level:

    There are two sublevels here. "Lower" level-one reading is that of matching a visual pattern, a "word" or logograph, to an object. Chimpanzees can be taught to read at this level, as can 10- to 12-month-old human infants. One of the earliest and most common examples of reading at this level would be recognizing the "golden arches"—the McDonald's hamburger sign. "Upper" level-one reading is the matching of the visual pattern of the word with a sound pattern and recognizing its meaning through language. So when the child sees "car," he also knows that this particular combination *represents* something that can be identified in the real world. This stage can also be called reading "environmental print."

2. The Sentence Reading Level:

    This level can occur quickly, once a child knows only a few words, even only two words, since "She ran" is a perfectly acceptable sentence. Chimpanzees can attain this level of reading, and some of the sentences they can produce are quite complex—an eloquent testimony, I think to the mental energy (g) that is common to purposeful beings. (Perhaps it is even possible to "speak with" and "read" many forms of life, once the correct "codes" are discovered.)

3. The Story Reading Level:

    At this level, children can read stories with plots; and prediction, which is such an integral part of mature reading, enters the picture. Children can anticipate a particular sequence of events and guess what comes next.

4. The Independent Reading Level:

    This is reading for its own sake. Once we have learned to read, we then read to learn. This level of reading is probably not open to chimpanzees, but it is open to humans as young as three or four years old in some cases. The mature reader at this level is constantly making predictions and deriving meaning. At this level of reading, the meanings of words and phrases are primary. In fact, the mature reader does not even recognize characters (letters of the alphabet), as such, when reading. The process is very automatic, and understanding or comprehension becomes paramount.

    Reading at this level also involves thinking. "Thinking" is a larger universe than "speaking," and larger still than "reading," although all are related. In terms of relating reading to intelligence theory in general, we have already seen that language is largely related to "intelligence"—indeed, an integral part of it. We would therefore expect reading to be largely related to intelligence as well. This, too, is true. As I have pointed out, the two are correlated, but not in any one-to-one way. There are some intelligent children who have never learned to read very well, and vice versa. However, all children can learn to read, provided that we understand that the *level* of reading is open to, say, a child with a measured IQ in the lower trainable mentally handicapped range may be considerably lower than for someone in the gifted range.

The process is similar, though, at all levels of intelligence. Mature reading involves an *interaction* of top-down and bottom-up strategies; an interaction between the reader's knowledge (schemata) base and the text itself. For example, the student who does not know who discovered America has no "script" or a weak "schema base" to draw upon when asked to read and answer questions related to any texts about Columbus. Reading comprehension depends on this interaction between concept-driven and data-driven processes. John McNeil explains:[2]

A concept-driven process is a "top-down" strategy in which the reader's goals and expectations determine what is said. In contrast, data-driven processing occurs when the reader attends to the text and then searches for structures (schemata) in which to fit the incoming information. The reader monitors the information from the bottom-up, replacing initial expectations with new ones triggered by the text. Different words and sentences suggest new expectations.

Good readers approach text with top-down strategy, and then use selected schemata to integrate the text, discarding schemata that are inappropriate. Less able readers tend to over-rely on either a top-down strategy or a text-driven process, which has a deleterious effect on comprehension. An overemphasis on top-down processing results in inferences that are not warranted by the text, while an overemphasis on bottom-up processing—staying close to the print—results in word calling.

Learning to read, then, is a very complex act. I would like now to consider just two models of reading and draw out some initial educational implications of each. The first, the Psycholinguistic Model (PL), is more developed and is quite widely subscribed-to presently. The other is the Bilateral Cooperative Model (BLC), a very recent addition to the numbers of reading models that have been developed over the years.

The Psycholinguistic Model of Reading

The PL model of reading emphasizes that efficient, mature reading involves the use of three types of information, in concert, as shown in Figure 4.1.

FIGURE 4.1. Schematic diagram of the psycholinguistic model of reading.

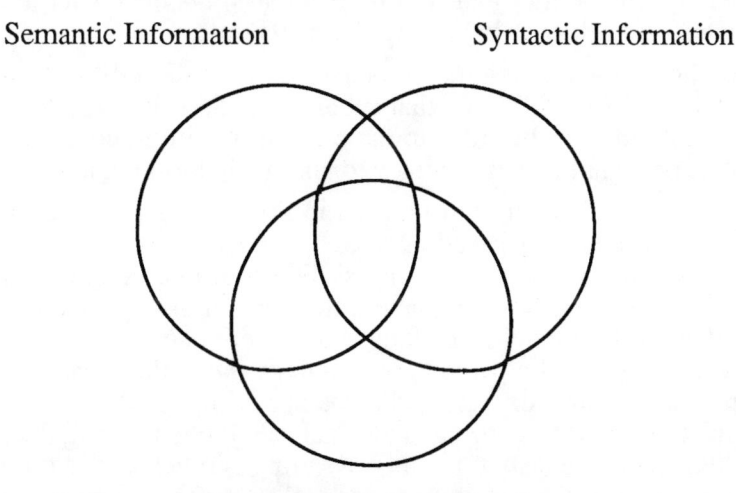

Semantic information is provided by our knowledge of the meanings of words in the real world, including their meanings in various contexts. So, "schema" development is an important asset the student brings to the act of reading. Specific "schemata" may be well developed or poorly developed in specific children.

Syntactic information comes from our knowledge of how word order affects meaning. It is the difference between a "blind Venetian" and a "venetian blind." Or, as every child knows, "There girl went the," does not make sense; but, "The girl went there," does.

Grapho-phonemic information (i.e., sound-symbol relationships) is what we would call knowledge of phonics, or how sounds and print go together. It is *not* the same thing as being able to state phonics rules. It is being able to use them when reading, even if one cannot state them explicitly.

Says Pearson:[4]

> Real reading occurs when all three kinds of information are utilized in concert. Efficient readers maximize their reliance on syntactic and semantic information in order to minimize the amount of *print to speech* (call this decoding, phonic, or grapho-phonemic analysis) they have to do. They literally predict what is coming and get enough grapho-phonemic information to verify their predictions. A single letter or a single syllable may be enough information to verify their predictions. For example, it doesn't take much visual or grapho-phonemic information to confirm the hypothesis that "telescope" fits into the sentence, "The astronomer looked through the _____." Readers must vary the amount of attention they pay to the graphic information according to their familiarity with the content. . . .
>
> Novice or poor readers are so bound up in their search for phonic information that they have little chance to attend to meaning. Good readers, on the other hand, because they attend to meaning, may often make unimportant errors in decoding words accurately.

As you can see, the model views top-down and bottom-up skills such as decoding in concert, but with more emphasis on top-down processing.

Indeed, one aspect which is secondary in this model, but primary in others, is *automaticity*. "Automatic" behavior can be performed without attention, once it is learned. For example, when you first learned to drive a car, your attention was directed to the gear shift, clutch, brake, and listening to instructions. You had no attention left for listening to the radio. Once driving became an automatic habit, you were able to do several things at once—listen to the radio, flip stations, etc., and drive. Your "automatic pilot" took over. There are many examples of automatic habits in everyday life, including reading. The fluent reader, for example, may read a passage but not attend to its meaning. His decoding skills are on "automatic" at that time; but his mind has wandered, perhaps to the nice-looking girl he met that morning in class. David LaBerge and S. Jay Samuels stress the need for automatic behavior in reading. Samuels states:[5]

> For years, teachers of beginning reading have been satisfied if their students were accurate in decoding words. While it is true that accuracy in decoding is necessary in reading, it is not a sufficient condition. In order to have fluent reading and good comprehension, the student must be brought beyond accuracy to automaticity in reading.

The bottom-up skills, then, are not ignored in the PL model; but, usually, they are given secondary importance to a meaning-based approach. Indeed, most reading specialists who subscribe to this model take it as axiomatic that no skills should be taught in isolation. So phonics worksheets, in and of themselves, they say, have little value in this approach.

Closely allied to the PL model is the language-experience approach. The skilled teacher of reading is the one who brings the knowledge of language the child *already* has to the learning of reading. For example, an average six-year-old has a speaking vocabulary of about 5,000 words, but a reading vocabulary of next to nothing. The teacher's job is to bring the strong semantic and syntactic base the child has to the task of reading. Reading is much easier if it relates to the child's own language. So, children might be encouraged to tell a story about an experience they just had, such as a visit to a zoo. The teacher writes out the story the child tells about the experience, and then reads the story with the child. Sight vocabulary, prediction, sequencing, and phonics, are all integrated into the one lesson; but the primary focus is always on meaning and prediction. Any bottom-up skills training is drawn out of the lesson and practiced from it.

A very useful resource book based on this theory and suitable for beginning readers is Karen Clark's *Language Experiences with Children's Stories* (Braun and Braun, Calgary, Alberta, 1983).

"Prediction" is an integral part of reading, from this perspective, because that is exactly what we do, as well, when we listen to someone. We listen and predict what the person is going to say next. So, anyone who uses language is capable of predicting. Prediction is routinely practiced, say Kenneth Goodman and Frank Smith, by both beginning and fluent readers.[6] Two conditions must be met by teachers in order to help the student to use prediction in reading. The first condition is that the material itself must be at least potentially meaningful for the student. If it is not, then it is nonsense and therefore more difficult for the student. The second condition is that the student must feel free to predict, to make intelligent guesses and occasional mistakes. "The worst strategy for any reader who is having difficulty understanding text," says Smith, "is to slow down and make sure that every word is identified correctly."[7] Therefore, "anxiety" and "fear of failure" as discussed in Chapter 3, apply to the process of prediction.

Prediction is not reckless guessing. The guesser is the one who is trying to get every word right to please the teacher, with little emphasis on whether or not it makes sense. This kind of reader also overrates accuracy. Errors, says Smith, either distort meaning or they do not. If meaning is not distorted by a reading error in context (e.g., "home" for "house"), then it is of no consequence.

Prediction can be encouraged in at least these four ways:

1. "First skip, and second, guess," says Smith. That is the preferred strategy to encourage a student who meets an unfamiliar word. Striving for meaning is all-important in the act of reading. The teacher can see if the student is doing this by seeing if the student is self-correcting reading errors, using logical substitutions, indicating dissatisfaction in some way with a passage or word that does not make sense, or using one's own dialect to substitute when reading without distorting meaning. The student who accepts nonsense—and many students with reading difficulties and disabilities do—must go back to square one. Such a student perhaps feels that, as long as you say anything when you read, as long as you make the attempt, it will keep the teacher happy and off your back.

2. Deemphasize "correcting" a student who has made a reading error. The student may well go back in the next sentence and self-correct, which is to be encouraged. Do not say the correct word immediately.

3. If the student asks what the word is, turn it around by asking, "What do you think it is? What makes sense?"

4. Play reading games with the student wherein you stop suddenly when reading, or leave a word out, or make a deliberate mistake. Encourage the student to predict and correct as he follows along.

So, predicting and intelligent guessing are to be encouraged from the perspective of top-down processing. I believe this to be true in the general sense, and adequate for students whose reading is not seriously impaired. But for students whose sound-symbol correspondences are extremely weak, the whole process of reading seems to be nothing but reckless guessing. They cannot predict or make intelligent guesses because there is nothing *there* for them to predict or make guesses about.

So, bottom-up processing *is*, after all, important. But, does this mean we should all switch to, say, the Orton-Gillingham approach?

The Orton-Gillingham program is a very bottom-up method of teaching reading. This program is extensively used by special educators for problem readers. In it, students learn phonics skills in almost total isolation, beginning with a heavy dose of memorizing sound-symbol relations. Once these are mastered, students go on to blending sounds into words. From there, reading words in sentences; and finally, paragraphs. So, meaning is eventually built from the bottom, up. This approach deemphasizes the student's strengths (the language base), and gives a heavy dose of teaching to the weakness. A PL/language-experience approach would do the opposite.

In the beginning years of my consulting work, I saw many teachers using the Orton-Gillingham approach. I was not overly impressed. Students were subjected to tedious lessons lacking any spark, and there was a definite overreliance on the program. Students were not surrounded by books, but by phonograms. Some students learned to read better, but some students read better regardless of the method.

The PL model, with its emphasis on the richness of literature and "whole language," was a welcome relief. And I still believe teaching should occur within the context of the language-rich environment the PL model encourages. However, there still remain many students who don't learn to read from such classrooms.

Why is this?

Beginning Reading—Another Look

I have always been struck by the fact in my years of teaching and consulting work that, no matter what particular reading *model* a teacher or specialist adhered to, there were many youngsters who were still unable to read, even after many years of excellent teachers. It seemed to me, then, that no matter what particular *theoretical* position one adheres to, something is missing.

What can it be? I have said repeatedly in this book that I favor a language-rich or language-immersion approach, both in the regular and remedial classroom. However, I have also stated that I am very eclectic in this approach, and I see some room for integrating a variety of methods and techniques from that context. It is very important for the school psychologist—and all other educators—to have a number of arrows in the quiver, so to speak.

Although I believe that top-down processing occurs in the mature reader, I believe that that is only possible because of a very fluent basis in the bottom-up processes, in particular the quick deciphering of the phonics "code" of our language. In other words, reading is an interaction between the top-down and the bottom-up, just as stated by the PL theory, but often forgotten in practice.

What is necessary in beginning reading? What is necessary, of course, is for the student to "crack the code." However, we know from years of research that phonics-based instruction is not significantly superior to any other methods that have been attempted to teach beginning reading, including the language-experience approach. So, perhaps by looking in greater depth at that third circle in the PL model, the grapho-phonemic one, we might come up with some insights.

In recent years, some articles have surfaced in the research literature that have, I think, some profound implications for the teaching of reading in its initial stages. These articles have to do with the role of phonemic analysis as a necessary prerequisite to reading. What is phonemic analysis? It is the ability to recognize and *manipulate* the underlying basis sound units (phonemes) of our language. Once that skill is mastered, the student is then able to link the sounds with the symbols (graphemes). So the ability to recognize, discriminate, and manipulate sounds comes *first*. Perhaps this is why phonics instruction is not as successful as it could be. Phonics teaching really goes the other way around (from the grapheme to the phoneme), and assumes the child can manipulate the phonemes at an adequate level. If that ability is not there, however (and for many children of all intelligence levels, that is true), then the child will never become a fluent reader. He may be able to make some progress in reading because of the variety of ways in which he can learn to extract meaning from print (including guessing), but he will not be the fluent, self-correcting reader that we desire, nor is he likely to be a good speller, because a thorough knowledge of the sound-symbol connections is necessary for spelling.

Thus, encouraging poor readers to guess, may not be the most fruitful approach. The important debate regarding a strictly top-down approach to reading, versus a bottom-up approach, has recently been discussed by Tom Nicholson. I would urge the reader to consult the entire article regarding the "great debate," as he calls it. The essence of the debate, says Nicholson, is this:[8]

> Goodman sees reading as a sophisticated guessing game where the efficient reader uses linguistic knowledge as much as possible, and print as little as possible . . . . Gough, however, takes the opposite view, that the reader is not a guesser, and that linguistic knowledge only comes into operation after the print has been decoded. As he puts it:
>
>> A guess may be a good thing, for it may preserve the integrity of sentence comprehension. But rather than being a sign of normal reading, it indicates that the child

did not decode the word in question rapidly enough to read normally. The good reader need not guess; the bad should not.

Nicholson then reviews the recent studies which indicate that context cues do *not* improve word recognition. He says:[9]

The irony is that poor readers, not the good, are the ones most likely to guess, simply because they are less able to decode, and have to rely on context clues to help them.

I think that there is much to be gained from this particular analysis. In the initial stages of reading, the child may pick up a number of sight words from "environmental print," as mentioned earlier. However, this particular strategy becomes inefficient as the number of words rapidly increases and the number of distinctive visual cues from the words themselves decreases. The child must then make the transition from "environmental print" to "cracking the code" (which Gough calls the cipher). To break the cipher, four conditions must be met:[10]

1. The child must be aware of the letters in words, and their order, that is, the cipher text;
2. The child must be aware of the abstract sound segments, or phonemes, in words, that is, the plain text;
3. The child must recognize the nature of the cipher problem, that print is encoded speech, and try to solve it; and
4. The child must have sufficient data to work with—for example, the child needs not only to see the printed word *cat*, but also to hear its spoken form.

Each of these four conditions is somewhat "unnatural" for the child, but must eventually be met, before fluency in reading is attained.

In particular, condition 2, phonemic segmentation ability, seems especially important. Nicholson says:[11]

To me, the value of phonemic awareness training in the context of reading instruction is that it generates an explicit awareness of the nature of the cipher, and how to solve it. Although it is only one of the four conditions for breaking the cipher, it acts like fluoride in water. That is, it seems to prevent the teething problems of learning to read.

Even more importantly, there is evidence to suggest that early attention to phonemic awareness will lead to better reading comprehension.

Does this sound like more process-training to you? In a way, phonemic awareness training *is* a process training; but there is much better evidence of the direct connection between this process and reading than there ever was with, say, perceptual training and reading. In fact, in one extremely important study, Bradley and Bryant show a *causal* connection between early training in phonemic awareness and reading progress.[12] Such studies have quietly been going on since about 1972. There is now a good body of research to support the idea that lack of phonemic training awareness is directly linked to reading difficulties, and that training in phonemic awareness corrects them.

There are a number of ways to teach phonemic awareness or phonemic segmentation or "linguistic awareness" or "linguistic insight" (the process goes by all these different names in the literature). *One* of these ways, and certainly the most available because it is commercially developed, is the *Auditory Discrimination in Depth* (ADD) *Program*.[13] The ADD Program was developed by Pat and Charles Lindamood in their clinic in San Luis Obispo, California. It has been the subject of some research, and the results are most encouraging.

For example, the Santa Maria, California, Elementary School District started their students on the ADD Program in kindergarten, and continued it through the second grade. They were able to complete it over a three-year period with just 15- to 20-minute daily lessons for *all* students. Students were instructed in small groups for the lessons by trained aides.

Results have been most impressive. On the *Stanford Achievement Test*, students made very substantial gains over previous years on their reading scores. The kindergarten students jumped from the 50th to the 75th percentile on the average. Similar gains were posted in grades one and two. "The primary grades have shown the biggest increase in reading I've seen in ten years," Doug Palmer, the school psychologist, was reported as saying.[14]

Bob Howard, the principal of Arco Elementary School in Arco, Idaho, writes in an open letter:

> I am writing to urge your consideration of the Lindamood Program, *Auditory Discrimination in Depth,* as a proven tool for ameliorating problems learners may have in reading, and as an excellent way to teach beginning reading . . . .
>
> The program has proven its effectiveness in improved reading scores in many ways. Students taught with the program in kindergarten enter first grade with significantly better reading skills ($p < .001$) than students in our district who did not receive such training. Students taught the program in the first grade have significantly better reading skills ($p < .001$) than students who did not have the ADD Program techniques added to their curriculum. As the children progress through elementary school (grades two through eight), those who had ADD Program training in the first grade do better in reading than students in our district who did not have such training ($p < .0001$) . . . .
>
> As you can tell, we strongly promote the Lindamood Program as a valuable teaching technique for use with all children. Our support is based on long-term experience, careful monitoring of the program's results, and the trust school and community members feel for the program.

It would seem, then, that a very valuable key at the beginning stage of reading has been found. I believe that phonemic awareness training is a concept whose time has come.

I will also have more to say in a later chapter on the relationship between the WISC-R Digit Span subtest and phonemic analysis.

The WISC-R and the Psycholinguistic Model

In terms of the WISC-R and the PL model, the Verbal Scale is very important in showing whether or not the student has a well developed language base. It also provides some clues to the student's schema base. The content of the responses the student makes often reveals in a general way his knowledge of semantic and syntactic structures. Any difficulties the student is having with such structures should be pointed out to the teacher and reading specialist so that accommodations and/or remediation may take them into account. The school psychologist administering the WISC-R will find that Level V analysis (see Chapter 7) will be very helpful here. I will discuss more details in Chapter 7. But to provide one example here, suppose the student's answer to why an orange and a mango are the same is, because they both have skin. This response is not as abstract as one which indicates they are both fruits. If a teacher is doing a language arts activity that is semantic-based, such as categorization games, then she will be helping the student to "stretch" his categorization skills to a higher-level, more abstract way of verbal processing. Various reading activities using "word banks" can help to accomplish this.[15] (See also, Appendix 5-1.)

Another important contribution the WISC-R examiner can make is to observe how anxious the student is, and to what degree the student displays risk-taking and fear of failure. The student who is anxious and/or afraid to take risks will likely have the prediction process in reading disrupted, perhaps to a significant degree. If the examiner notes such behavior during the WISC-R, he should confirm with the teacher or see for himself whether or not it also occurs during the act of reading. If it does, then the suggestions just given for encouraging predicting will be helpful. So will those suggestions in Chapter 3, for providing a sense of purpose in reading. Finally, the relaxation exercises may have a place. Recommendations as to what suggestions will be best for a particular student must ultimately be made on an individual basis, taking into account *that particular student's reactions and needs.*

Another way in which the WISC-R and the PL model are linked, is in regard to background knowledge (schema base). Again, the WISC-R may be helpful in general because of the Verbal Scale. And, in particular, the Information subtest provides some insight into whether or not the student's knowledge base is appropriate for his age. The examiner can do an *item analysis* of the Information subtest to determine which items the student is actually getting wrong. In this respect, Cooper provides a very valuable grouping of the content of the 30 items of the WISC-R Information subtest, as follows:[16]

Groupings	*Item Numbers*
• Numeric Content	2, 3, 5, 7, 10, 20, 24
• Divisions of Time	7, 8, 11
• Directionality/Space/Distance	14, 19, 21, 27
• Sequential Processing	7, 8, 11, 15
• Self	1, 2, 13
• Environment	6, 9, 22, 30
• People	12, 16, 29
• Action	4
• History/Geography	12, 17, 19, 21, 23, 27, 28
• Science	4, 18, 22, 25, 26, 29

Note that some items fall into overlapping categories. In my experience, many younger learning-disabled students who score poorly on the Freedom from Distractibility factor often also "blow" the Time and Number items on the Information subtest. Again, try not to generalize too far. A low score on the Information subtest does *not* necessarily indicate weak background knowledge. Indeed, the student's schemata may be well developed in many areas, but weaker in the areas suggested by item analysis. Specific static bits of information in certain areas may not have been learned well by some student; but more dynamic background information, such as required on the Comprehension subtest, for example, may be very well developed. Remedial strategies such as semantic mapping, semantic feature analysis, and the Frayer model, should also be considered when weak background knowledge is hampering a student's reading.[17]

The PL model and its "cousins," then, have much to contribute to reading instruction and remediation. The model is practical at the classroom level, and considerable research has been generated from it. But bottom-up processing (which is really part of the model) is vital, as well.

CASE EXAMPLE

To this point, I have discussed a number of important considerations related to learning in general and to reading, specifically including affective states, cognitive processes, schemata, prediction, and automaticity. These factors overlap, of course, when it comes to sorting out the difficulties that individual students have in their academic subjects.

This is best illustrated by a case example. Jason (not his real name, of course) is a student in third grade who, at the time he was initially referred, was really struggling with reading. He was first assessed by the district's reading specialist and then, a year later, by the school psychologist. The reading specialist's summary of his reading was as follows:

Jason reads word-by-word, even at a preprimer level. His voice is flat and without expression. Listening to him read in this very slow, dull way, one has the impression that Jason neither enjoys reading nor understands what he is reading; and indeed, this appears to be true. When I asked Jason if he liked reading, he said, "No." I asked him what kinds of books he liked to check out of the library, and he said, "None of them."

Although Jason can recall words, and has a reasonably good sight vocabulary, his comprehension of what he reads is very poor. This may be due to a "slow recall" of vocabulary. There is very little evidence of chunking. He reads each word as a separate entity, pausing for close scrutiny each time. Although many of these same words appear to be at an automatic level when presented in columns, he has not learned to read sentences fluently.

When Jason has completed a story and is asked to retell the story, his retelling is extremely brief—often one or two sentences. When pressed to tell more, it is apparent that he has understood very little of what he has read. Yet as he reads, many of his miscues are syntactically correct. He knows it should make sense; and he does some self-correcting; but he seems to be disinterested in the story, it is as if he can't be bothered to become "involved" with the story. Jason complained about almost every reading and writing task he was asked to do. He grumbled without actually saying that he did not want to do it.

Jason asked almost no questions; and when asked a question, he was very quick to say, "I don't know," or shrug his shoulders. He showed no interest about anything we discussed, although he expressed considerable interest in the awards being presented over the loudspeaker by the principal.

Jason appears to have a fairly good visual memory, and visual perception/visual-motor coordination is not a problem. He has no difficulty with handwriting. I believe Jason has fairly good general knowledge, although it is difficult to be certain, because he was so reluctant to discuss stories.

Jason needs to hear himself as a *fluent* reader, and he needs to become *involved* with the stories. Assistance in the resource room is recommended.

A number of specific recommendations are made, as follows:

1. Developing Fluency:

    To help develop reading fluency, arrange for Jason to read along with tapes on a regular basis. Of particular value would be taping the story he will be reading with the class, and allowing him several opportunities to read with the tape before asking him to read a part he particularly likes, aloud.

2. Manzo's Request Procedure:

    To help Jason become involved in the story, our goals should be to:

    a. Have him formulate his own questions about the text material he is reading;

    b. Have him develop an *active, inquiring attitude* toward reading;

    c. Have him acquire purposes for reading; and

    d. Have him begin developing independent comprehension abilities.

    The Request Procedure involves the student and teacher in silently reading portions of the text material, and then taking turns asking and answering questions concerning the material. [Note: A more complete description of the Request Procedure was attached to Jason's report, and can be found in Gillet and Temple (see reference citation 15 for this chapter).]

3. Risk-Taking and Development of Prior Knowledge:

    Research indicates that good readers take more risks and are right more often, whereas poor readers take fewer risks and are wrong more often. Jason doesn't like to take risks because he is afraid that, once again, he'll be wrong. He needs reading material that will offer him a reasonable chance of being successful. Children who do not risk a guess when reading are slowed down so much that they derive little or no meaning from the words they read. Be sure his reading material is predictable and offers context clues in order to provide meaningful feedback. One way to make a story predictable is to provide a great deal of background information before the student reads, and provide a Directed-Reading-Thinking Activity. [The DRTA description was also attached to Jason's report. Again, see Gillet and Temple for a more complete description.]

FIGURE 4.2. Jason's WISC-R profile.

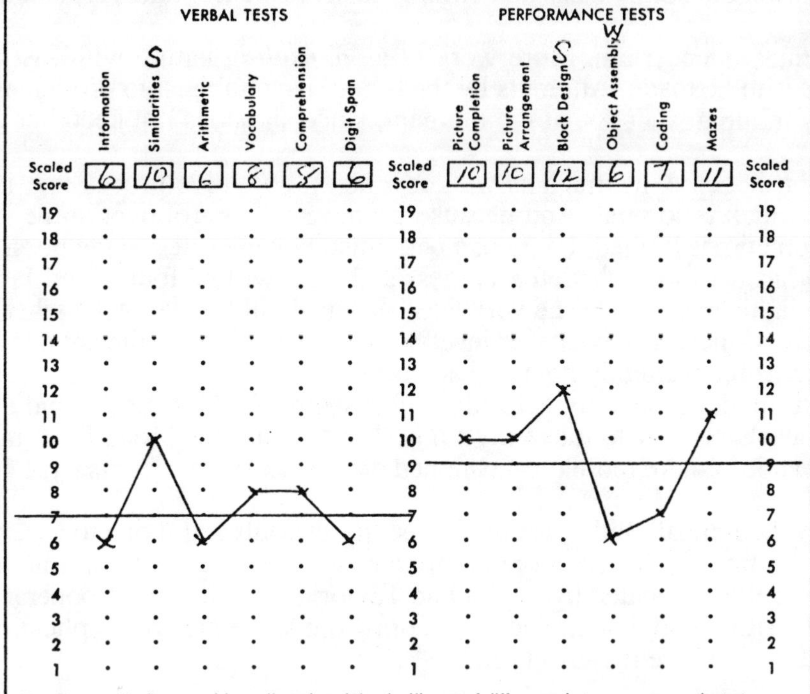

Probably paramount as you read Jason's case, is his *attitude*. Although many of the reading specialist's suggestions were faithfully carried out by the resource room teacher, and some improvements were noted, he continued to be uninvolved with reading.

In his second year in the resource room, Jason was referred to the school psychologist. A WISC-R was administered as part of the process. Jason's profile looked like the one shown in Figure 4.2.

Note the difficulties on the Verbal scale especially. The results of the WISC-R appear to dovetail with the processing difficulties noted by the reading specialist, except that his background knowledge was weaker than suspected. A parent interview was held between the school psychologist and Jason's mother, to discuss the test results, and to discover her *attitude* toward Jason and his reading problems. Jason's mother was very defensive. She steered away from answering any questions about his birth history and early development. As the interview progressed, she cried frequently. It seems obvious, then, that she felt very guilty and helpless about Jason's school difficulties. Two other children in the family had no problems in school—indeed, they often made the honor roll. Unfortunately, Jason's mother transferred her feelings of guilt to the school by blaming them for all of Jason's problems. Over time, the school discovered that Jason's mother was very inconsistent about helping him at home with any suggested activities. Because of her reluctance to discuss Jason's problems in an honest way, she held back his progress, probably conveying her disappointment to Jason on a daily basis and eroding his confidence, thus perpetuating the cycle of stress.

His future prognosis, thus, is uncertain. More work of a *counseling* nature with Jason's mother is vital, if any progress is to be made. Attempts by the school psychologist to provide this are being made, but with only minimal success, at the moment, since she does not keep her appointments.

I include this case report because, as much as we know about cognitive processing, it is often the *affective* component which is so vital. And because we have no control over home factors, success with students is sometimes limited. I am not a pessimist, however. It is quite possible that, at some point, the key to Jason's mother's defensiveness and guilt will be found, and Jason will truly make good progress in his reading. At the very least, Jason should be *enjoying* what he reads, and experiencing a feeling of success at whatever level he can handle. *That* is the issue in his case, and *that* is what his mother is inadvertently holding back for him.

I personally find the PL model especially helpful in discussing WISC-R results and recommendations with remedial teachers. I try to make my suggestions within the broad PL framework, but I tend to be quite eclectic. Where more old-fashioned drill work seems necessary, I certainly don't hesitate to say so.

The PL model, like any theoretical model, is not necessarily the only valid one to use, nor does it explain all there is to reading. In fact, a more comprehensive reading model (though, I think, a complementary one) recently advocated by Taylor and Taylor, is the Bilateral Cooperative Model (BLC). I will discuss the BLC model next, and again, draw out some general implications for reading and bring in the WISC-R where it seems to fit.

The Bilateral Cooperative Reading Model

This model was designed to provide a framework for every aspect of reading, from letter recognition, to understanding whole texts. As such, it is much more complete and complex than the PL model.

Taylor and Taylor describe the BLC model in this way:[18]

> ... Reading involves two parallel streams or "tracks" of interacting processes. The *left* track deals with functional relationships, sequentially ordered material, phonetic coding, syntax, and most functions we commonly think of as "linguistic." It is the analytic and logical track. The *right* track performs pattern matching functions, seeks out similarities between the input patterns and previously seen patterns, evokes associations, and relates

the meanings of words and phrases with real-world conditions. Its functions tend to be global, parallel, and passive. *Left* and *right* tracks cooperate in extracting the meaning from marks on a page (and indeed from speech as well . . .). The two tracks interact . . . . The *right* track makes quick guesses, and the *left* corrects the guesses as well as linking the results into phrases, clauses, and larger units.

The BLC model, then, is similar to the PL model in terms of the importance it gives to the language base and to prediction. Although it seems to be more bottom-up than the PL model, closer inspection indicates it is very much an interactive model. Both top-down and bottom-up processes are essential to reading (and speech) in the BLC model, too. The PL model seems to be more a "reading only" model, with language production already assumed; whereas the BLC model is more explanatory, and includes speech production in various languages in its explanatory process—an interesting feature.

A skeleton diagram of the BLC model for the first one-second (1 sec.) of reading is shown in Figure 4.3.[19]

The Taylors say the important features of the diagram are:[20]

- The processes on both *left* and *right* tracks can operate independently of one another between interconnection points.

- The interconnections occur only at discrete points, between which the processes on the two tracks perform related tasks on similar data. Five crossover points have been postulated, but the actual number is unimportant.

- It takes longer to transfer data from one track to the other at the higher stages because of an increase in processing required to translate the representations of one track to those of the other. The crossovers require complicated processing in their own right, especially at higher levels.

The processes in each track have a family resemblance: The low-level processes resemble the high-level processes within the same track much more closely than they resemble the same-level processes in the other track. [The diagram] lists some of the major differences between the *left* and *right* processes . . . . In each track, the lower levels deal with simple things such as letters or words; the higher levels with complex matters such as syntax or meaning. The *left* track links words together, in the manner discussed in grammar books. The *right* combines the ideas behind the words, and connects them with the current real-world context; it fleshes out the skeleton built by the *left*. Both tracks are heavily dependent on context, although it may not be evident from [the diagram]. The data gathered from lower stages serves [sic] largely to confirm or deny expectations derived from patterns or rules active in the higher stages. Each stage is thus firmly linked to higher and lower stages in its own track, and to parallel stages in the other track.

In addition, there is a table which specifies the functions of the *left* and *right* tracks, found in Figure 4.4.[21]

It is important to note that the left and right tracks do not correspond directly to the left and right hemispheres of the brain; but, at the higher comprehension levels, the parallel between tracks and hemispheres is much closer. Readers should also note the similarities to the "simultaneous/successive" distinction.

The model, say the Taylors, is supported by research on normal readers, those with brain damage, and experiments on split-brain patients.

Readers might have already been struck by the parallels of the left and right tracks in the BLC model, and the Verbal and Performance Scales of the WISC-R. I see the WISC-R as being only an "approximate fit" to the BLC model in that respect, and would not urge strict interpretations based on it.

FIGURE 4.3. The bilateral cooperative model of reading.

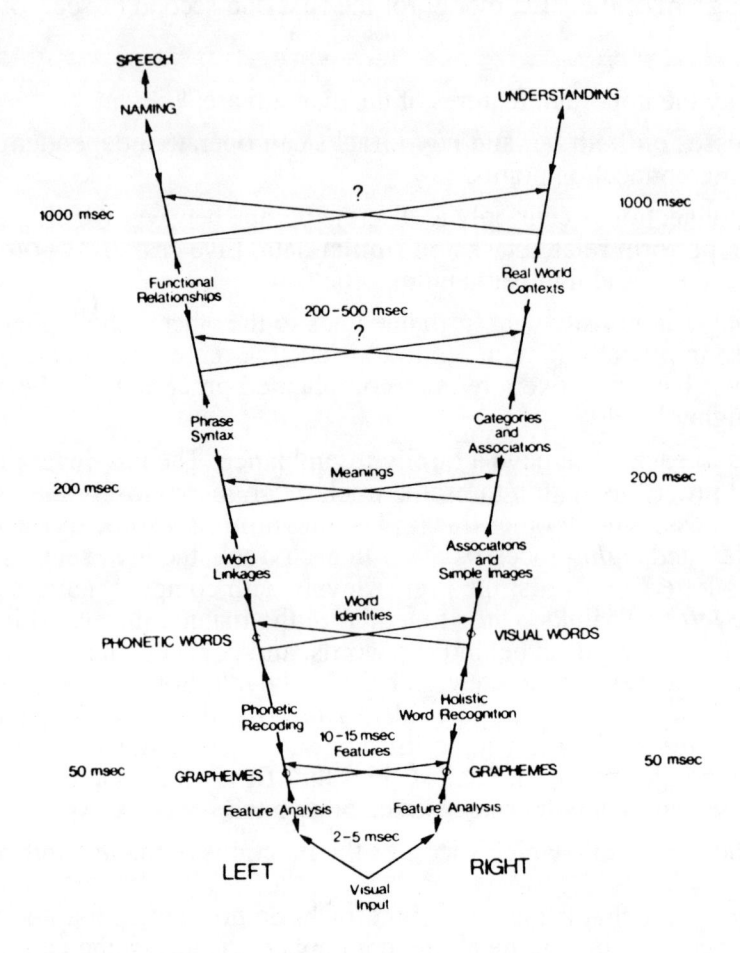

Left and right tracks and their interactions in the BLC model of reading. The two tracks are connected at a few discrete levels, but otherwise are independent. The right track works by global pattern matching and association, ultimately linking the sense of items to the state of the real world; the left works by analysis and rules, selecting appropriate pattern matches developed by the right, and inhibiting inappropriate ones. The left track is responsible for syntactic relations and phonetic coding of words.

From: Taylor, I., and Taylor, M. M. 1983. *The psychology of reading*, p. 234. New York: Academic Press.

FIGURE 4.4. Functions of tracks in the bilateral cooperative model.

	Left Track	Right Track
Cortical Location:	Left Hemisphere	Both Hemispheres, but mainly right in normal reading
Specialty	Labels, symbols, functional relationships, sequences	Patterns, colors, pictures, associations, collections
Processing style	Active, under attentional control Analysis into sub-units Seeks out differences Exact Unique result Serial, slow Handles material presented sequentially Time order Syntactic, rule based Pattern analysis Phonetically based Good short-term memory Speech output	Passive, automatic Global, wholistic Looks for similarities Approximate Many acceptable results Parallel, fast Handles material presented as a group Associations and spatial relations Meaning centered Approximate pattern matching Visually based Poor short-term memory Nonspeech output
Letter	Abstract letter identities Kanji phonetic and radical(?) Hangul and Kana	Isolated but not embedded letters Single or nonsense pairs of Kanji
Morpheme	Syntactic components Abstract elements	Content components Concrete elements
Word	Unfamiliar words Abstract words Embedded words Pseudowords	Familiar words Concrete, high-imagery words Words marked off by spaces
Sentence	Syntactic relations Make verbal gist	Meaning relations Visualization
Text	Functional and logical relations	Speed reading Humor and poetry

From: Taylor, I., and Taylor, M. M. 1983. *The psychology of reading*, p. 236. New York: Academic Press.

There are implications of the BLC model to reading disabilities (which the Taylors call developmental dyslexia). They say:[22]

> A deficient *left* track leads to poor phonetic coding, poor syntactic integration, poor sequencing, and poor STM [short-term memory]. A deficient *right* track leads to poor visual word recognition, poor comprehension of associations and real-world relationships, and perhaps poor LTM [long-term memory].

That paragraph certainly describes many of the students in resource rooms. Where does it leave the teacher, though, in terms of *how to teach* a student? The Taylors provide this overall suggestion:[23]

> Familiar words are recognized wholistically using a fast pattern-matching process, which can be done by both brain hemispheres, but is usually done by the right. Unfamiliar words and pseudowords are coded from their letters using a slow, analytic-phonetic process in the left hemisphere.
>
> In learning to read, both sets of processes must be developed and integrated, using whole-word and phonics methods. Learning proceeds in a series of three-phased cycles: recognizing a unit as a whole; analyzing it into subparts; and recognizing it as a whole again, based on securer recognition of its subparts. Poor or disabled reading results from failure to develop some part of the cycle.

More specifically:[24]

> The BLC model suggests that the learning sequence should have three phases: Learn a handful of words by their visual shapes (*right* whole-word recognition based on visual features); learn to analyze words into their parts (*left* analysis); learn once more to recognize the wholes, based on the securer knowledge of parts (*right* whole-word based on based on letter identities). Chinese children learn characters in the three phases, Swedish- and English-speaking preschoolers pick up reading in the three phases, and German children are taught to read at school in the three phases. School children in the United States are often taught by an eclectic approach mixing whole-word with phonics.
>
> Three-phased learning applies not only to words, but also to letters and to higher units of reading such as phrases, paragraphs, and whole texts. At the letter level, the child learns several letters by their gross shapes; then she notes the same and different features (configurational or fragmental) in the letters; and in the third phase she recognizes the whole letters again, now based on secure knowledge of the features.
>
> At the word level, teach a child a handful of words by look-say, ensuring that the vocabulary contains enough words with letters in common that the child can begin the analysis procedure. When the child notices that there is something similar between *cat* and *hat*, the analysis procedure should be encouraged, while at the same time, more look-say words are introduced to teach other letter-sound relations. By this means, the children develop both analytic and wholistic routes to word recognition. As fluent readers, they will read a familiar word as a whole visual pattern, and an unfamiliar word by phonetic analysis.
>
> At the passage level, the child already knows from speech something about elementary syntax and semantic associations among words, so that reading presents few problems of a new kind. But the syntax of writing can be more complex than that of speech, requiring a repeat of the same kind of three-phased learning. The three phases here are simple exposure to written syntax, its analysis into constituents, and the direct recognition of how words in common patterns fit together.
>
> Three-phased learning will happen no matter what a teacher does, but the teacher can encourage all three of the phases. At all levels, the analytic second phase is probably the one that can benefit most from formal training; the first phase requires exposure; and the third phase will follow the second automatically. If our observation is true, teachers should concentrate their efforts on phonetic word analysis, syntax, and story structure, but should allow the children to practice whole-word recognition, association, and story reading.

Effective learning requires not only the development of the analytic-phonetic *left* track and the wholistic *right*, but also their full integration.

The BLC Model and Automaticity

The Taylors seem to agree that reading is best learned by doing a lot of reading and practicing, but take issue with LaBerge and Samuels over their primarily bottom-up approach, one that emphasizes teaching each subskill to an automatic level before moving up to the next. They say:[25]

Subskills may be mutually facilitative rather than independent . . . . Instead of training each subskill to the level at which it becomes automatic before tackling the next one, as suggested by LaBerge and Samuels, we believe in training a few related subskills together, emphasizing one or another as conditions demand. The grounds for our belief are: (a) There is no clear boundary where the need for one subskill ends and another starts; (b) The smaller and lower the subskill, the less meaningful and interesting it tends to be; (c) The more finely and definitely is word decoding divided into subskills, the more difficult it will be to integrate the subskills again; (d) When one skill is learned, a cluster of its subskills may be partially acquired. For example, selecting, scanning, and unitizing letter features seem to be acquired largely spontaneously in the learning of letters and words. Calfee and Drum (1978) point out that prereading kindergartners handle graphic symbols in much the same way as do adults, when allowance is made for the role of memory and encoding, and that programs for enhancing visual perception are seldom effective. Sensitivity to orthographic structure might be considered as one of the subskills involved in word recognition. But is it sensitivity that facilitates word recognition, or vice versa?

As well as their excellent review and insights on word recognition, the Taylors provide a succinct summary of comprehension skills, where comprehension simply means extracting an idea conveyed in a sentence or passage. They say that:[26]

Similar comprehension subskills are involved in whatever languages or scripts children, or adults for that matter, may read.

In reading sentences, children must learn to:
- Recognize words;
- Assign syntactic and case roles to words;
- Construct a message based on content words, with the help of function words, if necessary;
- Identify the referents or anaphora;
- Organize words into larger syntactic units, such as phrase and clause;
- Extract the gist from a sentence.

In reading stories, children must learn to:
- Identify the motive or a hero or heroine;
- Follow the sequence of events or plot;
- Anticipate an outcome or climax;
- Extract a theme or moral.

In reading expository prose, children must learn to:
- Identify the topic;
- Distinguish important from unimportant idea units, processing the former more than the latter;
- Follow a sequence of directions or logical ideas;

- Draw inferences or conclusions;
- Sort out cause/effect relations;
- Extract the gist of a passage.

A reader has other, higher-level tasks. She must separate facts from opinions; evaluate the relevance of materials to the author's thesis or to her reading goals; appreciate the beauty, aptness, or novelty of expressions; grasp the point of a joke, irony, or sarcasm; and above all, retain at least the main points of what has been read.

The list above dovetails nicely with McNeil's flowchart for reading comprehension.[27] Finally:[28]

> Teachers can help children to develop comprehension skills by explaining syntax and text structure, by using plenty of examples of good and bad sentences and paragraphs, and by asking questions that test these skills. Children can develop the skills by reading a lot of stories and passages, as well as writing examples for comment or correction by teachers. The Greek philosopher and teacher Epictetus (first century A.D.) advised: "If you wish to be a good reader, read."

When I became a school psychologist, I had no idea of how complex the job was and the degree of understanding required for even seemingly "simple" things like reading. I hope that, by exposing you to both the PL and BLC models, some of this complexity is more comprehensible to you and, more importantly, that it suggests teaching strategies you can recommend. The PL and BLC models are complementary in many ways, although there are some obvious divergences which are likely to surface with more thought and research regarding the implications of each model.

Remedial Teaching Strategies

This is a good place at which to discuss some generalizations regarding teaching strategies for remedial readers. These generalizations seem to arise in many studies of good and poor readers:[29]

1. Good readers benefit under almost *any* instructional procedure. The "almost" is important here, however, because some conditions will not be as good as others. Good readers seem to learn even *despite* some kinds of instruction, in other words.
2. On the other hand, poor readers will benefit *only* under some instructional procedures and strategies. Unfortunately, the gap between good and poor readers is not necessarily narrowed. The reason for this is that both good and poor readers will benefit from an instructional strategy, good readers usually more so.
3. Some readers will remain behind, *despite* various teaching methods.

School psychologists and remedial teachers, then, need to continually evaluate their reading programs and strategies, and change them for poor readers through such practices as flexible groupings; diagnosis and program development; and the test-teach-test method, among others. More importantly, they need to remain open to new possibilities (such as phonemic analysis), but *without* jumping on bandwagons.

Finally, I should mention that it is quite possible to integrate a skill-development approach with a language-immersion approach in remediating reading problems. Following is an IEP in Figure 4.5 and a case example which illustrates this.

FIGURE 4.5. Individual education plan (following 4 pages).

ROCKY VIEW SCHOOL DIVISION NO.41

ESC 122/84

INDIVIDUAL EDUCATION PLAN - Pupil Services

Student's Name: "Michael" **Grade Placement:** Two **Date:** September

Subject Area: Language Arts **Level of Performance:** Beginning Reading Stage

Long Term Goals:
1. To learn to read using information gained from print
2. To be able to record ideas in a legible, clear, written manner
3. To perceive words as a particular organization of phonemes that occur in print as they do in speech

This form has been completed by: Debbie McLaren **Title:** Resource Room Teacher

Specific Teaching Objectives	Methods and Materials	Evaluation	Date Achieved
1. To learn both upper and lower case letters at a production level	Direct instruction of letters and sounds	Has mastered all except f, j, g, q, p	
2. To learn beginning consonant sounds and demonstrate by producing the letter	Use of sound stories, alliterative sentences. Reinforce through word sorts.	Needs to learn f, g, q	
3. To learn ending consonant sounds and demonstrate by production	Word Sorts Spelling Program-McCracken		
Word Identification			
1. To learn the short vowel sounds and practice them in context	Word Sorts Frisky Phonics I, a word families; T-scopes, short vowel sentences	a (November)	a (Nov/
2. To learn consonant blends and digraphs and demonstrate through reading and spelling	Word Sorts Spelling Program Frisky Phonics Teach Auditory Analysis Skills (Rosner)—Level III-beginning grade one too difficult—needs to go back to Level II (November		
3. To become aware of and begin using VCe rule in spelling and reading			

ROCKY VIEW SCHOOL DIVISION NO.41

INDIVIDUAL EDUCATION PLAN - Pupil Services

ESC 122/84
Page 2

Student's Name: _____ Grade Placement: _____ Date: _____

Subject Area: _____ Level of Performance: _____

Long Term Goals:
1. _____
2. _____
3. _____

This form has been completed by: _____ Title: _____

Specific Teaching Objectives	Methods	Materials	Evaluation	Date Achieved
Sight Words To develop and maintain a sight vocabulary that is recognized in various print contexts	Daily review of word cards made from basal readers Extended reading—other pre-primer books Methuen readers, Solo books Sight word puzzles Instruction of Dolch words—good progress—first 54 mastered using the Klatt method Sunny Sentences (grade 1) Story word cards; word families		Retention 43/47—not automatic (Nov.	
Comprehension 1. To use Michael's good verbal skills to predict story events, then attend to print to confirm predictions	Directed Reading Thinking Activity		Completed first preprimer (Mac-Millan R). Half-way through the second. Michael is very aware of story patterns. He uses the former, pictures and his highly developed understanding of language to over-ride print (Nov.	
2. To organize story events into proper sequence	Follow-up story activity involving cutting out sentences and rearranging		Successful if sentences are identical to those in the story. Finds it difficult when paraphrases are used.	

WISC-R COMPANION

ROCKY VIEW SCHOOL DIVISION NO.41

INDIVIDUAL EDUCATION PLAN - Pupil Services

ESC 122/84
Page 3

Student's Name: _____ Grade Placement: _____ Date: _____

Subject Area: _____ Level of Performance: _____

Long Term Goals:
1.
2.
3.

This form has been completed by: _____ Title: _____

Specific Teaching Objectives	Methods	Materials	Evaluation	Date Achieved
3. To begin to develop complete sentence answers to story questions orally—in phrases in written production	Self Directed Writing Program—unknown words are sounded out then underlined. Spelling conferences.		Beginning to look back in the story to find needed words (Nov.)	
Spelling				
1. To develop spelling awareness	McCracken; Sound Foundations I			
2. To develop beginning spelling skills through sound/symbol associations				
3. To develop a repertoire of high frequency words	Dolch—Klatt method		First 54 taught with 93% retention (Nov.)	
Written Expression				
1. To be able to record ideas in a clearly sequenced manner. To be able to reread a written piece.	Self Directed Writing Program—use of sequence of pictures drawn before writing. Verbalization of ideas very important.		Production level difficult; requires closeness to instructor to develop self discipline	
2. To be able to use capital letters at the beginning of a sentence, for names, and for the word "I".				
3. To develop a sense of sentence.	Rereading of stories and conferencing.			

ROCKY VIEW SCHOOL DIVISION NO.41

INDIVIDUAL EDUCATION PLAN - Pupil Services

ESC 122/84

Page 4

Student's Name: _____ Grade Placement: _____ Date: _____

Subject Area: _____ Level of Performance: _____

Long Term Goals: 1. _____
2. _____
3. _____

This form has been completed by: _____ Title: _____

Specific Teaching Objectives	Methods	Materials	Evaluation	Date Achieved
Speaking To gain self confidence through sharing of good vocabulary in group activities while learning to be less impulsive	Oral response times—language experience; choral speaking		Enthusiastic in sharing ideas. Beginning to learn to allow others to express ideas. Magnified expression in choral speaking (Nov.)	
Listening To develop listening skills so that Michael can appreciate a selection and ask questions to clarify.	Writing conferences		Consistently asks questions for clarification. Needs to eliminate self-distractors	
Printing To print legibly using uniform-size letters	Daily written work on interlined paper Direct printing practice		Tremendous improvement shown. Requires much self-control. Affected negatively by fatigue (Nov.)	

CASE EXAMPLE

Perhaps the IEP shown in Figure 4.5 belies how this resource room teacher truly integrates the methods. Following here, is her first-term report to the student's mother. (I would like to thank Debbie McLaren, the resource room teacher in this instance, for her permission to use this information. "Michael" is not the real name of the student, of course.) In it, you can see that she has a superb grasp of many of the principles we have been discussing:

Michael has become very comfortable in the resource room setting. [Note: This is a second-grade student who receives all of his language arts instruction in the resource room, but is otherwise mainstreamed.] He is beginning to gain self-confidence in the small group situation. Recognition of Michael's good verbal skills—extensive vocabulary, and wealth of information—is an important part of the oral response time each day. At that time, Michael is also encouraged to allow others to participate and share their ideas. Michael is very sensitive to others' accomplishments, and is quick to praise them. However, he is easily threatened by someone near him accomplishing something he has not quite attained. The emphasis in the resource room is to compete with yourself and to pat yourself on the back for your accomplishments, rather than compare yourself to someone else. Throughout the year, I hope Michael will begin to see himself in this light. The amount of seat work Michael can now accomplish independently has improved since September. Frequent checks by the teacher are necessary to keep him on task.

Michael has gained a sight-word repertoire of over 80 words. Recognition is not yet automatic, and retention occurs through daily review. Michael is beginning to attend to print and use his sight-word knowledge to gain meaning. He has completed the first preprimer reader and is more than half-way through the second. Controlled vocabulary material is used for instruction, so that Michael is very familiar with the words, therefore balancing his use of reading cues (semantic, syntactic, and word knowledge). When confronted with too-difficult material, Michael disregards the latter and imposes his own meaning upon the print. Frequent guided opportunities to read varied material at the preprimer level are very important to consolidate this delicate balance of cues. Letter identification and beginning and ending consonants are being reviewed. Short vowel instruction will be the emphasis in word analysis and spelling, so that Michael may begin to develop a word identification strategy to aid the sight words, semantic, and syntactic cues he already uses. Comprehension of stories is Michael's strength. Predicting and reading to confirm those predictions is emphasized. Sequencing of more than three story events proves challenging for Michael, especially if the events are paraphrased.

In the spelling program, Michael has studied the first 54 words with 93 percent retention. As mentioned previously, his spelling program will now expand to include learning to spell regular (predictable) words using short vowels. Michael is also developing spelling awareness, as evidenced by his looking back in stories to find a previously spelled word.

The writing program required Michael to "write" for approximately 20 minutes per day. He is currently at the stage where he draws pictures to clarify the main points of his story, then writes to the pictures. Animals, and his wealth of information about them, are his sole topics at present. Michael has much to contribute to the conferences and proves to be a good, active listener.

Printing practice is also a part of Michael's program, as he needs to develop consistent letter size, formation, and appropriate spacing. Already, there has been marked improvement.

[To Michael]: *Michael, you are an absolute delight to teach, because you have so much to offer to the class and to me. I am proud of how you are now able to listen to a request to get back to work and do so immediately. You are also beginning to read—truly read—every word, and you have now "published" one book. Give yourself a pat on the back!*

During our interview, Michael's Individual Education Plan, which details teaching techniques and materials appropriate to his level and learning style, will be available to you. Any concerns and/or questions can be addressed during that time.

Michael's second-grade WISC-R profile was as shown in Figure 4.6.

FIGURE 4.6. Michael's second-grade WISC-R profile.

WISC-R RECORD FORM

Wechsler Intelligence Scale for Children—Revised

NAME: Michael AGE: ___ SEX: ___
ADDRESS: ___
PARENT'S NAME: ___
SCHOOL: ___ GRADE: 2
PLACE OF TESTING: ___ TESTED BY: ___
REFERRED BY: ___

	Year	Month	Day
Date Tested			
Date of Birth			
Age	8	01	

Scaled Scores (Profile):
Verbal Tests — Information: 11, Similarities: 15, Arithmetic: 8, Vocabulary: 17, Comprehension: 15, Digit Span: 9
Performance Tests — Picture Completion: 11, Picture Arrangement: 18, Block Design: 13, Object Assembly: 10, Coding: 10, Mazes: 13

VERBAL TESTS	Raw Score	Scaled Score
Information	11	11
Similarities	16	15
Arithmetic	8	8
Vocabulary	35	17
Comprehension	18	15
(Digit Span)	(9)	(9)
Verbal Score		**66**

PERFORMANCE TESTS	Raw Score	Scaled Score
Picture Completion	16	11
Picture Arrangement	36	18
Block Design	27	13
Object Assembly	16	10
Coding	30	10
(Mazes)	(21)	(13)
Performance Score		**62**

	Scaled Score	IQ
Verbal Score	66	119
Performance Score	62	117
Full Scale Score	128	121

*Prorated from 4 tests, if necessary.

Chapter 5

WISC-R Interpretation: Levels I and II

Jerome Sattler suggests that the WISC-R can be interpreted in successive levels, as follows:[1]

- Level I—The Full Scale IQ
- Level II—Verbal and Performance IQs (I also include three-factor splits in this level)
- Level III—Subtest strengths and weaknesses
- Level IV—Patterns within a subtest
- Level V—Analysis of content responses and response styles

This interpretive approach corresponds closely to the Burt-Vernon hierarchical model of intelligence, with the primary emergence of *g* as the mental energy common to all human endeavors. It corresponds, as well, to the complex statistical work known as factor analysis that has been done extensively on the WISC-R. Additionally, this "successive-level" approach considers the difficulty associated with subtest reliability. It is a fact that, when a student is retested on the WISC-R, the Full Scale IQ will remain as the most stable score. The subtest scale scores themselves will vary considerably more. Therefore, beginning a WISC-R interpretation from the bottom, up, with a subtest-specific interpretation, is the *least* reliable approach to interpretation. On the other hand, remaining at Level I is not terribly helpful in terms of generating educational implications, since all we can really say at that level is how the student ranks on overall ability (*g*), compared to the standardization sample. (However, in some cases, that is only as far as one can legitimately go.)

Some combination of top-down and bottom-up interpretation is therefore desirable. One way around the bottom-up problem is to combine subtests into meaningful clusters, as combined subtests will be statistically more reliable than a subtest by itself. For example, if you look back at Table 1.1 (in Chapter 1), you will see that Planning Ability is a cluster that is shared by both Picture Arrangement and Mazes. If the interpretation that a student has good planning ability can be given, then that interpretation takes precedence over the *unique* abilities that each subtest has (sequencing and anticipating consequences and foresight and following a visual pattern, respectively). This means that *educational implications* suggested by Planning Ability would also take precedence over unique-ability implications. Readers should be familiar with the approach taken by Alan Kaufman in *Intelligent Testing with the WISC-R*, as his detective-work approach is very similar and complementary with what I am advocating here.[2]

There are yet other valid interpretative approaches using this successive-level model. For example, Blaha and Wallbrown reviewed a number of hierarchical factor solutions of the WISC-R.[3] They found considerable confirmation of Vernon's model (see their page 28). How the model looks in relation to the WISC-R is presented in Figure 5.1.

As one can see in Figure 5.1, these two authors present an interpretation of the WISC-R factors (in particular, Coding does not "load" on the Freedom from Distractibility factor in this approach) which is at slight variance with Kaufman's factor analysis. However, I believe that it is necessary to be eclectic, and not get stuck in one model. (This caveat is particularly important in factor analysis, since there are several ways in which factor analysis can be performed.) With the variety of student patterns you will encounter, it is necessary to become knowledgeable about a number of interpretive systems, each of which will have some merit.

The authors present four important implications for clinical interpretation of the WISC-R based on these findings. They suggest that profile interpretation be performed as follows. First:[4]

1. Account for child performances in terms of the broadest or highest-order factor(s) possible.

FIGURE 5.1. Hierarchical factor structure of the WISC-R.

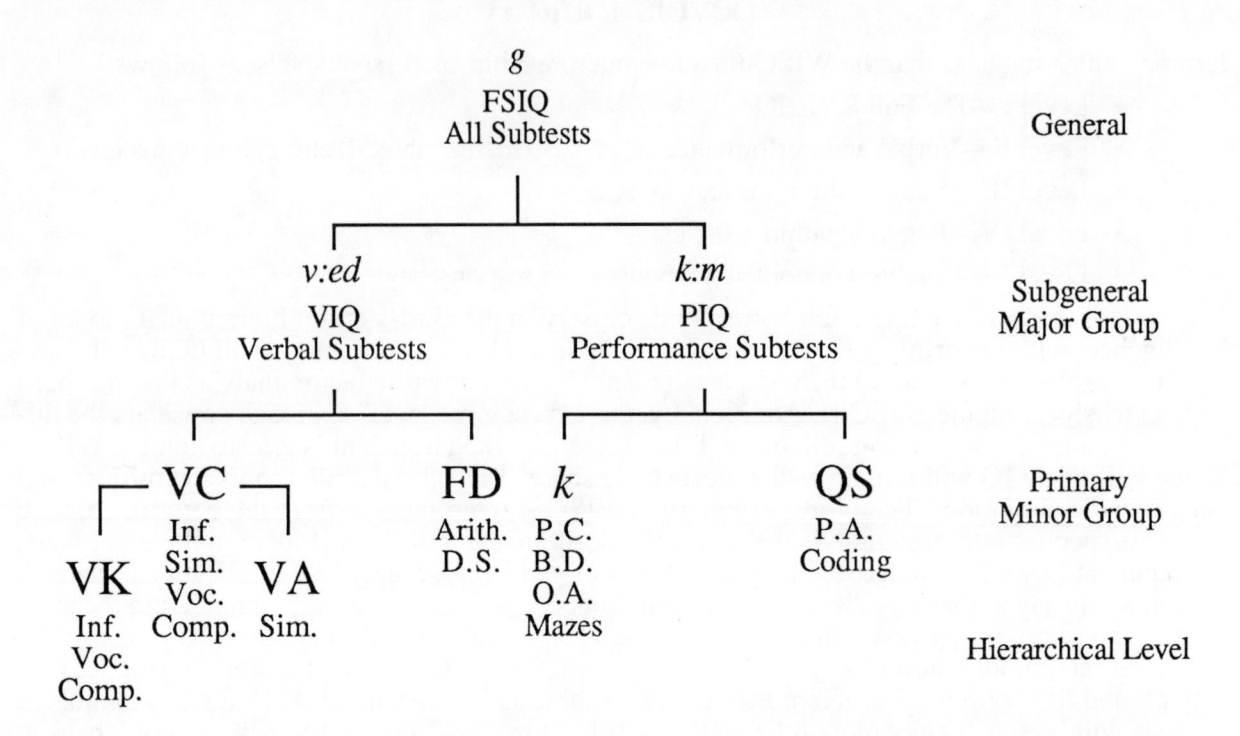

```
                        g
                       FSIQ                              General
                    All Subtests
                        |
           ┌────────────┴────────────┐
          v:ed                      k:m
           VIQ                      PIQ                  Subgeneral
      Verbal Subtests        Performance Subtests        Major Group
           |                         |
       ┌───┴───┐              ┌──────┼──────┐
      ┌─ VC ─┐                FD     k      QS           Primary
       Inf.                  Arith. P.C.   P.A.          Minor Group
       Sim.                  D.S.   B.D.   Coding
   VK  Voc.  VA                     O.A.
   Inf. Comp. Sim.                  Mazes
   Voc.                                                  Hierarchical Level
   Comp.
```

Composite hierarchical factor structure of the WISC and WISC-R derived from hierarchical analyses of 13 normal and atypical samples. (g = general intelligence, v:ed = verbal-numerical-educational, k:m = spatial-mechanical-practical, VC = verbal comprehension, FD = freedom from distractibility, k = spatial, QS = quasi-specific, VK = verbal knowledge, VA = verbal abstraction).

From: Blaha, J., and Wallbrown, F. 1984. Hierarchical analyses of the WISC and WISC-R: synthesis and clinical implications. *Journal of Clinical Psychology* 40:2, p. 563.

In other words, begin from the top, down. When a profile is relatively flat, then further calculation of factor scores may be redundant. Interpretation would have to stop at this level. However, if there is considerable variability among the subtests, then the Full Scale IQ should be deemphasized and the lower-order factors emphasized. Within each of the Verbal or Performance scales, variability is also important. For example, if there is a 12-point (or greater) difference between the Verbal and Performance Scales, but there is much variability within each scale, then the discrepancy may not be as important as the variability. The next step is:[5]

2. Determine the internal validity of a factor by examining the factor's variance. The greater the variance of the subtests that comprise a factor, the less valid that factor is in accounting for the child's performance.

As an example, they say:[6]

> ... If the scaled scores for the Arithmetic and Digit Span are 11 and 13, respectively, one can conclude that the student is above average in the ability to maintain numerical items in short-term memory and manipulate them without being distracted by extraneous stimuli. However, if the scaled score is 7 for Arithmetic and 17 for Digit Span, it would not make sense to consider the two scores together and relate them to other in-

formation about the child. Regardless of the weighting procedure used, we still would end up with a mean score on the FD [Freedom from Distractibility] factor and mask the huge differences (variance) between the two subtest scores.

Next:[7]

3. Determine the external validity of a factor by examining the degree to which the factor estimate agrees with other information about the child.

This is a point I have emphasized throughout this book. As the last major step in the analysis:[8]

4. If a higher-order factor analysis does not provide a valid estimate of a child's performance, then move down the hierarchy and attempt to account for the child's performance in terms of lower-order factors.

They elaborate on this point by stating:[9]

If the variability among the six subtests that compose either the v:ed or k:m factors is noteworthy, then it makes sense to move down the hierarchy of the major group factors whose validity is questioned and investigate the primary factors under its domain. Therefore, if the Verbal subtest variability is substantial, then attention should be drawn away from the VIQ [Verbal IQ] and toward the Verbal Comprehension (VC) and Freedom from Distractibility (FD) primary factors. The Information, Similarities, Vocabulary, and Comprehension subtests should be used to evaluate performance on the VC factor, and Arithmetic and Digit Span should be used to evaluate performance on the FD factor. When there is substantial variability within Performance subtests, then the Spatial (k) and Quasi-Specific (QS) primary factors should be investigated. Picture Completion, Block Design, Object Assembly, and Mazes should be used to evaluate performance on the Spatial factor, while Picture Arrangement and Coding should be used on the QS factor.

And, finally, when substantial variability exists within any of the primary factors, then, and only then, should rely on subtest-specific interpretation.

The approach advocated by Blaha and Wallbrown, then, is an elaboration of Sattler's Levels I and II.

For the remainder of this chapter, let's continue with Level I and II interpretations and some of their educational implications.

Level I—The Full Scale IQ Score

The Full Scale WISC-R IQ is the most valid and reliable of all the WISC-R scores. However, it should always be reported with its "confidence band." The confidence band will be larger or smaller, depending what level of confidence we wish to have for the score. We can increase the level of confidence by increasing the confidence band, but doing so results in a confidence band that could be so large that it becomes useless for educational purposes. We therefore need to make a reasonable trade-off. Usually, the 95-percent confidence level is required for educational purposes. The confidence level is also different at different ages. There are tables prepared for this; but, again, we will simply round-off, and accept ± 6 as the common confidence level (95 percent) for the Full Scale IQ at all ages of the WISC-R. So, if a 14-year-old student obtains a Full Scale IQ score of 96, it should be reported as "96 ± 6." The accompanying interpretive statement should be something like: "There is 95-percent confidence that the range of scores from 90 to 102 contains _____'s 'true' Full Scale IQ score."

Each Full Scale IQ score has a corresponding percentile. These percentiles enable us to see how that student ranks at that particular time against the standardization sample. The standardization sample of the WISC-R is already dated, since it was based on the 1970 U.S. Census, but is still the one against which all other of the student's peers are also compared; so, as far as *relative ranking* is concerned, the 1970 sample group does not affect interpretation. The WISC-R is a norm-referenced, not a criterion-referenced test. There is no "zero point" for intelligence test scores, so *there are no absolute criteria for discriminating individuals in terms of intelligence*—only relative ones.

Percentile scores are therefore very meaningful when interpreting the Full Scale IQ. However, one must bear in mind that a percentile score also has a "confidence interval." Table 2.2 at the close of Chapter 2 gives the percentiles for each Full Scale IQ score and the subtest scale scores.

The confidence band for percentiles is larger than for the standard scores themselves. For example, if a student scores a Full Scale IQ of 100, the confidence interval in terms of standard score points is from 90 to 102. The corresponding percentiles are from 25 to 55! This is substantial, and should be mentioned when interpreting results to teachers and parents.

Educational Considerations of the Full Scale IQ

1. General Considerations

Certain cautions must be born in mind in interpreting the Full Scale IQ. The first, as already mentioned, is the confidence level; the other is the fact that, for any individual student, we have a picture of his cognitive profile only at that point in time. The picture is neither complete nor unchanging.

One of the widest uses of the WISC-R is to help determine a placement in a special education program. You should remember that such decisions should never be made *exclusively* on an IQ score. Such scores are only part of the picture. You need also to bear in mind that any "cut-off points" that are used for placement are entirely arbitrary and will depend on how states and provinces best feel they can meet the needs of particular groups. The following classifications for WISC-R Full Scale IQ scores are the ones I prefer to use:

90+	Average and above
80–89	Low average
51–79	Educable mentally handicapped
31–50	Trainable mentally handicapped
<30	Dependent mentally handicapped

You need to become familiar with the classifications used in your local area.

Ignoring confidence levels for the moment, I have generally found that Full Scale IQs in the 80s are too low to be considered average. In placing an average expectation on such students, I feel we do them a disservice. Many such students are considered learning-disabled, and are therefore given programs where an implicit expectation of "catching up to their grade level" is made in reading and/or other subjects. As these students grow older, they are denied an opportunity to get into an excellent alternative program, such as a vocational one, because everyone "expects more" of them, and the LD label has stuck. It is much more difficult, in such cases, to convince parents that a nonacademic program is better for their child.

In practice, I have found educational systems quite flexible; so, even if a student *is* placed in a nonacademic program, there is usually the opportunity to switch to a more academic route later on, if circumstances change. These days, education is for life. Even if a person does not complete an academic program during his school years, there are more than ample opportunities to do so as an adult. For example, many colleges and universities open their doors to mature students who never completed an academic program in high school, but who now wish to continue their education at the university level.

High intelligence and good grades, then, are not *necessarily* prerequisites for university entrance, profession, or success in life. And, in fact, intelligence correlates very poorly with income level.

That is not to deny that intelligence has an important bearing on occupational status. When average IQ scores are calculated for various occupational groups, results such as those found in Table 5.1 are common.[10]

TABLE 5.1. Mean IQ of different professional and occupational groups.

140	Higher professionals, top civil servants, professors, and research scientists.
130	Lower professionals, physicians and surgeons, lawyers, engineers (civil, mechanical).
120	School teachers, pharmacists, accountants, nurses, stenographers, managers.
110	Foremen, clerks, phone operators, salesmen, policemen, electricians, precision fitters.
100+	Machine operators, shopkeepers, butchers, welders, sheet metal workers.
100−	Warehousemen, carpenters, cooks and bakers, small farmers, truck and van drivers.
90	Laborers, gardeners, upholsterers, farmhands, miners, factory packers and sorters.

From: Eysenck, H. J. (ed.). 1973. *The measurement of intelligence*, p. xi. Baltimore: Williams and Wilkins.

Expectations for various categories of mental handicap based on Full Scale IQ scores are illustrated in Table 5.2.[11]

TABLE 5.2. AAMD classifications of mental retardation, with descriptions of developmental characteristics.

IQ	Degree	Preschool Age 0-5 Maturation and Development	School Age 6-20 Training and Education	Adult Age 21 and Over Social and Vocational Adequacy
55-69	Mild	Can develop social and communication skills; minimal retardation in sensorimotor areas; often not distinguished from normal until later age.	Can learn academic skills up to approximately sixth-grade level by late teens. Can be guided toward social conformity. "Educable."	Can usually achieve social and vocational skills adequate to minimum self-support but may need guidance and assistance when under unusual social or economic stress.
40-54	Moderate	Can talk or learn to communicate; poor social awareness; fair motor development; profits from training in self-help; can be managed with moderate supervision.	Can profit from training in social and occupational skills; unlikely to progress beyond second-grade level in academic subjects; may learn to travel alone in familiar places.	May achieve self-maintenance in unskilled or semi-skilled work under sheltered conditions; needs supervision and guidance when under mild social or economic stress.
25-39	Severe	Poor motor development; speech is minimal; generally unable to profit from training in self-help; little or no communication skills.	Can talk or learn to communicate; can be trained in elemental health habits; profits from systematic habit training.	May contribute partially to self-maintenance under complete supervision; can develop self-protection skills to a minimal useful level in controlled environment.

24>   Profound   Gross retardation; minimal capacity for functioning in sensori-motor areas; needs nursing care   Some motor development present; may respond to minimum or limited training in self-help.   Some motor and speech development; may achieve very limited self-care; needs nursing care.

Adapted from Kirk, S. 1972. *Educating exceptional children*, p. 165. Boston: Houghton-Mifflin.

These are extremely important general educational implications of Level I WISC-R interpretation. School psychologists and teachers must remain flexible in their thinking, however, and remember that:

1. All expectations based on IQs are very rough guidelines only. Individual variation is considerable, and can change dramatically with time.
2. Individual students should never be labeled or placed in special education programs and forgotten. Periodic updating of scores and review of placements is vital.
3. Students should never be placed in special education programs based on IQ scores alone.
4. The goal of mainstreaming students should be upheld where feasible and desirable.

Full Scale IQ scores *do* change as a result of many factors, including cognitive growth and stimulation, and extraneous factors, such as measurement error and regression effects. The value of a Full Scale IQ score is to help set reasonable expectations based on the individual's overall ranking at a particular point in time.

2. Implications of the Full Scale IQ for Teaching Reading

Here, I will discuss some general implications of Full Scale IQ scores for teaching reading to mentally handicapped students. The learning-disabled group will be dealt with separately. Another special-needs group, the gifted, typically do not have difficulty with reading, though one group, gifted underachievers, might. I will also discuss some strategies appropriate to this group elsewhere in this chapter.

It should be kept in mind that the group of mentally handicapped students are all individuals. They are as heterogeneous a group (despite the fact that their measured IQ scores might fall below some arbitrary cut-off level) as, say, the learning-disabled or any other group of students. As such, then, careful individual diagnosis and good recordkeeping, preferably using a criterion-based system, is essential. I have found the Brigance inventories to be especially useful in this respect.[12]

As far as teaching reading to mentally handicapped students is concerned, no one particular "best" method exists. Each student has his own learning style and achievement level. Therefore, IEPs are essential, and structured programs like *Distar* may form part of the overall educational process for this group.

Materials themselves should be as concrete as possible, and much repetition is usually required. Mentally handicapped students typically have difficulty transferring what is learned in one context to another. So, not only is more repetition required; so is more teaching in a variety of contexts. Task analysis and teaching-for-transfer becomes particularly important for this group.

The Full Scale IQ is a good predictor of overall academic achievement, including reading. Brighter children will tend to read better; slower children, including the mentally handicapped, will tend to read much more poorly. Recall our regression effects, however. The relationship is by no means perfect. Bear in mind individual differences, as well.

Nevertheless, for students whose overall WISC-R IQ falls in the EMH or TMH range, and who are placed in special classes, we have to adjust our expectations and objectives for their reading program—in some cases, considerably so. Their overall cognitive handicap may set some limits as to what levels of reading they eventually attain. But the teacher's objectives should always be to stretch the student as far as possible.

In some provinces and states, the "reading" objectives are subsumed within the general "language arts" or "communications" curricula. To provide you with a typical picture of some communications objectives and expectations at the EMH level, I have included some from the Alberta Department of Education's *EMH Curriculum Guide* in Figure 5.2.[13] This is not to say that other provincial and state education departments do not have equally acceptable curricula. I am simply more familiar with the Alberta ones. In Alberta, the regular language arts curriculum is based on six primary modes of communication—listening, viewing, speaking, reading, spelling, and writing. The Alberta *EMH Curriculum Guide* describes the characteristics of the EMH student in each of these six areas.[14]

A sample of a few specific objectives and strategies for reading comprehension is shown in Figure 5.3.[15]

FIGURE 5.2. Characteristics of educable mentally handicapped students.

There are many characteristics which are common among EMH students in terms of the degree of development and level of competency of their communication skills. Age-appropriate materials and activities should be used.

1. *Listening*—Due to the lower level of reading ability found in many EMH students, it is very important to develop other receptive communication skills. It is necessary to teach these students to become competent and discriminative listeners. It is through listening that much informal and practical learning takes place. Therefore, the ability to listen and interpret what is heard is a very crucial skill to develop in the EMH student.

2. *Viewing*—Again due to limited reading skills, EMH students rely heavily upon the visual media to obtain information about their world. They watch more television than the average student, and are often found to be more gullible in accepting the standards and values of what they see on television or in movies. Reliance on pictures to get the context of a story, a news happening, or an advertisement, further justifies the need to teach these students how to interpret information experienced visually.

3. *Speaking*—Speaking is one of the communication skills which is utilized each day. For the EMH student, difficulty in expressing himself and verbalizing his wants and needs is a common problem. Part of this problem is often due to specific articulation deficits or maturational lags in language development. Regardless of the nature of the deficit, a specific sequential language development program should be followed daily to assist these students in their speech and language development.

4. *Reading*—EMH students generally learn to read at a later age and at a slower pace than their nonhandicapped counterparts. They often have great difficulty generalizing concepts and rules associated with reading skills. Although these students can learn the various reading skills in the same order and through similar teaching methods as regular students, they often require more teaching time and extensive practice in the various skills. The approach utilized in teaching to these students should emphasize a practical or functional point of view.

5. *Spelling*—There is often a relationship between reading ability and proficiency in spelling. Therefore, the extent of development of reading skills of the EMH student has a direct bearing on the student's ability to master spelling skills. Cognitive functions such as discrimination, perception, and memory must be developed within the spelling program to assist the EMH student in learning to spell competently. Often a pattern of says, points, reads, and writes, is most effective in the teaching of spelling to these students.

6. *Writing*—For the EMH student, learning to print and write is sometimes slower to develop, due to a slower rate of motor development or deficits in cognitive functions such as perception and discrimination. It is recommended that both manuscript and cursive writing be taught to EMH students. The teaching of cursive writing, however, should not be dependent upon mastery of manuscript writing.

Learning Approaches

The needs of the EMH student to function adequately within society do not differ greatly from those of a regular student. However, due to the fact that their rate of progress in learning is much slower, and their potential for mastery is not as great, programs designed in the teaching of communication skills must be modified in terms of instructional approaches and techniques.

It is recommended that an "eclectic approach" be utilized with these students. This approach necessitates that the teacher be adept at utilizing a variety of teaching techniques and methods (e.g., language experience, kinesthetic, phonetic) within each program. The eclectic approach makes use of the most appropriate program in terms of methods and materials for each individual student in order to facilitate maximum growth and development.

When teaching communication skills to EMH students, the teacher should relate instruction whenever possible to the tangible and concrete. In addition, one should not assume that a particular skill or concept is learned or has been mastered simply because the student can apply the use of the skill in one situation. By utilizing a wide range of instructional techniques, the teacher can facilitate generalization of skills across various situations. The rate of learning for the EMH student is very often much slower than one would expect of a regular student. When teaching communication skills to these students, then, repetition of instruction is often necessary. Maintaining interest is essential for the students.

The Alberta *EMH Curriculum Guide* is very extensive and has been very valuable in the special education of this group of mentally handicapped students. There is a similar guide for the TMH level.[16] The guides are thorough and extremely useful references.

In the previous chapter on reading theories, I discussed the Psycholinguistic (PL) and Bilateral Cooperative (BLC) Models of reading.[17] For the severely mentally handicapped, the BLC model has one very important implication. Even students in the low TMH range (Full Scale IQs below 45) should be able to acquire some Level I reading skills by emphasizing the *right* track (though a severely deficient *left* track, which many students have, will hinder progress). To do so, some form of logography would be most appropriate. *Blissymbols* and simple line drawings, or rebuses, have all been used successfully.

Both models also emphasize that a strong language base is necessary in reading. This is very pertinent for the mentally handicapped, since language disorders are far more prevalent in this group than in other handicapped groups. Therefore, a language-immersion approach, as outlined in Appendix 2-1, is also very appropriate to this group. This should include even more in the way of discussions, sharing experiences, developing basic verbal classification skills, semantic mapping, and development of background information. Of course, all of this must be modified to the level of the student.

Predicting is just as important a process in reading for the mentally handicapped as for any other group. A language experience approach serves this purpose very well. W. T. Fagan says:[18]

> Using this approach, the teacher transcribes a child's story or account of his experiences. Attention may be drawn to certain word sequences that could be modified or elaborated in further instruction. For example, the sentence, "I was at the party," could be modified by the child in response to questions read, "Bob was at the party," "Jane was at the party," and, "I was at the party that the teacher gave." Sentences might be printed on strips and cut into words or phrases and scrambled. With direction, the child could be asked to put various sentences together. The word cards "Bob" and "was" may be presented, and the child

then asked to read these and state (predict) what comes next. The words "at the party" could then be found to complete the sentence.

FIGURE 5.3. Reading comprehension development strategies for educable mentally handicapped students.

Objectives	Teaching Strategies	Materials
The student:		
Finds main idea in a story or paragraph.	Duplicate paragraphs. Have students either find or draw pictures to illustrate them. Have pictures pasted on cards which the students can use for this activity. Have student summarize the paragraph he has read by choosing a suitable picture.	Main Ideas and Details, Levels K-1 (S1-2); Working with Facts and Details (S2-4) A Nelephant Named Godfrey (S1-2-3)
Organizes events in proper sequence.	Cut story into paragraphs. Paste the paragraphs on cardboard and code so that the students may correct their work with a key. Have students read the paragraphs and place them in proper sequence.	Organizing Information (S2-4); Serial Sequencing Cards (S1-4)
Predicts outcomes from material read.	Paste short stories on cardboard sheets. Place conclusions of these stories on another card. Have students read the stories and the conclusions, and then match the stories with the endings.	Increasing Comprehension (S2-4)
Uses the index to find specific information.	List words from the reader's index on the chalkboard. Have students find each word in the index and write the number of the page on which information about each subject is found.	Using References (S3-4)
Skims to locate specific information.	Have student reread a story to answer specific questions.	Increasing Comprehension (S3-4); Working with Facts and Details (S2-4)

The word bank (see Appendix 5-1) can also be modified for the mentally handicapped reader. I would also include a good number of rebuses, since many students have shown that mentally handicapped populations do better on spatial tasks on the WISC-R (Picture Completion, Object Assembly, and Block Design) than they do on Acquired Knowledge tasks (Arithmetic, Information, Vocabulary). Any relative strength in these subtest for an individual student should be noted and woven into instructional programming whenever possible.

Meaning associations will usually be very weak for mentally handicapped students. Therefore, associations must be taught in the context of the reading program. Procedures like semantic mapping, to be discussed later, could be adapted and used in a class. Associations can also be encouraged by oral discussion, using examples and nonexamples of the concept in question. For example, if the student's task is to learn to read a *No Smoking* sign, then:[19]

A picture with signs incorrectly placed may be used for pupils to tell what is wrong with the picture. For example, pictures might show "No Skating" in an airplane, or "No Smoking" on an ice-covered lake.

Although the Full-Scale IQ is a good predictor of reading achievement, we should bear in mind what was said earlier about the scores not being cast in concrete. Teachers should *not* allow the Full Scale IQ to become a self-fulfilling prophecy, nor should they give up on a student with a low IQ score. The Full Scale IQ is usually a realistic *starting point* for educational planning. For those with lower IQ scores, the programming must be even more intense and more directive. Don't get caught in the "label trap." Douglas Carnine cautions:[20]

> Several researchers have found that when students are given a special education label, teachers rate behaviors more negatively. A description of a child is more likely to result in the label "mentally retarded" if the teacher is told the child is from a low-income background.... Poor attitudes and expectations for children can also affect peers' attitudes and the behavior of teachers, leading to segregation as well as fewer and less effective instructional interactions.

In the same article, Carnine goes on to give some very impressive and compelling data on the effects of the "Direct Instruction Model" on some 8,000 "high-risk" students from low-income homes in 20 U.S. communities.

The major building blocks of the Direct Instructional Model are the *Distar* programs. Many professionals I know cringe at the very term, *"Distar,"* since it is seen as too rigid and too structured a program. More recent criticisms attack the very bottom-up approach that *Distar* uses in teaching reading especially. I see the criticisms as lacking substance, however, especially for mildly mentally handicapped and possibly learning disabled populations, where the solid learning principles on which *Distar* was based, are especially applicable. In addition, Carnine et al. present some impressive research evidence to show just how effective implementation of the Direct Instruction Model can be.

School psychologists and special educators must work with such students daily. On a very practical level, then, these results should be taken seriously. *Distar*, or any other program, will not "work" if the teacher is emotionally cold or aloof, or has low expectations, or does not believe in the method. Speaking about expectations, Carnine says:[21]

> One of the most important findings from [Direct Instruction Follow-Through] was that students entering kindergarten who would typically be expected to fail in school could achieve at close to the national average. Direct Instruction Follow-Through students, all of whom were from economically disadvantaged homes and who were over 90-percent minority, scored about as well as the median of the test's norming sample. This finding and similar ones with special education populations is important because it justifies higher expectations on the part of educators.

And for those concerned about the rigid, bottom-up approach of *Distar*, it is necessary to cast off the shackles of preconceived pet theories and become more eclectic in outlook. Carnine tested students in kindergarten to third grade who had learned to read via *Distar* using "miscue analysis." Miscue analysis is a PL model approach that looks at errors made when reading to determine whether children are using semantic/syntactic/grapho-phonic cues when reading, or over-relying on one strategy and, in general, just seeing if the student is predicting and knowing that reading is something that must make sense. He found that:[22]

> ... Even though the children continue to work on the analysis of words in isolation, teacher-directed exercises on sentence and story reading led to a covertization of a set of reading skills; the children anticipated meaning, self-corrected words that apparently made no sense, and made the kind of mistakes that are possible only if the semantics and syntax of the passage are understood.

Direct Instruction was compared to eight other major instructional approaches covering a six-year study of using them with various economically disadvantaged groups across the U.S. I will not discuss the different approaches here. A brief description of each can be found in the Carnine article. What is important for our purposes are the following results comparing the programs on a complex set of measures collectively called the "Index of Significant Outcomes," as shown in Figure 5.4.

FIGURE 5.4. Index of specific outcomes (ISOs) for basic skills (B), cognitive skills (C), and affective measures (A).

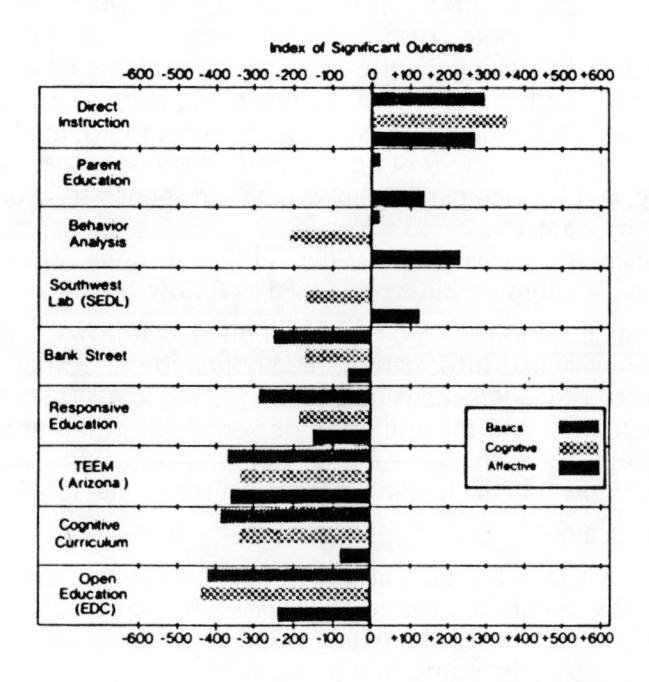

From: Carnine, D. W. 1979. Direct instruction: a successful system for educationally high-risk children. *Journal of Curriculum Studies* 11:29-45.

Of these results, Carnine says:[23]

The first four programs are the only programs with more positive than negative outcomes on some measures. Direct Instruction is the only model that shows consistently positive outcomes across measures. The more open-ended, child-centered programs show consistently negative outcomes.

These findings concerning Direct Instruction deserve particular attention. First, Direct Instruction students achieved well not only in basic skills ... but also in cognitive skills—reading comprehension, math problem solving, and math concepts. Second, Direct Instruction students' scores were quite high in the affective domain, suggesting that competence enhances self-esteem and not vice versa.

In this book, I do not intend to advocate *Distar* or any one program above others. I do feel, however, that there is a place for Direct Instruction *principles*, many of which have already been discussed in the "Teacher Effectiveness" portion of Chapter 3. This is particularly true for disadvantaged and mentally handicapped whose present Full Scale IQs would otherwise suggest a poor academic prognosis. I am *not* in favor of using *Distar* for *all* students, but I can certainly see a place for it for students who could be considered at-risk. *Distar* principles can be part of the language-immersion environment I describe more fully in Appendix 2-1.

Level II—Verbal and Performance IQs; Three-Factor Splits

The Verbal and Performance Scales of the WISC-R measure two separate factors or underlying cognitive abilities. The Verbal scale depends heavily on language usage and background of experiences. The student listens to the questions and responds to them verbally.

The Performance scale is different. It measures a student's ability to solve unique problems. The output is primarily motor (use of hands); and the materials are primarily nonverbal (pictures, blocks, puzzles), but which require some verbal explanation on the part of the examiner. The student does not reply verbally except on Picture Completion—though, even here, the student may simply point. However, the examiner should watch for rapid, automatic naming on the student's part. Rapid, automatic naming (not on Picture Completion, specifically, however) is a correlate of good reading, and is often part of the student's response style on the Picture Completion subtest. More on this in Chapter 7.

In summary, then, the Verbal Scale of the WISC-R is quite broad in its sampling of verbal ability (v:ed). Blaha and Wallbrown summarize v:ed as follows:[24]

> ... The Vernon definition of v:ed may be applied as follows: Verbal information as indicated by Vocabulary and Information, the application of verbal skills and information to situations that require judgment as indicated by some items from Comprehension and Similarities, the retention and manipulation of verbal information in short-term memory as indicated by Digit Span and Arithmetic. This illustrates the breadth of this major group factor directly below *g* in the hierarchy, which is somewhat less broad than the *g* factor.

While the Performance scale:[25]

> ... is a gross estimate of a child's ability to think in terms of visual images and manipulate them with fluency, flexibility, and relative speed. In the classroom, one might expect that a child with a high Performance IQ would respond to visually oriented modes of instruction such as graphs, charts, diagrams, and pictures.

Much attention has been given over the years to Verbal/Performance discrepancies (i.e., when one scale of the WISC-R is "significantly" higher or lower than the other). The key word is "significantly." To reach *educational significance*, the difference between the Verbal and Performance Scale IQs should be 12 points or more in either direction.[26] Such a difference forms the basis for a number of educational hypotheses important for the student's educational program or placement.

Discrepancies of 12 points or more suggests a broad preference for one or the other modes of reasoning as we have described, and suggest other differences, such as in cognitive style, in information processing strengths or weaknesses, in difficulty in working under time pressure, or in differences in aptitudes and interests. Consideration also has to be given to the possibility of brain damage or emotional disturbance.[27] However, since discrepancies of 12 points or more occur in a significant number of students in the normal population, the discrepancy, by itself, should *never* be used to make such a diagnosis. If other corroborating evidence suggests it, then of course, further testing becomes imperative. As ever, corroborating evidence for *any* of the hypotheses is necessary.

This brings us to a small but important digression. Much has been made of the fact that Verbal/Performance discrepancies (and other WISC-R clusters) occur so frequently in the normal population, that their diagnostic value is nil. I do not agree with such interpretations. It is true that Verbal/Performance discrepancies occur frequently in the normal population. Additionally, in the WISC-R standardization sample, it was found that:[28]

Verbal/Performance IQ differences were not related significantly to either sex or race, but were related significantly to parental occupation and to intelligence level. Children of professional parents tended to have higher Verbal than Performance IQs, while children of semiskilled and unskilled workers tended to have higher Performance than Verbal IQs. More Verbal/Performance differences were observed in the brighter groups than in the duller groups. At all levels of intelligence, it was about as likely that Verbal IQ would be higher than Performance IQ, as that it would be lower.

These are important facts that every school psychologist should be aware of. It suggests to me that a combination of genetic and environmental factors influence the development of the two major factors tapped by the WISC-R. Now, as for the validity of interpreting such differences, Sattler makes a statement that I think is very pertinent:[29]

> Verbal/Performance differences may be significant and yet occur with some frequency in the population. Thus, the discrepancy may be a reliable one but not a unique one. The probability-of-occurrence approach is dependent on the correlation between the two scales, while the reliability-of-difference approach is based on the standard error of measurement of each scale. I recommend that when reliable (significant) differences occur between the child's Verbal and Performance scales, hypotheses about the child's cognitive strengths and weaknesses may be formulated. This recommendation is made because discrepancies may provide a meaningful profile (or pattern) of abilities, even though they may occur in a large segment of the population.

So, the examiner should always carefully consider a number of possible hypotheses when the Verbal/Performance discrepancy is 12 points or greater. Besides the ones already mentioned, Sattler also suggests the relationships between Verbal and Performance scale scores shown in Figure 5.5.[30]

FIGURE 5.5. Verbal-Performance relationships.

Verbal > Performance	Performance > Verbal
1. Verbal skills better developed than performance skills.	1. Performance skills better developed than verbal skills
2. Auditory processing mode better developed than visual nonverbal mode.	2. Visual nonverbal mode better developed than auditory processing mode.
3. Possible difficulty with practical tasks.	3. Possible difficulty with reading.
4. Possible performance deficit.	4. Possible language deficit.
5. Possible limitations in motor nonverbal output skills.	5. Possible limitations in auditory conceptual skills.

From: Sattler, J. 1982. *Assessment of children's intelligence and special abilities*, 2nd ed., p. 200. Boston: Allyn and Bacon.

The student with the V > P pattern will not be as likely to have as much a problem with *academic* subjects as the student with the P > V pattern, in my experience.

For example, let's suppose two students obtain the following WISC-R IQ scores:

Michael		*David*	
Verbal IQ	85	Verbal IQ	115
Performance IQ	115	Performance IQ	85
Full Scale IQ	99 ± 6	Full Scale IQ	99 ± 6

Both students obtain exactly the same Full Scale IQs, and both students show markedly discrepant Verbal/Performance patterns (30 points). However, Michael is far more likely to have problems with reading, because language facility is such an integral part of it. In the upper years, if the pattern remains, Michael may benefit far more from a placement in a vocational school, because the "hands-on" training he gets in such a setting is far more matched to his strengths. Students like Michael are likely to be classified learning-disabled or dyslexic; however, there is an underlying assumption that, somehow, he can "catch up." This may or may not be true.

David may encounter some problems in school as well, but they are likely to be quite different than Michael's. David's verbal strengths will likely lead to higher academic expectations on the part of teachers and parents alike. They are bound to notice his verbal facility and expect him to match it in academic tasks. If the situation is one of oral discussion, he may very well do so. His reading may also be consistent with the Verbal IQ. But he could also have problems organizing himself on paper. Therefore, his written output may be more akin to his Performance IQ, rather than his Verbal *or* Full Scale IQ.

Again, such generalizations are not perfect, so caution must be observed in such interpretations. Behavioral observations and teacher comments about how the student works under different task demands are very important considerations in each case.

For students whose Verbal/Performance discrepancies are also associated with written output problems, the handwriting and compensations suggested in Appendix 5-2 could be applicable. Some research also supports the use of EMG biofeedback for improvement in handwriting, other academics, and self-concept.[31] The improvements occurred in as little as ten one-hour sessions. One practical drawback, however, is the special biofeedback training required.

For most school situations, then, the Verbal/Performance discrepancies merit careful attention. Remedial attention in the P > V profile should focus primarily on language and reading development in the elementary grades. This pattern also corresponds closely to the one that Vance, Wallbrown, and Blaha call "Pervasive Language Disability."[32] The prognosis, according to these authors, in a reading clinic where the student received three to five hours of individual instruction per week for two years, is very poor in terms of catching up to grade level. So the objective of having the student catch up may be unrealistic in such cases. That does *not* mean that the effort should not be made.

Language development, especially as applied to reading, becomes a major objective in my mind for such students in the primary grades. I will now discuss some semantic and some experience- and mnemonic-based strategies for vocabulary development in reading. Such strategies are integrated in their approach. They require the student's background of information and their abstract reasoning, as well as their lexical knowledge. As such, they draw on many of the language aspects tapped by the Verbal Scale of the WISC-R.

Vocabulary Development Strategies

Building associations among words is building a meaning base, stretching and expanding the student's schemata (internal cognitive structures). Therefore, building a student's vocabulary is an important part of every student's normal development and formal schooling. For those whose Full Scale IQ scores are low, this is even more true.

A number of methods have been used to develop reading vocabularies. These methods are applicable, with modifications, at practically every level of intelligence.

Experience-Based Strategies

An experience-based strategy for vocabulary-building emphasizes—just as we might expect—students' own experiences. These strategies are closely related to the semantic ones I will discuss next, though some of the semantic strategies do not build on experience as a cornerstone.

Why is an experience-base important for building vocabulary? Frederick Duffelmeyer writes:[33]

> The more firmly rooted in experience each schema is, the more integrity it has. Thus word meanings that are rooted in experience would result in more substantial schemata than word meanings that lack an experiential foundation
>
> All of this suggests that vocabulary instruction should be experience based. Otherwise, students are likely to end up with a store of words that Dale refers to as "floating items unattached to real experience [where] the *shell* of meaning is there, but the *kernel* is missing."

There is some research to support the notion that experience-based vocabulary learning is superior to non-experience approaches such as using context or using the dictionary.[34] Duffelmeyer explains four different strategies using this approach in a teaching lesson. I will quote only one of them here. The method involves using synonyms and examples.[35]

Strategy 1: Synonyms and Examples

- Planning. Select a word you wish to teach. Decide on a simple synonym for the word, find several familiar examples that illustrate the concept, and write a sentence containing the word.

    Example:

    Word: renowned

    Synonym: famous

    Examples: Christopher Columbus, Reggie Jackson, Michael Jackson

    Sentence: If you discovered a cure for the common cold, you'd be renowned.

- Teaching.

    Teacher: (Displays *renowned*, pronounces it, and has students pronounce it.) *Renowned* means the same thing as *famous*. A person becomes *renowned* by doing something that no one else has ever done or by doing something very, very well. For example, Christopher Columbus is renowned for . . . .

    Student: Discovering America.

    Teacher: Reggie Jackson is renowned for . . . .

    Student: Hitting a lot of homers.

    Teacher: Another example of someone who is renowned is Michael Jackson. What is he renowned for:

    Student: "Thriller," that real scary video.

    Student: The millions of records he sold.

    Teacher: What other person do you know of who is renowned?

    Student: Sally Ride.

    Teacher: What is she renowned for?

    Student: She was the first woman astronaut from the United States to go into outer space.

    Teacher: (Displays sentence.) Read this sentence silently. (Pause.) Why would you be renowned if you discovered a cure for the common cold?

    Student: Because right now there is no cure.

    Student: And it would help millions and millions of people all over the world.

The other strategies that are mentioned in the article are: positive and negative instances, example and definition, and definition and use. Each is discussed in the same practical detail as the one I just quoted. Readers can refer to the article for complete details. Another useful reference is Carl Braun's and Victor Froese's (eds.) book, *An Experience-Based Approach to Language and Reading* (Baltimore, University Park Press, 1977).

Another useful and related vocabulary-building strategy is the word bank, complemented by word sorts. Word banks are just that. The student selects words from his own experience- and language-base, writes or prints them on file cards, and keeps them in a "bank" of some sort. A number of teaching activities can be done with the words in the bank. These are described in Appendix 5-1.

Semantic-Based Vocabulary-Building Methods

There are a number of general semantic-based techniques used by regular and special education teachers for reading. Some of them are based on analysis of context clues. These can be used in isolation or in the act of reading itself. These strategies may not be as effective as the experience-based ones, but they need to be taught in any case. They are commonly used strategies and do not take nearly as much teaching time as the experience-based ones. Kenneth Goodman provides the following seven strategies and principles, all of which are semantic-based:[36]

1. The way the word or phrase is used is a good clue to its meaning in the particular passage.

2. Authors frequently provide simple definitions right in the text: "To measure wind speed, meteorologists use an anemometer."

3. If a word is important, it will occur several times. Each subsequent occurrence will provide a new context to help the reader zero in on its meaning.

4. If the word is unimportant to the reader's comprehension, he will only need a vague notion of its meaning to go on. Usually its context provides that. Most proficient readers have learned to be undisturbed by a few unimportant words, the meanings of which are uncertain.

5. Dictionaries are most helpful for confirmation when the reader has formed a fairly strong notion of a word's meaning from the context.

6. If the word or phrase is a name difficult to pronounce or a foreign word, it may be sufficient to use a place holder to facilitate reading. Calling the character with the Slavic name Ivan may be good enough—and save a lot of time while avoiding distraction.

7. One need not be able to pronounce every word to get its meaning. Most proficient readers have many words in their reading vocabularies they do not use or have not heard used orally.

    Our research has shown that less proficient readers dissipate a lot of energy working at every word while more proficient readers have the confidence that they can get the meaning without word-by-word accuracy.

The foregoing strategies are all derivatives from PL theory. They are excellent, day-to-day semantic strategies that can be used by regular teachers and, with modification, by special educators. Their intent is to help build reading vocabulary levels in all groups of students, regardless of intelligence level. However, in most special education classes, a good deal more structure is required to help students acquire the same strategies that good readers seem to pick up incidentally. This structure can be provided by modeling and a great deal of "thinking out loud" on the part of the teacher. For example, if a teacher is working with a student who comes to a word he doesn't know, the teacher could pause and think out loud by asking:

"OK. Here's a word that's new (difficult) for you. What are some things you could do to figure out what it means?" Try to elicit the following kinds of strategies from the student:

- "I could read the other parts of the sentence. That's a good clue."
- "I could see if the word is used anywhere else in the paragraph. Sometimes that helps."

- "I could see if the author gives a definition."
- "I could ask the teacher." (This strategy should be used only infrequently.)
- "I could skip over it if it's not that important anyway."
- "If it's a name that's hard to pronounce, I could substitute an easier name for it every time I see it."

These are the same strategies listed by Goodman. But, whereas students who are good readers seem to pick them up incidentally, the poor reader frequently needs to have them taught. If the student cannot verbalize the strategies as in the example just shown, then the remedial teacher can do so first. Then have the student follow suit. The idea is to model first, then have the student eventually internalize the strategies. Many students with reading problems will learn to internalize such strategies with time. But they often must be encouraged to do so in a very direct manner by the teacher.

There are additional factors to consider at different levels of reading. For example, at the beginning stages of reading, children need to build a sight vocabulary for reading, again regardless of their intelligence level. (Most children in our culture are exposed to, and remember, certain signs such as "McDonald's," "Exit," etc., which become part of their initial reading vocabulary.)

When children are taught to read, basal readers are almost always used. These all have a controlled vocabulary, and the vocabulary is almost always selected on the basis of frequency of occurrence. That is the basis of the Dolch word list, for example. But are there many cognitive factors which affect the "learnability" of a word which school psychologists should know? One such major factor is the categorization level of the word, which is explained thus:[37]

> . . . Children as well as adults have fairly stable hierarchies for concept and category members. That is, they are aware that *apple* and *banana* are related, and at some stage of cognitive development, know that both are fruit. A unique aspect of this approach is that within these hierarchies there exists a basic level of categorization which is more salient than category levels which are superordinate or subordinate relative to the basic level. *Chair, flower,* and *car* are basic level objects because they represent their respective categories at highly discriminable levels. Car cues are highly differentiated from chair or flower cues. *Furniture, animal, plant,* and *vehicle* are superordinate. They share very few salient attributes and therefore, comparisons between them yield little usable information. They have low cue validities. *Kitchen chair, poodle, petunia,* and *sports care* are subordinate. These more specific examples have many overlapping attributes with other category members at this level of categorization and therefore have a lower cue validity than the basic level objects.

A number of studies show that categorization by *basic* levels is very facilitative. We therefore might expect *basic* words to be learned easier by sight than superordinate, subordinate, or high-frequency words. This prediction was confirmed by James King, who found that *basic* words were learned faster and recalled better after 24 hours.[38]

Teachers of beginning readers and special education teachers dealing with students who have difficulty acquiring sight vocabulary, should try to develop their own basic word lists for their students and use them as needed. High-frequency or concreteness are insufficient criteria to include a given word.

The implications of this study for school psychologists and teachers are:

1. Be aware that basic nouns in basal readers are much easier to learn than super- or subordinates.
2. Use super- and subordinate names with care for beginning readers.
3. Discuss the relationship between unknown nouns and known, basic nouns where appropriate in the reading lesson. Semantic mapping, discussed next, may be helpful in this respect.

4. Pictures which illustrate basic concepts should also be at a basic level. So a flashcard with *chair* on it that is illustrated, should have a very basic, generic illustration. A beanbag chair, for example, would be inappropriate and harder to learn initially.
5. Categorization and classification skills should begin with basic words and move to super- and subordinates. Children *can* classify from higher levels, but this is more difficult for them.

For children who have some difficulty on the Similarities subtest of the WISC-R, the findings just listed might be useful.

Semantic Mapping

Semantic mapping is a widely used, highly advocated method of developing reading vocabulary. This technique activates what students already know about a word. Students generate "maps" which link the unfamiliar or target word to existing words and concepts.

There are a number of variations of the technique. I will present an example here, the steps of which might be employed in the construction of a semantic map on the seasons of the year. (My thanks to Marilyn Znider, Reading Specialist, for her preparation of the example):

1. Hand each child a piece of paper on which is written one of the seasons of the year. Have each child write on his paper all the things that come to mind when he thinks of that season. Allow a short period of time for this.
2. Have the children read their lists. Compile these on the chalkboard in a manner like that shown in Figure 5.6.
3. The semantic maps may be expanded as the children think of additional items to be added.
4. The semantic maps can be refined and extended in the following manner.

    For example: Ask the children if they could group any of the items related to winter. It may be necessary to ask questions such as, "What do cold, snow, and blizzards tell about?

    So, a refined semantic map for winter may look like the one shown in Figure 5.7.

Verbalizing. Discussion should be encouraged to go from the top, down (deductively), or from general to specific (i.e., there are four seasons of the year; one of them is winter; in winter, it is cold; etc.). They should also be encouraged to go from the specific to the general (inductively), or from the bottom, up (i.e., skating, skiing, and playing hockey are all things that you can do in winter; winter is one of the four seasons of the year).

Extension and practice. To make sure the child does understand the relationships, practice is needed. Many activities could be designed for this. Here are just two examples: (1) Keep the structure of the map intact, but remove the words, and have children write them in the correct place (flashcards can be used if desired). (2) After studying lessons, children may be asked to use their maps to help them write a paragraph about the topic.

5. Similar semantic maps can be constructed for spring, summer, and autumn—or virtually any other theme consistent with your program.

An important ingredient of semantic mapping is the group process involved between teacher and students. It is this very feature which makes semantic mapping such a useful classroom procedure in both regular and special education classes with students of varying verbal abilities. Readers should keep in mind that what was discussed earlier regarding basic versus super- and subordinate word learning. Perhaps basic words should most frequently be used as the target word in semantic mapping in order to facilitate learning.

FIGURE 5.6. Semantic mapping of the seasons of the year.

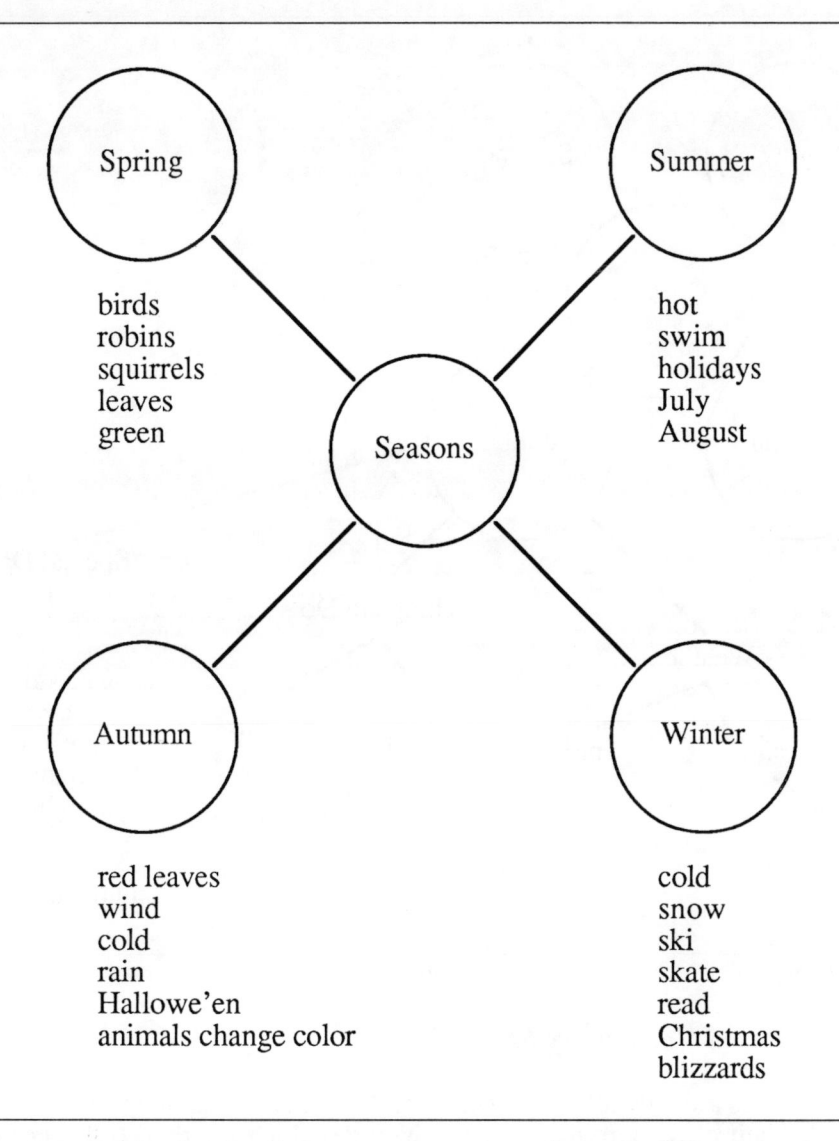

```
        Spring                    Summer

   birds                      hot
   robins                     swim
   squirrels                  holidays
   leaves                     July
   green      Seasons         August



   red leaves                 cold
   wind                       snow
   cold                       ski
   rain                       skate
   Hallowe'en                 read
   animals change color       Christmas
                              blizzards
        Autumn                    Winter
```

One very interesting variation of semantic mapping is the ENIGMA Program (Engineering Individual Growth through Manipulative Associations).[39] The teacher uses a high-quality picture (from a magazine, for example), and cuts it into pieces. Vocabulary items are taken from the picture, and the teacher writes an appropriate accompanying story. The vocabulary items are printed separately on cards (concrete words can be placed on white paper, and more abstract words on another color), and can be repeated as often as possible in the story. In a small group, students are then given the picture puzzle pieces and asked to arrange the pieces correctly. Word cards are then matched to the picture. (This is not only a semantic map; it is a visual map.) Students then take turns reading the story. Difficult words can then be practiced by the student for homework; the student may also draw an appropriate picture to accompany the difficult word. A number of other excellent activities can be developed that are appropriate to the age and reading level of the student. More details can be found in the journal article I cited.

FIGURE 5.7. Refined semantic map of one of the seasons of the year.

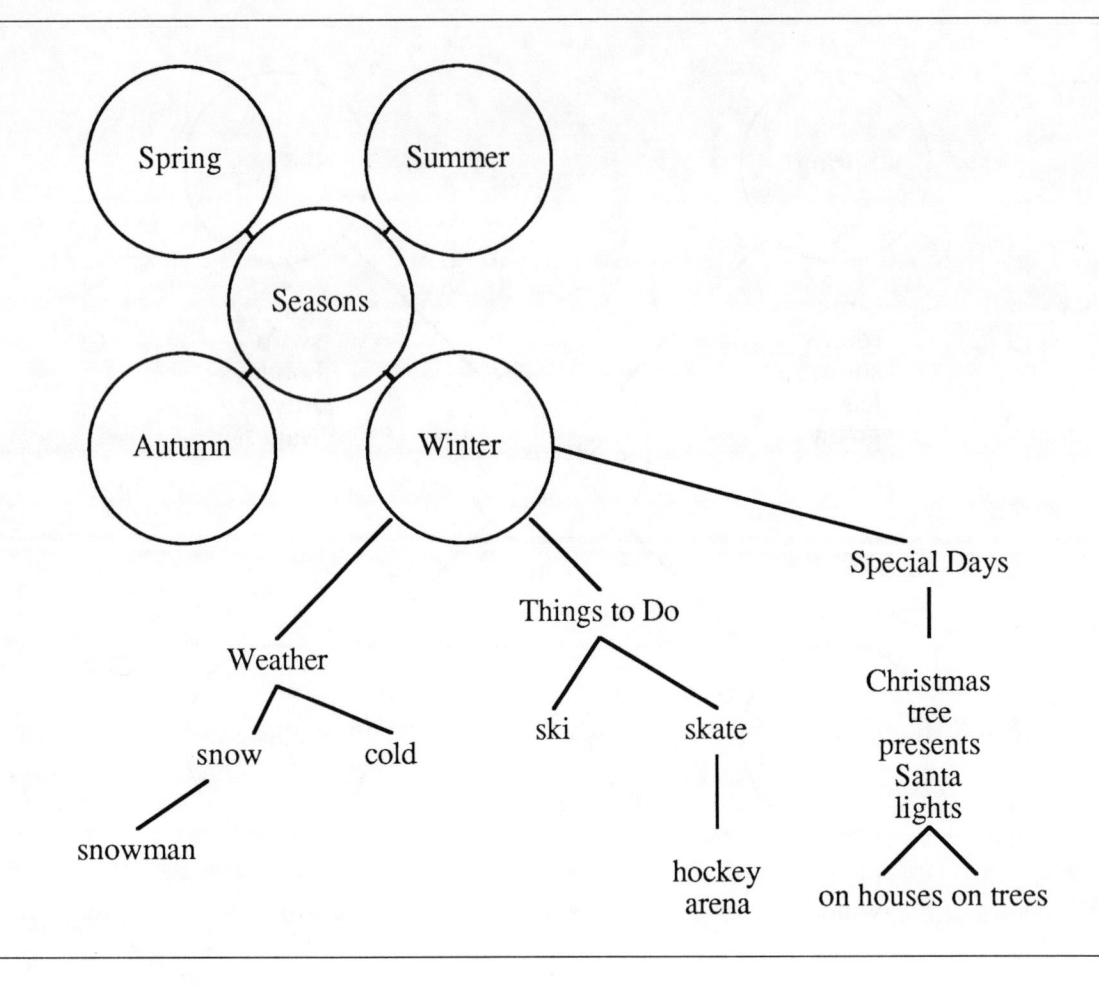

Mnemonic-Based Vocabulary Strategies

These techniques are radically different from the semantic- and experience-based techniques already discussed. Their classroom use is not as well developed, either, but school psychologists and special educators should become aware of them and begin using them more often. Research shows that the mnemonic strategies are *superior* to the semantic ones for learning new words, particularly for low achievers and/or learning-disabled populations.[40] This does not mean that they should be used exclusively. A combination of methods and approaches need to be recommended by school psychologists and used by remedial teachers as they seem appropriate to the problems and situations they face with individual students. Students with low verbal patterns on the WISC-R will benefit from an eclectic approach using a variety of procedures.

The major mnemonic strategy for vocabulary development is called the *keyword* approach. It is quite unusual, but is based on the idea that a word is better learned and stored in memory if it is more effectively encoded in the first place.

The procedure for developing a keyword is to use a word that is acoustically similar to the target word. For example, if the new vocabulary item to be learned is *angler*, an acoustically similar word such as *angel* might be appropriate. Then—and this is most important—the parallel acoustic word and the target word are illustrated together. *They need to interact in some way.* So, for our *angler*, the drawing shown in Figure 5.8 might be appropriate.

FIGURE 5.8. Using a keyword (1).

[Cartoon: Two angels on a cloud. One says "That ANGEL down there sure knows how to catch a lot of fish". The other replies "That's because he's an expert ANGLER". Below, an angel sits on a cloud fishing into a pond, catching fish.]

ANGLER (ANGEL) a person who likes to go fishing

From: Levin, J., Johnson, D., Pittelman, S., Levin, K., Shriber, L. Toms-Bronowski, S., and Hayes, B. 1984. Vocabulary learning strategies. *Reading Psychology* 5:4.

Or, if one were teaching new vocabulary, items in a foreign language, such as the Spanish word for *duck* (*pato*), a good, acoustically similar word in English might be *pot*, or perhaps *potato*. Then, the pot and the duck are drawn so that they are interacting in some way, as shown in Figure 5.9.[41]

FIGURE 5.9. Using a keyword (2).

Mnemonic Illustration of pato = duck.

| Pato (pot) | Duck |

From: Scruggs, T., and Mastropieri, M. 1984. Improving memory for facts: the "keyword" method. *Academic Therapy* (November) 20:2, p. 160.

The student must also be taught how to retrieve the appropriate response. For the example in Figure 5.9, it might go something like the following:[42]

> When the student is asked what the meaning of *pato* is, he is told first to think of the keyword for *pato* (*pot*) and then told to think back to the picture with the pot in it, and what was happening in that picture. In this case, the learner thinks of the picture of the duck with the pot on its head, and, therefore, is able to respond that *pato* means *duck*.

These same authors emphasize:[43]

> The most important thing to remember, whenever using the strategy, is to think of a good keyword that sounds as much as possible like the word to be learned and to picture it in some interactive way with the information to be learned. Just to think of a duck and a pot together to recall the Spanish word *pato* is not sufficient. The duck and the pot must actually be doing something together. This makes retrieval of the picture much easier.

The keyword method has been successfully used in a variety of content areas. History, science, social studies, language, and foreign language concepts have all been taught using this approach.

A related method to the keyword approach is called *pegword*. The pegword strategy is best applied to learning *sequenced* information, such as the order of U.S. presidents or Canadian prime ministers, or the hardness level of minerals. It therefore may be a useful strategy for those students who show sequencing difficulties on the WISC-R, and for whom sequencing is difficult on academic tasks. The strategy is described as follows:[44]

> This is a rhyming scheme in which a pictured word, which rhymes for each number, is given—that is, *one* equals *bun, two* equals *shoe, three* equals *tree, four* equals *door, five* equals *hive* . . . . Learners are told to memorize these pegwords. Then, if students need to learn any information in sequence, they tie each item to its associated pegword. In learning hardness levels of certain minerals, for example, learners can think of a keyword for the mineral and picture it interacting with the associated pegword. Therefore, to recall that *bauxite* is number one on the hardness scale, learners can think of a keyword for bauxite, which could *box*, and imagine a picture of a box full of buns. Then, to retrieve the information when they hear the word *bauxite*, they can think back to the box, remember that it was full of buns, remember that *bun* equals the number *one*, and respond with that number.
>
> The keyword/pegword procedure can be used in learning the order of the U.S. presidents. For example, to remember that Jackson was number 7, learners first think of a keyword for Jackson, which could be *jacks*, and associate it with its pegword for *seven*, which is *heaven*. An image could be pictured of angels playing jacks in heaven . . . .
>
> The pegword method has other uses besides remembering numbers associated with objects or people. It can be used to remember any type of information that is given in order. For example, the first ten amendments of the Constitution, the six reasons why Shakespeare may not have written his own plays, the five causes of a particular war, and so on, can all be adapted to the pegword retrieval system.

If learners have to learn more than 10 items, the pegword/keyword approach is limited. However, it can be extended by using the *method of loci*, which is actually a very old technique, used frequently by Greek orators. One method of loci involves relating each season of the year to a decade of numbers. So, "spring" can include the numbers 1 to 10, and be associated with a spring garden scene. To complete the "Jackson" scene, the angels playing in heaven with jacks can be doing so above a spring garden. When the student retrieves this scene, because it includes the spring garden, he knows it must be in the first 10 numbers. For "summer," the primary scene might be a summer beach scene. "Summer" would include the numbers 11 to 20. So, for example, to remember that Fillmore was the thirteenth president:[45]

> . . . First, one thinks of a keyword for Fillmore, which could be *film*, and the pegword *three* plus its seasonal referent, which would be a summer beach scene to make it the second decade of three, or thirteen. Therefore, to recall that Fillmore is president number 13, one could think of a film in a tree in a summer beach scene.

Including the seasons extends the number of sequences that could be learned to 40. However, the Greeks extended it to infinity by simply increasing the number of scenes in some integrated way. For example, if one had to memorize a great deal of information, such as *Hamlet*, one could visualize a house with any number of distinct rooms. In each room, one could place a scene until one had the whole play covered. The Greek orators were said to memorize their speeches in this fashion, and were specifically trained in the method of loci.

Obviously, there are other ways to memorize text or sequences. However, this method is unique and intriguing, and could be especially useful for students who have difficulty memorizing specific items.

Attribute Learning

Another related mnemonic method is called *attribute learning*. This strategy, it seems to me, is very similar to semantic mapping; but it is primarily visually based, rather than verbally based.

Semantic mapping delineates how words are related to each other in a verbal way. Attribute learning visually demonstrates and expands a concept. For example:[46]

... It may not be enough to know simply that bauxite is number one on the hardness scale. It may be important to know several other things about bauxite, such as its color and what it is used for. The learning of such attributes has also been increased with the use of the keyword method. For example, to remember that bauxite is number one on the hardness scale, white in color, and used in making aluminum, one could picture the keyword for bauxite, *box*. In addition, the box may be colored white to represent the color. Aluminum foil in the box with the buns can represent the use, and the buns themselves can represent the hardness level. Similarly, to recall that pyrite is six on the hardness scale, yellow in color, and used for making acid, the learner can picture a yellow pie (keyword for pyrite) resting on sticks (pegword for six) with acid being poured into it. Other content areas for which attribute learning may be helpful include biology (for example, organs of the body and their functions) or social studies (for example, famous people and their accomplishments).

Attribute learning goes well beyond vocabulary development. However, a big drawback at the present time to using these mnemonic strategies is the lack of commercially available, teacher-made materials.

Comparing Semantic to Mnemonic Strategies

In special education, it is important to know whether or not a strategy works, since time is such a precious commodity. But that is not enough. If one strategy works better than another for a special education population, that strategy should be carefully considered for joining the repertoire of strategies the special education teacher needs at her disposal.

When comparing semantic mapping to the keyword approach in research studies, the keyword approach wins out. In one study, for example, the keyword method was compared to semantic mapping and contextual analysis. High achievers were compared to low achievers on the three methods. For the low achievers, the keyword approach was significantly superior to the other methods in all outcomes of recall tested. Indeed, except in one area, the low achievers *matched* the high achievers in all outcomes. This is strong evidence of a powerful tool![47]

In another study, junior high school learning-disabled students (WISC-R Full Scale IQs ranging from 72 to 129) were taught the hardness levels of minerals (a science concept; but, as we have seen, this strategy can be used in many content areas) using the keyword/pegword approach as compared to a traditional teacher-questioning/drill method and a free study condition in which students were shown how to study the hardness levels and given materials to do so. Results were as shown in Table 5.3.[48]

The high achievers and low achievers in this group were simply those learning-disabled students whose reading comprehension scores on the *California Achievement Test* were at or above the 40th percentile, compared to those below the 30th percentile.

Note again the superiority of the mnemonic techniques for *both* groups. It should be remarked that mnemonic strategies require much more processing time, but may well be worth it, since recall after a 24-hour delay is substantial.

TABLE 5.3. Comparison of methods with achievement in terms of percent-correct.

	Condition			
	Mnemonic	Questioning	Free Study	Across Conditions
Lower Achievers	70.0	25.7	27.6	41.1
Higher Achievers	80.5	30.0	44.8	51.7
Across Achievement Levels	75.2	27.8	36.2	

Note: $MS_E (84) = 289.12$

From: Mastropieri, M., Scruggs, T., and Levin, J. 1985. Mnemonic strategy instruction with learning-disabled adolescents. *Journal of Learning Disabilities* (February) 18:96.

Strengthening and Stretching Recall Ability: An Appeal for an Eclectic Approach

I began this section by focusing on low Verbal versus Performance WISC-R scores. These students are particularly difficult to remediate in terms of ever bringing them up to grade level. However, as we have seen, there are ways of building and stretching these students' vocabularies by a judicious use of both semantic and mnemonic techniques. *Both* are necessary, although some preference might be given to the mnemonic strategies in some circumstances for some students. These techniques are good for *all* learners; but, as the evidence suggests, they are especially effective for the lower-achieving student.

One more factor that needs to be considered in teaching vocabulary is the *multiple meanings* of words. For example, even at the primer level, there are 37 meanings of the simple word *run*, 21 meanings of *sound*, 20 meanings of *play*, and 17 meanings of *cut*. About 90 percent of basal word lists in reading series have multiple meanings.[49]

The number of words a child knows correlates strongly with reading comprehension; but, in addition, the number of different meanings known for a single word and the ability to select a particular meaning in a given context, are two further dimensions of vocabulary that also relate to reading comprehension.[50]

How can a teacher help students recognize multiple meanings? A good part of every primary teacher's and every special education teacher's time is spent on vocabulary development. Searls and Klesius offer some excellent instructional strategies to help the teacher teach multiple word meanings.

First, their list of the 99 most common multiple-meaning words is shown in Figure 5.10. These are all taught in first grade and occur frequently in later grades.[51]

FIGURE 5.10. Basic list of 99 multiple-meaning words.

about	cook	house	paper	stay
as	cry	how	picture	stop
at	cut	in	place	story
away	dance	it	play	tail
back	do	just	pot	take
ball	down	kind	rain	time
basket	duck	leave	rake	to
bear	end	let	ride	too
bed	fall	like	right	tree
big	fast	live	roll	up
book	fish	long	room	use
by	fly	look	run	wait
call	for	make	saw	walk
can	game	may	school	want
care	get	mean	see	way
clean	give	nose	sentence	will
coat	go	on	show	word
cold	have	out	sit	work
color	head	over	so	yellow
come	help	paint	sound	

From: Searls, E. and Klesius, J. 1984. Multiple-meaning words for primary students and how to teach them. *Reading Psychology* 5:58.

FIGURE 5.11. Semantic map of a multiple-meaning word.

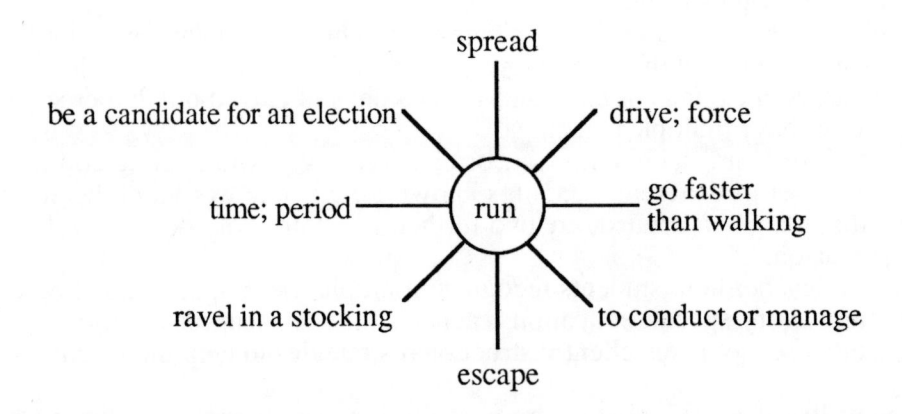

```
                    spread
be a candidate for an election \    / drive; force
                                \  /
        time; period ――――――――( run )―――― go faster
                                /  \        than walking
                               /    \
        ravel in a stocking   /      \ to conduct or manage
                          escape
```

From: Searls, E. and Klesius, J. 1984. Multiple-meaning words for primary students and how to teach them. *Reading Psychology* 5:60.

These authors suggest that multiple meanings can be taught using pictures and objects. For example, *duck* could be illustrated by a picture of a duck, or a person who ducks going through a doorway. The student and teacher share an oral discussion and provide examples of their own. This, as we have discussed, is very important, since it draws in the experience base of the students. (In addition, the group process allows those students who have weak experience bases to profit from hearing the students who are stronger.) Definitions could be listed in various ways. Children could be encouraged to bring in their own pictures, and have the other students guess which of the meanings the word represents.

A variation of semantic mapping could be used. Figure 5.11, for example, shows the map for *run* which illustrates some of its many meanings.[52]

Students could be grouped and develop their own semantic maps for a particular word. Each meaning could also be illustrated, acted out, or posted in some way. I believe this step is extremely important for the remedial student because it provides a direct link from experience to word. All the groups' words could then be shared and displayed around the room or school.

Context could also be used, because it provides clues to word meaning. Sentences such as the following could be created to show how syntax affects meaning:[53]

- The *cook* will *cook* a delicious meal.
- Jane wants to *dance* at the *dance*.
- The *rain* may *rain* all afternoon.

Prepositions have multiple meanings, too. These are best taught in context as well. Here are some examples:[54]

- Bill was reading a book *by* the tree.
- The book was *by* his favorite author.
- Bob said he would come *by* my house.
- He said he would be there *by* three o'clock.
- We went to the football game *by* bus.
- Our team won the game *by* one point.

The authors suggest that blank playing cards could be given to students with one of the words. Various card games could be played with them. Furthermore, writing activities could be drawn out of the words:[55]

(a) One student can write a sentence in which one multiple-meaning word is used in two different ways. The sentence is read aloud, omitting the target word. Other students can guess the words. (b) Using a multiple-meaning word identified by the teacher, each student writes a sentence on a 3x5 card. The cards can then be sorted and put in envelopes on which are written different meanings of the word. (c) Children can write stories incorporating as many different meanings of a target group of words as possible.

Variations of some of the mnemonic strategies could also be attempted, I might suggest. These should probably be used only for particularly troublesome meanings for an individual student.

In all the activities I have discussed so far, the students' background of information, their abstracting ability, and their vocabularies are used, and stretched. These are integral components of the verbal factor tapped by the WISC-R.

Teaching takes time; and, for those students whose language facility is weak, time is at a premium. School psychologists and remedial teachers must therefore be continually vigilant for new methods which might be more effective for special education students.

Three-Factor Splits

Three-way splitting of WISC-R profiles is, I believe, a Level II interpretation. The split is often masked, and has to be teased out. It is a very common pattern in referred students.

Let's look at some scores from a nine-year-old student's WISC-R profile which illustrate the pattern very distinctly. Sara obtained the following WISC-R results:

Verbal IQ: 102

Performance IQ: 96

Full Scale IQ: 100 ± 6

Notice, there is no significant discrepancy (12 points or more) between the Verbal and Performance IQs. The Full Scale IQ indicates average ability. To end the interpretation at this point would be a great disservice to Sara. Here are her subtest scale scores, first presented in Chapter 2 in reference to my discussion of the zone of potential difference.

Verbal		*Performance*	
Information	10	Picture Completion	11
Similarities	14	Picture Arrangement	10
Arithmetic	6	Block Design	13
Vocabulary	15	Object Assembly	9
Comprehension	7	Coding	5
Digit Span	6	Mazes	(not administered)
Verbal Average	10	Performance Average	10
(Percentile 50)		(Percentile 50)	

Notice that some of the subtests (notably Arithmetic, Digit Span, and Coding) are particularly low. This triad of subtests is called the Freedom from Distractibility factor, as explained earlier. To calculate whether or not the differences between the three factors are significant, we must calculate the average scale scores on the subtests which load on each factor. These have been listed previously. For Sara, these are:

Factor I		*Factor II*		*Factor III*	
I	10	PC	11	A	6
S	14	PA	10	DS	6
V	15	BD	13	C	5
C	7	OA	9		
Avg. 12		Avg. 11		Avg. 6	
(Percentile 75)		(Percentile 63)		(Percentile 9)	

(See Tables 2.1 and 2.2 at the close of Chapter 2.)

Factors I and II are about evenly developed; even so, the Comprehension subtest is weaker within that factor. This is consistent with the Verbal and Performance IQs in the first place, and is to be expected. But the Freedom from Distractibility factor is very much lower than either of the other two.

Whenever the Factor III average is three points lower than the average of *either* Factor I *or* Factor II, then, Kaufman suggests, it is interpretable psychometrically, and should be considered as educationally significant.[56]

I find this pattern repeatedly in referred students. It is somewhat a misnomer, to call it Freedom from Distractibility, however, because distractibility may not be the reason a student scores low on Factor III. It may also indicate a developmental delay in selective attention, impulsivity, poor facility with numbers, a simultaneous-successive information processing discrepancy, poor short-term memory—or a combination of these. It may also suggest poor ability for phonemic manipulation. Again, careful observation, more testing, and/or discussion with the student's teacher and parents are important to confirm or deny the hypotheses suggested.

I will now examine each of these hypotheses in terms of the educational strategies they suggest.

Distractibility

Let's suppose it can be determined that the student's primary problem *is* distractibility. A number of intervention strategies could be employed, if that is the case. Some of the ones I have found *particularly* useful are the "Good Behavior Game Plus Merit" described in Chapter 3, and the self-monitoring technique described in Appendix 2-4.

Drug and/or diet therapy is also often advocated for distractible students. I personally do not advocate drug therapy as an approach, primarily because drug therapy does *not* improve learning, even though it may have a dramatic, positive effect on the distractible behavior itself. Also, it creates a kind of implicit message to the student which says, "I can *only* function when I'm on medication. I'm *better* when I'm on medication." The results of many research studies indicate that the common drugs such as Ritalin® and Cyclert® do *not* enhance student learning. If they do, the actions are drug-specific. That means that, if a student does better on a Maze while on Ritalin, the improved performance will not generalize to when the student is off the drug. So, the bottom line is that students must learn to deal with their distractibility. And that is, admittedly, a difficult, long-term process.

Though there is a limited place for drug therapy with hyperactive/distractible students, I do not feel it should be a treatment advocated by school psychologists.

Vitamin therapy is also often touted as a treatment for hyperactive/distractible youngsters. Unfortunately, most of the reports and claims are anecdotal in nature. There is very little in the way of well-controlled research to confirm or deny potential benefit or harm. We have one recent double-blind study, in which the authors have this to say:[57]

> We concluded from the study that large doses [Note: children were given doses 10 times in excess of the RDA {recommended dietary allowance} of the vitamins niacinamide, vitamin C, vitamin B_6, and calcium pantothenate] have no beneficial effect for children with ADD [Attentional Deficit Disorder]. Furthermore, many children had a significant elevation of blood sugar tests during the vitamin administration and many withdrew from the study because of gastrointestinal complaints, indicating that megadoses of these vitamins are potentially toxic and could cause severe liver injury. Because of their ineffectiveness and possible serious side effects, megavitamins should not be utilized in the management of children with ADD.*

Developmental Delay in Selective Attention

The terms *distractibility* and *attention span* are often used interchangeably. Attention can be described as the ability to focus our awareness selectively. In many special education students, such ability seems to be lacking, for whatever reason. I have found A. O. Ross' explanation of the development of selective attention to be very helpful at times. Figure 5.12 illustrates the three developmental phases of selective attention.[58]

In the Overexclusive Phase, the child sees the trees, one might say, but not the forest. Attention is focused on one salient feature of the object, and the child excludes the rest. Some students seem overwhelmed, for example, by the multisensory impact of a rich environment. Perhaps they only focus on one (often irrelevant) feature of the task at hand.

In the Overinclusive Phase, the opposite happens: The child attends to many aspects of the stimulus. This happens to all children; but, in those for whom the phase lasts longer than normal, the label "distractible" applies, according to Ross.

---

* As an aside, I find the label "Attentional Deficit Disorder" of limited value in the school system. It is a clinical term (and often leads directly to drug treatment); it completely implies a defect in the student; and it does not specify in any way the *nature* (etiology) of the so-called attention disorder.

FIGURE 5.12. The effect of individual differences in the development of selective attention at various age levels.

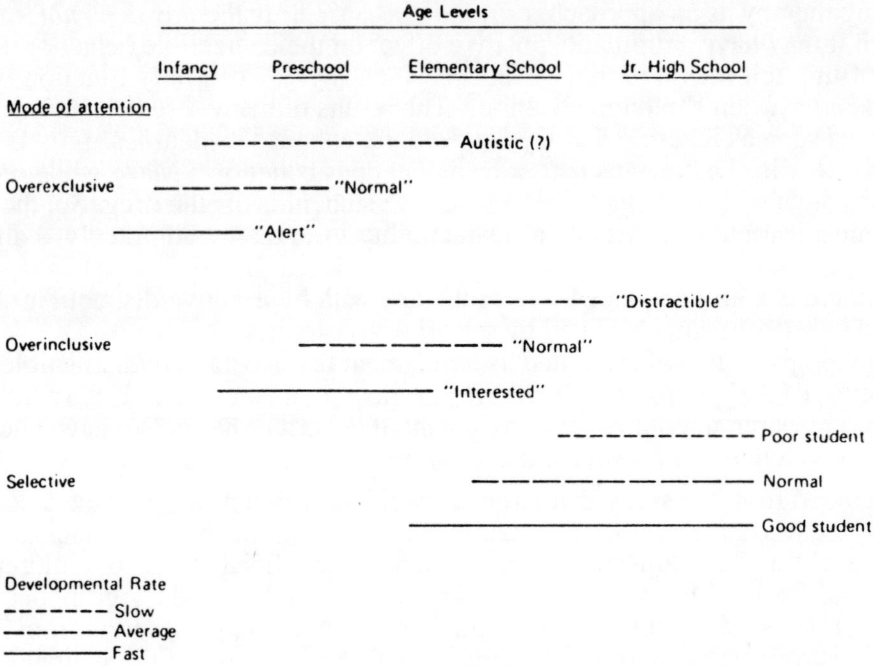

```
                          Age Levels
              ─────────────────────────────────────────
              Infancy   Preschool   Elementary School   Jr. High School
Mode of attention
                        — — — — — — — — — Autistic (?)
Overexclusive           — — — — — "Normal"
                        ─────── "Alert"

                                     — — — — — — "Distractible"
Overinclusive                        — — — — — "Normal"
                                     ─────────── "Interested"

                                              — — — — — — Poor student
Selective                                     — — — — — — Normal
                                              ─────────── Good student

Developmental Rate
    — — — — — Slow
    — — — —  Average
    ──────── Fast
```

From: Ross, A. O. 1976. *Psychological aspects of learning disabilities and reading disorders*, p. 55. New York: McGraw-Hill.

Finally, the child (around age 12, on the average) enters the selective attention phase. Here, he is able to focus attention on the appropriate feature of the stimulus necessary to the task at hand. This involves also being able to suppress or inhibit what is irrelevant and unnecessary.

Children, particularly the learning-disabled group who are slow to enter this phase, are described by Ross:[59]

> It may be that the learning-disabled child, and particularly the disabled reader, is again slow in acquiring this skill (selective attention). Such a child might still be using the overinclusive mode of attention when his or her peers are already functioning at the level of selective attention. Such children would respond to all manner of irrelevant stimuli, making them appear impulsive, distractible, and hyperactive.

The major remedial implication that arises from this perspective is that students who are having difficulty attending to a task must be taught to attend to the relevant features of the task at hand. One way to do this is by increasing the salience of the stimulus:[60]

> If one wishes to teach a child to differentiate between *b* and *d*, for example (or various sight words), it is preferable to present these letter pairs in a variety of sizes and degrees of brightness, as well as in different parts of the writing surface, than to repeat the presentation of the same pair over and over again.

Repetition, in other words, is not enough. Novelty and assisting the child by helping him direct his overinclusive attention to salient features, is important. External reinforcements are also useful, since these will increase novelty and help to reverse what may be a very aversive situation for the student. Encouraging "rehearsal" is also useful from this point of view. (See Appendix 2-5.)

Impulsivity

Impulsivity is closely related to distractibility. Students who score poorly on the Freedom from Distractibility triad may do so because they consistently rush through their work, giving whatever comes to mind as an answer, with little reflective thinking evident. I also find that their response style on Picture Completion and Mazes can supplement this hypothesis. Impulsive students tend to be fast on these subjects, and may or may not be accurate. Their speed actually helps them on many of the easier items; and they may even end up with elevated scores on these subtests; or, their speed may hinder them so that they end up with lowered scores. It is, to my mind, a question of *response style*, not the scaled scores themselves. For example, on the Picture Completion items, it is relatively easy to determine how long the student scans each picture. During Mazes, the student will rush up blind alleys. On Arithmetic, he will quickly say, "I don't know," or make rapid but inaccurate calculations. On Coding, such students have a tendency to begin the task before you complete the instructions. The same is true for Digit Span. Such a response style may mean that the student has very poorly developed plans, or strategies for "stopping, looking, and thinking through," before beginning a task. In fact, forcing such students to spend some time (five seconds has been found to be the optimal amount) reflecting before they answer can raise subtest scores on the WISC-R. The authors of one study used only four of the WISC-R subtests to determine this (Information, Vocabulary, Picture Arrangement, and Block Design); surprisingly, they found that the five-second forced delay was effective for the Verbal, but not the Performance, subtests. Forced delay did *not* raise the scores of the already reflective students, only the impulsive ones.[61]

It is imperative, then, that when a student is perceived by the examiner as displaying a high degree of impulsivity throughout the testing, that the report of findings contains a statement that the Full Scale IQ score is definitely an underestimate of the student's cognitive ability. School psychologists can also supplement their diagnosis of the student's "conceptual tempo" by using Kagan's *Matching Familiar Figures Test*.[62]

For such students, a number of cognitive self-control techniques have some research support as being effective. The basic steps in *any* self-instructional procedure involve:[63]

1. Modeling appropriate strategies for the task and describing it simultaneously to the student by "thinking out loud";
2. Having the student perform the task as the teacher verbalizes it;
3. Having the student "think out loud" as he performs the task;
4. Having the student whisper (subvocalize) the appropriate self-statements; and
5. Having the student silently rehearse the appropriate self-statements.

The student can also be taught some coping self-statements to use when an error is made, and some self-monitoring procedures to evaluate how he is doing. Any procedure which helps students become aware of their own thinking processes, whether it be in reading comprehension tasks or in doing a maze, can be described as metacognitive in nature.

Poor Facility with Numbers

Because Arithmetic, Digit Span, and Coding all involve numbers, it is possible that poor facility with numbers, rather than any other reason (such as short-term memory difficulty), lies behind the student's low scores on the triad. However, it is not all that easy to separate the two, since limits on short-term memory are also associated with arithmetic processing! Such "confounding" of variables makes the job of diagnosis much more difficult, of course.

For example, some researchers examined the link between memory span, Piagetian tasks, and arithmetic tasks. They showed that there is a correspondence between Piagetian stages and digit span. Preoperational performance requires a memory span of 2 items; concrete operational performance requires a span of 4; and the formal-operations level requires a span of 8.[64] In other words, age-related changes in the ability to do complex arithmetical questions to some extent is determined by the limitations of the short-term memory span. There are many students in special education who, when tested on Digit Span, seem to have spans that are below those expected for their chronological age. This makes it difficult for them to remember information presented orally.

Different types of special education populations seem to make slightly different kinds of computational errors in their arithmetic operations, as shown in Table 5.4.[65]

TABLE 5.4. Error types: comparison of percentage total error for regular, educable mentally handicapped, and learning-disabled student groups

Error Type	Regular Students (Englehardt 1977) (N = 198) % Total Error	EMH Students (Janke 1980) (N = 370) % Total Error	LD Students (Safran 1980) (N = 37) % Total Error
Basic facts	32	37	28
Grouping	19	5	33
Inappropriate inversion	17	3	7
Incorrect operation	4	24	15
Defective algorithm	16	21	2
Incomplete algorithm	6	4	6
Identity of 0 and 1	1	1	2
Zero	5	5	7

From: Frost, R. 1982. The arithmetic achievement of learning-disabled students: a training study, p. 232. Doctoral dissertation. Calgary: University of Calgary.

In the study from which this table was taken, Dr. Ruth Frost suggested that the *affective* component is very important in terms of remediating the arithmetic difficulties of the severely learning-disabled group. They had "coded" some very negative feelings toward subtraction, in particular, which proved to be a stumbling block to mastering basic facts. Why subtraction in particular? Well, perhaps it is the idea of "taking away" which the students subconsciously disliked. In any case, Dr. Frost devised an ingenious remedial program using Cuisenaire rods that were decorated to resemble robots, families, and ethnic groups. Teachers were trained to use the materials with an emphasis on tapping into the students' feelings of "rescuing," "overcoming," and "helping." The students learned that the operation of "taking away" in arithmetic could be used to "rescue" someone in distress. So, the negative affect associated with subtraction was turned into something positive. This extremely intriguing approach produced *very* significant growth in arithmetic skill areas for students. Unfortunately, the arithmetic program itself remains unpublished to date.

Self-instructional training can also be useful as a remedial strategy for students if poor facility with numbers is a problem for them. The basic steps outlined previously can be adapted quite easily to arithmetic problems. An example is outlined for you in Appendix 5-3.

Anxiety

Should anxiety be a primary factor in poor performance on the Factor III subtests, the school psychologist could suggest a number of helpful strategies. These will depend on the source of the anxiety. A useful supplementary test for this is the *Frost Self-Description Questionnaire*, which breaks "anxiety" down into several components, providing the examiner with helpful hints as to remedial directions.[66]

The general strategies of stress reduction I described in Chapter 3, particularly relaxation training (see Appendix 3-5), can be very helpful. Deep relaxation training can be incorporated into any of the self-instructional procedures given in the appendices. A very helpful program which ran successfully for several years in the San Diego (California) Unified School District, is called "Teaching Children Self-Control." The program consisted of training in deep relaxation and general problem solving. Structured lessons were developed, and manuals prepared, for grades 1-3, 4-6, and 7-9. Dr. Dan Watson of San Diego still conducts training sessions for school psychologists and special educators in the procedures.[67]

Since anxiety also constricts short-term memory, the examiner must decide whether short-term memory difficulty, or anxiety, is foremost. Frequently, it is a combination of the two.

Simultaneous and Successive Information-Processing

For students who are significantly stronger on Digits Forward versus Digits Backward on the WISC-R Digit Span subtest ("significant" means a difference of 3 or more on the student's span), the hypothesis of a strength/weakness in simultaneous or successive information processing should be examined. The Performance scale of the WISC-R can be used to cross-check the hypothesis as follows:

Simultaneous	*Successive*
Picture Completion	Picture Arrangement
Block Design	Coding
Object Assembly	Mazes

If the average of the three subtests on each of the dimensions is 3 points or more, then a significant strength or weakness is psychometrically interpretable. If the student also seems to proceed in a "wholistic" fashion on Block Design, working rapidly from the gestalt, he may be a "simultaneous" processor. If the student seems to work in a very methodical, logical fashion, rotating the blocks until the correct design is formed, then the student may be more a "successive" processor. It is therefore quite difficult at times to use the subtest scale scores as the basis for diagnosis. Keen observation on the part of the examiner is necessary. Kaufman admits the same problem even with the *Kaufman Assessment Battery for Children* (K-ABC). Because it is possible to solve what is primarily a successive task in a simultaneous fashion, or vice versa, the scores themselves cannot be used as the sole basis for diagnosis. The school psychologist could also administer the K-ABC itself (which is designed to help determine whether a student is significantly stronger or weaker in one or the other of the processing styles), and/or a battery devised by Dr. J. P. Das of the Department of Educational Psychology at the University of Alberta, Edmonton.

I personally find the distinction useful in the case of some students. It seems to me, though, that both types of processing are involved in all learning, just as both halves of the brain are always involved in learning. For that matter, Kaufman himself says that students who are stronger in one of the styles still require instruction in the other style. Others I have talked to insist that all learning is successive in nature, that it is simply not possible to do *any* simultaneous processing.

Whatever one's theoretical stance, I do find merit in saying that some students appear to be more comfortable with certain kinds of teaching/learning styles, and that an awareness of the individual differences among students can help a teacher with that student. It may not even be that the student performs better academically when taught consistently with his style—but the student may find learning a lot more enjoyable.

Since the simultaneous/successive split can be considered a learning style, it fits into Level III WISC-R interpretation. I will therefore return to the distinction and some of its educational implications in the next chapter.

Short-Term Memory

The Digit Span subtest uniquely measures auditory short-term memory. What exactly does this mean? To me, it has always fundamentally meant that the "trace" itself is weak; that, somehow, the individual with a "weak" memory simply forgets what was said. If it is visual memory, the same thing applies; the individual simply forgets information that is presented visually. I always look closely, therefore, at the *span* of the student. Is it significantly below that of his peers? The score itself tells me that. Next, I look at the *kinds of errors* that the student makes on the Digit Span subtest. For example, if the sequence of numbers presented was 5-2-3-7 and the student says 5-3-2-7, then the span is not the problem for the student. This student has made a reversal (sequencing) error, but has in fact remembered all the numbers. If, on the other hand, the student had said 5-2-7, then one of the numbers was completely forgotten; and that, in my mind, is stronger evidence of a weakness in auditory short-term memory, since one of the numbers and a "slot" completely disappeared. Both students will fail the trial and receive the same score, but the kinds of errors they make are quite different. Next, I look back to the Arithmetic subtest. Did I have to repeat a given question in order for the student to answer it (again, evidence of short-term memory difficulty)? The student might get the correct answer and might even have a scaled score that is average for age; but if my notes say that nearly all the questions had to be repeated, then facility with numbers may not be the problem; difficulty with auditory short-term memory is more likely.

"Memory" from an information-processing viewpoint can be divided into three components: encoding, storage, and retrieval. Encoding is the initial acquisition of information. Storage is the length of time the information is available (which may be brief [short-term] or delayed [long-term]). Retrieval can occur by recognition, by cued recall, or by free recall.[68] Memory ability in general increases with age, perhaps because knowledge in general increases with age. (Because the knowledge base expands, incoming information is more meaningful and the student remembers it better.) In information-processing theory, memory is not a single entity, but is closely tied to the development of other cognitive strategies, which also increase with age. These strategies include rehearsal (basic and complex); elaboration (basic and complex); organization; and comprehension monitoring.

Students with learning disabilities have a number of problems with these areas. For example, they do not recall as much relevant information as does a group with no learning problems. In addition, before the age of eight, children with learning disabilities do not spontaneously rehearse material that is presented. The results of several memory studies on learning-disabled groups are summarized as follows:[69]

> Children with learning disabilities recalled and recognized fewer items when compared to those without learning problems when auditory or verbal stimuli were employed. Problems discriminating and attending selectively to relevant stimulus features impaired performance. In addition, these children generated fewer correct responses, resampled disconfirmed responses following negative feedback, and used fewer rehearsal strategies spontaneously. This latter finding was interpreted from the lack of primacy effects obtained with eight-year-old children with learning disabilities.

Remedial Implications

There are a number of remedial strategies that are appropriate and which the school psychologist can recommend, depending on the individual student:

1. Chunking and rehearsal can be encouraged in acquiring sight words (see Appendix 2-5) and other academic activities.

2. Sorting by categories is an important teaching and learning strategy (see Appendix 5-1). A variation of the suggestions in Appendix 5-1 would be to have the student sort a series into categories. Then, take the words away and have the student recall the items (free recall). If the student has difficulty, the teacher can make it easier by providing the student with the categories (cued recall). If the student still has difficulty, then present the words again and ask the student to group the words according to the categories provided by the teacher (recognition).[70] These procedures can be added to the Word Sort activities at any point.

3. The student could also be encouraged to use a semantic cue to help encoding. For example, if the words to be learned are *cowboy* and *horse*, then the student could be asked to relate the two in a sentence, such as, "The cowboy rides a horse." Then, ask the student to recall the word pair without any cues (free recall). If the student has difficulty, present one of the pairs (cued recall).[71]

4. Another elaborative strategy is mental imagery. This was discussed in relation to reading comprehension and recall in Appendix 2-2. The strategy can also be used in learning sight words. An important variation is the keyword approach discussed earlier. The keyword approach also eliminates the primacy effect, since all items are recalled equally well. Perhaps learning-disabled groups have particular difficulty with semantic encoding, and is the reason why the more visual encoding of the keyword approach works better for them.

5. Complex elaboration can also be encouraged, where appropriate. This kind of elaboration involves connecting new information to old in some way, such as by:
   a. Creating analogies
   b. Developing images
   c. Considering implications
   d. Paraphrasing with an emphasis on the relationship between the two ideas or words.

Meta-Memory

Part of the remedial process is to involve the student in some way in helping himself. The student has to become aware of when to use a particular memory strategy. This is called meta-memory. One such awareness strategy involves the student's own knowledge of his span. For example, when nursery school and kindergarten children are asked to predict how many pictures they will remember of a series presented to them, the gap between the prediction and actual recall is enormous. This gap narrows with age, however, so that by the time the student is in fourth grade, the predictions are as accurate as those of adults. This suggests a developmental meta-memory process.

This does have a practical application. For example, ask the student to make a prediction about how many words he thinks he can remember when a series of sight words is presented. Then present the words and see how close the student came to his prediction. Award points for close predictions. This procedure is apt to be quite motivating for some students. Another helpful modification is to tell the student something like, "The average student your age can remember ____ words."

It is also important, when you are working with individual students, that they receive some feedback regarding their use of a procedure. For example, if the teacher wants to teach the student how to use rehearsal, then the *strategy plus meta-memory training* will be more effective than strategy training alone. This can be accomplished by appropriate feedback like: "You did so much better when you whispered those words over and over. I guess whispering helped you remember the words better." Similar feedback should be given when training students in the use of any other memory strategy.

Phonemic Manipulation

In a previous chapter, I mentioned the importance and very exciting possibilities regarding remediation and prevention of reading problems by increasing students' awareness of and ability to manipulate the basic phonemes of our language.

The ability to discriminate and manipulate phonemes can be directly assessed using the *Lindamood Auditory Conceptualization Test*.[72] This test is a useful adjunct to WISC-R testing, particularly when Digit Span is depressed (though not limited to this situation alone).

Digit Span in particular from the Freedom from Distractibility triad seems to be related to phonemic analysis. The relationship is by no means a direct one, but it is definitely there. For a full discussion of this point, I refer the reader to Cohen, Fil, Netley, and Clarke. In the article, the authors make the link as follows:[73]

> Cohen and Netley (1981) have pursued the serial aspect of phonetic processing, suggesting that the poor reading and poor serial STM [short-term memory] abilities of reading-disabled children are the result of a deficiency in their ability to process serial strings of speech sounds which these authors call phonological patterns.

When the school psychologist feels that poor phonemic analysis is a hypothesis that should be investigated, than the Lindamood test, as mentioned, is the test of choice. There are other more informal methods for assessing this particular skill, but the *Lindamood* is the one most fully developed at this time.

Remediation of this skill is not restricted to the ADD Program as discussed earlier. (There are at least four other ways of training this skill [see Williams 1984].)[74] But again, the ADD Program is the most commercially available of them. Most of the training programs require only a modicum of time-investment—usually about 15 to 20 minutes daily.

Gifted Students and the WISC-R

School psychologists are frequently asked to assist in the selection of students in upper ability levels. As school divisions increase their level of program services to the upper ends of "exceptionality," this demand will increase. An important tool in this identification is the WISC-R. However, as with other areas, it should not be the only assessment instrument administered.

In our present discussion, I will use Joseph Renzulli's definition of giftedness, a state which:[75]

> ... consists of an interaction among three basic clusters of human traits—these clusters being above-average general abilities, high levels of task commitment, and high levels of creativity. Gifted and talented children are those possessing or capable of developing this composite set of traits and applying them to any potentially valuable area of human performance.

Of the three components mentioned by Renzulli, the WISC-R measures only the first—general abilities. Both task commitment and creativity need to be assessed by other methods, though the examiner might get some feel for the student's task commitment by observing his test behavior. It is quite possible that students who score in the top 5 percent on a WISC-R lack the task commitment to do well academically. Such students might be called gifted underachievers. They pose unique problems for school psychologists and other school personnel who must deal with them. I will discuss a general plan for dealing with such students in the next section.

The basic school needs of gifted students could be stated as follows:[76]

1. Maximum achievement of basic skills and concepts.
2. Learning activities at an appropriate level and pace.
3. Experience in creating thinking and problem-solving.
4. Development of convergent thinking and problem-solving.
5. Stimulation of imagery, imagination, and spatial abilities.
6. Stimulation to pursue higher-level goals and aspirations.
7. Development of self-awareness and self-acceptance.
8. Development of independence, self-direction, and discipline in learning.
9. Experience in relating to other gifted/talented students.
10. A large fund of information about diverse topics.
11. Exposure to a variety of fields of study, arts, professions, and occupations.
12. Access and stimulation to reading.

As you read through the list, you might be struck by the fact that these needs are not radically different than those for *any* child. That is true, to a point. What needs to be taken into account is the general ability of a particular student. Certainly, maximum achievement of basic skills and concepts, for example, is as much a need at the trainable mentally handicapped level as it is at the gifted level. It is obvious, however, that the gifted learner will require a qualitatively different kind of stimulation than the TMH student.

I believe the needs of the vast majority of gifted students can be met at the local school level by using Renzulli's Enrichment Triad Model, shown in Figure 5.13, as a framework.[77]

The various activities within the model can be described as follows:

- *Type I*. These are activities which *all* students should be exposed to within the regular classroom program. They include the range of good, basic teaching, and extend to interest centers, field trips and visits, guest speakers, library research, and so on.

- *Type II*. These are activities especially suitable for the top 15 to 20 percent of the student population, and include special skills training. Training can be best accomplished by a joint regular classroom and partial pull-out enrichment program coordinated by the school's gifted program teacher. The training activities would include critical thinking, divergent/convergent thinking, creative problem solving, deductive and inductive reasoning, and so on.

- *Type III*. These activities are best accomplished through a part-time program within the regular school day. Type III enrichment usually means an independent research study done on an area of interest to the student. Perhaps about half the time that the top 5 percent of the student population spends in such programs should be devoted to the pursuit of a Type III activity.

FIGURE 5.13. The enrichment triad model.

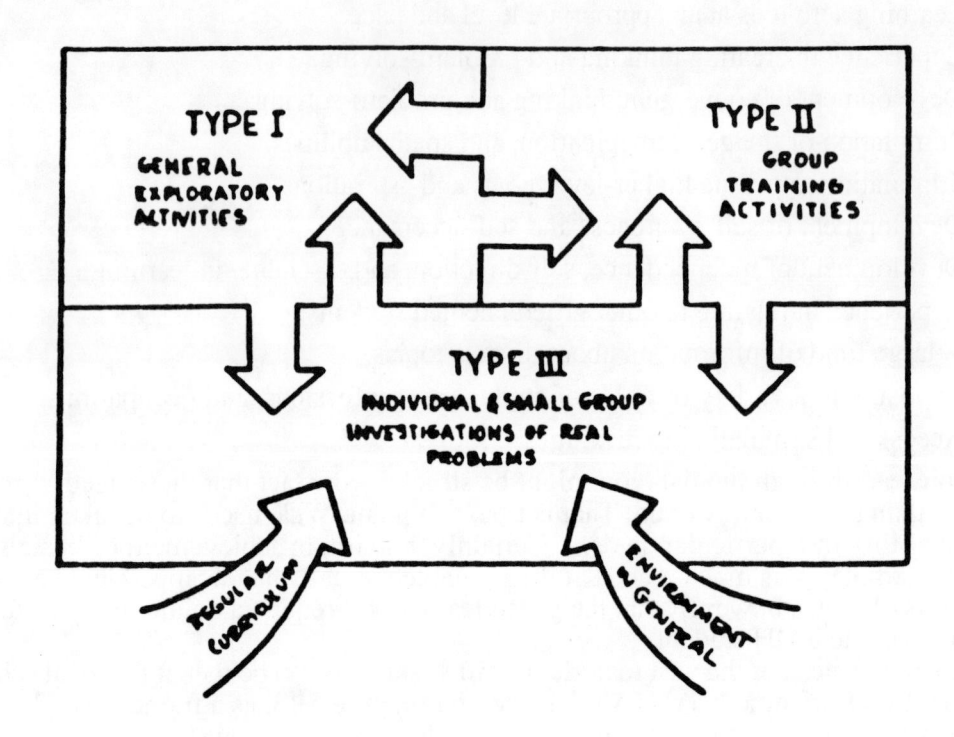

```
┌─────────────────────────────────────────────┐
│                                             │
│   TYPE I          ⬅              TYPE II    │
│   GENERAL         ⬇              GROUP      │
│   EXPLORATORY   ⬆  ➡  ⬆          TRAINING   │
│   ACTIVITIES                     ACTIVITIES │
│                                             │
│      ⬇           TYPE III           ⬇       │
│              INDIVIDUAL & SMALL GROUP       │
│              INVESTIGATIONS OF REAL         │
│                    PROBLEMS                 │
│                                             │
└─────────────────────────────────────────────┘
         ⬈                          ⬉
     REGULAR                    ENVIRONMENT
    CURRICULUM                   IN GENERAL
```

From: Renzulli, J. 1977. *The enrichment triad model: a guide for developing defensible programs for the gifted and talented.* Mansfield Center, Connecticut: Creative Learning Press.

A systematic, reasonably accurate selection process is therefore necessary to identify the top 5 percent of a school's population. Clearly, if we use Renzulli's definition of giftedness, an IQ test should only be part of that process. In one school system for which I do consulting work, the following three-step process is used:[78]

- *Step 1.* Identification of the top 15 percent of students on a composite index. *All* students in the district are given a group IQ test, a group achievement test, and rated using the Renzulli scales. A weighting factor is used for each source of information, and local T-scores are calculated. Cut-off scores are established to pick up the top 15 percent.

- *Step 2.* Identification of the top 5 percent of students is done by further evaluation of the top 15 percent. This further evaluation includes a parent inventory, a self-rating inventory, and a test of higher cognitive/critical thinking. The results are also weighted, and the top 5 percent identified. Furthermore, a teacher or parent could still be an advocate for any particular student who was felt to be missed by the process. Usually, such students are then further assessed on an individual basis. A decision is made on the basis of a number of factors.

- *Step 3.* Administration of an individual IQ test (usually the WISC-R) to the top 5 percent of students, to further pinpoint cognitive strengths and weaknesses, if required. Students within each school in the district are then provided enrichment according to the

Renzulli model. One teacher for each school is designated as the gifted program teacher, and is responsible for the overall program in that school.

Other models and other processes may be equally effective. I have chosen this one because I am familiar with it, and because the selection process is a top-down one, with all students forming the initial pool. The chances of mis-identification are greatly reduced. Some districts use only one source of information, such as teacher nomination, then perhaps followed by an individual assessment. Although some gifted students are identified by this process, a great many are not, since teachers tend to nominate high-achieving students who are teacher-pleasers.

It occurs to me that Renzulli's model and the three-step identification process could be modified to identify learning-disabled students more accurately. Unfortunately, most school districts still work only on a referral basis. As a result, many school psychologists simply test and rubber-stamp a student as learning-disabled. Because of this, I believe many students with IQ scores of 100+ and who show a discrepancy between achievement and ability, are never diagnosed; while those students who are simply "slow" are given special service. That is because school districts place students who are below grade level in special education classes. A student with an IQ of 80 is *bound* to be below grade level. The proper questions that need to be asked here, are: (1) "Is there a *discrepancy* between the student's ability and achievement?" and (2) "Is this discrepancy a *significant* one?" These questions can now be answered with much greater psychometric precision and sophistication.[79] As a result, school psychologists would be better able to discriminate those students who require a Type II remedial program from those who require only modification within the classroom (Type I remediation) or who require some special skills training (Type II remediation).

Figures 5.14 and 5.15 represent WISC-R profiles of two students who have been referred as possibly gifted.

The first student, Michael, was already in the talent pool (top 15 percent). On the basis of the WISC-R results and other pertinent data, it was recommended that Michael remain in the talent pool. Note in particular Michael's lower scores on the memory subtests of the Verbal scale. Though he was in the talent pool, Michael had some academic difficulties that would have precluded success in the more demanding Type III activities.

The other student, Jonathan, was referred on an advocacy basis. The screening procedure had missed him, and some teachers and a supervisor felt he might still be a Type III candidate. Jonathan *was* placed in the gifted program on the basis of these results and other sources of information. He is now busily engaged in a Type III activity of his choosing.

Gifted Underachievers

This group, also sometimes called the gifted learning-disabled, poses special problems for the school psychologist. I have found the guidelines presented by Fine and Pitts to be particularly helpful for this kind of problem.[80]

First, they describe the gifted underachiever as a ". . . kind of intellectual delinquent who withdraws from goals, activities, and social participation."[81] Further descriptors of such a student and some of the dynamics include the following:[82]

1. Low self-esteem, including an accompanying unwillingness to take risks. Social isolation is also present. The student may show a very great interest in something like rock-collecting. This is interpreted as the student finding school boring. However, it maintains the social isolation.

2. Deficient academic skills—most often, this student is truly behind academically; but, because he is recognized as very bright, he is seen by teachers simply as someone who "won't try." Although this is true, the "won't/can't" attitude usually does lead to a true deficit in academics.

FIGURE 5.14. Michael's WISC-R profile.

FIGURE 5.15. Jonathan's WISC-R profile.

3. Passive-aggressive behavior, with frequent attempts to "get back" at other students and teachers by nonachievement. This causes extreme anger and frustration for parents and teachers alike.

4. Motor delays or deficiencies—many of these students would rather talk than play. In fact, the verbal strengths the students have are greatly reinforced at home and school. As a result, the student may avoid paper-and-pencil or gross-motor tasks.

5. "Adultizing the child"—again, because of the student's verbal strengths, parents and teachers begin treating the child on an adult level (where the child does well) and are thereby constantly deflected from the real issue, which is the continual avoidance of academic tasks.

6. Attribution of blame—the student typically blames others by intellectualizing and rationalizing any wrongdoing on his part. "Verbally reasoning" with the student is therefore not likely to be effective—only confusing.

7. Family conflict—sometimes such a student *causes* severe family conflicts, and sometimes such a student is the *scapegoat* in a family which unknowingly acts out their own conflicts via or "around" the student. The dynamics of family interaction around school assignments are such that the parent winds up spending much time and energy tracking down the assignment. Much concern and anger is present. The assignment itself is usually done quickly, once the student puts his energy into it.

8. Parent/school conflicts—each side usually blames the other for not motivating the child. This conflict can really be severe and sustained for years.

9. Interpersonal attitudes—Fine and Pitts state that the student seems to work from an "I'm OK—You're not OK" stance. This component is something that teachers see continually. The student ridicules others and puts them down constantly. By provoking others, he invites rejection, but of course denies any responsibility when others reject him. Again, parents often perceive this situation as the child being "picked on" by other students, thus inadvertently maintaining the rejection because, of course, they reinforce the student's belief that "It's not my fault."

CASE EXAMPLE

To illustrate this problem, I will describe the case of Thomas in detail. Thomas was originally referred to me in first grade. The concerns stated by the school at that time were:

Thomas exhibits antisocial behavior both in the classroom and on the playground; this pattern has existed since playschool. Thomas appears to be bright to the point of being brilliant.

I began by administering the WISC-R, the *Human Figure Drawing Test*, and the *Kinetic Family Drawing Test*. The WISC-R results are shown in Figure 5.16.

Note the high score on Block Design. Other than this subtest score (95th percentile), there were no other indicators of giftedness. The projective drawings were also very clean. Thomas' behavior in the testing situation was impulsive. He "tested *my* limits" frequently, and tried to gain control. However, he was easily manageable at the time. His responses on the Comprehension subtest reflected a lack of social sensitivity.

FIGURE 5.16. Thomas' first-grade WISC-R profile.

These results were discussed with Thomas' parents. In the interview, they pointed out Thomas' unusual interest in medical books and his curiosity. Of course, they felt his behavior problems in school were caused by boredom. Unfortunately, the WISC-R results did not support that he was particularly bright. (What makes diagnosis more difficult is that very bright students exhibit much more variability on retests of the WISC-R than do less bright students.) Because of Thomas' behavior problems, family counseling was recommended but, unfortunately, was not acted-upon by the parents. Thomas' social problems continued in school, but were manageable enough until fourth grade, when another referral came in on him. This time, he was referred primarily because of a "short attention span" and "inability to complete many simple tasks." By this time, as well, Thomas' father was *livid* with the school. He saw his son as brilliant, and blamed the school entirely for all of Thomas' social problems. Thomas was still interested in medical books, and had extended his interest to a number of other scientific areas. However, he got a D in Science on his report card, which was incomprehensible to the parents. Understandably so. In a one-to-one situation with adults, and on a topic of interest to him, Thomas would work quite well. Even then, he was distractible; but the parents did not interpret it as distractibility—only as further evidence of his brilliance. The father would frequently phone the school and hurl a torrent of abuse on the principal. The situation had deteriorated to a crisis level.

This time, the referral went to the district reading specialist, who performed a thorough academic assessment, and then cross-referred to me. I decided to readminister the WISC-R (Would I find anything this time to confirm the parental insistence on Thomas' brilliance?) and do a classroom observation.

The WISC-R profile, represented in Figure 5.17, was indeed very different this time.
Notice the three-factor split this time:

- Factor I—95th percentile
- Factor II—91st percentile
- Factor III—37th percentile

The reading specialist had Thomas write a story. His story was about "making a battery." It was written beautifully and finished in about 15 minutes. The vocabulary was consistent with his high verbal ability. No difficulty was noted on the writing task in terms of attention span or distractibility. Thomas' written work on this occasion was as good as any student's in the school's gifted program—showing that he could, at times, perform at a high level. He also scored very high on some *Peabody Individual Achievement Test* (PIAT) subtests, but showed genuine weaknesses on reading comprehension and planning ability in terms of organizing his thoughts on paper on another writing task. On a second testing occasion, the reading specialist found Thomas *much* more distractible, even though the story he was writing was in the science area.

These results, overall, presented a very different picture than those in first grade. Note also, how reasonably well Thomas did in a one-to-one setting this time, so long as the activity was of high interest to him (even so, his performance was variable).

His behavior in a classroom setting was another story. I went to observe him, and found him very fidgety and restless. He seemed continually in motion, though never actually out of his seat. He made inappropriate noises. When the teacher gave him a look of disapproval, he looked at me to see how I would react. (This kind of attention-seeking behavior was very typical for Thomas, I learned from the teacher—it wasn't just because I was there.) At one point, a student next to him dropped her pen top. It rolled under Thomas' desk. She picked it up. Thomas let go a string of ridicule because the girl would now get "germs." He went on and on about it. When the poor girl finally said, "No, I won't," Thomas let forth an encyclopedic explanation which in no uncertain terms proved he was right and she was an idiot. It was very easy to see from that instance how Thomas invited rejection from his peers; he was certainly operating from an "I'm OK, you're not OK" attitude. Interestingly, when I described this to his parents, they laughed and did not really see a problem.

FIGURE 5.17. Thomas' fourth-grade WISC-R profile.

How does one go about trying to assist in straightening out such a mess? Fine and Pitts suggest the following steps. These were followed in Thomas' case with modifications appropriate for the situation. The guidelines for intervention suggested, are:[83]

1. Involve the parents in a "high confrontation / high-accountability" program. Involve the parents deeply in a program where goals are clearly established and where they are involved in planning the courses of action to be taken. The "accountability" part included follow-up conferences, modification of original plans, keeping good records, and establishing someone as a "case manager." All of this needs to be done in a nonpunitive, matter-of-fact way. In Thomas' case, a very long conference was held, and the issue placed "on the table" both by the parents and the school. We discussed a number of options and courses of action. One thing that had to happen was for the parents to see Thomas in action in a classroom, since their view of him was exclusively in a one-to-one home setting. The parents volunteered to come into the classroom twice a week. The first week they did so, Thomas was, as usual, very distractible, and did not complete his work in class. I believe this was a real eye-opener for his parents.

2. Family dynamics cannot be ignored. If the student himself is included in the planning, then it is quite likely that the underlying manner in which he is able to manipulate will surface. Thomas was included in the first meeting only toward the end. He agreed to the plan of action and was very pleased that his parents would be in the classroom, because now "they could help me with my work." This was despite the fact that it had been explained that they would be there like any other parent volunteer to help with the whole class. The major difficulty here was to help the parents see that Thomas was more than "bored" in school. This, I believe, they are starting to see. The father, in particular, was very unrealistic. He wanted Thomas to be marked and tested on the work he completed, not what was assigned, for example. So, if Thomas did three of fifteen arithmetic questions and got them all correct, he was to receive a mark of 100 percent from the teacher. (This strategy does have *some* value if used judiciously.)

3. Follow-up conferences are vital. Fine and Pitts suggest once-a-week conferences for the first while. Because his case is ongoing at the moment, the outcome is uncertain. However, the conferences are being held; and there is, at the moment, better communication between home and school. The major focus on the conferences and daily assignments is simply to help Thomas get them done. If he begins to show some consistency, the school is quite prepared to let him join in some enrichment activities.

4. Fine and Pitts also caution about "sabotage" by either parents or teachers in such cases. They state:[84]

> The literature has made it abundantly clear that the underachieving gifted child is often more than just a child bored with a mundane school experience. Also the pattern of underachievement can become pervasive and diminish not only the child's school satisfaction but have a serious and negative impact on peer-social relationships and the child's place within the family.

Profile Analysis of Very High IQ Students

In this final section, I would like to briefly outline a method of profile analysis developed by Reynolds and Clark which the school psychologist may find very useful for some profiles.

Reynolds and Clark make the valid point that it is very difficult to find intra-individual strengths and weaknesses (using Kaufman's method) when all subtests are in the very high range. For example, if the mean of the subtests is 18, then how can a significant strength even be determined?

The authors recommend a seven-step procedure, which I will present in abbreviated fashion here. For a full discussion of the rationale and process, readers are encouraged to consult the reference.[85]

1. First, administer and calculate all standard scores on the WISC-R in the usual fashion. Formulate any relevant hypotheses. Next, determine the *age equivalents* for each of the WISC-R subtests (these can be found in the test manual, p. 189) which most closely correspond to the student's raw scores.

2. Calculate the *median* age equivalent for the subtests. Eliminate any subtests from this calculation on which the student exceeded the mean performance of the oldest group.

3. Now, treat the median age equivalent as the chronological age for the purpose of *recalculating* the subtest scaled scores. For example, if the student was 10 years old, and you found the median test-age to be 13 years, you would enter the 13-year-old table in the WISC-R manual.

4. Recalculate subtest scale scores, and the major IQ scores. Reynolds and Clark state that such recalculated IQ scores should not deviate much from the range of about 94 to 106. If they do, then recheck your calculations, as there is likely to be a clerical error.

5. Finally, proceed with profile analysis as suggested by Kaufman. Remember, however, that you cannot make *inter-individual* comparisons using this process—only ipsative (*intra-individual*) ones.

Readers should make every attempt to become more familiar with the kinds of profiles and problems exhibited by the "gifted LD" group of students. In one article, the *emotional* problems exhibited by such students come to the fore:[86]

Many of these uneven gifted youngsters exhibited talents in art, music, poetry, electronics, business, and the sciences . . . .

Despite these talents, and average or above-average performance in math and reading achievement, the group of children tended to be emotionally upset and disorganized. All expressed a sense of unhappiness, and many felt they did not fit in anywhere. They often complained of being isolated or scapegoated; images of being corroded, out of control, monster-like, or dumb prevailed. Virtually all had some idea that they could not make their brain, body, or both do what they wanted each to do. They often reported organizing difficulties in simple mathematical calculations, spelling, and handwriting. They reported extremely upsetting feelings with physical education and gross-motor activities, and they often perceived themselves powerless in a fearsome and attacking world. Many sought angry revenge against teachers or children who made fun of them or picked them last in games. The emotional complications of the group as a whole included inadequate impulse control, defective self-concept, narcissistic hypersensitivity, and poorly developed integrative functions . . . .

These descriptions from the study match closely the kinds of experiences I have had with such students over the years. Such students are very challenging indeed.

Chapter 6
Level III and IV Interpretations of the WISC-R

Level III Interpretation

Level III interpretation of the WISC-R involves examining individual subtest strengths and weaknesses. Since the focus is on the individual, it is intra-individual strengths and weaknesses that are of primary concern here. This level of interpretation is often fascinating, since many patterns of cognitive abilities are possible.

I would like to discuss the difference, though, between patterns for diagnostic purposes, as opposed to educational purposes. Certainly, there is more than enough evidence to show that the different patterns on the WISC-R I have discussed so far—such as Verbal-Performance discrepancies, three-factor splits, and ACID profiles—cannot be used to diagnose a student as learning-disabled, educationally disadvantaged, or whatever. That is because such patterns are also present, often in significant proportions, in the normal population. Many students with no academic problems will exhibit significant "scatter," for example. Conversely, some students with academic problems show *no* "scatter" on the WISC-R. Therefore, it is impossible to diagnose a condition from a WISC-R score or sets of scores. However, that is surely not the end of it. If a student with or without academic difficulties, for example, shows a split of scores on the WISC-R indicating a strong field-dependent cognitive style, then there are certainly educational implications for both students.

I believe, in such cases, that profile analysis is valuable in suggesting educational strategies for that student. Again, though, the WISC-R, by itself, will not be as valuable as information from a variety of sources. Recommendations for any one student are likely to be better when a team approach is used. This way, the benefits of a number of lines of expertise can converge and serve the best interests of the student.

The distinction between what is diagnostically significant and what is educationally significant is an important one. As I have said repeatedly throughout this book, one cannot diagnose a student as such-and-such based on a WISC-R profile; but to ignore what lies in a particular profile in terms of educational hypotheses will have the effect of "freezing" all WISC-R interpretations at Level I. This point of view is indeed espoused by some researchers. Kavale and Forness, for example, say:[1]

> Despite long-standing cautions, suggestions about grouping WISC subtests into new clusterings have been advanced repeatedly. However, the present findings offer no empirical support for the existence of such groupings. On the contrary, nonsignificant findings show the WISC profiles as possessing no external validity for LD diagnosis. Kaufman suggests that the search for WISC profiles requires good detective work employing "ingenuity, clinical sense, and thorough grounding in psychological theory and research to reveal the dynamics of a child's scaled-score profile." In reality, the problem faced by the WISC detective appears to be the lack of any case to be solved. Thus, the LD group was found to exhibit neither sufficient variability nor singular uniqueness requiring any detective work.

And:[2]

> The present findings should not be construed as negative, however. Although WISC profile and scatter analysis is not defensible for diagnosing LD, the WISC remains a valuable tool for *global* IQ assessment and should be restricted to this purpose.

The reasoning that Kavale and Forness offer is this: Learning-disabled groups and normal groups do not differ on WISC-R profiles. The profiles therefore cannot be used to diagnose learning disabilities (and, by extension, any other condition). I agree with this point, even though many clinicians abuse it.

However, their next step is: When a student *does* have a profile of strengths and weaknesses, ignore it. There is nothing to explore, no more detective work to be done. This, I certainly do not agree with. To leave interpretation at Level I for students whose WISC-R profiles show certain clusters, is ludicrous. Kavale and Forness seem to assume that diagnosis, only, is the name of the game. They also assume a very static assessment process (i.e., that, somehow, the differences between a learning-disabled student and a normal student will be found in the standardized numbers themselves). As every school psychologist knows, students' behavior on some subtests provides many valuable clues, even though the scale score itself may fall in the average range. So, a student may score a 10 on Mazes, but still be very "impulsive" in his approach. The WISC-R must be used in a very dynamic way. It is from the overall impressions (the "detective work") and, of course, from the numbers themselves, that recommendations of an educational nature can be made.

To begin Level III interpretation (assuming that all Level I and II hypotheses have been explored), I recommend Kaufman's approach.[3] The examiner calculates a Verbal average (using all six subtests and rounding the scaled score average to the nearest whole number). The same is done for the Performance Scale. Any Verbal or Performance subtest which deviates ± 3 points from its respective mean is considered a significant strength or weakness *for that student*. An example follows in Figure 6.1.

Note that, for this student, the Verbal average is 7, which is significantly weaker than the population average to begin with. But *within that scale*, the Information subtest is significantly weaker than the others, while the Vocabulary subtest is significantly stronger.

The next step is to see if any of the significantly strong or weak subtests cluster in some meaningful way. One can consult Kaufman's work directly for a more detailed explanation of the process and implications, and/or consult the modified table in Chapter 1 for an overview of some of the hypotheses suggested by this kind of detective work. Again, in the foregoing example, Information, Arithmetic, and Digit Span all have "memory" in common, so "memory" aspects might be further explored in regard to this student.

But much of what is uncovered in this way about a student can best be discussed in terms of learning styles.

The WISC-R and Learning Styles

What is a learning style? Rita Dunn says, simply, that:[4]

> ... Learning style is the way in which each person absorbs and retains information and/or skills; regardless of how that process is described, it is dramatically different in each person.

"Learning style" and "cognitive style" are often used interchangeably, but the former is the umbrella term; so, learning style can include affective and physiological states, as well as strictly cognitive ones. That makes the whole issue very complex. Indeed, the diagram of the Dunn and Dunn learning style model, shown in Figure 6.2, amply illustrates the complexity.[5]

I find the model in Figure 6.2 interesting, but exceedingly complex. In fact, there are 2,304 *different* combinations that are possible from the model! How can the school psychologist or teacher possibly become familiar with the various implications of each combination? More importantly, would it really make any big difference to the student's achievement? Here, we would expect research to provide some answers, but we find controversy instead. For example, Rita Dunn says:[6]

> In every case [of the research studies she cites] students were matched with methods, resources, or environments that complemented their reported strong preferences achieved statistically higher; they achieved statistically less well when they were mismatched with their preferences.

FIGURE 6.1. Example of profile of strengths and weaknesses.

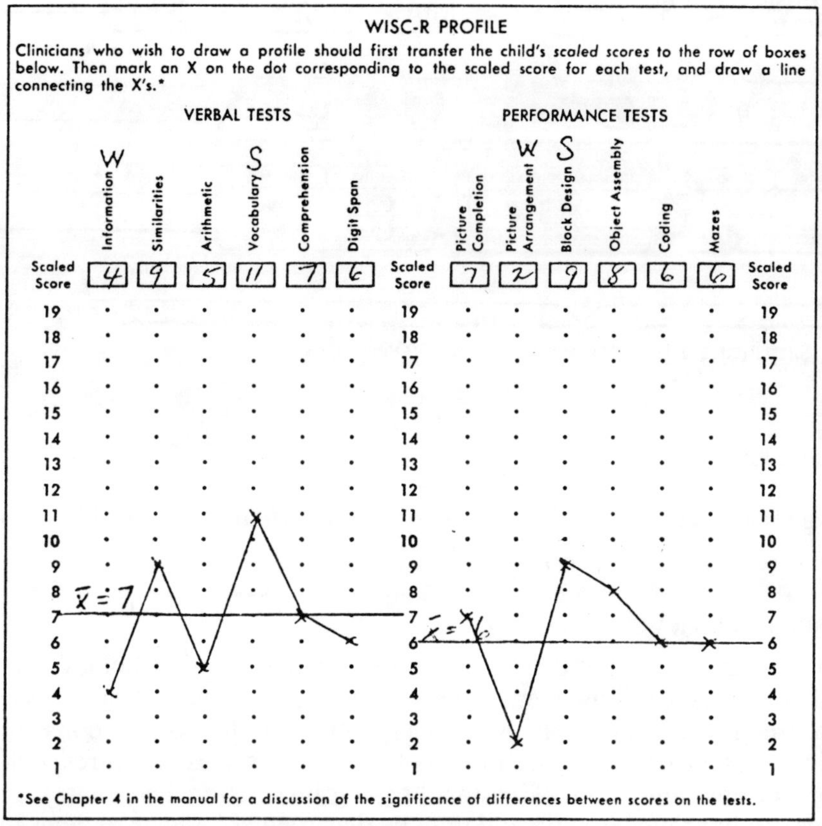

FIGURE 6.2. Diagnosing learning styles.

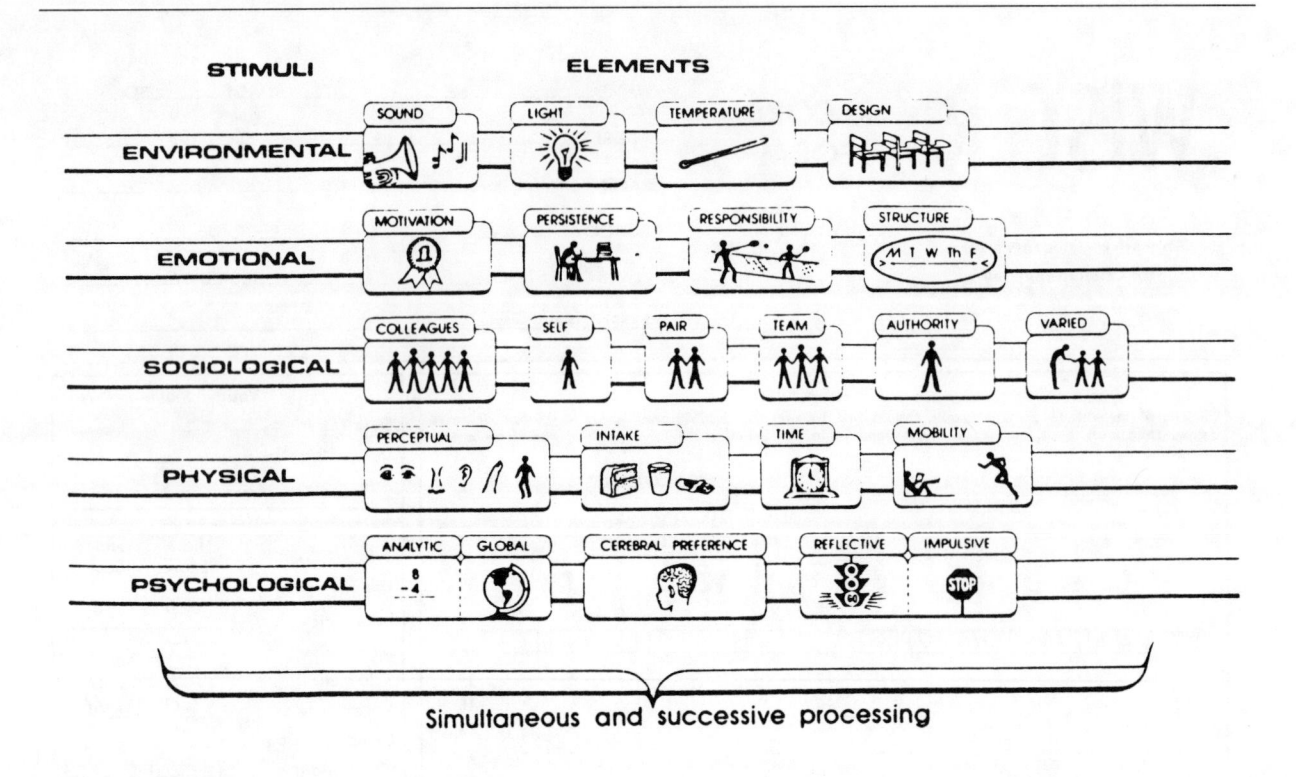

[Figure: Diagnosing learning styles diagram with STIMULI and ELEMENTS columns, showing rows for ENVIRONMENTAL (Sound, Light, Temperature, Design), EMOTIONAL (Motivation, Persistence, Responsibility, Structure), SOCIOLOGICAL (Colleagues, Self, Pair, Team, Authority, Varied), PHYSICAL (Perceptual, Intake, Time, Mobility), PSYCHOLOGICAL (Analytic, Global, Cerebral Preference, Reflective, Impulsive). Bracket at bottom labeled "Simultaneous and successive processing".]

Note: Designed by Rita Dunn and Kenneth Dunn.

From: Dunn, R. 1984. Learning style: state of the science. *Theory into Practice* 23:1, p. 11.

Doyle and Rutherford give the opposite view:[7]

> Advocates of matching models often claim that their methods increase student achievement. The weight of the evidence does not, however, support such claims. In a massive review of research on attribute-treatment interactions, Cronbach and Snow found few consistent results for programs matching instructional treatments to learning styles. With respect to learner preferences, for example, they concluded that "basing instructional adaptations on student preferences does not improve learning and may be detrimental." Other reviews and studies report similar results. Peterson found weak effects for achievement, although she did identify effects of matching on noncognitive variables such as self-esteem and motivation. Kampwirth and Bates reviewed 22 studies on the effects of matching modality preferences with teaching methods. Only two studies reported significant effects on achievement. The remaining 20 studies found either no significant interaction effects or support for the effectiveness of teaching to the nonpreferred modality.

What is the school psychologist or classroom teacher to make of such conclusions? (Certainly, the first recommendation is to proceed with caution!) Once again, there are no black-and-white answers. Consideration must be given to the *individual* student. It is my experience that the learning style rationale is often one way to at least turn a teacher's or parent's attitude around. For example, if a student *does* find that working with music in the background helps, while a parent insists on quiet *and is in conflict with the student over it*, then a learning style explanation may help reduce the conflict and lead to improved academics or homework habits. In this case, improved learning has as much to do with attitude changes (in support of Kampwirth and Bates, cited in the foregoing excerpt from Doyle and Rutherford) as it does with learning style per se. There *is*, however, some evidence that some students do indeed perform better in noisy versus quiet environments. I have found in my consulting work that carefully thought-out recommendations based on a learning style analysis can and do improve the situation for a student. Sometimes, it is not academic improvement, per se, that improves, however. Improvement may occur in less tangible, more difficult-to-quantify ways.

Here are some important considerations to keep in mind, then, about learning styles:[8]

1. There is no single dimension of learners that unambiguously dictates an instructional prescription. Thus, accommodating cognitive style, which is likely to influence motivation primarily, does not necessarily account for other critical variables in learning, such as ability and prior knowledge. Indeed, concentrating exclusively on a single dimension could even be harmful for learning because other aspects of instruction are neglected. Moreover, there is no compelling evidence that *matching* instruction to learning style is always beneficial. In fact some studies suggest that a mismatch is best under particular circumstances.

2. There are higher-level interactions between learner characteristics and instructional treatments. Thus, the effect of learning style on achievement is likely to be affected by the nature of the learning task, the relationship between teacher and student, the time of the year, and other local conditions. It is difficult, therefore, to predict a simple linear connection between learning style and instructional dimensions.

3. Most students can adapt to a variety of instructional modes, even if they are not preferred. The central issue is whether the instruction provided is of sufficiently high quality, in terms of such dimensions as task clarity, feedback, and opportunities for practice, to facilitate learning.

4. In a classroom, uniform instructional treatments are often superior to differentiated treatments because they are compatible with the teacher's skills and are easier to manage. In addition, whole-class instruction is not necessarily "uniform" at a process level. Teachers often present information in a variety of formats (discussion, lecture, questions) and adjust to the attributes of learners during individual contacts. Thus, opportunities are provided for different learners to gain access to instruction.

In other words, teaching style needs to be considered, too—particularly, *effective* teaching techniques. And what is effective may be different for different students. For example, if we take Dunn and Dunn's "Emotional" stimulus category, and look under "Structure," we find good evidence that lower-ability students respond better to structured versus unstructured tasks. High-ability students learn well under either condition. "Structure" means, in this case, direct teaching, explicit guidance, and immediate feedback, with plenty of opportunities for practice. This kind of learning/teaching style match is certainly at a practical level for the classroom.

It seems to me, then, that the issue of learning style means, "*What* learning style are we talking about?" and "How does it apply in *this* student's case?"

Diagnosis can be quite important. Most theorists state that learning styles are quite pervasive and stable over time. Such dimensions as field-dependence/independence, for example, which is a well researched cognitive style, seems to be quite stable over time for individuals. Therefore, while certain WISC-R patterns may suggest learning styles, these hypotheses should be explored with teacher input, behavioral observations, and further, supplementary tests when necessary.

Some learning styles seem to have better research-based support than others. I cannot deal with all possible learning styles in one chapter, so I have selected the following: modality preference; field-dependence/independence; simultaneous-successive; conceptual tempo; right-left brain and Letteri's approach.

Modality Preference

This particular type of learning style approach developed in the early days of remedial education. Students were classified as "visual," "auditory," or "tactile-kinesthetic" learners based on their preferred mode of information input. A number of reading programs were developed stressing one or more of the modalities. Little formal research was available at the time to determine whether or not any one method was superior to another and for what learners. There is still a dearth of research on the subject.

The Verbal Scale of the WISC-R could be interpreted as "auditory-vocal," since all items require the student to listen and respond orally. The Performance Scale is primarily "auditory-visual/manual," since input is both auditory (verbal instructions) and visual (pictures, blocks, puzzles, etc.), while output is mainly manual (pointing, manipulating items, paper and pencil tasks, etc.). Therefore, a Verbal/Performance discrepancy on the WISC-R could be interpreted, for example, as a strength or weakness, depending on the direction of the difference, in auditory versus visual learning.

Such an interpretation I find useful on occasion in some individual cases. Most often, the underlying verbal or performance strengths should be the dominant interpretive hypothesis.

There are a number of significant problems with the "modality" interpretations. A primary difficulty is the fact that only a small percentage of students show a clear-cut preference for one modality over another (about 10 percent). Second, there are very few reliable instruments to measure such preferences; and, finally, there is a confounding with other, likely more important, variables.

For example, in one recent research report, learning-disabled students were taught sight words using a VA (visual, auditory) approach (the teacher read the word, students repeated it, then said the sound of each syllable, then said the word again), or a VAKT (visual, auditory, kinesthetic, tactile) approach (the teacher said the word, students separated it, traced the word with their index finger while saying the sounds, underlined the word, and said it again). After five words were completed this way, students said the words again, traced each word over with their pencils, and underlined the word while repeating it). The VAKT approach produced better results both in terms of on-task behavior and number of words correctly read.[9] However, when *praise* was added to either the VA or VAKT method, results improved dramatically for both methods, with a slight advantage to the VA method! So, praise was a very significant addition to the modality teaching. It seemed to have as much effect as the modality approach itself.

It is hard to imagine any teacher spending more than a few minutes a day in such a modality drill to begin with. Notice how completely bottom-up the drill is. It completely ignores the meaning and syntactic cues that could be added. Modality approaches ignore the fact that words are meaning-based, regardless of which modality is primary as an input source. Otherwise, how would Helen Keller have learned to read and comprehend?

Barbara Larivee reviewed a number of studies done on method-by-modality studies for beginning-reading instruction, and concluded:[10]

> ... Differentiating instruction according to modality preference does not appear to facilitate learning to read or the acquisition of specific beginning reading skills .... One might infer that adapting the instructional mode to the learner's preferred modality is not important for teaching beginning reading and/or that the tests used to assess modal preferences do not in fact determine a preference, but rather reflect the child's experience with the particular type of task measured.

My own conclusion regarding modality training is that, if such an explanation and training are to be used at all, a multisensory approach is best because it is simply more interesting, and therefore helps students attend. It involves the student more, if all senses are engaged.

Although the divisions are somewhat arbitrary, the following classifications might be helpful to you:

- *Visual:* chalkboard, overhead, dittos, posters, charts, maps, video, films, filmstrips.

- *Auditory:* lecture, questioning, discussion, audiotapes, music, listening centers.
- *Kinesthetic:* tracing, drawing, role-playing, experiments, printing/writing, drama.

Any teacher using a variety of such teaching activities and aids is likely to meet any modality needs of students.

Field-Dependence/Independence

The construct of field-dependence/independence arose from Herman Witkin's work with World War II pilots. Witkin noticed that some pilots were much more capable of orienting themselves to upright positions during complex flying manoeuvres than were others. Witkin and his coworkers then developed some rather elaborate testing mechanisms, including tilting chairs and rooms to help them discriminate those individuals who were more adept at repositioning themselves.

After the war, Witkin continued his research, and coined the terms "field-dependent" (FD) and "field-independent" (FI). He found that the ability to experience the environment in global (FD) or more analytic (FI) ways was a pervasive and essentially stable characteristic of individuals— a cognitive style, if you will. The style pervaded many aspects of the individual's functioning in the environment, certainly not just in orienting to an upright position. The FD/FI construct is considered an important variable. It has been well-researched; in fact, it may be *the* most well documented of the cognitive styles. It is a variable which needs to be considered with a number of individual students.

In general, FIs tend to perceive individual items in their environments as separate from the background context; whereas, FDs are much more influenced by the backgrounds and see less *differentiation* and more *fusion* with the environment. (Perhaps many of the so-called "perceptual problems" that students have are simply manifestations of a more FD cognitive style.)

The WISC-R Performance Scale can be used to suggest an FD or FI orientation. Scores on Picture Completion, Block Design, and Object Assembly can be added and averaged. If their average differs from the other three Performance subtests by ±3 points or more, then a FD or FI hypothesis can be considered. Higher scores on these three subtests suggest the FI orientation. The Verbal Scale has not been analyzed in this way. However, since FDs have a more general differentiation in their environment, we would expect high-level, more abstract, *quality* responses on the Verbal items. The examiner can confirm or deny the FD/FI hypothesis by further testing with such tests as the *Rod and Frame* or *Embedded Figures Test* or *Group Embedded Figures Tests*, or *Children's Embedded Figures Test*.[11] Note, however, that this same triad is involved in the simultaneous/successive dichotomy, and is related to Bannatyne's Spatial category. Which hypothesis is dominant for the student needs to be decided by the examiner.

People with FI orientations tend, as the name suggests, to see their world from an internal point of view, and to impose their own structure and organization upon it. FDs, on the other hand, tend to see the world from an external point of view, one from which they can employ the already existing structure as their own. FDs tend to be much more adept at interpersonal relationships, however.

Figure 6.3 shows a WISC-R profile which suggests an FD orientation.

Notice how Picture Completion, Block Design, and Object Assembly are significantly lower than Picture Arrangement, Coding, and Mazes. In addition, even though the Vocabulary and Similarities subtests are in the average range, the quality of responses was not good. The student earned 2 points on many of the Vocabulary items by naming several attributes, rather than using one good synonym.

FIGURE 6.3. A WISC-R profile which suggests a field-dependent orientation.

In terms of learning and education, a number of studies suggest the following learning differences between FD and FI students:[12]

The FD/FI differentiation extends into many areas of human activity, including learning and education. Ruble and Nakamura, for example, suggest that FD children are more able than FI children to solve problems containing social cues. In the area of concept formation, a differentiation is also noted. Witkin et al. cite several studies that suggest that FD learners tend to focus on salient cues when developing concepts. FI learners, on the other hand, tend to objectively sample from the full array of available cues in order to form concepts. Goodenough suggests that motivation is also an area of differentiation. Field dependents tend to be more attentive to intrinsic motivators and self-defined goals. Field dependents tend to be more responsive to extrinsic motivation and goals.

In terms of reading, specifically, the research suggests that FIs are generally better readers than FDs. Learning-disabled students are typically FD.[13]

What, then, makes for the difference in reading ability between FD and FI students? Some studies have been done relating to the psycholinguistic reading model (PL) discussed in Chapter 4 to the FD/FI construct. Mature reading involves word knowledge, word decoding, and comprehension. The mature reader seems to use both top-down and bottom-up processes interactively. The evidence in general seems to suggest better reading at all levels by FIs. As well, there is evidence to suggest that the FD reader uses a more bottom-up approach; whereas the FI reader uses more top-down processing. In terms of reading vocabulary, word boundaries are learned more effectively by FIs, a result we might expect from theory, since FIs are better able to disembed items from the background—a process which is certainly necessary in differentiating words from the surrounding lines of print while reading. FD readers pay more attention to the surface features of the word, and are misled by primary word cues when secondary meanings are more appropriate. As an example, an FD reader might choose "knock" for the meaning of "know" in a multiple-choice situation, because "knock" is a surface feature distractor.

When oral reading miscues are used to determine word recognition strategy, it has been found that:[14]

. . . Field independents made more grammatically acceptable miscues, demonstrated stronger grammatical relationship patterns, and had better retellings of the text than field dependents. Both groups used graphophonic cues in reading; however, the field independents used semantic and syntactic cues to a greater extent. The field dependents responded to the text in a passive and observant manner rather than applying what they knew and integrating it with the text. They seemed more concerned with the surface structure of the text and less with meaningful predictive strategies. This accords with Goodenough's conclusion that field dependents, in general, tend to take a "spectator" approach to learning, while independents assume a more "participant" or hypothesis-making role. This also suggests that field dependents may have a greater reliance upon bottom-up, text-driven strategies for word recognition and accessing word knowledge. Field independents, however, employ more interactive strategies. Complementary findings were reported in a study that looked at the silent text readings of ninth-graders using analysis of a cloze procedure task. This investigation found that the patterns of miscues varied the greatest by cognitive style with frustration level texts. At this level the FI students demonstrated, through miscue analysis, a greater control over meaning (semantic acceptability of errors) and syntax (syntactic acceptability of errors), than the FD students. Similarly, Rounds found that field independent second-grade students were more able to gain from grammatical awareness training than dependents. The FI children apparently had greater proficiency in disembedding or abstracting relevant grammatical generalizations and structures than the FD children.

In summary, then, when we look at the relationship between FI/FD and word knowledge in reading, there is a clear trend for superiority for the FIs. FIs seem to use more effective cognitive strategies and are better able to predict and use top-down processing to guide their reading. FDs are easily misled by surface features and do not allow meaning acquisition to guide their reading as forcefully as do FIs. We might therefore expect that reading *comprehension* will also be a problem for FDs.

This prediction is supported by a number of research studies showing better reading comprehension for FIs. Some of the identified reasons for this are:

1. FIs impose a structure onto the passage and therefore organize the material much more readily than do FDs.

2. FIs comprehend high-importance information in passages more effectively than FDs.

3. FIs can more easily provide unambiguous interpretations of ambiguous material than FDs. This is an important finding. It seems that the ability to effectively organize verbal sets is related to the ability to do likewise with nonverbal sets. In other words, the student who shows an FI pattern on the Performance scale of the WISC-R is *likely* to handle verbal language effectively as well.

4. FIs have more effective working memory, it seems, than FDs. So, in reading tasks where complex ideas require the storage of more propositions, the FDs are likely to suffer, and comprehension will drop.

In addition, FDs are not as successful in using their background knowledge when reading passages, as are FIs. This applies to schema activation in particular. In other words, FIs may have no more background knowledge on a subject than do FDs; but they can certainly apply it more effectively when reading.

Helping Field-Dependent Students
Become Better Readers: Suggestions and Strategies

1. Become more aware of which students in your class are probably FD and those that are FI. Many students, of course, will fall somewhere in the middle. However, it is quite likely that many of your poorer readers will also be FD. The WISC-R Picture Completion, Block Design, and Object Assembly cluster, as already mentioned, can suggest the hypothesis, but further testing may be necessary.

2. Once identified, grouping for instruction is very important. Here are some considerations:[15]

   The research literature shows quite clearly that field dependents tend to be poorer readers than independents. Consequently, these students will tend to be found in the lower reading groups in their classrooms. The work of Allington and Collins suggests that the type of reading instruction provided students in lower reading groups is markedly different than that provided [to] the higher groups. Specifically, when contrasted to high reading groups, the low group readers do less reading, read more orally than silently, get interrupted more often by the teacher for errors made in reading, and are given a greater instructional focus on decoding as opposed to comprehension. These observed practices are in almost complete contradiction to what the research reviewed here points to. The FD/FI research shows that field dependent readers attend too closely to the salient, surface-level cues in texts and that they pay relatively less attention to meaning. The logical implications of this suggest that FD readers should be given help in paying more attention to meaning and less attention to code as they read. They should be helped in using the less obvious meaning and contextual cues to aid word recognition and vocabulary improvement. They should be encouraged to make meaningful predictions about words in texts. Further, predictions about the meaning of whole texts should be encouraged. Directed Reading Thinking Activities (DRTA) would be highly appropriate here. Scott and his associates recommend too that field dependent students should not be required to read orally in the classroom, since this places high priority on accuracy over meaning for them. For the same reason, teacher interruptions to correct reading errors, especially those errors that do not affect meaning, should be deemphasized.

The suggestions given in the foregoing passage dovetail very nicely with those provided in this book, particularly in the appendices, and are consistent with the language-immersion approach to reading.

3. Help the FD student become a more active reader. The technique of reciprocal teaching (see Appendix 6-1) may be quite effective for this purpose.

4. Help the student develop strategies for organizing text. An advance organizer, for example, has been shown to be useful for both the FD and FI students in terms of improving reading comprehension. There is, however, also a significant interaction between type of treatment and cognitive style. *FD students who are given advance organizers together with prompts within the lesson which draw attention to the organizer, will make the most impressive gains.*[16] The gains are such that FD students who are given these additional organizers within the text and prompted to use them can increase their reading scores to match the FI students' normal performance. (This is also a good example of a teaching strategy which helps the student perform higher in his "zone of potential difference.") While an advance organizer is one way of imposing more organization on text, another way is the use of imagery (see Appendix 2-2). If FD students are given instruction on how to make a mental picture of a story, this will help them in their comprehension—moreso than just listening or even using pictures that accompany the text. Other organizational strategies, such as instruction in note-taking and the SQ3R method, could be helpful, as well.

5. Because FD students have well-developed interpersonal skills, capitalize on this strength as much as possible by using and encouraging:

— Reading partners and teams (emphasize cooperation, deemphasize competition)

— Reading clubs

— Book discussion groups

— Collaborative language arts assignments

— Book conferences

As well, books with "people" and social situations as the primary content should be appealing to FD students.

6. When students are reading texts, draw attention to the headings and subheadings already there. Have them pay attention to key concepts and words, and remind the students of them as they read along.

Simultaneous/Successive Information Processing Styles

I have already introduced this distinction in conjunction with the Freedom from Distractibility triad. If a student shows a split on the appropriate Performance subtests, then the hypothesis should be considered. Cross-checks include a split of ± 3 digits or more on Digits Forward versus Digits Backward (in terms of span) and behavioral observations. For example, some students seem to solve the Block Design and Object Assembly items in a very sequential manner—perhaps even assembling parts of the whole before attaching them into a coherent unit; while other students seem to see the whole design or object immediately, and assemble it from the "top, down."

The profile following in Figure 6.4 illustrates a simultaneous/successive split on the Performance scale in favor of simultaneous processing.

What is simultaneous and what is successive information processing? Alan Kaufman, author of the *Kaufman Assessment Battery for Children* (K-ABC), which was designed to differentiate students on these two processing styles, says:[17]

> A problem requiring sequential processing emphasizes the consecutive, one-after-the-other order in which small amounts of information must be arranged. Sequential processing is logical and analytic; it usually employs language and chronological order, since both depend on arrangements in time. When you listen to a lecture, scribbling notes as the speaker moves from point to point, you are acquiring information sequentially. Later, when you read over your notes in light of the completed lecture, you'll probably use simultaneous processing to integrate and synthesize all the items of information you've jotted down.
>
> A problem requiring simultaneous processing emphasizes complete units, wholes, integrated pieces of information that all must be considered before a problem can be solved or a conclusion reached. Simultaneous processing is holistic and synthetic; it usually employs visual images and spatial arrangements, since perceiving many details at once involves seeing or imagining the entire problem or situation. When you stand appreciatively before a painting, perhaps admiring the overall artistic balance or responding to the mood conveyed by the total scene, you are "processing" simultaneously, perceiving the picture all at once. However, if you concentrate on various details of the picture, moving from one aspect to another systematically, you are analyzing it in a more sequential way.

The distinction stems from the Russian psychologist A. R. Luria, and has been developed more fully in North America by J. P. Das and Alan Kaufman. From the latter, following are general teaching guidelines for each learning style:[18]

For the sequential learner:

1. Present material step by step, gradually approaching the overall concept or skill. Lead up to the big question with a series of smaller ones. Break the task into parts.

2. Get the child to verbalize what is to be learned. When you teach a new word, have the child say it, aloud or silently. Emphasize verbal cues, directions, and memory strategies.

3. Teach and rehearse the steps required to do a problem or complete a task. Continue to refer back to the details or steps already mentioned or mastered. Offer a logical structure or procedure by appealing to the child's verbal/temporal orientation.

    For example, the sequential learner may look at one or two details of a picture, but miss the visual image as a whole. To help such a student toward an overall appreciation of the picture, start with the parts and work up to the whole. Rather than beginning with, "What does the picture show?" or "How does the picture make you feel?" first ask about details:

— "What is the little boy in the corner doing?"

— "Where is the dog?"

— "What expression do you see on the woman's face?"

— "What colors are used in the sky?"

— "What is the cow looking at?"

Lead up to questions about the overall interpretation or appreciation:

— "How do all these details give you cues about what is happening in this picture?"

— "How does this picture make you feel?"

The sequential learner prefers a step-by-step teaching approach, one that may emphasize the gradual accumulation of details.

WISC-R COMPANION

FIGURE 6.4. Simultaneous/successive split, favoring simultaneous processing.

WISC-R RECORD FORM

Wechsler Intelligence Scale for Children—Revised

NAME _____ AGE _____ SEX _____
ADDRESS _____
PARENT'S NAME _____
SCHOOL _____ GRADE _____
PLACE OF TESTING _____ TESTED BY _____
REFERRED BY _____

WISC-R PROFILE

Clinicians who wish to draw a profile should first transfer the child's *scaled scores* to the row of boxes below. Then mark an X on the dot corresponding to the scaled score for each test, and draw a line connecting the X's.*

VERBAL TESTS

	Information	Similarities	Arithmetic	Vocabulary	Comprehension	Digit Span
Scaled Score	4	11	7	9	9	7

$\bar{x} = 8$

PERFORMANCE TESTS

	Picture Completion	Picture Arrangement	Block Design	Object Assembly	Coding	Mazes
Scaled Score	5	9	4	5	8	8

$\bar{x} = 7$

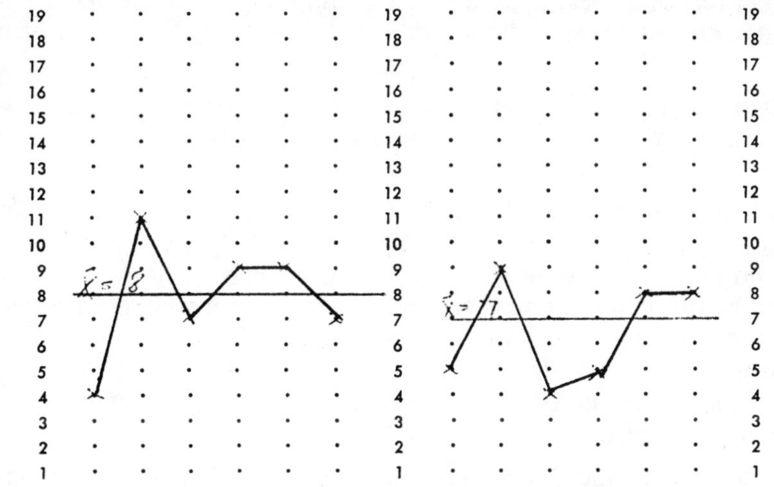

*See Chapter 4 in the manual for a discussion of the significance of differences between scores on the tests.

NOTES

	Year	Month	Day
Date Tested			
Date of Birth			
Age	13	6	26

	Raw Score	Scaled Score
VERBAL TESTS		
Information	11	4
Similarities	19	11
Arithmetic	11	7
Vocabulary	35	9
Comprehension	22	9
(Digit Span)	(10)	(7)
Verbal Score		40
PERFORMANCE TESTS		
Picture Completion	14	5
Picture Arrangement	27	9
Block Design	14	4
Object Assembly	15	5
Coding	49	8
(Mazes)	(21)	(8)
Performance Score		31

	Scaled Score	IQ
Verbal Score	40	87
Performance Score	31	74
Full Scale Score	71	80*

*Prorated from 4 tests, if necessary.

Copyright © 1971, 1974 by The Psychological Corporation.
All rights reserved. No part of this record form may be reproduced in any form of printing or by any other means, electronic or mechanical, including, but not limited to, photocopying, audiovisual recording and transmission, and portrayal or duplication in any information storage and retrieval system, without permission in writing from the publisher. See Catalog for further information.

Printed in U.S.A.   The Psychological Corporation   74-103AS   9-990334

For the simultaneous learner:

1. Present the overall concept or question before asking the child to solve the problem. Continue to refer back to the task, question, or desired outcome.

2. Get the child to visualize what is to be learned. When you teach a new word, have the child write it and picture it mentally, see it on the page in the mind's eye. Emphasize visual cues, directions, and memory strategies.

3. Make tasks concrete wherever possible by providing manipulative materials, pictures, models, diagrams, graphs. Offer a sense of the whole by appealing to the child's visual/spatial orientation.

The simultaneous learner may react to a picture as a whole, but may miss details. To help such a student notice the parts that contribute to the total visual image, begin by establishing an overall interpretation or reaction:

— "What does the picture show?"

— "How does the picture make you feel?"

Then, consider the details:

— "What is the expression on the woman's face?"

— "What is the little boy in the corner doing?"

— "What colors are used in the sky?"

Relate the details to the student's initial interpretation:

— "How do these details explain why the picture made you feel the way it did?"

The simultaneous learner responds best to a holistic teaching approach that focuses on groups of details or images, and stresses the overall meaning or configuration of the task.

I personally find the simultaneous/successive distinction useful many times, but it seems to me that most learning requires the integration of the two styles. This Kaufman admits when he says:[19]

It seems clear that very little learning calls exclusively for one process. We are constantly switching from one to the other, depending on the task before us. Many school-related activities, such as reading and arithmetic, require the integration of both processes. Still, many of us have a favorite learning style, one that we feel most comfortable with when we're confronted with an unfamiliar problem or new information. Our students, particularly those with special learning difficulties, may also have preferred styles. They can begin to feel more successful in school if new tasks are presented to them in ways that are congenial to their mental processing strengths.

Since the simultaneous/successive distinction is also relatively new, there is little research support which shows that teaching to the preferred style for a student will truly help him academically. This flaw is shared by many of the cognitive styles, however, as I have already discussed. But school psychologists and teachers who use a learning-styles approach must always ask themselves: "If I teach exclusively toward the student's preferred style, will I harm him by *not* exposing him to the nonpreferred style?" In general, teachers are probably better off using a variety of strategies and approaches, including both simultaneous and successive techniques, while making some adjustments for individual students when a clear-cut preference in one style is known.

Although primarily the Performance Scale of the WISC-R provides data on the simultaneous/successive split, some of the Verbal Scale subtests have also been researched using the Luria/Das model.[20] Unfortunately, not all the WISC-R subtests were used in this study (Information, Vocabulary, Comprehension, and Arithmetic were omitted because of the influence of school achievement on them). For the *normal standardization sample* of the WISC-R, here is how the subtests "regrouped" on the two dimensions:[21]

Simultaneous Subtests   *Successive Subtests*
- Similarities
- Picture Completion
- Picture Arrangement
- Block Design
- Object Assembly
- Mazes

- Digit Span
- (Similarities)
- Coding

Note how Similarities "loads" on both dimensions (however, it loads more heavily on the simultaneous factor).

The picture changes quite dramatically, however, when subgroups of special education students are sampled. In this study, separate groups of mentally handicapped, and students referred for learning and behavior problems, were used. The authors conclude:[22]

Whereas the emergence of factors for the WISC-R resembling the Luria/Das successive/simultaneous dichotomy for three groups of children is the main result of this investigation, there is another finding of almost equal value. The factor solutions for the two exceptional populations were highly similar to each other, but both differed from the results for normal youngsters as follows: (a) Similarities had a clear-cut simultaneous component for normals, but was strongly successive for the exceptional groups, especially the retarded; (b) Picture Arrangement was a simultaneous task for normals, but was clearly successive for the two exceptional groups; and (c) Coding was a successive task for normal children, but not for either exceptional population.

Why is this, one might ask? The authors speculate:[23]

... One possible explanation is that normal and exceptional children attack the same problems using different modes of processing. If we assume that normal children use the preferred or more efficient processing style, then it is conceivable that retarded youngsters or children referred for learning problems are using inefficient strategies.

It would seem, then, that simultaneous and successive processing is used differently in solving problems by different groups of students. In particular, very poor performance on Similarities, Digit Span, and Picture Arrangement seems to speak for severe problems in successive processing, particularly in exceptional populations.

The educational implications are stated as follows:[24]

... The teaching of more appropriate problem-solving strategies may well be a logical addition to remedial programs for children with learning problems. Similarly, recommendations for prescriptive teaching follow logically from the Luria/Das model. Instruction may be geared toward capitalizing on a child's particular strength (whether it be simultaneous or successive) in processing information, thereby circumventing the problems associated with the weaker mode. For example, consider the child who has not performed well in reading and shows evidence of a successive processing deficit coupled with a strength in simultaneous processing. This is the type of child who may benefit from a sight word instructional approach which emphasizes the holistic nature of word recognition rather than the analysis of discrete phonetic units and their proper ordering. Obviously, such speculation requires careful empirical investigation before these notions should be implemented.

In fact, some studies have been done which indicate that direct training in the processes of simultaneous and successive strategies has a positive effect on reading.[25] Adding such training to the resource teacher's repertoire, then, seems desireable. I would also refer the reader to the excellent article by Judy Gunnison which gives more detail on developing educational interventions from this model.[26]

In summary, then, the simultaneous/successive model is another area to explore when the Perceptual Organization factor is high and the Freedom from Distractibility is low on the WISC-R, since these two factors from the complete WISC-R battery closely fit this dichotomy.

Conceptual Tempo
and Planning Ability

Conceptual tempo refers to a "speed/accuracy" problem-solving approach. I also discussed this in more detail in the previous chapter. It is most often measured by the *Matching Familiar Figures Test* (MFFT) developed by Jerome Kagan. On the WISC-R, it is a behavioral observation made by the examiner. Students who do the MFFT quickly and make many errors are on the "impulsive" side insofar as cognitive tempo goes, while those who are slow but accurate are called "reflective." In any random sample of students, about one-third will fall into the "impulsive" end of the scale. The planning and scanning strategies of such students is often unsystematic, random, and global. Most often, such students do not "stop and think." This can cause problems in three ways:[27]

1. The student may not comprehend the problem sufficiently to recall relevant past experience.

2. The student may have the previous experience relevant to the problem, but fail to recall it, and/or

3. The student may not be in the habit of relying on past experience to guide present behavior.

If students are impulsive, it also implies that they are failing to inhibit an immediate response. They are acting without fully analyzing the options. This may result from a reluctance or inability to:[28]

1. Engage in search-and-scan activities,

2. Generate response alternatives, and

3. Delay actions until consequences are evaluated.

On the WISC-R, the examiner might note many instances of "impulsivity," all the way from such behaviors as grabbing the stopwatch the instant the student enters the examining room, to rapid, inaccurate scanning on Picture Completion, to rapid, haphazard planning on Mazes, to quickly saying, "I don't know," to any questions where no answer immediately comes to the student's mind. This kind of behavior leads to an underestimate of the student's potential.

Where behavior and teacher comments warrant a hypothesis of "impulsivity," appropriate educational activities need to be recommended. The whole field of cognitive behavior modification comes to bear here. Impulsive students typically do not plan well. Therefore, remedial attempts need to focus on helping the student to stop and think. Talking-out-loud, self-instruction, self-control, and modeling techniques are some of the means by which this can be accomplished.

Planning Ability

Closely related to conceptual tempo is planning ability. The inability to plan and organize is a pervasive characteristic of learning-disabled and low-achieving students, and can be viewed as part of the student's style or approach to problem-solving.

On the WISC-R, low scores on Picture Arrangement and Mazes may reflect poor planning ability.[29] However, I find this term a little too global.. Moreover, many students whom I have tested do *not* have significant strengths or weaknesses on these two subtests in terms of the actual scaled scores, yet are very poor at planning in a classroom situation. In fact, some of them seem to achieve quite high scaled scores on Mazes, especially—but nevertheless display erratic planning skills on other WISC-R tasks or in the classroom.

What, then, *is* "planning"? Two researchers, Carole Kops and Ira Belmont, devised an interesting experiment to help isolate which features of planning were difficult for a group of second-grade low achievers (LA) and average (or better) achievers (AA). Twenty LAs were paired with 20 AAs in terms of age, PPVT and DAP scores, sex, and social class. Each student had to perform five classroom-like tasks and two standardized tasks—Mazes from the WPPSI, and the *Trail*

Making Test. Overall, the LAs scored significantly worse on the five classroom tasks in terms of (a) the number of trips taken to complete the tasks, (b) number of correct items brought on the first trip, and (c) time taken to complete the task. The LAs scored significantly *higher* on Mazes, however, but significantly worse on the *Trail Making Test*. To give you some idea of the task requirements in the study, the instructions for Task I were as follows:[30]

> Task I: (Showing picture display board) "These are some of the materials we would need if we were to make a cake today: a pan, mixing bowl, mixing spoon, measuring cup, and cake mix (pointing to each item on the display board). You will find all of these around the room. Can you find them? Bring them back and place them over here (pointing to a place on the examiner's table) in exactly the same order as these" (indicating the picture display board).

The authors discuss the poorer results of the LAs in terms of planning with reference to:

1. Planning and set
2. Planning and spatial organization
3. Planning and language
4. Planning and memory
5. Planning and attention

I would like to discuss these findings briefly in each of these areas, since I believe there are implications for teaching.

Planning and set. The authors give the following interpretation of the differential performance of the two groups in terms of set:[31]

> Children of both groups appeared to begin the tasks by attempting to recall all of the items. The average school achievers showed better recall ability than the low achievers as shown by their bringing both more correct items and fewer incorrect ones on the first trip. Crucial for success, however, was the children's subsequent performance, after their return with items on the first trip, since the task was still incomplete. On failing to bring all the necessary items at one time, most average achievers directly consulted the pictures on the display board to remind themselves of missing items. This can be seen as a shift in strategy (plan) from a set for total recall to a set for incorporating the pictures as an integral part of the task .... The low achievers appeared unable to entertain an alternative method (to change set) and tended to be bound to the original, more demanding strategy (to remember all of the items and use the pictures only as a "crutch").

Many school psychologists are familiar with the term "perseveration," or an inability to switch sets. Some of this kind of behavior is displayed on the WISC-R. It seems to me that the inability to switch sets is a metacognitive one, so that pairing a student who has difficulty switching sets with one who does not would be an effective remedial strategy in terms of peer modeling. If that proved ineffective, then more direct teaching and thinking-out-loud by the teacher or a peer could prove helpful.

Planning and spatial organization. On Mazes, the LAs did *better*. The authors interpreted this as a possible strength in solving visual, nonverbal tasks, in contrast to the language-related, school-type tasks involved in the study. They also felt the AAs had developed more careful work habits, which they applied even when it resulted in less efficient (in terms of speed) performance. They did not feel it was because of impulsivity, in this instance.

Planning and language. Trail-making is a language-related spatial task. Here, the LAs took longer to complete the task, and received lower scores. While doing this task, the authors note that the LA students talked aloud more frequently, and asked more questions about what was to be done. Relating this to language and planning, they say:[32]

> Meichenbaum and Goodman found that the expression of overt language developmentally precedes the use of covert language in problem solving, a developmental sequence postulated earlier by Vygotsky and developed further by Luria. Low achievers could be said to

be at a lower language developmental level than are average achievers. Such deficient or lagging language development could be a critical factor in the poorer organizational skills shown by the low school achievers. This is of particular importance if one accepts the view developed by Vygotsky that by school entrance age, language has taken on a dominant role in initiating, directing, regulating, and organizing cognitive functions and behavior.

Planning and memory. Low achievers evidence poorer memory on the school-like tasks, in that they brought fewer correct items and more incorrect ones on the first trip of each task. But:[33]

> . . . It may not be poorer memory alone that was the basis of poorer performance by the low achievers, but, rather, less flexibility in reorganizing the tasks . . . . The low achievers' continued attempt to recall all of the items may have created an additional burden leading to poorer organization (or partial disorganization), thus producing memory "failure," which was a critical variable illustrated by an average achiever who unhesitatingly and quickly from the beginning brought one item at a time as she consulted the display board each time to determine which item was to be sought next.

However, on the *Trail Making Test* it is probable that slower and poorer recall of the sequence of numbers and letters was central to the low achievers' performance.

Planning and attention. Planning in part also means being able to direct one's attention appropriately to the task at hand and is described thus:[34]

> Directed attention . . . concerns the controlled, sequential shifting of focus from one task element to the next until the task is completed. For this, the child must be able to (a) develop an end goal, (b) develop related subgoals, and (c) maintain these simultaneously in relation to each other as each subgoal is achieved. The child must be able to redirect attention in an orderly fashion, searching first for selected objects and when found to discard it (them) as a focus while shifting attention to the remaining objects as a new focus and so on, all within the context of achieving the end goal.

Low achieving students do not have an independent attentional deficit, according to the authors of the above study, but rather a:[35]

> . . . failure to develop a more effective strategy which led to less well-organized direction and redirection of attention. Yet, where their approach was more adequate to the task (Mazes) the low achievers selected, organized, and sequenced the relevant elements more effectively than did the average achievers.

And they conclude, with reference to planning and attention, that:[36]

> . . . The low achieving children were able to maintain goal direction, decide on a course of action, and monitor and check their performance sufficiently well to complete the tasks. However, they tended not to redefine or alter their original course to improve efficiency.

In light of all of the foregoing, the authors conclude:[37]

> . . . that planning and organizing is not a unitary set of skills but is, instead, developed in relation to specific cognitive functions. If so, the issue of understanding low achievement is more complicated than now envisioned, and requires careful delineation of the particular demands of given tasks and the related cognitive and strategic competencies required of the child.

And the major implication in terms of teaching is that:[38]

> It requires that we search both for specific cognitive inadequacies underlying poor learning and for related deficient or inadequate methods used in organizing, retrieving, and using knowledge. This duality of skills requires increased attention to the creation of teaching methods which help the child to link specific material to be learned with methods for organizing, storing, and using knowledge.

As you can see, this kind of analysis is *far* more helpful than a global diagnosis of "attention deficit disorder." The implications for the school psychologist seem to be consistent with the kinds of strategies advocated in this book.[39] In particular, in terms of planning, it implies that teacher modeling by thinking-out-loud, followed by the student doing the same, is an important one. *However, the thinking-out-loud strategy needs to be adjusted to the specific task demands being made on the student at the time.* These will vary from classroom to classroom, as well as from task to task.

Finally, one of the major controversies in the learning disabilities literature at the moment is whether or not such students have a "strategy" or a "capacity" deficit. The results of this study indicate that the two are closely linked, and the search for strategies to remediate both kinds of problems needs to continue.

Right- and Left-Brain Processes

There has been considerable neurological work done in the last 15 years to create a simplistic notion of right- and left-hemisphere specialization. When I say "simplistic," I mean that many people—educators included—now think that the left hemisphere does x and the right hemisphere does y in some sort of autonomous way. It is true that there are certain activities that are specialized or favored by one hemisphere or the other, but we cannot neglect the fact that the brain works in an integrated fashion all the time. All learning involves both hemispheres, though the activity of one hemisphere for certain tasks may be higher. But the hemispheres always act in concert.

If you refresh your memory right now by looking back at the Bilateral Cooperative Reading Model, I think you will see what I mean. The right and left tracks (which are associated with the right and left hemispheres at the higher processing levels) must work in a cooperative, integrated fashion for efficient learning of reading.

On the WISC-R, two subtests on the Performance Scale seem to involve primarily right-hemisphere functioning. They are Picture Completion and Object Assembly.[40] The other subtests involve primarily integrated functioning. Occasionally, one does come across WISC-R profiles, such as the one shown in Figure 6.5, where such a split seems educationally relevant.

This particular student, as you can see, did exceptionally well on the integrated subtests:

Right Brain	*Integrated*
PC = 6	PA = 12
OA = 7	BD = 14
	Cd = 15
	M = 19
Avg. = 7	Avg. = 15
(Percentile 16)	(Percentile 95)

Additionally, this student shows Verbal Conceptualization which is solidly in the average range.

It's possible to teach reading comprehension using some integrated strategies. I will review three from a journal article which I find appealing.[41]

Strategy 1—Predicting Maps

I have said that predicting is an integral and important aspect of mature reading. A prediction map is like a semantic map, only it conceptualizes the internal process of prediction/revision on the chalkboard. Seeing the process charted this way would, I think, appeal to both hemispheres, so to speak. Sources of information from both the student (reader-based inferences) and the text (text-based inferences) are integrated. The process, when drawn out, might look like the one shown in Figure 6.6.[42]

FIGURE 6.5. Picture Completion / Object Assembly split in WISC-R profile.

FIGURE 6.6. A prediction map.

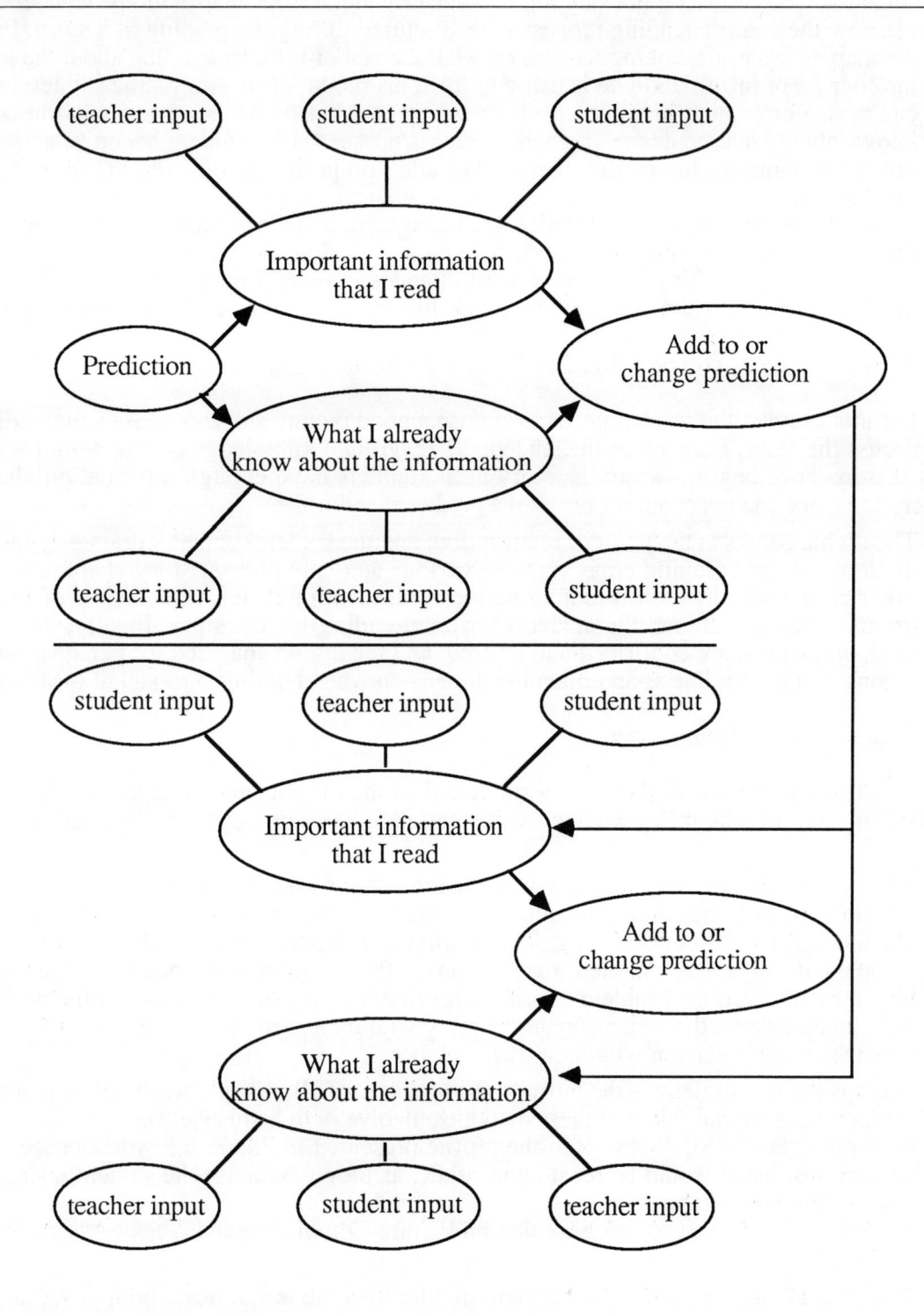

From: Walker, B. 1985. Right-brained strategies for teaching comprehension. *Academic Therapy* (November) 21:2, p. 137.

It is described as follows:[43]

Initially, the teacher takes an active role by mapping her own constructive process of comprehending as the story is read. The predictions, important textual information, and personal interpretations are mapped interchangeably in the flow chart with the teacher modeling how the comprehending process is restructured during the reading of a story. In using the map, teacher questioning focuses on what the reader is understanding about the text and the sources of information he is using to form his model of meaning. She suggests that he can revise or expand his prediction according to what he has read and what he already knows about what he has read. As the process proceeds, the student becomes actively involved in building his model of meaning and comparing it with the author's intended meaning.

In this technique, the information is displayed in a visuo-spatial orientation and offers the reader more flexibility of options, revisions, and additions during the reading of a story . . . . This engages his divergent, yet simultaneous processing of verbal information and displays his information in a spatial organization which is similar to his thinking style.

Strategy 2—Story Dramatizing, Emphasizing Predicting

For this activity, the teacher needs to choose a good picture storybook. As a prereading activity, discuss the story, drawing in the students' background knowledge as you would with any reading lesson. Then begin reading the story until students have enough information about the characters and story line to act out (dramatize) a predicted ending:[44]

The drama begins at the point of interruption, and the students actually dramatize their predictions in a roleplaying experience as various students present story characters. In the process of dramatization, predictions are revised through the roleplaying of the story drama. After the drama, the students write an ending for the story. Finally, the story is read, predictions are confirmed and revised, and the drama analyzed for personal interpretations of the story line as an influential dimension when building a model of meaning.

Strategy 3—Guided Imagery

This technique involves choosing a story, and taking the students through a guided "mental journey" designed to evoke their own internal images about the story. Specifically, Barbara Walker writes:[45]

The story is read in a calm, serene voice using many pauses so the imagery of the journey can flow through the conscious mind of the student. Usually, the student's eyes are closed and the lights are dimmed. The guided journey is left open-ended so that the students can complete the experience in their imaginations. After the journey is complete, students write how they resolved the problem . . . . As a result of writing how they solved the problem in their imaginations, the students read the story with increased involvement in order to compare the author's version with their own.

Perhaps the last strategy is the most "right-brained" of all, though the distinction, as I have noted, is somewhat artificial. Most of these activities involve both hemispheres.

In terms of the WISC-R results in the profile presented in Figure 6.5, you can see that the three strategies just listed would be most appropriate, as they would use the student's strength in the integrated brain functioning areas.

But *why* is the student so much weaker on Picture Completion and Object Assembly? Alan Kaufman writes:[46]

The right hemisphere seems to be more mature than the left at birth, both physiologically and functionally, and is also a more pervasive force in the very early stages of life. An infant perceives and learns nonverbally, sensorily, and spatially to a large extent during the first year of life, styles of learning that are congruent with the processing mode of the right cerebral hemisphere. Although less mature than the right brain, the left brain is more adaptable at birth and has the capacity of subsuming complex and analytic functions. The greater adaptability of the left hemisphere may conceivably render it unusually vulnerable to the impact of cultural deprivation. Hence disadvantaged children may have a right-brain leaning, at least in part, because of the resilience of the right hemisphere in the face of deprived environmental conditions.

Here, we have a student exhibiting the opposite pattern—an integrated, rather than a right-hemisphere leaning. Did this student not rely on the right hemisphere during infancy? That explanation seems unlikely. Is there a subtle, neurological right-hemisphere deficit? Without neurological testing, it's not even possible to begin to answer that question, and was not done in this case.

The importance of the right hemisphere to reading, however, is said to be as follows:[47]

The right hemisphere may be indispensable in beginning reading when children are learning to recognize letters and words as gestalts. The left hemisphere meanwhile may convert these symbols into phonological units and into meaning.

This explanation seems to apply to the student we are discussing. He had to have a special program within the classroom in first grade which emphasized sight word acquisition, where he was very weak right from the start. Once he learned the word, his teacher notes, he seemed to remember it. He continued to struggle with reading, however. The WISC-R that you see in Figure 6.5 was administered when he was in fourth grade. He was in the school's resource room program at the time. His resource teacher said that Michael (a pseudonym, of course) seems to have difficulty when meeting new words, such as polysyllabic ones. His predicting in reading is sometimes meaningless; and, despite his good verbal ability, he has trouble with some word meanings, such as the meaning of the word "moccasin." He did not recognize this word in context; but, even when he did, he did not know what it meant.

The resource teacher continues to emphasize meaning and predicting in reading, and finds visualization a good strategy with him. She continues to emphasize the meaning-base of words with him. Michael is making gains in reading, but also continues to require extra assistance, and is still well behind in his reading. Does the "right-brain weakness" make the transfer of symbols into meaning more difficult for him?

Finally, it is important to state again that the WISC-R profile *cannot* be used to diagnose "brain damage" in either hemisphere. If the examiner feels a pattern and/or the student's behavior is peculiar, and there is other evidence (such as history of trauma) to indicate the possibility, then of course a neuropsychological referral should be made.

Letteri's Approach

Charles Letteri has developed a very comprehensive and intriguing approach to the field of learning styles. Even though his approach does not use the WISC-R per se, I would like to provide an overview for the reader.

So far, I have discussed each of the cognitive style variables suggested by WISC-R profiles and behavioral observations as single variables. Students can be grouped as simultaneous/successive, impulsive/reflective, and so on. What happens, though, when we combine some of these constructs? In other words, instead of treating them as unidimensional variables, treat them as a multidimensional composite. That is Letteri's approach. Using it, he shows that there are characteristic profiles which can be used to classify students in terms of academic achievement with a high degree of accuracy. He calls the profiles Type 1, Type 2, and Type 3. Each is described as follows:[48]

The Type 1 cognitive profile, significantly associated with high achievement levels in academic performance as measured by standardized tests, indicates a subject articulated in a majority of the following dimensions: analytical, focuser, narrow, complex, reflective, sharpener, tolerant. [Note: I have not discussed many of these cognitive styles in this book.] The Type 3 cognitive profile, significantly associated with low achievement levels in academic performance as measured by standardized tests, indicates a subject articulated in a majority of the following dimensions: global, nonfocuser, broad, simple, impulsive, leveler, intolerant. The Type 2 cognitive profile, significantly associated with average academic achievement performance, is either a nonarticulated profile, that is not articulated at either extreme of the seven cognitive dimensions, or is a mixed profile indicating an inconsistent pattern or articulation with no majority matching a Type 1 or Type 3 profile.

The remedial implications of this approach are the ones of most interest to school psychologists. Letteri writes:[49]

In contrast to current research that attempts to identify learning deficits on the basis of a unidimensional construct, the cognitive profile can accurately identify those specific dimensions of subjects' thinking and learning patterns that contribute significantly to their levels of academic performance. As a result, teachers or other professionals have an accurate statement concerning where the specific deficit is located and can direct their efforts in a more focused and efficient manner to help ameliorate learning deficits. As a result of continuing research, specific strategies and materials have been developed that are capable of augmenting an individual's cognitive profile, that is, moving an individual's articulation from a Type 2 or Type 3 profile to a Type 1 profile. In doing so, an individual's thinking and learning pattern becomes compatible with academic tasks. Results, thus far, indicate that for subjects included in the experimental augmentation group ($N = 10$), as opposed to the control group ($N = 20$), augmented profiles did move from a Type 3 profile to a Type 1 profile with a corresponding significant ($p = .01$) change in achievement scores.

I, for one, am looking forward to hearing more from Dr. Charles Letteri and his Center for Cognitive Studies. The implications for education are exciting. He says:[50]

. . . The curriculum for school-age children should . . . incorporate this information, so that while we build on children's strengths, we can accurately and specifically designate their weaknesses and employ efficient strategies to change these weaknesses to additional strengths. In doing so, every child can hope to have equal intellectual access to learning materials and environments and not just the equal opportunity to sit in their presence.

Level III Interpretation:
Subtest-Specific Strengths and Weaknesses

Kaufman suggests that any subtest which deviates ± 3 points from its respective Verbal or Performance average be considered a significant strength or weakness respectively. He also recommends that, when subtests are grouped together into a cluster, that all the subtests which fall into that grouping be at or above the average for that scale. So, for example, if Picture Completion, Block Design, and Object Assembly suggests a field-dependent interpretation, then each of the scaled scores in that cluster should be below the Performance average or close to it for that student (as well as being significantly lower than the average for the other three subtests, of course). If the cluster suggests field independence, then the opposite holds. Each of the subtests should be at or above the Performance average for that student. If they are not, then some of the hypotheses suggested by Sattler in the list following the next paragraph of text may be worth checking out.

At this point the examiner may want to compare certain of the WISC-R subtests with each other. Sattler provides examples, following. They are not meant to be exhaustive, nor are they meant to do anything more than *suggest* a hypothesis concerning a student. (There are *no* studies of which I am aware which confirm or deny these hypotheses.) Further observations or testing or sources of information may be necessary to verify or confirm any of them. Furthermore, the educational implications need to be drawn out by the artistry of the examiner. To aid in more hypothesis-generation (but with the foregoing cautions in mind), Sattler suggests the following:[51]

1. Information and Comprehension. This is a comparison of the amount of information retained (Information) and the ability to use information (Comprehension). Information requires factual knowledge, while Comprehension requires both factual knowledge and judgment.
    - I > C: High Information and low Comprehension may suggest that children have general knowledge but are not able to synthesize and use information to solve problems involving the social world.
    - I < C: Low Information and high Comprehension may suggest that children have been limited in their exposure to factual material, but use their limited knowledge to make appropriate judgments.
2. Comprehension and Arithmetic. Both the Comprehension and Arithmetic subtests require reasoning ability or, more specifically, the ability to analyze a given set of material and then to recognize the elements that are needed for the solution for the specified problem.
    - C > A: High Comprehension and low Arithmetic may suggest that reasoning ability is adequate in social situations but not in situations involving numbers.
3. Arithmetic and Digit Span. Both the Arithmetic and Digit Span subtests require facility with numbers and ability in immediate recall. Comparing the two subtests may provide an index of the relative balance between attention (Digit Span) and concentration (Arithmetic).
    - DS > A: High Digit Span and low Arithmetic may suggest that attention is better developed than concentration.
4. Similarities and Comprehension.
    - S > C: High Similarities and low Comprehension may suggest that children have the ability to do abstract thinking but cannot apply their conceptualizing ability to solve problems in the social world.
5. Vocabulary and Similarities. Both Vocabulary and Similarities measure level of abstract thinking and ability to form concepts, but Similarities is a better measure of these abilities.
    - S > V: High Similarities and low Vocabulary may suggest that children have the mental ability to do abstract thinking but have had restricted opportunities to learn new words.
6. Vocabulary, Information, and Comprehension.
    - V,I > C: High Vocabulary and Information coupled with low Comprehension may suggest that the individuals are not able to use fully their verbal facility and general knowledge in life situations; they therefore may have impaired judgment.
7. Digit Span—Forward versus Backward.
    - DS(F) > DS(B): High Digits Forward and low Digits Backward may indicate that the child did not put forth the extra effort needed to master the more difficult task of recalling digits backward in sequence.
    - DS(B) > DS(F): High Digits Backward and low Digits Forward may occur when children see Digits Backward as a challenge rather than as a task which consists of a mere repetition of numbers.
8. Similarities and Digit Span.
    - S > DS: High Similarities and low Digit Span may reflect good conceptualizing ability coupled with poor rote auditory memory for digits. Children with this pattern may do poorly in acquiring reading decoding skills that are highly dependent on

memorization of sound-symbol relationships. However, their listening comprehension may be strong.

9. Comprehension and Picture Arrangement. Both the Comprehension and Picture Arrangement subtests contain stimuli that are concerned with social interaction. Scores on the two subtests permit comparison of knowledge of social conventions (Comprehension) with the capacity to anticipate and plan in a social context (Picture Arrangement).
   - PA > C: High Picture Arrangement coupled with low Comprehension may indicate that the individuals are sensitive to interpersonal nuances, but disregard social conventions.
   - C > PA: An adequate Comprehension score coupled with a poor Picture Arrangement score suggests that the children can understand social situations in the abstract, but once they are involved in them they may be unable to decide what they may mean or how to act.

10. Picture Completion and Picture Arrangement. This comparison provides an estimate of attention to detail versus organization of detail. Both tasks involve perception of details, with Picture arrangement requiring logical ordering of details or sequencing.
    - PC > PA: High Picture Completion and low Picture Arrangement may suggest that perception of details in nonsequencing tasks is better developed than that in tasks requiring sequencing and organization.

11. Picture Completion and Block Design. This comparison involves an estimate of visual perception versus visual-motor-spatial coordination.
    - PC > BD: High Picture Completion and low Block Design may suggest that children have adequate nonspatial visual perceptual ability but have difficulty in spatial visualization.

12. Object Assembly and Picture Arrangement. This comparison provides an estimate of inductive reasoning versus sequencing. Both tasks require synthesis into wholes without a model to follow, with Picture Arrangement involving sequencing in addition.
    - OA > PA: High Object Assembly and low Picture Arrangement may suggest that visual inductive reasoning skills are better developed than visual sequencing skills.

13. Object Assembly and Block Design. This comparison provides an estimate of inductive reasoning (Object Assembly—working from parts to a whole) versus deductive reasoning (Block Design—working from a whole to parts). Both tasks involve perceptual organization and spatial visualization ability.
    - OA > BD: If Object Assembly is higher than Block Design, it may suggest that nonverbal inductive reasoning skills are better developed than nonverbal deductive reasoning skills.

14. Block Design, Object Assembly, and Coding. The Block Design, Object Assembly, and Coding subtests require visual-motor coordination; that is, they involve motor activity guided by visual organization. A visual direction is involved in the execution of the tasks. The role of visual organization differs in the three subtests. In the Block Design subtest, visual organization is involved in a process consisting of analysis (breaking down the pattern) and synthesis (building the pattern up again out of the blocks). In the Object Assembly subtest, the motor action consists of arranging parts into a meaningful pattern. In the Coding subtest, visual organization is of the same kind that is found in such activities as writing or drawing. Thus, the name "visual organization" does not refer to the same function in every case.

- BD > Co: High Block Design and low Coding may suggest that visual organization skills involving analysis and synthesis are better than those involving visual-motor coordination.

Once the clustering of subtests into the various learning style categories has been sifted through, and the various groupings such as those in the foregoing list have been analyzed, there may remain some profiles which simply have some subtests which are significantly elevated or depressed, and which do not seem to fit into any particular larger grouping. At this point it may be necessary to give a subtest-specific interpretation. For example, if the student has Similarities and Arithmetic as the only two subtests significantly elevated on the Verbal scale, then these could reflect specific strengths in abstract categorical reasoning and mental computational skills respectively. (See Table 1.1).

Level IV Interpretation:
Patterns within a Subtest

There is not a great deal to say about interpretation at this level. The examiner should be alert to the student who is internally inconsistent on a subtest. For example, if a student gets the first two items wrong on the Picture Arrangement subtest, then the next two correct, and the next three wrong, it may suggest attentional problems or perhaps anxiety about the item content of certain social situations. The same holds true for the other subtests. On Information, as another example, if the student shows an erratic pattern of correct and incorrect responses, and obtains the same scaled score or raw score as another student the same age who simply reaches the ceiling of five incorrect in a row with no previous errors, the former student may have higher "potential." Again, perhaps anxiety or knowledge of certain items tapped by the questions may be missing, and is interfering with test performance. Look at the item content to see specifically if there are certain *kinds* of problems the student consistently gets incorrect before categorically stating that he or she has a "weakness in background knowledge."

This type of interpretation of the WISC-R is very close to, and perhaps indistinguishable from, Level V interpretation, to which we now turn.

Chapter 7

Level V WISC-R Interpretation

Most school psychologists simply do not have time to go through an item-by-item analysis of WISC-R responses. They should have some background on this kind of analysis, however, and be aware of additional hypotheses such an examination reveals.

There is one very excellent reference for this chapter from which I will be quoting extensively. That is Shawn Cooper's book, *The Clinical Use and Interpretation of the Wechsler Intelligence Scale for Children–Revised*.[1] Cooper goes through an exhaustive, question-by-question analysis of every WISC-R item. I cannot go into, nor is there any need, for the same detail as Cooper gives. School psychologists should consult Cooper's book if they want more information in this regard. What I *will* do, is highlight, subtest by subtest, some important Level V considerations for each.

Level V analysis truly changes the WISC-R administration and interpretation from a static to a dynamic nature. It is this aspect which also illustrates how much WISC-R interpretation is truly the "art of synthesis," based on the knowledge and experience of the examiner.

Even though the actual administration of the WISC-R alternates Verbal with Performance subtests, I have found it more useful for this chapter to discuss all the Verbal subtests, and then, all the Performance ones.

Verbal Subtests

Information

In Chapter 4, I introduced you to Cooper's general classification of the Information questions into various categories. This classification is useful in determining *which* background items a student has difficulties in. For example, many students I have assessed seem to have difficulty with the time, number, and directionality items (depending on their age). This could provide the impetus to offer or suggest to the teacher that such concepts be reinforced for that student. The same recommendation can be given to parents, some of whom do not directly show their children how the calendar works, how the year is divided into months, days, and weeks, as well as more subtle concepts such as "leap year." Since the Information subtest contains items which are directly teachable, this is a reasonable line-of-approach. The purpose, however, is not to teach to the WISC-R subtest, but to help fill important voids which may exist for a particular student in critical areas of background knowledge.

Additionally, *how* the student handles each subtest can be observed.

For example, if the student says the items are very easy, it may indicate, Cooper says, a bolstering of "... his own sense of adequacy in anticipation of questions he may be unable to answer."[2]

Or, if the student says he "doesn't know" the answer to a question, is this a simple statement of fact, or did the student make this statement a little *too* quickly, indicating a careless or incomplete memory search, or impulsivity? To what extent does it affect the WISC-R score? If many of the student's responses are impulsive, the WISC-R score definitely underestimates the student's ability.

Another frequent response is, "We haven't taken that yet," or, "My teacher hasn't taught that yet," or some similar kind of response. This response may indicate an avoidance or denial of personal responsibility in learning. Is this a characteristic of this student? Useful supplementary tests to investigate this hypothesis include the *IAR Scale*, or perhaps a locus-of-control measure.[3] Perhaps the student just shrugs, rather than directly saying, "I don't know." Again, is this avoiding the admission of a perceived personal inadequacy?

Perhaps the student does say, "I don't know," but feels badly about it. This is generally communicated nonverbally and should be noted on the protocol.

Perhaps the student guesses. Is this good risk-taking on the student's part? If the guesses are unusual or bizarre, what's going on? Is the student trying to impress you? Is the student simply too uncomfortable to admit that there are things that he just doesn't know?

What is the student's reaction to several failures in a row? To success? To praise? Does the student quickly retreat and show discouragement? Is there an obvious positive reaction to praise and a negative one to failure? Does this mean the student is unnecessarily externally motivated? If so, the distinction between *praise* and *encouragement* made by several writers, may be an important one for the teacher. A praise statement such as, "That's great," "You're a good student," etc., may be used excessively by a parent or teacher. The student then becomes "hooked on praise," so to speak, and begins to feel his own worthiness *depends on meeting someone else's standards*. Encouragement, on the other hand, is an acknowledgment of effort. It focuses on the student's strengths, his progress; and it helps the student evaluate his own efforts.[4] Phrases like, "I like the way you handled that," "I'm glad you're happy with your work," and "Your drawing makes me feel happy; how do you feel about it?" are ones which show your acceptance and are apt to help the student become more internally motivated. I do not mean that praise should never be used. It is important, in my experience, that students know when standards *are* being met. Some students, however, are excessively competitive; and with them, encouraging statements may help temper some of the excess zeal. They are also very useful with students who do not experience much in the way of academic success. For such students, encouraging effort and helping them recognize the gains they are making, is very important.

Cooper also suggests that, for each WISC-R subtest, there are responses which may indicate psychopathology, anxiety, or defensiveness. Although certain responses on the WISC-R may indicate disturbances in cognitive processing or affect, once again, by themselves, they cannot be used to diagnose any particular condition. Examiners need to be very cautious in giving a teacher any feedback about a student's possible "abnormal responses." If the examiner suspects psychopathology, then an appropriate clinical referral needs to be made.

With that important caveat, Cooper suggests that the content of some students' responses may indicate very distorted ideas, concepts, or beliefs. *Be cautious with your own values* and how they may be influencing your interpretations, however.

Very confused responses that seemingly have nothing to do with the question also may indicate disordered thought. Again, though, cautious probing is very necessary to determine what, exactly, the student has meant. Many students' responses are seemingly bizarre on the surface, but may make perfect sense, once the student is given the opportunity to explain himself.

Additional Examiner Strategies

Cooper makes, I think, one very good suggestion regarding the Information subtest, and that is to time the response time—the interval between the question asked and beginning of the student's answer. This can be very important, since some students simply need more processing time to come up with an appropriate answer. The teacher can encourage higher-level cognitive thinking by increasing her own "wait-time" in between asking questions of students. This concept has been well researched and has some important educational implications. For example, in a typical reading lesson, the following occurs:[5]

1. In an average 25-minute reading lesson, a teacher will ask 36 questions, or, about one question every 43 seconds.

2. Some 63 to 75 percent of the questions are "text-based," requiring mainly literal recall. The remainder are "scriptal-based," and require higher-level processing on the part of the students. Higher-level processing requires more *time*, however.

3. Once a teacher asks a question, *less than one second* of "think-time" is given before the teacher asks another question or another student. This is clearly inadequate. Research

shows that waiting four to five seconds is necessary, and clearly improves student responding.

4. Worse, "high ability reading groups" receive a better balance of text versus scriptal questions (about 50%/50%), but the average and low groups receive significantly fewer scriptal questions.

There are also large individual differences in "think-time" for students. I recall examining many students whose response times were exceedingly slow. This information, together with the research data on "wait-time," is clearly important in making recommendations to a teacher about a specific student.

The strategy of timing the student can be used, obviously, for any of the WISC-R subtests. Is there a discrepancy between "think-time" for some subtests over others? If so, what implications are there for the student in a specific classroom setting?

Similarities

Because of a 2, 1, or zero scoring system on this subtest, examiners may miss some of the verbal classification possibilities. Students do grow in classification skills with age, and their concepts can be stretched by teaching activities.

Sylvia Farnham-Diggory provides a good description of various types of verbal groupings:[6]

1. Superordinate Concept Formation. (E.g.) "Orange and peach are the same because they are both fruits." The superordination may also be itemized by the student (e.g.), "A banana you eat, and a peach you eat, too." This type of superordination is less generalized than the first. (It is a more concrete response and, of course, receives a lower score on the WISC-R.)

2. Complex Formulations. In these types of responses, the student selects one attribute and tries to group the other items using the same attribute. There are five different kinds of complex formulations:

    a. Association complex. (E.g.) "A bell makes a sound and a drum does, too."

    b. Key ring complex. (E.g.) "A bell is silver and sometimes a drum is, too."

    c. Edge matching complex. This consists of forming associations between pairs of words which then pile up in linked pairs. These formations are easier to observe when there are three or more items to be classified. Since there are only two stimulus items on each question of the Similarities subtest, this formation cannot easily be observed. But let's suppose the student had to tell you why an apple, peach, and potato were the same. An edge matching response might be, "Apple and peach look alike; potato and peach are round."

    d. Collection complex. The student finds an attribute that relates the pair, but does not quite make the link. (E.g.) "A grape is purple and a pineapple is yellow."

    e. Multiple grouping complex. Again, several stimulus words are necessary to observe this type of grouping. What the student does, is form several subgroups, but the bridge among them is not built. Suppose the list consisted of banana, peach, meat, and milk. An example of a multiple grouping complex would be: "A banana and peach, you eat; meat and milk, you drink."

3. Thematic Groupings. This kind of grouping is the lowest form of classification. In fact, it is not classification at all. It relates two or more items in some idiosyncratic way, usually in the form of a story (e.g., "A boat and a car are the same because you can pull the boat with your car").

Research clearly shows that, as students grow older, their groupings definitely move from complex formations to superordinate ones. However, teaching activities designed to enhance and encourage classification and sorting can be done by the teacher. One excellent strategy is the Word Bank and Word Sort described more fully in Appendix 5-1. For example, a teacher can have the students find all the . . .

- Color words
- Feeling words
- Food words
- Listening words, etc.

. . . from their banks. Such sorts are called closed sorts. In an open sort, the student is asked to form a classification scheme of his own (a more difficult task). Students can share their groupings and the types of formations just listed can be more closely observed by the teacher.

In terms of affective states and the Similarities subtests, watch for responses like "they burn you" for item number 2, and "they're enemies" for item number 7. Cooper suggests that the student's handling of the task in such cases is being dominated by aggressive or anxious feelings. However, I think that this hypothesis should be cross-checked by the examiner by other WISC-R items (item number 6 on the Comprehension subtest is particularly good), and, of course, by spontaneous comments made by the student throughout the testing, and observations from significant others in the student's life.

Cooper also suggests that very high scores on Similarities, in contrast to low scores on the other Verbal subtests:[7]

. . . would suggest that the individual is very much able to deal with objects or events as verbal ideas but that the individual has lacked the broader development of his/her intellectual functioning across the wide range of cognitive tasks sampled by the entire Wechsler Intelligence Scale.

Cooper calls this an indicator of psychopathology; but, again, I would be *extremely* cautious about such a hypothesis. I have seen a number of students with surprisingly elevated Similarities subtests, in contrast to the other Verbal subtests. I prefer the foregoing interpretation, but without the "psychopathological" implication.

Arithmetic

I have already discussed a number of facets of the Arithmetic subtest, particularly in regard to Level II analysis of Arithmetic as part of the Freedom from Distractibility factor.

Because most of the problems on this subtest involve mental manipulation of numbers, the subtest by itself may not correlate very well with actual classroom-based arithmetic operations. However, informally testing the limits would prove useful in some cases. For this subtest, I would suggest the following procedure.

1. If the student fails an item, go back and repeat it. If he says he "doesn't know" the answer, ask him to repeat the question (this is to test whether the difficulty is in short-term memory).
2. If the student does not know the answer, give the components, and see if the student can perform the calculation(s). Classify the errors, using Sternberg's analysis, into:
   a. Lack of metacomponent awareness (i.e., the student has no idea of what operations are to be employed to solve the problem);
   b. Lack of performance awareness (i.e., the student knows what operations are to be used, but makes a mental calculation error such as adding 10 and 18, and getting 29);

    c. Lack of learning components (i.e., the student has not learned the basics of, say, addition, to begin with).

Sometimes these distinctions become blurred; but the examiner should at least make a rough attempt at it, since the implications for teaching are different, depending on the kind of error the student is generally making.

Here is a rough classification of each *item* on the Arithmetic subtest, in terms of the operations involved:[8]

1. Basic serial counting with a visual stimulus.
2. Segmenting a set—visual stimulus present.
3. Same as item 2, but more complex because a larger set is involved.
4. Mental addition using visual information.
5. Transition item—could easily be on the Information subtest. No real math operation involved.
6. Subtraction. (Watch, on this item and others, to see if the student is using his fingers as an aid—often, students hide their hands under the table!)
7. Addition.
8. Addition with sum > 10.
9. Subtraction—2-digit number, less a 1-digit number.
10. Multiplication.
11. Multiplication with verbal complexity.
12. Subtracting 2-digit numbers.
13. Division.
14. Addition, followed by subtraction.
15. Division.
16. Multiplication.
17. Manipulating fractions.
18. Calculating simple fractions sequentially (could be simpler than item 17).

It is only by working with the regular or special education teacher, however, that the particular combination of strengths and weaknesses on each item of the subtest can be translated into remedial strategies. William Levy writes:[9]

> It is clear that the psychologist and classroom educator must attend to the presentation and response requirements of the task. Through holding the mathematical content constant and varying the presentation and response behavioral requirements of the subtest, instructional pathways are identified. The identification of the specific presentation and response combinations, which are associated with strengths and weaknesses in WISC-R Arithmetic subtest performance, possesses obvious instructional implications for both the regular and special education teacher.

This means, then, comparing and contrasting how the student performs on the Arithmetic subtest where most items are presented orally, to paper-and-pencil math, where most items are always visually present to the student.

As with other Verbal subtests, the response time of the student for each item can be noted. Individual differences will appear, of course; and inordinately lengthy response times can be noted. It is very valuable to a teacher, for example, to know that a student can properly answer the question, but that he requires extra processing time.

Testing the limits is important for some students on the WISC-R and on academic tests. An excellent set of probe questions can be found on page 53 of the manual for the *Diagnostic Achievement Battery* (Austin, Texas: Pro-Ed).

Vocabulary

Cooper notes:[10]

Glasser and Zimmerman note that Vocabulary is probably the best single measure of general intellectual level, and that it provides an indication of the child's learning ability, fund of information, richness of ideas, kind and quality of language, degree of abstract thinking, and character of thought processes. It also reflects a child's level of education and environment. The Vocabulary subtest is of value because of the qualitative aspects that may be seen in different individuals' unique definitions of the same item, which may vary in abstractness, detail, or degree of sophistication. Glasser and Zimmerman note that from the clinical point of view, the most important feature of verbal definitions is the insight they can provide into the nature of a child's thought processes, particularly among those children who display poor orientation to reality.

In terms of psychopathology, anxiety, or defensiveness, Cooper says the examiner should look to the content of the responses, particularly the kinds of associations the word has for the student. This, he says:[11]

. . . can provide information regarding the extent to which the definitions the child offers are conventional, consensually valid, or more individualistic and idiosyncratic; in this sense, the examiner can observe the extent to which the child's definitions are more typical or less typical, more normal or more deviant.

Again, though, it is very important to note that diagnosing any form of psychopathology from such responses is not valid. It is only suggestive. In my experience, it is quite common for students to give responses suggesting aggressive/hostile feelings. When they occur and fit with other descriptions from other sources about the student, then they may take on greater significance.

Another aspect of response content to watch for is any self-derogatory statements the student might make in replying to Verbal subtests, or spontaneously. They should be followed-up by the examiner. Self-concept inventories can be quite useful here for providing supplementary information and triggering a good clinical interview with the student. I have found the *Culture-Free Self-Esteem Inventories*, by Dr. James Battle, to be very useful in this respect.[12] These inventories are not time-consuming, and break the global construct of "self-esteem" into General, Academic, Parental, and Social areas. Percentile scores can be calculated for each area. Discrepancies from one area to another are clearly visible and valuable in terms of providing a direction for a recommended course of treatment. For example, a student who scores very poorly on academically-related self-esteem, but high in all other areas, will likely require a different type of support or intervention than a student who scores low in *all* areas. This inventory also has a built-in social desirability scale. It can be administered to elementary students, through high school and adult levels.

Speech articulation and syntax are other areas the examiner will be able to observe as the student responds to each item. Is the student competent in language use? Is articulation normal? If not, does it merit the attention of a speech therapist? Are the responses the student makes direct, or roundabout? Are there many associations involved that are vague? If the student does not have rapid naming ability, this may interfere to some extent with reading and writing.

Examiners also need to note the quality of responses. This is very important in terms of its relationship to the school environment. Cooper notes:[13]

. . . Even if the individual achieves, for example, a low average Vocabulary subtest score, but fails a number of definitions or obtains partial credit on a number of words, the examiner would conclude that the individual will have difficulty with a variety of language-based aspects of school learning, including reading, expressive writing, understanding complicated written or spoken instructions, and perhaps even with verbal expression. On the other hand, to the extent that the individual's Vocabulary score is average or above, one would conclude that the individual has a greater comfort in using language for understanding and/or communicating and that the individual is much more likely to be successful in various verbally weighted school subjects, such as reading, expressive writing, or various kinds of classroom discussion.

Comprehension

I find this subtest particularly valuable in providing insight into a student's knowledge of some social standards. The early items of the subtest directly ask for such knowledge or awareness of appropriate behavior in social situations.

Additionally, since rather lengthy verbal responses are required, an excellent sample of the student's facility with language is obtained. The student who gives correct responses but who requires frequent probing as the subtest allows, may be a more nonverbal communicator. This information is very valuable to a teacher who wants to know whether a student can "handle" the language arts curriculum. This particular type of student can handle the curriculum on a cognitive level much better if additional nonverbal strategies such as drama, role-playing, puppetry, and drawing are incorporated into the activity. Risk-taking in purely verbal situations, in other words, needs to be encouraged.

I have also often found that many aggressive youngsters who are referred because "they just don't seem to know social rules" in fact display a good knowledge of what they *should* do. Their difficulty lies not in lack of awareness of standards, but in complying with them.

A very useful and inexpensive resource for this particular problem is the *Getting Along with Others* program.[14] This program or relevant portions of it can easily be incorporated into resource and remedial behavioral programs as needed. It can also be used in the regular classroom program where it "fits" (such as in the Health curriculum), or for an individual or small group of students. Over 17 sessions, students are taught the basics in such skills as following directions, interrupting a conversation, joining a conversation, handling name-calling and teasing, saying "no" to stay out of trouble, etc. Another valuable portion of the program is the five teaching strategies that are suggested. Again, these strategies can be used by any teacher in a variety of classroom situations. Opportunities for transfer of the skills into home and school environments is provided and can be observed each time in the way of "homework" assignments.

If students score very low on the Comprehension subtest, they may have poorly developed social awareness and/or understanding. These youngsters, too, can profit from the kinds of skills taught in *Getting Along with Others*.

I frequently find myself watching for the locus of orientation of the student. For example, the student who consistently answers with such replies as, "Tell my Mom," has not internalized any self-responsibility. This student may be very passive and lack a good sense of an internal locus of control that is important to both social and academic success. Responses suggesting an external orientation are more common among younger students (which is normal, since the growth from externality to internality is age-related), so age should be taken into account before seriously entertaining this hypothesis. It can also be cross-checked using the IAR or similar scale.

In general, then, the responses to the Comprehension subtest allows the examiner:[15]

. . . to observe the individual's knowledge of social rules, the clarity or confusion that characterizes his/her expression of this knowledge, the certainty or uncertainty the individual displays in selecting among possible responses, and the differential response the individual may reveal in dealing with neutral or more emotionally arousing questions on this subtest.

Digit Span

Since I have covered most of the educationally relevant aspects of this subtest in other chapters, there is little to add here.

Performance Subtests

Picture Completion

One strategy I always use on this subtest is timing how long the student takes to respond to each item. This is relatively easy, of course, because the subtest itself is a timed one. From the length of time it takes the student to respond and the accuracy of the response, I make an initial judgment regarding the student's cognitive tempo (see the commentary on this in Chapter 6). This becomes a working hypothesis which I then modify in light of further observed behavior.

Another response to watch for is whether or not the student says, "I don't know," to an item, or, "There's nothing missing." If the response is the former, how quickly does the student say that? If said too quickly, it may suggest a feeling of inadequacy, together with low task persistence. This is to be distinguished from a realistic "I don't know," which is done after careful scanning, and simply reflects an honest self-appraisal in light of a difficult item. Usually, the tone and manner in which the student says, "I don't know," conveys to the examiner which of these is the more likely hypothesis. Clinical impressions, together with supplementary testing, can suggest very important avenues of remediation. Simple responses like "I don't know" can convey a wealth of meaning.

Figure 7.1 is a graphic representation of how high and low academic achievers differ in the way they judge the outcome of their efforts on a task.

In the flowchart displayed in Figure 7.1, if a student is given an arithmetic task, for example, and the student obtains the correct answer, the high achiever will typically attribute success to himself, whereas the low achiever will attribute it to something outside himself, such as luck, or the task being an easy one. Contrariwise, if the high achiever does poorly on a task, then the high achiever attributes it to task difficulty, luck, or poor effort. Hence, he is more likely to try harder the next time. The low achiever, by contrast, sees failure more as the lack of ability leading to self-punishment and negative expectations, and perhaps more likel to avoid the task in the future. Involving the student in goal setting and goal assessment, together with changing the "learned helplessness" response (see Appendix 3-4) can be very helpful.

If the student says, "There's nothing missing," he is redefining the task slightly, and projecting responsibility outside himself. If the student says, "I can't find anything missing," notice the subtle difference. The second student has accepted responsibility for himself.

Cooper makes a good point regarding the item content of Picture Completion. Items 2, 4, 6, 12, 15, 17, 19, and 25 all have human contents and ". . . hence may set off specific anxiety in the individual regarding interpersonal relationships or regarding the individual's noticing visual information or cues regarding people."[16] I talked in the previous chapter about the field-dependent/independent distinction. One strength of field dependent students is usually their "people orientation." Looking at how the student performs on the cited items (relative to their age, of course), as well as on item 4 of Object Assembly, may be helpful in providing suggestions as to a field dependent or field independent cognitive style.

Another useful supplementary test (besides the *Embedded Figures Test* mentioned earlier) in this regard is *The Bicognitive Inventory*, which has two versions.[17] One can be filled out by the teacher to determine her own degree of field independence or "field sensitivity" (these authors work from a slightly different version of Witkin's construct). The other version can be filled out by the teacher on particular students or the whole class to see how field independent or field sensitive the student is.

FIGURE 7.1. An attributional model of achievement motivation.

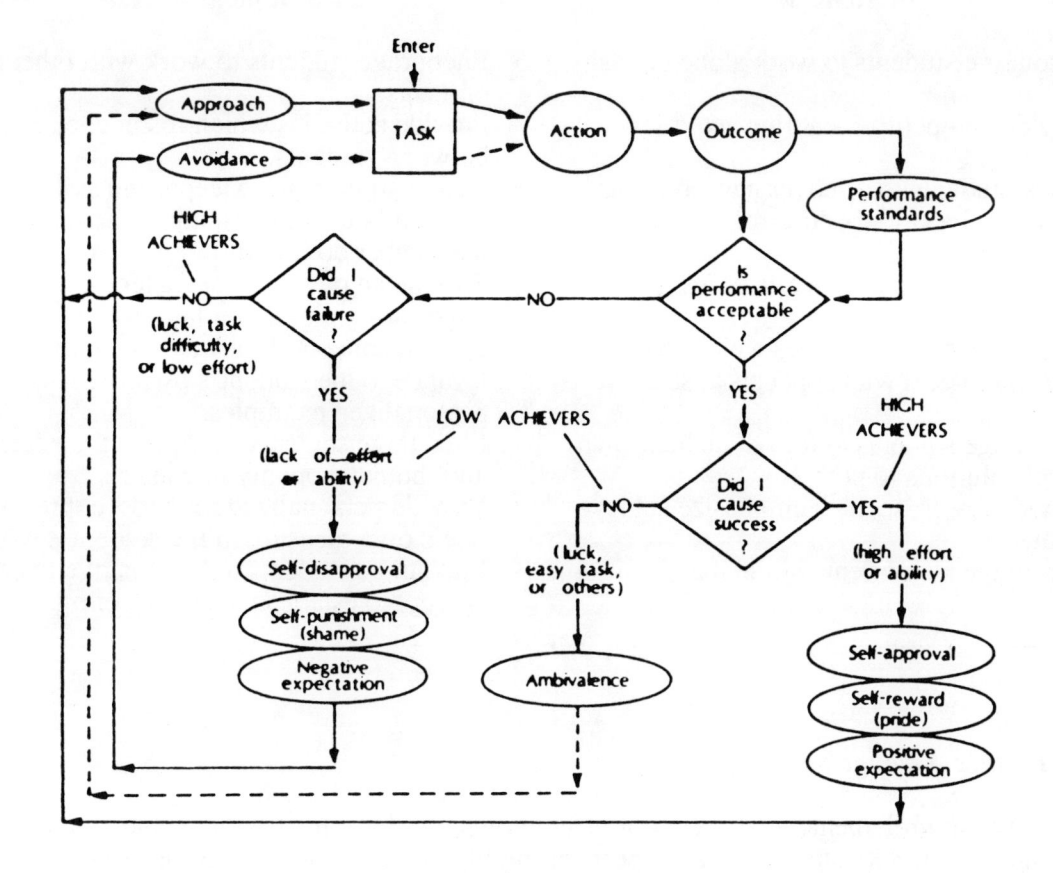

From: Cook, R. 1983. Why Jimmy doesn't try. *Academic Therapy* (November) 19:2.

    The authors suggest that teachers need to be more aware of where students are on the dimension and try to balance their teaching activities to cater to both ends of the spectrum. In particular, they suggest the strategies which follow in Figure 7.2.
    The authors emphasize, and I would agree with them, that there is no point in always trying to match a student's learning style with a similar teaching style. Students need exposure to both, to try to achieve a healthier balance.
    A further behavior I watch, as mentioned earlier, is whether or not the student names the missing items (and how quickly), or whether or not he merely points. I call this, rapid naming ability. The student who is poor at it is likely to have some difficulties with both oral expression and writing.

FIGURE 7.2. Field sensitive and field independent teaching strategies.

FI Strategies	FS Strategies
• Encourage students to work alone on tasks.	• Encourage students to work with others on tasks.
• Provide competitive learning activities.	• Provide activities which foster cooperation between students.
• Allow students to discover new concepts by tyemselves; trial-and-error.	• Demonstrate new concepts and skills personally to students; allow them to see the teacher do it first.
• Emphasize facts and details of lessons.	• Provide an overview of material, discussing major principles and relationships.
• Provide learning exercises which require students to deal with concepts abstractly.	• Present concepts in a way which has relevance to the student's own life. Use personalized examples.
• Encourage students to formulate their own novel solutions to problems.	• Encourage students to express their feelings and thoughts openly in class.
• Provide rewards which emphasize achievement.	• Provide personalized rewards, expressing one's own pleasure in the student's work.
• Encourage task-orientation in the classroom.	• Encourage students to be sensitive to others; attempt to establish a group feeling.

Picture Arrangement

A worthwhile behavior for school psychologists to look for on this subtest is whether or not the student "thinks out loud" while performing the tasks. This information is valuable to the teacher, since thinking-out-loud can be an aid to problem solving in some situations. It also gives the examiner some ideas as to the student's level of "internal language." If the student uses a lot of thinking-out-loud, it suggests a certain immaturity in the problem-solving process.

Another observation that can be made here (as on many of the other Performance subtests) is whether or not the student persists beyond the time limits of the item and solves it. If he does, then, again, such information is valuable to the teacher, in that the student may be able to solve difficult academic tasks if given slightly more time to complete them.

Cooper also suggests that one should observe whether or not the student displays a very uneven sequence of successes and failures before reaching a ceiling. If it is uneven, then, he says, this ". . . would suggest that the individual's social understanding is disrupted by inattention, anxiety, variable social comprehension or even confusion in dealing with interpersonal stimuli."[18]

The specific items the student worked incorrectly should also be looked at to see which areas may be causing difficulty. The Picture Arrangement items can be classified as to affective/social themes, as follows:[19]

- Aggression—items 1, 3, 8, and 11
- Theft—items 2, 5, and 8
- Dealing with Authority—items 3, 5, 10, and 12, and (to some extent) item 9
- Inadequacy/Self-Image—item 7
- Item 4 does not fit any of the foregoing categories.

Again, using the WISC-R in this fashion is a means of providing possibly fruitful hypotheses, *not* to "diagnose," per se.

Finally, comparing the Picture Arrangement subtest to its Verbal counterpart, the Comprehension subtest, provides some information on whether or not a student can verbally state what is an appropriate response to certain social situations, versus indicating the extent to which a student can recognize the logical flow of social events. Sometimes a low Comprehension, high Picture Arrangement score indicates more ability to use visual than verbal cues in the environment. Thus, the student could be described as socially alert, even though he cannot express social rules verbally.

Block Design

Block Design is an excellent measure of reasoning with nonverbal input. The task itself is unique, and allows the examiner to observe a number of things about the student. One of the things I try to do is draw the design the student makes for each item right on the WISC-R protocol. I also make notes regarding the types of errors made, like reversals and transpositions. This lets me know whether or not the student has made a careless or impulsive error like a reversal, or simply had no idea how to solve the puzzle. Some students seem to work the entire time in a seemingly random fashion, never using a systematic strategy. Would thinking-out-loud and the four-step planning process suggested in Appendix 5-3 be suitable for such a student?

One can also observe whether or not the student uses one hand, switches hands, or uses both to solve the problem, thereby getting an impression of the student's neurological maturity. I also note how the student reacts as more stress is introduced by way of task complexity, particularly for older students when item 9 is introduced. Does the student display uncertainty or inadequacy, or does the student react to the more complex task as a challenge with, say, a delightful gleam in the eye?

Impulsivity and task persistence can also be observed here. Does the student give up quickly or go beyond the time limits?

Some suggestion as to a simultaneous or successive information processing style (see Chapter 6) can also be partially observed on Block Design. Does the student move to a rapid solution by grasping the overall pattern (a more simultaneous style), or does the student seem to examine each part carefully, as if distributing it into its components, then checking back to see that it is correctly rotated, etc. (a more successive approach)? Or, is it some combination of the two that the student successfully integrates?

Cooper notes that some students will accept an obviously inaccurate design as correct, even if pressed. They may just shrug, or say it's correct, thus deflecting responsibility for their performance because they won't acknowledge it in the first place. Such students can be expected to have difficulty in handling correction or constructive criticism, he suggests.

Cooper also notes that high scores on Block Design may reflect high energy and an orientation to things, rather than people. This makes sense if we use the field-independent, field-dependent style approach, since Block Design loads on the field-independent side. Field-independent students, as noted earlier, are less sensitive to a "people" orientation. If that is so, is it a problem for the student? Is he too thing-oriented? Would some of the teaching strategies relating to field sensitivity be helpful in this particular student's situation?

Another behavior that should be noted is the student who frequently checks the sides of the blocks. Such a response may indicate an excessive concreteness which would impede general adaptive ability, notes Cooper.

There is some relation between Block Design and some academic areas. Geometry, for example, which deals with abstract visual-spatial reasoning and manipulation, would seem to involve similar processing as in Block Design. The student who does well in Block Design might also do well in vocationally oriented courses like shop, home ec., etc., where manipulation of concrete objects is called for; or, at a higher level, in engineering courses. This does not mean that a high score on Block Design automatically means the school psychologist should recommend vocational or engineering courses! Nor does it mean that a student with a low score on Block Design should be excluded from such courses. However, if a school psychologist has to make, say, a vocational placement recommendation, then certainly the student's strengths and weaknesses need to be taken into account, including, of course, his performance on Block Design.

Object Assembly

Object Assembly, like Block Design, involves motor coordination to solve a visual-input problem. Unlike Block Design, Object Assembly involves "meaningful" items in that the student, in all likelihood, has some visual schema for the items. The student must integrate the visual pieces into a meaningful whole. Speed becomes a factor, especially with older students. So, students who do very well on Object Assembly may be able to channel their intellectual energy "through their hands" to solve such problems. Again, this would suggest the student who does well on the task would also do well in shop, crafts, and possibly dramatic activities.

Similar questions about student behavior on this subtest can be asked by the examiner as on the Block Design subtest. Does the student persist, or only make feeble attempts? Is the student angry or upset with himself if he cannot do a puzzle? Or a student may not integrate a piece, and claim that it "doesn't fit," thereby shifting responsibility away from himself.

Sometimes I turn Object Assembly into a game-like setting by asking the student either to turn around or close his eyes as I put out the pieces. I observe the student's reaction to this. Many students respond favorably, a valuable piece of information for the teacher in some cases. Some, however, are very solemn throughout the administration, and even this game they treat in the same, almost affectless, way. Such students tend to be quite passive, and will likely ask you what the pieces are supposed to make, for example, rather than guessing themselves. Some students "peek" when they close their eyes, a behavior also worth noting.

I also make some note of the kinds of errors the student makes on each item. The commonest for the first item are reversals. The errors made may be due to carelessness or, Cooper suggests, to a more disturbed body image if all the pieces are reversed or if the mid-section is omitted (this is very rare, however). He also suggests that when the legs are reversed, the girl appears to be running, which a more active child might see as being more appropriate. Inverting the door in item 3 is another common error. Does the student also reverse the legs on the girl, the mid-piece on item 2, and have trouble with the eye-piece on item 4? If so, is it mainly carelessness with fine detail and a lack of self-correction? Is impulsivity contributing to this? If so, then again, many of the self-control procedures in Appendix 5-3 could be helpful.

Is the student rigid or flexible in solving the puzzles? Does he try various other rotations when his choice is obviously incorrect, or does he rigidly try the same approach over and over. The nose-piece on the face often reveals this. Some students try to force the piece, or rotate through every possibility except the correct one.

Does the student use form and line cues when doing the puzzles? Item 2 is the only item with no line cues, so performance on this item can be compared to the others. In particular, watch to see how the student handles the front end of the car. The hood has few line cues, so it is mainly form on which the student must rely, while the back end is mainly line cues, with form being less important. Can the student shift from one cue to the other easily?

The examiner can also observe whether or not the student seems to use a more simultaneous or successive approach in solving the puzzles.

Coding

I have already spent considerable time in discussing the cognitive aspects of Coding in relation to the Freedom from Distractibility factor. Additionally, low scores may suggest poor paper-and-pencil coordination, and could have implications for the student's printing and cursive handwriting ability, and/or performance on timed paper-and-pencil tasks of any kind in a school setting. Since I presented a number of strategies for writing and spelling in Appendix 5-2, I will not deal with any more academic implications of the Coding subtest here. Instead, I will again focus on what the examiner can look for in a student doing the task.

The first is handedness. Left-handed students (15 percent of the population, or less—Ed.) are at a disadvantage for this subtest, because the most efficient strategy for doing it involves identifying the number, looking for the correct shape in the key, and then marking it. As the student does more of these, he may memorize some of the associations and thereby do the task even more quickly. A left-handed student, however, will find the task awkward, however, because his hand will cover the key as he progresses. For left-handers, it is therefore perfectly acceptable to provide an additional key which they can place above or beside the protocol.

Frequently, students who perform poorly on Coding also do poorly on Digit Span. Perhaps it is because their choice of strategies is the same—memorization—and they aren't very good at it. However, you also come across some students who do poorly on Digit Span, but do not on Coding, or vice versa. Perhaps it is a result of their using some feature of each task to their advantage. Digit Span involves trying to memorize numbers given orally by the examiner. If the student forgets the numbers, he cannot do the task. On Coding, however, the student may still be able to perform well because the key is always there. Does the student take advantage of this and, therefore, do better on Coding? If the reverse is true, is it because auditory memory is better for the student than visual memory?

Note how the student handles the task. Does he think-out-loud while doing it? This strategy can sometimes be an aid, but may slow the student down and hamper his efforts after some time, since thinking-out-loud is developmentally less mature.

Sometimes the student stops after working the first row. Is is because he did not listen or process the instructions? Or is it part of a more pervasive, passive orientation, where the student requires more adult structure and guidance to complete the task?

Cooper suggests an interesting examiner strategy, and that involves keeping track of how many items the student completes after every 20-second interval. Presumably, if learning is occurring, performance will be more rapid, or at least remain constant as time progresses. One could see how many items the student performs in each of the 20-second intervals, or compare the first minute to the second. Attention or mood may be behind any variations noted. So is self-correction. A student who stops to correct an error will be severely penalizing himself. One could also allow the student to complete the whole subtest (noting where he was after two minutes, of course), and compare the number of items completed over selected time intervals.

When using this strategy, Cooper says that it is important to note that the numbers 1, 2, and 3 predominate in the first line, while the remaining digits appear in the second line and are more frequent thereafter. The frequency of 1, 2, and 3 in the first line may therefore account for some variability over timed intervals, presumably because the first line is easier for the student simply due to repetition.

Finally, I have found that a similar and useful supplementary test is the *Basic Visual-Motor Association Test* (BVMAT)[20] This standardized test uses a task very similar to Coding, but involves letter-like shapes rather than numbers and shapes. The author, Dr. James Battle, provides data to show that the BVMAT can be used as a guide to predicting reading, spelling, and arithmetic achievement. The BVMAT can also be used as an effective and very quick screening device where the situation demands, or can be a useful supplement or posttest where the testing integrity of Coding needs to be preserved, or when the retest interval is too short.

Mazes

Mazes is an optional and supplementary task on the WISC-R, like Digit Span. However, I invariably administer both, primarily for the additional information (and, of course, without Digit Span, the third factor cannot be calculated).

Impulsive behavior can easily be noted on Mazes. The student may race up blind alleys, cut corners, or wander off the lines in his rush to get the job done. Such a student may indeed even score quite high on the subtest as a consequence, but at the sacrifice of neat work. I have already discussed in detail the educational implications of both the planning and impulsivity aspects of the Mazes subtest.

Sometimes I run across students who do exceptionally well on this subtest in contrast to the others. My first question to such students is whether or not they play a lot of Pac-Man or other, similar, maze-like video games. Very often, they do, which affects my interpretation of the results.

Examiners sometimes encounter students who start the Mazes from the exit and go back to the middle. Is this type of response a clever strategy or a deliberate circumvention of the stated rules? Examiner judgment based on student reaction to the other WISC-R subtests can help to answer this question. The examiner must, of course, correct the student who uses this exit-first procedure.

Does the student show task persistence as the complexity of the Mazes increases, or does he have an "Oh, no, I can't do this" reaction (verbally or nonverbally)? In other words, does he retreat and surrender in the face of some stress, or mobilize his efforts to the challenge?

Cooper suggests some interesting contrasting of Mazes to other WISC-R subtests, in terms of comparing the student's handling of auditory or visual information with personal or impersonal information. So, in this respect:[21]

- Mazes vs. Coding—linear, sequential performance involving linguistic symbols (Coding) vs. linear, sequential information which excludes linguistic information (Mazes).
- Mazes vs. Picture Arrangement—dealing with visual, sequential information with social content (Picture Arrangement) vs. visual, sequential information only (Mazes).
- Mazes vs. Digit Span—external, visual, sequential processing (Mazes) vs. internal, auditory, sequential processing (Digit Span).
- Mazes vs. Comprehension—visual, abstract, sequential reasoning (Mazes) vs. person-relevant, verbal, sequential understanding (Comprehension).

In each case, I would look for a ± 3 scale score point discrepancy before concluding that any difference was statistically significant. As well, such information is dormant unless it can be coupled with a remedial recommendation. And remedial strategies based on such constructs as "visual sequential memory," "auditory closure," etc., have not proven to be very educationally fruitful avenues. The preceding contrasts, then, should be employed with caution and used with discretion in certain individual cases. Sometimes, for instance, it is helpful for a teacher to know the student can do well if a memory constraint is removed, such as if Mazes were significantly higher than Digit Span.

Temporal Plotting

The WISC-R, unlike the WISC, alternates Verbal and Performance subtests when the test is actually administered to a student. When a WISC-R profile is plotted on the face-sheet of the test protocol, therefore, the sequence of the subtests as listed under the Verbal and Performance Scales appears different from the actual administration sequence.

The purpose of temporal plotting is to determine whether or not the actual sequence of presentation of the subtests is a factor more important than other hypotheses suggested by a traditional analysis. The procedure was introduced by Glenn DiPasquale in the *Canadian Journal of School Psychology* (1986, 2:55-60) and has some interesting ramifications.

Let's use a case example provided by DiPasquale himself. "Emma" was a seven-year-old referred because of difficulties coping with the second-grade program in her school. During testing, she presented herself as a pleasant youngster, but also as pale and lethargic. She tired easily, and her motivation waned. The results of the WISC-R, using the traditional profile, are shown in Figure 7.3.

FIGURE 7.3. A traditional graph of "Emma's" WISC-R performance.

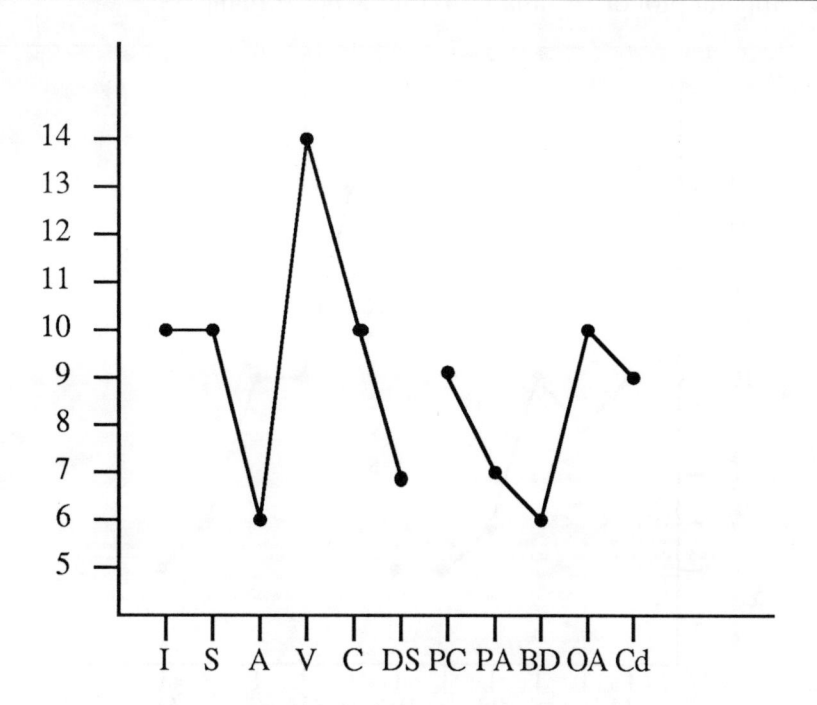

From: DiPasquale, G. 1986. The temporal plot: another tool for WISC-R profile interpretation. *Canadian Journal of School Psychology* 2:1, p. 56.

As you can see, there is a strong presence of the "third factor" on the WISC-R profile. In her case, the Verbal IQ was 100; the Performance IQ, 86; and the Full Scale IQ, 92 ± 6. The average for Factor I was 11; for Factor II, 8; and for Factor III, only 7. Thus, Factor III (as well as Factor II) is significantly lower than Factor I. However, DiPasquale was not happy with an interpretation of distractibility in Emma's case, nor with any of the alternate interpretations of Factor III. It is only when the WISC-R subtests were plotted temporally (i.e., in the order administered), that another explanation made sense. The temporal plot is presented in Figure 7.4.

Of this, DiPasquale says:[22]

As can be seen in Figure 2 [i.e., Figure 7.4], a major role appears to be played by the passage of time, and by the recess break which was over twenty minutes in length by the time Emma returned to the test room. From this simple rearrangement of the data, an entirely new hypothesis presents itself. It appears possible that Emma is a youngster who is subject to fatigue over time, and not a distractible or anxious child at all. The third factor has been inadvertently affected because two of the three subtests comprising it were administered last, and the third, Arithmetic, happened to fall just prior to the recess break. If this hypothesis is correct, it has implications not just for diagnosis, but also for remedial programming. To remediate distractibility, many authors prescribe exercises that resemble the weak WISC-R subtests, or encourage the use of games like Concentration. While such remedial approaches are controversial at the best of times, they are inappropriate in the extreme if, like Emma, a child exhibits a "distractibility" profile because of fatigue.

Using the temporal plot proved to be extremely helpful in Emma's case. It resulted in a medical intervention which focused the parents on issues of nutrition, diet, exercise, and appropriate bedtime. Follow-up at a later date suggested promising progress.

FIGURE 7.4. A temporal plot of "Emma's" WISC-R performance.

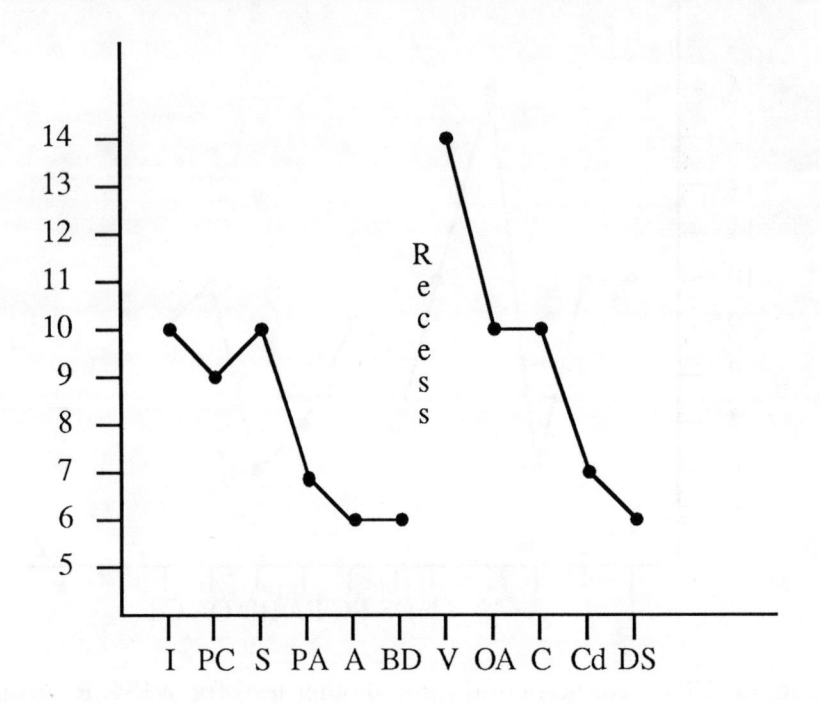

From: DiPasquale, G. 1986. The temporal plot: another tool for WISC-R profile interpretation. *Canadian Journal of School Psychology* 2:1, p. 57.

DiPasquale presents two other case examples which I will not reiterate here. Needless to say, this approach has considerable merit in my opinion, and should definitely be incorporated into the analysis of a WISC-R profile where it seems appropriate to do so (this does not happen frequently, in my experience). Temporal plotting is a nice complement to the five-level approach I have suggested in this book. It may suggest further hypotheses and remedial approaches, and provide insights not afforded by the other levels.

For your convenience, I have included a figure, Figure 7.5, with the WISC-R subtests arranged temporally, so you can do your own plotting.

FIGURE 7.5. WISC-R subtests arranged temporally.

I	PC	S	PA	A	BD	V	OA	C	Cd	DS	Mz

Afterword

As you can appreciate by reading to this point, a remarkable degree of background knowledge, sophistication, clinical judgment, and expertise is necessary to do justice to a full WISC-R interpretation. Furthermore, the school psychologist must be able to link hypotheses with remedial strategies in a way that makes sense for the classroom or remedial teacher and parent.

In previous chapters, I covered a lot of ground in an attempt to help you uncover *some* of the hypotheses which are generated in the level-by-level interpretation I have used for the foundation for this book.

I realize that most school psychologists simply do not have the time to pore over each WISC-R protocol with a fine tooth comb; nor do they necessarily have the time to write brilliant and complete reports. Most of the good consultation and information transpires verbally in the parent and teacher interviews. However, every school psychologist needs a sound data base to begin with. It is my sincere hope that the *WISC-R Companion* helps you achieve a greater depth of interpretive understanding, which will assist you in your role as a consultant and helper.

Sources and Annotations

Chapter 2

1. Pyle, D. 1979. *Intelligence, an introduction*, p. 9. London: Routledge and Kegan Paul.
2. Cited in Vernon, P. 1979. *Intelligence, heredity, and environment*. San Francisco: W. H. Freeman.
3. Meeker, M. N. 1969. *The structure of intellect*. Columbus, Ohio: Charles E. Merrill. [Diagram from Pyle, D., op. cit., p. 11.]
4. SOI Institute, 214 Main St., El Segundo, California.
5. Kaufman, A. 1979. *Intelligent testing with the WISC-R*. New York: John Wiley.
6. Vernon, P., op. cit.
7. Ibid., p. 204.
8. Ibid., p. 207.
9. Ibid., p. 240.
10. Holmes, B. J. 1985. A critique of programmed WISC-R remediations. *Canadian Journal of School Psychology* 1:1.
11. Ibid, p. 13.
12. Cited in Vernon, P., op. cit.
13. Clark, A. M. 1984. Early experiences and cognitive developed. In *Review of research in education*, ed. E. W. Gordon. Washington, D.C.: American Educational Research Association.
14. Ibid.
15. Cited in Vernon, P., op. cit.
16. Sternberg, R. 1984. How to teach intelligence. *Educational Leadership* pp. 38-48. [Vide: Sternberg, R. J., and Ketron, J. C. 1982. Selection and implementation of strategies in reasoning by analogy. *Journal of Educational Psychology* 74:339-413.]
17. Ibid. [Readers interested in pursuing some of the Instrumental Enrichment literature should read: Feuerstein, R. 1980. *Instrumental enrichment*. Baltimore: University Park Press.]
18. Ibid.
19. Flesch, R. F. 1949. *The art of writing*, p. 183. New York: Harper.
20. Naisbitt, J. 1982. *Megatrends*. New York: Warner.
21. Cited in Sattler, J. 1982. *Assessment of children's intelligence and special abilities*, 2nd ed. Boston: Allyn and Bacon.
22. McCall, R., Appelbaum, M., and Hogarty, P. 1973. Developmental changes in mental performance. *Monographs of the Society for Research in Child Development* 38:3, serial 150 1-83.
23. Cited in Sattler, J., op. cit.
24. Sattler, J., op. cit.
25. Vance, II., Wallbrown, F., and Blaha, J. 1978. Developing remedial hypotheses from ability profiles. *Journal of Learning Disabilities* 12:8, pp. 557-561; 1978. Determining WISC-R profiles for reading-disabled children. *Journal of Learning Disabilities* 11:10, pp. 657-661.

26. Bannatyne, A. 1974. A note on recategorization of the WISC scaled scores. *Journal of Learning Disabilities* 7:272-274. [Vide: Bannatyne, A. 1971. *Language, reading, and learning disabilities.* Springfield, Illinois: Charles C. Thomas.]

27. Badian, N. A. 1981. Can the WPPSI be of aid in identifying young children at risk for reading disability. *Journal of Learning Disabilities* 17:10, pp. 583-587.

28. Kaufman, A., op. cit.

29. Cooper, S. 1982. *The clinical use and interpretation of the* Wechsler Intelligence Scale for Children–Revised. Springfield, Illinois: Charles C. Thomas.

30. Torgeson, L. M., and Houck, D. G. 1980. Processing deficiencies of learning-disabled children who perform poorly on the Digit Span test. *Journal of Educational Psychology* 72:141-160.

31. Carrier, C., Joseph, M., Krey, C., and LaCroix, P. 1983. Supplied visuals and imagery instructions in field independent and field dependent children's recall. *Educational Communications and Technology Journal* 31:3, pp. 153-160.

32. Gardner, R. 1981. Digits forward and digits backward as two separate tests: normative data on 1567 school children. *Journal of Clinical Child Psychology* pp. 131-135.

33. Mishra, S., Ferguson, B., and King, P. 1985. Research with the Wechsler Digit Span subtest: implications for assessment. *School Psychology Review* 14:1, pp. 37-47.

34. Cone, T., and Wilson, L. R. 1981. Quantifying a severe discrepancy: a critical analysis. *Learning Disability Quarterly* 4:4, pp. 359-371.

35. Reynolds, C. 1984-1985. Critical measurement issues in learning disabilities. *Journal of Special Education* 18:4.

Chapter 3

1. Selye, H. 1974. *Stress without distress.* New York: Signet.
2. Ibid.
3. Rogers, C. R. 1951. *Client-centered therapy: its current practice, implications, and theory.* Boston: Houghton-Mifflin.
4. Battle, J. 1982. *Enhancing self-esteem and achievement: a handbook for professionals.* Seattle: Special Child Publications.
5. Dinkmeyer, D., McKay, G., and Dinkmeyer, D. 1980. *Systematic training for effective teaching.* Circle Pines, Minnesota: American Guidance Service.
6. DeBruyn, R., and Larson, J. 1984. *You can handle them all.* Manhattan, Kansas: The Master Teacher.
7. Truch, S. 1980. *Teacher burnout and what to do about it.* Novato, California: Academic Therapy Publications.
8. Abrams, J. C., and Smolen, W. O. 1973. On stress, failure, and reading disability. *Journal of Reading* 16:462-466.
9. Reichurdt, K. W. 1977. Playing dead or running away—defense reactions during reading. *Journal of Reading* 20:706-711.
10. Downing, J., and Leong, C. K. 1982. *Psychology of reading.* New York: Macmillan.
11. Ibid.
12. Lansdown, R. 1974. *Reading, teaching, and learning.* London: Pitman.

13. Gentile, L, and McMillan, M. 1987. *Stress and reading difficulties: research, assessment, intervention.* Newark, Delaware: International Reading Association.
14. Taylor, I., and Taylor, M. M. 1983. *The psychology of reading*, p. 370. New York: Academic Press.
15. Smith, D. E. P. 1969. Increasing task behavior difficulty in a language arts program by providing reinforcement. *Journal of Experimental Child Psychology* 4:8, pp. 45-62.
16. Darveaux, D. 1984. The good behavior game plus merit: controlling disruptive behavior and improving student motivation. *School Psychology Review* 13:4, pp. 510-514.
17. Downing, J., and Leong, C. K., op. cit., p. 254.
18. Smith, H. K. 1972. Reading for different purposes. In *Literacy at all levels*, ed. V. Southgate. London: Ward Lock.
19. Maier, A. 1980. The effect of focusing on the cognitive processes of learning-disabled children. *Journal of Learning Disabilities* 13:3, p. 35.
20. Morris, J. M. 1966. *Standards and progress in reading.* Slough, England: National Foundation for Educational Research.
21. Hansen, H. S. 1973. The home literacy environment—a follow-up report. *Elementary English* 50:97-98, 122.
22. Downing, J., and Leong, C. K., op. cit.
23. Ibid., p. 294.
24. Ibid., p. 295.
25. *Intervention assistance teams: a model for building-level instructional problem solving.* Available from: National Association of School Psychologists, Publication Office, 10 Overland Drive, Stratford, Connecticut 06497.
26. Hamachek, D. E. 1975. *Behavior dynamics in teaching, learning, and growth.* Boston: Allyn and Bacon.
27. Downing, J., and Leong, C. K., op. cit., p. 297.
28. Schunk, D. 1984. Enhancing self-efficacy and achievement through rewards and goals: motivational and informational effects. *Journal of Educational Research* 78:1, pp. 29-34.
29. Shelton, T., Anastopoulos, A., and Linden, J. 1985. An attribution training program with learning-disabled children. *Journal of Learning Disabilities* 18:5, pp. 261-265.
30. Benson, H. 1975. *The relaxation response.* New York: William Morrow.
31. Jacobson, E. 1938. *Progressive relaxation.* Chicago: University of Chicago Press.
32. Frey, H. 1980. Improving the performance of poor readers through autogenic relaxation training. *Reading Teacher* 33:928-932.
33. Stroebel, E., Stroebel, C., and Holland, M. 1980. *Kiddie QR: a choice for children.* Available from: QR Institute, 119 Forest Drive, Wethersfield, Connecticut 06109.

Chapter 4

1. Taylor, I., and Taylor, M. M. 1983. *The psychology of reading.* New York: Academic Press.
2. McNeil, J. 1984. *Reading comprehension: new directions for classroom practice*, p. 4. Glenview, Illinois: Scott, Foresman.

3. Pearson, P. D. 1976. A psycholinguistic model of reading. *Language Arts* 53:3, pp. 309-314.
4. Ibid., p. 310.
5. Samuels, S. J. 1976. Automatic decoding and reading comprehension. *Language Arts* 53:3, p. 323.
6. Smith, F. 1975. The role of prediction in reading. *Elementary English* 52:3, pp. 305-311.
7. Ibid., p. 310.
8. Nicholson, T. 1986. Reading is not a guessing game—the great debate revisited. *Reading Psychology* 7:197-210.
9. Ibid., p. 199.
10. Ibid., p. 200.
11. Ibid., p. 203.
12. Bradley, L., and Bryant, P. 1983. Categorizing sounds and learning to read—a causal connection. *Nature* 301:419-421.
13. Lindamood, P., and Lindamood, C. *Auditory discrimination in depth.* Allen, Texas: Developmental Learning Materials. Available in Canada from Teaching Resources.
14. Quoted in *Santa Barbara News-Press*, Friday, August 29, 1986. More information is available from Leroy Small, District Superintendent, Santa Maria Elementary School District, 321 North Thornburg Street, Box 460, Santa Maria, California 93456, phone (805) 928-1783.
15. Schoenfelder, P., and Skriba, F. 1979. Activities for young word bankers. *Reading Teacher* (January) pp. 453-457. [Videque: Gillet, J. W., and Temple, C. 1982. *Understanding reading problems, assessment, and instruction*, p. 137. Boston: Little, Brown. This book is an excellent reference for the school psychologist interested in knowing more about the reading process and reading remediation.]
16. Cooper, S. 1982. *The clinical use and interpretation of the* Wechsler Intelligence Scale for Children–Revised, p. 33. Springfield, Illinois: Charles C. Thomas.
17. McNeil, J., op. cit.
18. Taylor, I., and Taylor, M. M., op. cit., pp. 233-234.
19. Ibid., p. 234.
20. Ibid., p. 235.
21. Ibid., p. 236.
22. Ibid., p. 421.
23. Ibid., p. 429.
24. Ibid., pp. 385-386.
25. Ibid., pp. 390-391.
26. Ibid., pp. 393-394.
27. McNeil, op. cit.
28. Taylor, I., and Taylor, M. M., op. cit., p. 394.
29. Downing, J., and Leong, C. K., op. cit., pp. 318-319.

Chapter 5

1. Sattler, J. 1982. *Assessment of children's intelligence and special abilities*, 2nd ed., p. 193. Boston: Allyn and Bacon.
2. Kaufman, A. 1979. *Intelligent testing with the WISC-R*. New York: John Wiley.
3. Blaha, J., and Wallbrown, F. 1984. Hierarchical analyses of the WISC and WISC-R: synthesis and clinical implications. *Journal of Clinical Psychology* 40:2, pp. 556-571.
4. Ibid., p. 567.
5. Ibid., p. 567.
6. Ibid., p. 569.
7. Ibid., p. 567.
8. Ibid., p. 567.
9. Ibid., p. 568.
10. Eysenck, H. J. (ed.). 1973. *The measurement of intelligence*, p. xi. Baltimore: Williams and Wilkins.
11. Kirk, S. 1972. *Educating exceptional children*, p. 1655. Boston: Houghton-Mifflin.
12. Brigance, A. H. 1978. *The Brigance diagnostic inventory of early development*. Curriculum Associates, 5 Esquire Road, North Billerica, MA 01862-2589.
13. *Curriculum Guide (EMH)*. 1980. Edmonton, Alberta Education.
14. Ibid., pp. iii-iv.
15. Ibid., p. 34.
16. *Curriculum Guide (TMH)*. 1982. Edmonton, Alberta Education.
17. Taylor, I., and Taylor, M. M., op. cit.; Pearson, P. D., op. cit.
18. Fagan, W. T. n.d. Reading and the mentally handicapped. *Mental Retardation for Special Educators*.
19. Ibid., p. 237.
20. Carnine, D. 1983. Direct instruction: in search of instructional solutions for educational problems. In *Interdisciplinary voices in learning disabilities*. Austin, Texas: Pro-Ed.
21. Ibid., p. 19.
22. Ibid., p. 35.
23. Ibid., pp. 13-14.
24. Blaha, J., and Wallbrown, F., op. cit., p. 559.
25. Ibid., p. 559.
26. Kaufman, A., op. cit.
27. Sattler, J., op. cit., p. 199.
28. Sattler, J., op. cit., p. 198.
29. Ibid.
30. Ibid., p. 200.
31. Carter, J. L., and Russell, H. L. 1985. Use of EMG biofeedback procedures with learning-disabled children in a clinical and an educational setting. *Journal of Learning Disabilities* (April) 18:4, pp. 213-216.

32. Wallbrown, F. H., Blaha, J., and Vance, B. 1980. A reply to Miller's concerns about WISC-R profile analysis. *Journal of Learning Disabilities* 13:6, pp. 340-345.
33. Duffelmeyer, F. 1985. Teaching word meaning from an experience base. *The Reading Teacher* (October) 39:1, pp. 6-9.
34. Ibid.
35. Ibid., pp. 7-8.
36. Goodman, K. 1973. Strategies for increasing comprehension in reading. In *Improving reading in the intermediate years*, ed. H. M. Robinson, p. 66.
37. King, J. R. 1984. Levels of categorization and sight-word acquisition. *Reading Psychology* 5:130-131.
38. Ibid.
39. Sachs, F. G., and Banas, N. 1985. The ENIGMA reading program. *Academic Therapy* 20:4, pp. 481-485.
40. Levin, J., Johnson, D., Pittelman, S., Levin, K., Schriber, L., Toms-Bronowski, S., and Hayes, B. 1984. Vocabulary learning strategies. *Reading Psychology* 5:4.
41. Scruggs, T., and Mastropieri, M. 1984. Improving memory for the facts: the "keyword" method. *Academic Therapy* (November) 20:2, p. 160.
42. Ibid., p. 160.
43. Ibid., p. 162.
44. Ibid., p. 163.
45. Ibid., pp. 163-164.
46. Ibid., p. 165.
47. Levin, J., et al., op. cit.
48. Mastropieri, M., Scruggs, T., and Levin, J. 1985. Mnemonic strategy instruction with learning-disabled adolescents. *Journal of Learning Disabilities* 18:2, pp. 94-100.
49. Searls, E., and Klesius, J. 1984. Multiple-meaning words for primary students and how to teach them. *Reading Psychology* 5:55-63.
50. Ibid.
51. Ibid., p. 58.
52. Ibid., p. 60.
53. Ibid., p. 61.
54. Ibid., p. 62.
55. Ibid., p. 62.
56. Kaufman, A., op. cit.
57. Haslam, R. H. A., Dalby, J. T., and Rademaker, A. W. 1984. The effect of megavitamin therapy on children with attention deficit disorders. *Pediatrics* 74:103-111.
58. Ross, A. O. 1976. *Psychological aspects of learning disabilities and reading disorders.* New York: McGraw-Hill.
59. Ibid., p. 55.
60. Ibid., p. 58.
61. Walker, N. W. 1981. Modifying impulsive responding to four WISC-R subtests. *Journal of School Psychology* 19:4, pp. 335-339.
62. Kagan, J. 1966. Reflection-impulsivity: the generality and dynamics of conceptual tempo. *Journal of Abnormal Psychology* 71:17-24.

63. Meichenbaum, D., and Goodman, J. 1971. Training impulsive children to talk to themselves: a means of developing self-control. *Journal of Abnormal Psychology* 77:115-126.

64. Halford, G. S. 1978. An approach to the definition of cognitive developmental stages in school mathematics. *British Journal of Educational Psychology* 48:298-314.

65. Frost, R. 1982. The arithmetic achievement of learning-disabled students: a training study. PhD dissertation, p. 232. Calgary: University of Calgary.

66. Frost, B. P. 1973. *The Frost self-description questionnaire.* Order from: B. P. Frost, 628 Station Street, Carlton North, Australia VIC 3054.

67. Dr. Watson can be contacted through the San Diego Unified School District, 6401 Linda Vista Road, San Diego, California 92111.

68. Parill-Burnstein, M. 1981. *Problem solving and learning disabilities, an information-processing approach.* New York: Grune and Stratton.

69. Ibid., p. 109.

70. Adapted from Parill-Burnstein, M., ibid., p. 110.

71. Ibid.

72. Lindamood, C., and Lindamood, P. 1979. *The LAC (Lindamood Auditory Conceptualization) test*, rev. ed. Allen, Texas: DLM Teaching Resources.

73. Cohen, R., Fil, D., Netley, C., and Clarke, M. 1984. On the generality of the short-term memory/reading ability relationship. *Journal of Learning Disabilities* 17:216-221.

74. Williams, J. 1984. Phonemic analysis and how it relates to reading. *Journal of Learning Disabilities* 17:240-245.

75. Renzulli, J. 1978. *Phi Delta Kappan* (November) p. 261.

76. Feldhusen, J. F., and Wyman, A. R. 1980. Super Saturday: design and implementation of Purdue's special program for gifted children. *Gifted Child Quarterly* 24:15-21.

77. Renzulli, J. 1977. *The enrichment triad model: a guide for developing defensible programs for the gifted and talented.* Mansfield Center, Connecticut: Creative Learning Press.

78. The gifted program in Rocky View School Division, Calgary, Alberta, is called the Pegasus Program. It is coordinated by Mrs. Jo-Anne Koch.

79. Vide, e.g.: Reynolds, C. 1984-1985. Critical measurement issues in learning disabilities. *Journal of Special Education* (Winter) 18:451-476.

80. Fine, M., and Pitts, R. 1980. Intervention with underachieving gifted children: rationale and strategies. *Gifted Child Quarterly* (Spring) 24:2, pp. 51-55.

81. Ibid., p. 51. First defined by Gowan, J. 1955. The underachieving gifted child—a problem for everyone. *Exceptional Children* 21:247-249, 270.

82. Adapted from Fine, M., and Pitts, R., ibid.

83. Adapted from Fine, M., and Pitts, R., ibid.

84. Ibid., p. 55.

85. Reynolds, C., and Clark, J. 1986. Profile analysis of standardized intelligence test performance of very high IQ children. *Psychology in the Schools* 23:5-12.

86. Schiff, M., Kaufman, A., and Kaufman, N. 1981. Scatter analysis of WISC-R profiles of learning-disabled children with superior intelligence. *Journal of Learning Disabilities* 14:7, p. 403.

Chapter 6

1. Kavale, K., and Forness, S. 1984. A meta-analysis of the validity of Wechsler scale profiles and recategorizations: patterns or parodies? *Learning Disability Quarterly* 7:150.
2. Ibid.
3. Kaufman, A. 1979. *Intelligent testing with the WISC-R*. New York: John Wiley.
4. Dunn, R. 1984. Learning style: state of the science. *Theory into Practice* 23:1, p. 12.
5. Ibid., p. 11.
6. Ibid., pp. 12-13.
7. Doyle, W., and Rutherford, B. 1984. Classroom research on matching learning and teaching styles. *Theory into Practice* 23:1, p. 22.
8. Ibid., p. 22.
9. Thorpe, H., and Borden, K. 1985. The effect of multisensory instruction upon the on-task behaviors and word reading accuracy of learning-disabled children. *Journal of Learning Disabilities* 18:5, pp. 279-286.
10. Larrivee, B. 1981. Modality preference as a model for differentiating beginning reading instruction: a review of the issues. *LD Quarterly* 4:188.
11. Witkin, H. A., Oltman, P., Raskin, E.,, and Karp, S. 1971. *Children's embedded figures test*. Palo Alto, California: Consulting Psychologists Press.
12. Rasinski, T. 1984. Field dependent/independent cognitive style research revisited: do field dependent readers read differently than field independent readers? *Reading Psychology* 5:306.
13. Ibid.
14. Ibid., p. 309.
15. Ibid., p. 315.
16. Satterly, D. J., and Telfer, I. 1979. Cognitive style and advanced organizers in learning and retention. *British Journal of Educational Psychology* 49:169-178.
17. Kaufman, A., and Kaufman, N. 1984. *Training packet for sequential or simultaneous mental processing*. Circle Pines, Minnesota: American Guidance Service.
18. Ibid.
19. Ibid.
20. Naglieri, J. A., Kamphaus, R., and Kaufman, A. 1983. The Luria-Das simultaneous-successive model applied to the WISC-R. *Journal of Psychoeducational Assessment* 1:25-34.
21. Ibid., p. 28.
22. Ibid., p. 31.
23. Ibid., p. 31.
24. Ibid., p. 31.
25. Das, J. P., Leong, C. K., and Williams, N. H. 1978. The relationship between learning disability and simultaneous-successive processing. *Journal of Learning Disabilities* 11:618-625.
26. Gunnison, J. 1984. Developing educational interventions from assessments involving the K-ABC. *Journal of Special Education* 18:325-343. [Even though the author fo-

cuses on the K-ABC as the primary diagnostic instrument, the educational strategies are similar, regardless of how the diagnosis is originally made.]
27. Meichenbaum, D. 1975. *Cognitive behavior modification.* New York: Plenum.
28. Kendall, P., and Finch, A. 1976. A cognitive-behavioral treatment for impulse control: a case study. *Journal of Consulting and Clinical Psychology* 44:852-857.
29. Kaufman, A., *Intelligent testing with the WISC-R*, op. cit.
30. Kops, C., and Belmont, I. 1985. Planning and organizing skills of poor school achievers. *Journal of Learning Disabilities* 18:1, p. 9.
31. Ibid., p. 12.
32. Ibid., p. 13.
33. Ibid., p. 13.
34. Ibid., p. 13.
35. Ibid., p. 13.
36. Ibid., p. 14.
37. Ibid.
38. Ibid., p. 14.
39. I would refer the reader to: Fry, P., and Lupart, J. 1986. *Cognitive processes in children's learning.* Springfield, Illinois: Charles C. Thomas. [This is an excellent reference for more educational strategies for helping students to organize, store, and retrieve knowledge.]
40. Kaufman, A., op. cit.
41. Walker, B. 1985. Right-brained strategies for teaching comprehension. *Academic Therapy* (November) 21:2, pp. 133-141.
42. Ibid., p. 137.
43. Ibid., p. 138.
44. Ibid., p. 138.
45. Ibid., p. 139.
46. Kaufman, A., op. cit., p. 160.
47. Ibid., p. 162.
48. Letteri, C. 1980. Cognitive profile: basic determinant of academic achievement. *Journal of Educational Research* 73:4, p. 196.
49. Ibid., p. 198.
50. Ibid., p. 198.
51. Sattler, J., *Assessment . . .* , op. cit., pp. 201-203.

Chapter 7

1. Cooper, S. 1982. *The clinical use and interpretation of the Wechsler intelligence scale for children–revised.* Springfield, Illinois: Charles C. Thomas.
2. Ibid., p. 34.
3. Crandall, V., Katkovsky, W., and Crandall, V. 1965. Children's beliefs in their own control of reinforcements in intellectual-academic achievement situations. *Child Development* 36:91-109.

4. Vide: Dinkmeyer, D., McKay, G., and Dinkmeyer, D., jr. 1980. *Systematic training for effective teaching*. Circle Pines, Minnesota: American Guidance Service. [An excellent resource for this topic.]
5. Gambrell, L. 1983. The occurrence of think-time during reading comprehension. *Journal of Educational Research* 77:2, pp. 77-80.
6. Adapted from: Farnham-Diggory, S. 1978. *Learning disabilities*, pp. 128-132. Cambridge, Massachusetts: Harvard University Press.
7. Cooper, op. cit., p. 72.
8. Adapted from: Cooper, ibid., pp. 109-114.
9. Levy, W. 1981. How useful is the WISC-R Arithmetic subtest? *Topics in Learning and Learning Disabilities* 1:3, p. 86.
10. Cooper, op. cit., p. 134.
11. Ibid., p. 141.
12. Battle, J. 1981. *Culture-free self-esteem inventories for children and adults*. Seattle: Special Child Publications. [Available in Canada from: Foothills Educational Materials, 13027 Lake Twintree Road SE, Calgary, Alberta T2J 2X2.]
13. Cooper, op. cit., p. 144.
14. Jackson, N., Jackson, D., and Monroe, C. 1983. *Teaching social effectiveness to children*. Champaign, Illinois: Research Press.
15. Cooper, op. cit., p. 180.
16. Ibid., p. 53.
17. Castenada, A., and Wolt, D. 1978. *The bicognitive inventory*. Hollister, California: Cybernetic Learning Systems.
18. Cooper, op. cit., p. 88.
19. Adapted from Cooper, ibid., pp. 92-95.
20. Battle, J. 1982. *Basic visual-motor association test [BVMAT]*. Seattle: Special Child Publications. (Available in Canada from: Foothills Educational Materials, 13027 Lake Twintree Road SE, Calgary, Alberta T2J 2X2.)
21. Cooper, op. cit., pp. 221-222.
22. DiPassquale, G. 1986. The temporal plot: another tool for WISC-R profile interpretation. *Canadian Journal of School Psychology* 2:1, pp. 55-60.

Appendix 2-1

The "Language-Immersion" Environment

I recommend a combination of top-down (i.e., meaning-based) and bottom-up (i.e., data-based) approaches to teaching reading in the regular and remedial classroom. The top-down, seeking-for-meaning approach is best served by what I call a "language immersion" environment, of which the language-experience approach is a part. The student is literally immersed in a total language environment, and his language/knowledge/experience base is used as the building block for the next step. The student is not taught skills in isolation in a special room in the corner of the school. Instead, remediation is based on what is meaningful and interesting to the student. The resource room becomes a lively and integral part of the total school environment. Close cooperation with the student's home-room teacher becomes necessary so that remedial lessons, if possible, are based on home-room or overall school-based themes. Additionally, the remedial teacher needs to tap into the student's interests and reading attitudes (see Chapter 3 and the accompanying questionnaires in this appendix).

Remedial reading lessons should, if possible, be designed around the key elements of themes; and students should be constantly encouraged to predict what will happen in stories. In this way, the search for meaning will always be foremost, because these elements are largely top-down. In addition, because so many disabled readers are passive learners, some attempt to make them more active participants should be built in. Finally, as much as possible, the teacher should try to link what the student already knows to what he or she still needs to know. This means tapping into a student's language and experience base.

It also means that teachers need to spend a great deal of time preparing their students before ever doing any actual reading, so as to make full use of this language and experience base. For example, Karen Clark makes the following program suggestions for prereading strategies using this approach:

I. Select the Instructional Reading Matter with Care

Select a text or passage that is neither too difficult nor too easy for the student(s) that is consistent with your current theme. Always know what the student's instructional reading level is. If you are using an ungraded text, be sure to do a readability test on it. In addition to examining vocabulary, check the passage for complexity of concepts. The key to this approach is using appropriate reading material.

II. Questioning

The following questioning procedures are designed to (a) stimulate student curiosity about a passage to be read, (b) activate prior content knowledge, and (c) lead the student to anticipate and elaborate upon what is read, or focus attention on specific information.

A. Teacher Questioning

Establishing specific reasons for reading a passage is crucial. (You may wish to review the discussion in Chapter 3 again about reading purposes.) Ask yourself what it is that you want your students to know after they read the selection. Once this is determined, purpose-setting questions can be developed to focus student attention on the relevant aspects of the story or text.

By asking questions at various levels of comprehension, teachers will activate prior knowledge. For example, if the story is about a coyote, the literal-level questions might be:

1. Where was Ben sleeping?
2. What did he hear?

The inferential-level questions might be:

1. Why was Ben afraid?
2. How is a coyote like a dog?
3. In what ways do you think they are different?
4. Why did Ben have nothing to fear?

These are not the only questions that might be asked, of course; but they are representative of the kinds of questions which can be asked to prepare the student for the concepts of vocabulary he will encounter when the story is read.

B. Teacher-Student Reciprocal Questioning

The objective of active comprehension is to have students learn to ask their own questions and to guide their own thinking in learning from the text before, during, and after reading. Student-generated questions can lead to improved comprehension. In order to generate questions, there must be deep processing of the text. If the teacher models good questioning behavior, then—eventually—the student will learn to formulate his own questions. This might be done by having the student read the title of the story or look at an illustration. It may be accomplished by having the student progress through a lesson with teacher guidance, where the student is provided a safe atmosphere in which to ask his own questions in his effort to understand the story. Gradually, the teacher takes less and less of a role in question formulation. As the student begins to ask his own questions without teacher prompting, he is engaging in active comprehension.

The "request procedure" is one way of having the student learn to formulate questions. Begin with an expanded PReP (a Pre-Reading Plan—the PReP has been adapted by Karen Clark from Judith Langer's work at the University of California). The PReP assists the teacher in:

1. Determining the prior knowledge a student possesses about a specific concept, as well as the manner in which this knowledge is organized;
2. Becoming aware of the language a student uses to express knowledge about a particular concept;
3. Making judgments about how much additional background information must be taught before the student can successfully read the text; and
4. Developing the vocabulary and syntax with a group.

The PReP calls for an extensive group discussion before the students read the text. Let's go back to the example of the boy and the coyote to illustrate this:

Initial Associations with the Concept

1. Association Activity. You might say something like this to your group: "Tell me anything that comes to your mind when you hear the word *coyote* (or see this picture)." As each student in the group freely associates and tells what ideas come to mind, the responses can be written on the chalkboard.

    During this phase, the students have an opportunity to make associations between a key concept and what they already know. You should actually draw a schema, something like this on the chalkboard:

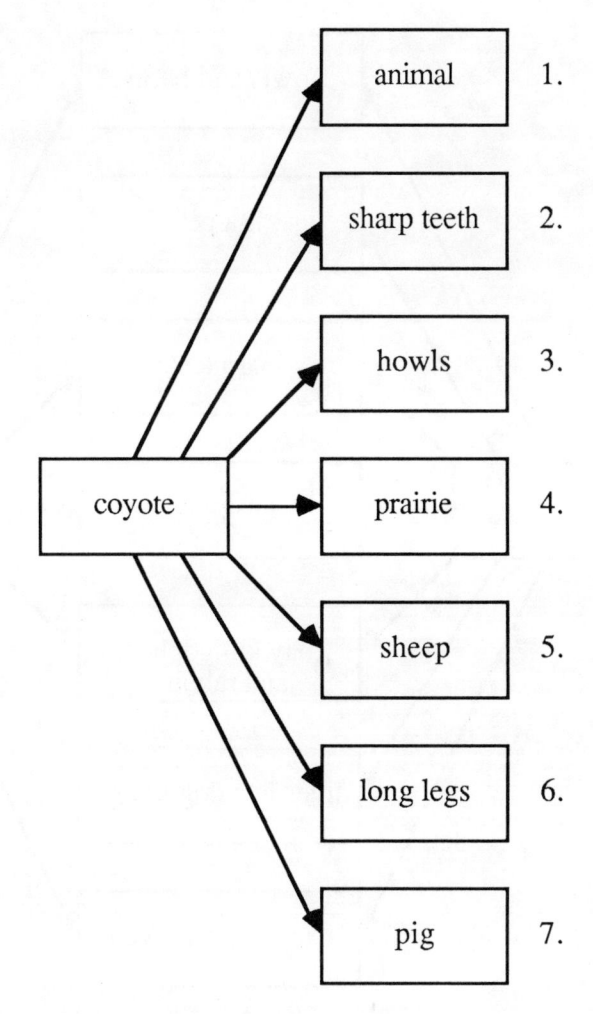

```
coyote → animal      1.
       → sharp teeth 2.
       → howls       3.
       → prairie     4.
       → sheep       5.
       → long legs   6.
       → pig         7.
```

2. Reflections on Initial Associations. Next, the students should be asked questions like, "What made you think of the coyote's sharp teeth?" This phase encourages students to become more aware of the associations they have made, to listen to each other's responses, and to become aware of their changing ideas. Through this procedure, they gain the insight which permits them to evaluate the usefulness of these ideas in the reading experience.

3. Reformulation of Knowledge. After each student has had an opportunity to think and tell their ideas concerning the concept, the teacher may read a short story about a coyote to the class, or show a filmstrip, or perhaps just show a picture of the coyote. Then the teacher returns to the first schema of the coyote, and asks if the students would like to add anything to the schema, or change anything. Usually, there is considerably more added; and, sometimes, the schema changes because a student wishes to delete an item.

Concept-Stretching

If the students still do not have a good schema for *coyote*, you may wish to stretch their concept of *dog* to include *coyote*. What you can encourage them to do, then, is to brainstorm about something they know well to help them relate as many characteristics of the known, to link with the unknown. Perhaps their brainstorming leads to the following schema:

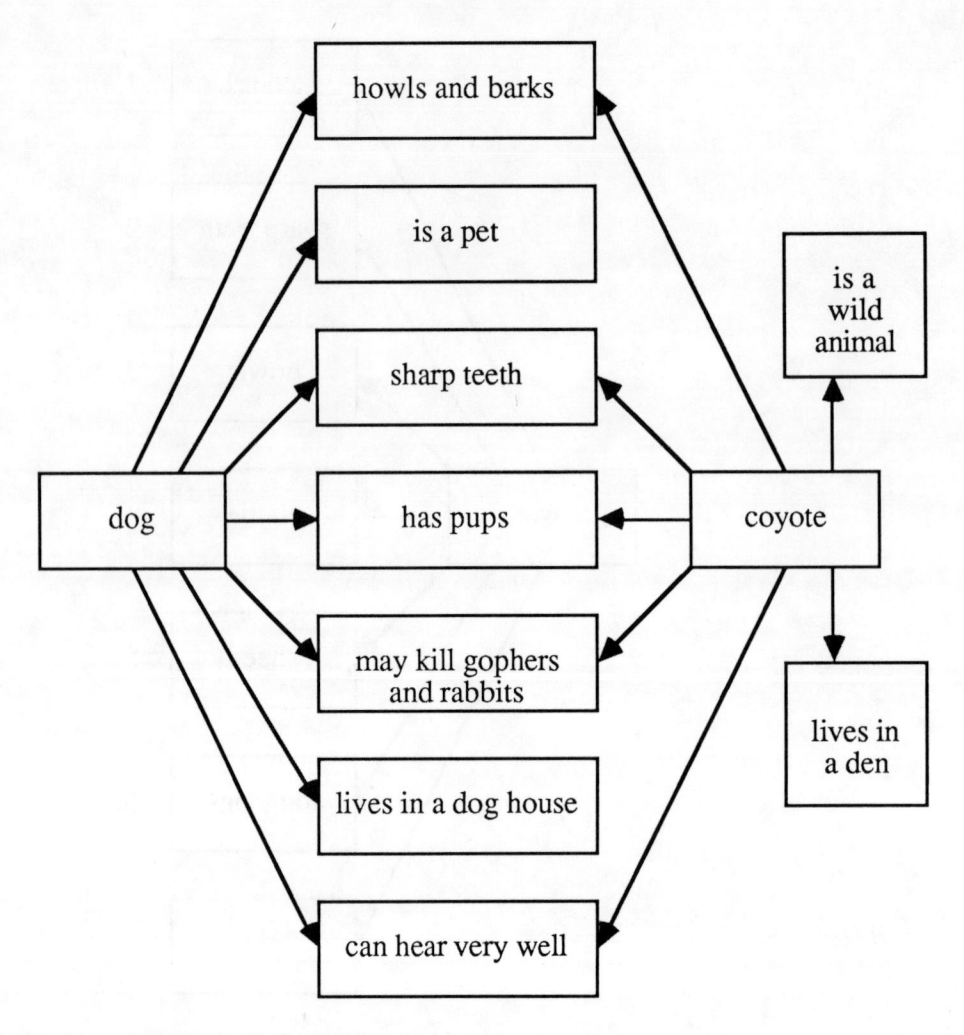

```
                    howls and barks
                          ↑
                       is a pet
                                              is a
                      sharp teeth             wild
                                             animal
        dog  →       has pups       ←  coyote
                                              ↓
                  may kill gophers          lives in
                   and rabbits               a den
                          
                  lives in a dog house
                          
                  can hear very well
```

Again, discuss responses as needed.

Vocabulary Development (videque Chapter 5)

At this point, the group might be ready to make some predictions about the vocabulary in the story. As the teacher, you could:

1. List key words as predicted by the students. Pronounce each word as it is written on the board.
2. Elicit sentences. Ask the students to use a word from the list and make up a sentence that might be in the story. Record the sentence verbatim and underline the word or words used from the list. Be sure to record the sentences exactly as stated, even if the information is not correct.
3. If necessary, have the students dramatize the vocabulary—that's always a lot of fun.
4. Read and verify the sentences. Have the students read the story and see if their predicted sentences are close to the ones in the story.

• • •

Notice how the foregoing lesson framework is truly a language-immersion one. The key elements of theme, predictability, and active student involvement are all beautifully woven together into a meaningful tapestry. In this particular example, there is also a strong emphasis on linking the known to the unknown.

It is also possible to adapt a basal reader to a language-immersion approach. The following steps are suggested for this purpose:

1. Determine all new and important vocabulary in the forthcoming basal story.

2. Identify the important concepts the students must have in order to understand the story.

3. Make up a story built around the list of vocabulary words. Use a theme in keeping with a concept you wish to stretch or expand upon, from the basal story.

4. Read or tell the story to the reading group.

5. After storytelling, have the students discuss the story. If appropriate, provide opportunities for the students to participate in some of the experiences they will encounter in the story. For example, if the story is about a child's new kite, have the students make kites and fly them. The experience will serve as a basis for language and concept development.

6. Have the students tell the story back to you, as you write it on the board or chart paper. Ask questions to elicit responses that contain the new vocabulary words if these do not come naturally from the students.

7. Have the students read the story in unison several times. Individual sentences or the whole story may be read by several or all of the students.

8. Have the students underline the new vocabulary words in the story one at a time, in response to questions such as:

    a. Find the word that describes how Tina felt when she could not find her puppy.

    b. Find the word that means the opposite of *found*.

    c. Find the word that begins with *h* and rhymes with *cold*.

9. The next day after choral reading of the language-experience story, provide any additional schema development that is required to understand the new basal story, and proceed with directed reading of the story. You will likely find that the students will be pleased to find words they already know and have so recently encountered. Since the new vocabulary is not a burden, the students are free to enjoy and appreciate the new story.

Please do not take all this to mean that there is no place for the old-fashioned drills. There is, because automaticity is an important ingredient of reading well. Perhaps five to ten minutes of each 40-minute lesson could be drill-based or bottom-up. Again, though, drills should be based on more meaningful work the student is engaged in, if at all possible. Selections from the story just read can form the focus for phonics, spelling, or writing, as required by the individual student. Drills can also focus on areas such as increasing the speed of reading.

How can you tell a teacher is using such an integrated approach in a remedial class?—usually, just by walking in the room. When I come to a resource room (or a regular class, for that matter) and I see stories, drawings, artwork, music, and drama related to the larger themes a teacher or a school has planned; when I see "tons" of children's books and reading lofts, reading corners, learning centers, calendars, and clocks; when I see small groups of students busily and happily engaged in writing letters, poems, stories, recipes, and so on (again, related to some larger, meaning-based activity)—then I know I am immersed in a total-language environment. That kind of classroom is definitely "on track." And when I see a few progress charts coupled with specific objectives within this language-immersion environment, then I know I'm really looking at a first-class resource room where top-down and bottom-up approaches are being used in concert for the benefit of the student.

By contrast, when I walk into a resource room and see barren walls devoid of students' work, straight rows of desks, few or no presence of children's literature, but plenty of busy-work worksheets, and little instructional time spent on anything but drills and more drills, I know I'm in a primarily bottom-up classroom.

The following seven-step model for small-group instruction will give you more ideas for the flavor of a whole-language approach for a reading lesson. It is based largely on Ethel Buchanan's *The Love of Reading*. This model can be used in a regular classroom as well as in a remedial setting:

1. Getting Ready. Prereading activities should include the entire group.

    a. Pose an open-ended question to bring out the group's knowledge of the subject. Brainstorm.

    b. If more background knowledge is required, you might do semantic mapping (see Chapter 3), beginning with what students know and leading them to what they do not know. You could show objects, a filmstrip, pictures, or read a story or poem. The objective is to build a schema of the topic *before* the student reads.

2. The Small Group. This will likely be a heterogenous group of two to ten children. Have them assemble in a circle to facilitate interaction. If more schema development is necessary, begin with a more hands-on approach to understanding the topic. This might include demonstrations or a walk-through of certain concepts that will be encountered in the story.

3. Identifying Purposes for Reading. (See Chapter 3 as well.)

    a. Have the students think about the title and look at the picture on the title page, or listen to a paragraph from the story. If they are age nine or older, this is also the place to use imagery training (see Appendix 2-2).

    b. Have the students predict:

        (1) Story type (narrative or expository):

        (2) What the story might be about (ask inferential questions). (Note: Questions for narrative material might deal with characters, events, setting, theme, and plot. Questions for expository material might deal with main classification, subheadings, details, and how this information is related to what is already known. Each question and the students' answers are discussed thoroughly so they reflect the group's thinking.

4. Silent Reading of the Story. Students read several pages of the story, then stop in order to:

    a. Answer the questions they have posed by providing proof from the text or illustrations.

    b. Formulate new questions based on the information already given in the story. This is the process of predicting, confirming, and comprehending the story. The teacher's questions at this point should be open-ended and should encourage thinking.

    c. Formulate more mental pictures (images).

5. Post-Reading Discussion.

    a. The group discusses the prereading questions.

    b. Consensus is reached, using proof from the text.

    c. Mental pictures (images) are discussed again. New ones can be introduced. Discussion at this point could become quite lively. Students may need to review their good manners in terms of listening to others, taking turns, not interrupting or monopolizing the conversation, and so on.

6. Individual Follow-Up. This should be an open-ended assignment designed to encourage high-level thinking. Students could write a new ending to the story, giving the

story another title, or consider what would happen if .... Different follow-up activities for each child might be planned.

7. Automaticity Drills ("BUDs"). These can be introduced at this point either with the whole group or with a few students who need it. The bottom-up drills (BUDs) could focus on sight-word acquisition (based on words from the story just read); rapid writing or reading drills (based on sentences from the story); spelling skills or any other skill which needs reinforcing. Since many of the students have difficulty with short- and long-term memory and symbol manipulation in general, short, daily drills over a long period of time are very important. Often, the WISC-R results are helpful in suggesting where a student might have a weakness :(e.g., memory, psychomotor output, etc.). It is important, though, that the BUDs that are used be academic in content. Just drilling a student on "memory tasks" is trying to teach a skill in isolation. And there is little evidence that such remedial work transfers to academic spheres.

The role of the teacher, then, in this approach, is to:
- *Activate thought* by asking, "What do you think?"
- *Agitate thought* by asking, "Why do you think so?"
- *Demand proof* by having students refer to the story.
- *Record the questions* asked by the group.
- *Guide discussion* by redirecting questions back to the group.

The role of the student is to:
- *Predict story content* by asking inferential questions before reading.
- *Form mental images.*
- *Discuss with peers* in order to clarify thinking or develop concepts.
- *Find answers to questions* to enhance comprehension.

WISC-R COMPANION

WHICH BOOK WOULD YOU CHOOSE?

Name_____Grade_____School_____Date_____

If you could choose four books from the following groups, which would you select? Mark your answers 1, 2, 3, or 4, in the order you would choose them (1 = first choice; 2 = second choice; 3 = third choice; 4 = fourth choice).

_____Adventure   _____People and Places in Other Lands

_____Animals   _____Poetry

_____Biography   _____Pre-Historic

_____Fairy Tales   _____Science

_____Frontier and Western   _____Science Fiction

_____History   _____Space

_____Mysteries   _____Sports

_____Myths and Legends   _____Stories about Boys and Girls

READING ATTITUDE QUESTIONS

1. When I read, I_____.
2. Reading makes me _____.
3. School is_____.
4. I wish teachers were _____.
5. When someone reads out loud to me _____.
6. Going to college or university_____.
7. To me, books _____.
8. I like to read about _____.
9. On weekends, I_____.
10. I'd rather read than _____.
11. Last night, I read_____.
12. To me, homework _____.
13. When I am in the Library _____.
14. Comic books_____.
15. When I take my report card home_____.
16. When I read arithmetic _____.
17. The future looks _____.
18. I think reading is_____.
19. I like to read when _____.
20. I would like to be _____.
21. For me, studying _____.
22. Reading science _____.
23. Reading poems_____.
24. I'd read more if_____.
25. When I read out loud _____.

    This survey is a very informal one. Student responses can be very interesting at times! Very often, you will find such surveys of value in planning your recommendations, IEPs, etc.

Appendix 2-2

Using Imagery to Improve Story Recall and Comprehension

1. Select the passage you wish your class, small group, or student to read. This passage could be any suitable story consistent with your objectives or one that is part of your regular curriculum. It should be at the reading level of the student:(s).

2. Instruct the group or student to form a "picture in their mind" either before or after they read the passage. Sometimes it is also necessary to remind some students to from mental pictures while they are reading the passage. (Of course, you should never introduce the passage without considerable oral discussion beforehand, emphasizing whatever other aspects of language development or reading is important for that group or student.)

3. Provide time (about five minutes) for a discussion of the students' "pictures" after they read the story. Be sure to respond positively to their "pictures" and provide other suitable images of your own that are consistent with the story.

4. If it is appropriate to do, test the students at this point, either verbally or with written questions, that sample both recall and inference.

5. You may need to give your students some practice in forming mental images before this technique can be used on a regular basis in your teaching. Once you are sure they have caught on, then simple instructions to have them use the technique are all that is necessary.

This very simple technique has been shown to bring dramatic improvement in students' recall of stories (percentage of correct answers nearly *doubled* on both recall and inferential questions over pretest scores). Additionally, the mental imaging technique was more effective than using the actual pictures which accompanied the text itself.

But the study from which this is drawn involved students at the sixth-grade level. Research has shown that imagery training does not appear to be effective until the student is nine or ten years old. For students younger than that, pictures in the text *will* help comprehension—provided that the pictures are consistent with or central to the overall message. Teachers of younger students should therefore assist them in deriving information from pictures in the text as an adjunct to reading comprehension.

Adapted from: Carrier, C., Joseph, M., Krey, C., and LaCroix, P. 1983. Supplied visuals and imagery instructions in field independent and field dependent children's recall. *Educational Communications and Technology Journal* 31:3, pp. 153-160.

See also: Levin, J. R. 1981. On functions of pictures in prose. In *Neuropsychological and cognitive processes in reading*, ed. F. J. Pirozzolo and M. C. Wittrock. New York: Academic Press.

Appendix 2-3

Teaching Sequencing

Perhaps the WISC-R results and parent and teacher behavioral observations suggest that sequencing is a problem for the student. If it is, the school psychologist's job is to provide recommendations that relate to academics. Here are two complementary methods (the first of them from Karen Clark) for emphasizing sequencing of time and story events.

Method 1

1. You may wish to begin with a clock. Show the students how to read a clock and stress the idea that one hour follows another. (You could incorporate both digital and analog time with older students.)

2. On the chalkboard, draw a circle and divide it into eight sections. Ask the students to think about the events of their daily routine, such as dressing, eating meals, and going to bed. Write these ideas, in sequence, around the circle. Discuss the repeated events of their daily lives.

3. You may wish to help the students construct time lines of their lives, beginning with birth and including important events up to the present.

4. Select an appropriate book from the great wealth of children's literature. For example, Tomie De Paola's *Strega Nona*, or Beatrix Potter's *Peter Rabbit* would be appropriate for a child in second or third grade. Read the book to the students, and then discuss the important events. List these events on a time line constructed as a group project.

5. Using discarded books, have the students search for "time" words or phrases. Ask them to locate and underline words such as *later, soon, tomorrow, in the future,* etc. Discuss the meaning of these words and how they relate to sequencing. For instance, a sentence beginning with *later* would not describe the first event of a series, while *in the evening* refers to the *end* of the day.

6. Have the student look at the illustrations in a story. Ask him or her why snow-covered ground would not be a suitable illustration for a summer story setting. Show the student the illustration from a picture-story book such as the old folk tale, "The Peddler and His Caps." Have the student tell the story through the ideas reflected. Encourage him or her to use sequence words such as *next, and then, at last,* and *later*. Then read the book to the student to see how accurate the student was in prediction concerning time. When questioning the student, wait for the response, and then ask, "And *then* what happened?" or, "And at *last* . . . ?" Use these language cues to help the student answer a question that requires that events be ordered sequentially.

7. Let the student draw his own illustrations for stories just read. The pictures should reflect the passage of time. A story such as *The Three Billy Goats Gruff* would be a good one to illustrate.

8. Write four or five sentence strips from the story being read. Mix them up and have the student read them, and then place them in the order in which they occur in the story. If the student is still a nonreader, use pictures from the story, rather than sentences. If the student has marked difficulty with sequencing, then an additional component is to have him "think out loud" while performing the task. If not, demonstrate the technique yourself. Encourage the student to try it on his own as he tries to sequence the pictures or sentences. Once he shows progress, reduce the thinking out loud to a whisper, and then fade it entirely.

Method 2

This method reinforces sequencing skills in a reading lesson, and can be adapted for any grade level.

1. Use a story from a theme you are currently working on.
2. Write the title on the chalkboard and ask the students to predict the subject matter of the story.
3. Present sentences from the story to the students. You could do this, for example, by placing them on strips. Prepare an envelope for each student that contains five or six sentences. Have the students individually try to put the sentences in order on the basis of what makes sense. If a student is still a nonreader, use pictures rather than sentences.
4. Have students compare and discuss their answers with two other students.
5. Discuss with the entire class the possible sequences, as well as the rationale behind each one. Be sure to emphasize natural-language sequencing words like *first, second, next, afterwards,* etc., present in the story.
6. Have students read the story from which the sequence statements were selected. While reading, they should be encouraged to compare other sequences with the text and change them as they consider appropriate.

You will also note this strategy highlights and strengthens the student's abilities to predict, confirm, and integrate information while reading.

Appendix 2-4

Distractibility

While the material in this appendix specifically relates to Chapter 2, it also has applications with respect to Chapters 3 and 5.

Distractibility—A Behavior

Distractibility is a behavior. As such, it is observable both in the classroom and at home. It is also observable when the student is being tested with an instrument like the WISC-R. The cluster of scores on the Freedom from Distractibility factor (Factor III) on the WISC-R also may have distractibility as the cause of low scores. Again, this hypothesis must be verified by sources of information that lie beyond the WISC-R scores themselves.

If distractibility is a major problem for this student, then the "Good Behavior Game, plus Merit" mentioned in Chapter 3 should be considered. That approach involves the whole class, rather than just the distractible student.Behavior management approaches have also proven useful at times. Research on diet management of distractibility, and its associated problem, hyperactivity, has been equivocal. As an approach to the problem in the classroom, it is unlikely to be helpful. Treatment with drugs such as Ritalin™ and Cylert™ has consistently shown that, although the student's motor activity or overactivity settles down, there is no concomitant increase in academic achievement. The school psychologist is therefore still left with trying to suggest creative ways of managing the student's needs in the classroom environment.

Because distractibility is a behavior, it can be modified by encouraging self-control. Students may be described as being inwardly distractible or outwardly distractible. If they are inwardly distractible, they may give the appearance of attending; but, in fact, they are off-task, because they are daydreaming—lost in "inner space," so to speak. If they are outwardly distractible, the teacher usually knows it, because the student gazes at the wall or whatever else captures his fleeting attention—out-of-seat inappropriately, always restless and fidgety, or interrupting others inappropriately.

Both types of distractibility are harmful academically; but the latter is the more noticeable, and therefore the more likely of the two to be referred to the school psychologist for intervention. In this appendix, I will present two methods for dealing with the problem. The first is drawn from some suggestions by Karen Clark, and is useful for younger students with milder degrees of distractibility. It is not really a "method" as such, but some global suggestions for the teacher.

Method 1

This helps develop concentration skills in listening and reading.

1. Read or tell a story to the student. Ask him to retell the story. Follow-up with specific questions. Begin with factual questions that stress memory for detail. Then ask questions requiring the student to draw inferences. At the end of the story, ask the student what might happen next.

2. After the student reads or hears a story, show him pictures, and have the student put them in the order in which they occurred in the story. You could also include some of the thinking-out-loud procedures suggested in Appendix 2-3 for sequencing, for this particular activity.

3. Have the student read directions for making something. Have the student perform the task by following the directions.

4. Teach the student to use verbal and nonverbal cues when listening. For example, when reading a story, change the intonation of your voice as you read various characters' parts. Have the student listen attentively and determine which character you are portraying. Have the student become aware of special cues that will alert him to sequence, as suggested in Appendix 2-3.

5. Facilitate the student's learning of verbal materials by organizing oral instructions in a clear, logical sequence. It is often very helpful to write these in point form on the chalkboard. It is also helpful to have the same points typed or written and attached to the student's desk.

6. Give the student passages that contain irrelevant material, or nonsensical statements. Ask the student to read through the entire passage and then circle the statements that are inappropriate.

7. When presenting an oral lesson, or when the student must read or write, be sure that there are no distractors on the student's desk, and that background noise is at a minimum. As the student gains facility with paying attention, he will learn to "filter out" distractors automatically.

Method 2—The Random "Beeper"

This procedure can be used with a whole class or a single student as young as seven years old in virtually every subject area.

1. Prepare an audio-cassette tape which contains beeps or tones which come on the tape about every 45 seconds. There should be nothing else on the tape between the beeps. The interval between the beeps can be as short as 10 seconds or as long as 90 seconds. If you are using the procedure with only one student, place the tape recorder on his desk. If you are using it with the whole class, place it somewhere where everyone can hear it.

2. Explain to the students that, each time they hear the beep, they are to ask themselves, "Was I paying attention?" If the answer is *yes*, they are to record it under the "Yes" column of a self-recording sheet taped to their desks. If the answer is *no*, they are to record it in the "No" column. For younger students, happy and sad faces can be substituted for the words. (A sample sheet follows this text.)

Your job as the teacher is to define clearly what "paying attention" means; to show the students how to mark the recording sheet; and to ask the students to repeat your instructions to be sure they are clearly understood. It is also important to solicit their cooperation beforehand.

It is better to use this procedure with written, independent work, than during the oral part of a lesson. With larger groups, however, you could try wrist-counters, rather than recording sheets. Wrist-counters are minimally disruptive.

If you are concerned that students will "cheat," then create the illusion of surveillance, or include a reinforcement if their *yes* marks agree with yours. You may also wish to build-in some reinforcement as a back-up if the number of *yes* marks reaches a specified criterion.

This procedure has been researched and shown to be effective in improving the on-task/off-task behavior of learning-disabled students.

Adapted from: Hallahan, D., and Sapona, R. 1984. Self-monitoring of attention with LD children: past research and current issues. In *Annual review of learning disabilities*, ed. J. Torgeson and G. Senf, pp. 97-101.

WAS I PAYING ATTENTION?

1. Y N   11. Y N   21. Y N   31. Y N   41. Y N

2. Y N   12. Y N   22. Y N   32. Y N   42. Y N

3. Y N   13. Y N   23. Y N   33. Y N   43. Y N

4. Y N   14. Y N   24. Y N   34. Y N   44. Y N

5. Y N   15. Y N   25. Y N   35. Y N   45. Y N

6. Y N   16. Y N   26. Y N   36. Y N   46. Y N

7. Y N   17. Y N   27. Y N   37. Y N   47. Y N

8. Y N   18. Y N   28. Y N   38. Y N   48. Y N

9. Y N   19. Y N   29. Y N   39. Y N   49. Y N

10. Y N   20. Y N   30. y N   40. y N   50. Y N

Appendix 2-5

Assisting Sight-Word Acquisition

Here are two methods for helping students develop their reading vocabulary to an automatic level. The first method comes from Karen Clark; the second is my own.

Method 1

1. Select a master list of words that you wish the student to know on sight. This could be a list such as Fry or Dolch, or the words could be taken directly from the reading material the student is currently using. Be sure the words have been introduced within a proper context before the students begin using this method. It is no use learning a word by sight if you have no idea of what it means!
2. Divide the words into lists of not more than 25 words per list. Number the words, and provide two places to check the accuracy of the reader.
3. Each word on the list should also be written on a word card. Number the card to correspond with the word on the list sheet.
4. Tape the words on a tape recorder, at a normal rate of reading. Do not pause too long between words.
5. The student listens to the words read, as he reads along silently or aloud.
6. The student reads along with the tape as many times as needed to learn the words.
7. When the student is ready, he brings the list to the teacher, who randomly selects words from the card pack. Present the cards one at a time, and check the sheet to indicate if it was correctly identified immediately, or if a second exposure was required.
8. When the word on the list is known immediately, encourage the student, and provide some visual feedback by using a progress chart. Use the same method for the next list. If a cassette recorder is available at home, the student could do some extra practice for homework.

Method 2

This method uses rehearsal to assist in sight-word acquisition.

1. Select the words you would like to use (see Method 1).
2. Work on only five words on the first day. Present each word, one at a time. Have the student look-see-repeat the word. Then turn it face down.
3. Present the next word. Have the student look-see-repeat this word *and rehearse the previous word* (without looking at it).
4. Repeat this procedure for all five words. Each time, have the student rehearse the other words.
5. Repeat the next day. However, begin by asking if the student can retrieve any of the previous day's five words.
6. Repeat the process. Once you are certain that the student knows the words automatically, record the progress on a chart.
7. Introduce five new words in the same fashion. After 15 words are mastered to the automatic level, begin another set of 15 words.

8. Encourage the student to use rehearsal (whispering to himself) in the regular classroom, as well. Role-play situations where this strategy could be useful. This part of the process is very important.

Rehearsal can also be used in the same fashion with the multiplication tables. It is useful for very "stubborn" words.

Appendix 3-1

Self-Rating Scales for Teacher Effectiveness

Self-Rating Scale for Classroom Management

Respond to each item in terms of the extent to which it describes you:
- 1 = Not at all descriptive
- 2 = Descriptive to a small extent
- 3 = Descriptive to a moderate extent
- 4 = Descriptive to a large extent
- 5 = Descriptive to an extremely large extent

Classroom Set-Up and Organization

1.1. I arrange physical space and instructional materials to minimize disruptive movement around my classroom, and to facilitate easy access to high-use materials   1 2 3 4 5

1.2. I establish and implement minimally disruptive traffic patterns and procedures.   1 2 3 4 5

1.3. I establish and implement procedures for nonacademic class business (e.g., tardiness, material use, movement in and out of the room, distributing materials, talk among students, bathroom breaks, etc.).   1 2 3 4 5

1.4. I establish and implement procedures for academic business (e.g., seatwork, obtaining help, volunteer behavior in small groups, learning centers, set-up and take-down of lessons, etc.).   1 2 3 4 5

Teaching Rules and Procedures

2.1. I communicate clearly what behavior will be tolerated and what will not.   1 2 3 4 5

2.2. I give behavior reminders and statements of desired behaviors in advance of activity.   1 2 3 4 5

2.3. I clearly introduce rules, procedures, and consequences at the beginning of the school year and whenever needed.   1 2 3 4 5

2.4. I state rules, post rules, and provide discussion of rules and procedures.   1 2 3 4 5

2.5. I present examples and non-examples of rules and procedures.   1 2 3 4 5

2.6. I require student rehearsal of rules and procedures.   1 2 3 4 5

2.7. I monitor rule compliance and provide feedback.   1 2 3 4 5

2.8. I act upon noncompliance by stopping inappropriate behavior immediately, and require students to practice procedures until they are performed automatically.   1 2 3 4 5

Mainstreaming Rules and Procedures

3.1. I position myself in the room to provide a high degree of visibility (e.g., I can make eye contact with my students).   1 2 3 4 5

3.2. I scan the room constantly, and make eye contact with all my students on an equal basis.   1 2 3 4 5

3.3. I detect disruptive behavior early and cite the rule or procedure in responding to the disruptive behavior.   1 2 3 4 5

3.4. I reinforce appropriate performance through specific praise statements.   1 2 3 4 5

3.5. I administer praise contingently (contingent upon the behavior I want).   1 2 3 4 5

3.6. I include students in the management of their own behavior.   1 2 3 4 5

3.7. I use nonverbal signals to direct students when I am teaching other groups of students.   1 2 3 4 5

Self-Rating Scale for Instructional Organization

Respond to each item in terms of the extent to which it describes you:
- 1 = Not at all descriptive
- 2 = Descriptive to a small extent
- 3 = Descriptive to a moderate extent
- 4 = Descriptive to a large extent
- 5 = Descriptive to an extremely large extent

Allocated Time

1.1. I maximize time instruction by continually scheduling students in direct instruction (e.g., I interact with 70 percent or more of the students per hour).   1 2 3 4 5

1.2. I minimize time in noninstructional activities (e.g., I spend 80 percent or more of class time in instructional activities).   1 2 3 4 5

1.3. I keep transition time between lessons short (e.g., no more than three minutes between change of students and activity; no more than 30 seconds when changing activity only).   1 2 3 4 5

1.4. I establish procedures for lessons that signal a clear beginning and end.   1 2 3 4 5

1.5. I gain all students' attention at the beginning of the lesson and   1 2 3 4 5
maintain student attention during lessons at a 90-percent level.

1.6. I prepare students for transitions in advance by stating behavioral   1 2 3 4 5
expectations and informing students that the lesson is drawing to
a close.

Engaged Time

2.1. I maintain students' attention during seatwork at 80-percent   1 2 3 4 5
levels or higher.

2.2. I monitor seatwork of students continuously through eye-scanning.   1 2 3 4 5

2.3. I circulate among students between lessons to assist students and   1 2 3 4 5
monitor progress.

2.4. I maintain seatwork accuracy at 90-percent levels or higher.   1 2 3 4 5

2.5. I tell the rationale for seatwork and communicate the importance   1 2 3 4 5
of the assignment to students.

2.6. I provide active forms of seatwork practice clearly related to   1 2 3 4 5
academic goals.

2.7. I set seatwork and assignment standards (e.g., neatness, accuracy,   1 2 3 4 5
due-dates, etc.).

2.8. I use tutoring (e.g., peers, volunteers, aides) and other specialized   1 2 3 4 5
instructional technology to increase the opportunities for active
academic responding during seatwork.

2.9. I establish procedures for early finishers, students who are stalled,   1 2 3 4 5
and those seeking help.

2.10. I schedule time to review seatwork.   1 2 3 4 5

2.11. I require that students correct their work and make up missed or   1 2 3 4 5
unfinished work.

2.12. I give informative feedback to students in making written or oral   1 2 3 4 5
corrections.

Self-Rating Scale for Teaching Presentation

Respond to each item in terms of the extent to which it describes you:
- 1 = Not at all descriptive
- 2 = Descriptive to a small extent
- 3 = Descriptive to a moderate extent
- 4 = Descriptive to a large extent
- 5 = Descriptive to an extremely large extent

Lesson Presentation—Introductory Phase

1.1. I review prior learning by requiring active student recitation or practice of previous day's drill. 1 2 3 4 5

1.2. I state the objectives of the lesson and communicate to students what they will be expected to do to demonstrate mastery of a new skill. 1 2 3 4 5

1.3. I provide an overview of the lesson. 1 2 3 4 5

1.4. I relate new concepts to old ones by stating how a new skill is like or different from those the student already knows. 1 2 3 4 5

1.5. I use the student's prior experiences to aid comprehension and understanding. 1 2 3 4 5

1.6. I convey purposefulness for learning by stating the rationale. 1 2 3 4 5

Lesson Presentation—Demonstration Phase

2.1. I model behavioral responses for factual learning, and I model the steps of a procedure in procedural learning. 1 2 3 4 5

2.2. I require students to rehearse new behaviors and procedures based on imitation of my modeling. 1 2 3 4 5

2.3. I point out distinctive features of new concepts. 1 2 3 4 5

2.4. I state concept definitions and provide rehearsals. 1 2 3 4 5

2.5. I present many examples and nonexamples of new concepts or generalizations, and explain why they are examples or nonexamples. 1 2 3 4 5

2.6. I provide discrimination activities (e.g., series of examples and nonexamples to test student performance and understanding). 1 2 3 4 5

2.7. I ask students to give a rationale or explain decisions in determining why particular instances are examples or nonexamples of the concept. 1 2 3 4 5

2.8. I deliver specific cues and prompts prior to the initiation of student responses, to maintain accuracy above 80 percent. 1 2 3 4 5

2.9. I ask frequent questions to test understanding and provide opportunities for academic practice. 1 2 3 4 5

Extended Practice and Evaluation

3.1. I repeat practice opportunities until students are not making errors. 1 2 3 4 5

3.2. I use error correction procedures (e.g., prompts or models), rather than tell answers or call on another student. 1 2 3 4 5

3.3. I provide error drill by repeatedly presenting concepts on which   1   2   3   4   5
       students have erred.

3.4. I follow-up on correct responses with contingent and specific praise. 1   2   3   4   5

3.5. I maintain a brisk pace during the lesson.   1   2   3   4   5

3.6. I provide daily, weekly, and monthly reviews.   1   2   3   4   5

3.7. I provide frequent tests to determine students' mastery of academic 1   2   3   4   5
       objectives.

3.8. I reteach or make instructional decisions on the basis of students' 1   2   3   4   5
       performance on tests.

3.9. I maintain continuous records and graphs of student progress.   1   2   3   4   5

Adapted from: Englert, C. S. 1984. Measuring teacher effectiveness from the teacher's point of view. *Focus on Exceptional Children* (October).

Appendix 3-2

Potential Reinforcers

1. Ten minutes of extra recess.
2. Getting to talk to a group of friends during the last ten minutes of class.
3. Getting to choose a special seat partner at lunch.
4. Winning a "Super Student" badge.
5. Having a note sent home to parents praising the student's work.
6. Reading comic books for ten minutes.
7. Helping in the classroom.
8. Helping the caretaker or building-supervisor.
9. Helping the principal.
10. Cleaning the erasers.
11. Taking attendance in the morning.
12. Decorating the bulletin board.
13. Using a typewriter or computer.
14. Running the photocopier.
15. Stapling papers together.
16. Giving a message over the intercom.
17. Carrying messages to other teachers.
19. Cleaning the teacher's desk.
20. Picking up litter on the school grounds.
21. Handing out and collecting assignments.
22. Emptying the waste-paper basket.
23. Using an overhead projector, filmstrip or movie projector, or VCR.
24. Writing with a pen or colored pencils.
25. Correcting papers.
26. Recording the student's own behavior on a graph.
27. Working with clay.
28. Teaching/tutoring another student.
29. Doing special problems.
30. Reading the newspaper in class.
31. Learning a magic trick.
32. Reading or drawing a road map.
33. Listening to the radio with an earplug.
34. Arm wrestling.
35. Lighting or blowing out a candle (be careful!).
36. Being allowed to move desks.
37. Going to the library.
38. Helping the librarian.

39. Writing a letter to someone special.
40. Looking at a globe/atlas.
41. Making or flying a kite.
42. Popping corn.
43. Visiting with the principal.
44. Making a puppet.
45. Making a book.
46. Sitting next to the teacher at lunch.
47. Opening the teacher's mail/messages.
48. Weighing or measuring various objects in the classroom.

Other:

Adapted from: Wallace, G., and Kauffman, J. 1978. *Teaching children with learning problems.* Columbus, Ohio: Charles E. Merrill.

Appendix 3-3

Hints for Successful Study at Home

Dear Parent,

There are several ways you can help your child with his or her reading at home. A very important aspect of this help is to build a positive attitude toward reading. This can be done in a number of ways:

1. Become involved with your child when he or she reads. Put your arm around your child. Take an interest in your child's activities. *Show* your child that you are interested; and show approval. Laugh along with the story, and interject your own observations at appropriate moments.

2. Encourage frequent use of your local library. Take your child to the library. You don't necessarily need a lot of books at home of your own. Help your child select books appropriate to his or her own interests and reading ability. If a book is too difficult for your child to read, but interest is shown in it, perhaps that's the one you can read to him or her for that week.

3. Help set a purpose for your child's reading—but be sensitive to your child in this regard. Try not to make it too much of a "teaching situation." If your child is resisting you, don't force the matter; but, if you can do it in a positive atmosphere, have your child read a passage silently several times. Ask your child to read the passage each time for a different purpose, such as:

    a. What do you think is the main idea?
    b. What happens first in the story? Second? Third?
    c. Ask a specific question yourself, focusing on an important detail.
    d. Ask any other specific question about the story.
    e. If the story is a tale, or involves a problem of some sort, ask your child to focus on:
        (1) What was the problem?
        (2) How was it solved?
        (3) What is the lesson in the story?

    Your child may have difficulty if all the questions are asked at the end. If so, make the task easier by pointing out to the child what, in each section of the story, to focus on. "Now, in this part, watch for . . . ." These questions may be used whether you read the story to your child, or the child reads independently. Remember, however, that the atmosphere needs to remain pleasant. If you find yourself arguing with your child over reading assignments, consider using a tutor or an older, helpful student to do these activities instead.

4. Help your child look words up in dictionaries, encyclopedias, and other reference sources. Show your child how a dictionary is organized. If your child is interested, show him or her how to use a thesaurus works, as well. If you can afford the investment, a set of encyclopedias is a valuable asset to your home, so long as its use is encouraged, and you participate in that encouragement.

5. If your child has reading problems, then your attitude toward reading is crucial. You must be patient and satisfied with one step at a time, no matter how small that one step may be. Remember how pleased you were when your child took his or her first step. Convey that same pleasure as your child takes each small step toward better reading. Above all, do not show disappointment or convey to your child that he or she is not

meeting your demands and expectations. Equally damaging are attitudes of anger, hostility, or indifference.

Your child needs you. We are all working toward the same goals—improved reading and enjoyment of reading.

Appendix 3-4

Changing "Learned Helplessness"

Many students with learning difficulties exhibit signs of learned helplessness. Such students do not attribute success (or failure) on a task to their own efforts or lack of effort. If they do well, they tend to think it is just because the test was too easy or the teacher praised them just because the teacher was being nice to them. If they do poorly, they generally think it is because of a lack of their own ability, rather than a lack of effort.

Consequently, one characteristic of such students is that they "quit before they even start." They may be very slow to start their project or assignment, or may simply put their heads down, giving a nonverbal sign of defeat. They frequently require teacher prompting to keep going on a task if and when they do start, and are quick to give up when the first obstacle is reached. Frequently, they do not ask for assistance when they should. They may become destructive or withdrawn. They also exhibit little pride in their work, such as not sharing it with the teacher or peers.

A number of researchers have shown that it is possible to change the "internal thinking (attributions)" a student makes when faced with a difficult task. A relatively short training period has been shown to increase task persistence and change the negative attributions.

The following procedure has been adapted from one of the research studies in this area.

Time Required

A total of six hours spread over three weeks. Each session should be about one-half hour long, and done twice weekly. To begin, do the training one-on-one. As you become more adept, you will be able to work with small groups by making some adjustments.

Materials Required

1. Tape recorder. For the first two sessions (Week 1), the student is to listen to an appropriate model (a student the same age and sex) who reads a sentence correctly, and with errors. When the sentence is read correctly, the student says:

   - "I got that right. I tried hard and did a good job."

   When the student makes an error, the student says:

   - "No, I didn't get that quite right—but that's OK. Even if I make a mistake, I can go back and try harder to get it right."

2. Sixteen sentences of about the same length on individual cards or strips. Ten of the sentences should be within the student's reading level. These are designated as E for Easy. The remaining six should have three words above the student's reading level. These are designated D for Difficult. Since students become more familiar with the sentences through the training sessions, you may have to prepare a second set of sixteen sentences in the same fashion as the first.

3. A suitable space—together with patience, respect, and care.

Procedure

Session 1

Establish rapport with the student. Explain why you are working together. As much as possible, involve the student in the process. You might say something like:

- "..., you and I are going to work together on a project. I've noticed that when we do things in school, you sometimes put your head down and don't try it, or you seem to give up quickly after you start. Do you notice that about yourself?"

If the student responds "yes," continue; but, if "no," then do some mild confrontation using more examples. Usually, the student will just admit there could be a problem. Then you might say:

- "Well, sometimes part of the difficulty is just what we tell ourselves when we do something right or get it wrong. I'm going to have you listen to someone read some sentences to show you what I mean." [Play the recording.]

Ask:

- "Did you notice what the person said when he [she] got it right?" [Have the student repeat it.]
- "And what about when the person got it wrong? What did he [she] say?" [Have the student repeat it, or play the recording again.]
- "Now I'd like to have you give it a try. I'm going to show you some sentences, one at a time, that I'd like you to read out loud. Some of the sentences will be easy and others will be hard, but I want you to read all of them and do the best you can."

Introduce an Easy sentence. The student should get it right. Then say:

- "OK, what should you say to yourself when you get it right?"

Have the student say the appropriate phrase first out loud, then in a whisper, and then silently. This sequence is important, because it follows the natural way we internalize something modeled for us. The first three sentences should be Easy ones.

The fourth sentence should be a Difficult one. After the student makes his attempt, have him say the appropriate attribution out loud, then in a whisper, and then silently. At this point, you could also encourage an appropriate reading strategy such as rereading for context clues, using a suitable prediction, or trying to sound the word out. But try to place the onus on the student to do this. The dialogue or "self-talk" might go something like this:

- "Whoops, I didn't get that right, but that's OK. Even if I make a mistake, I can go back and try again. What should I do here? I could try to guess what the word should be that I got wrong because I know some of the other words in the sentence. Yes, that's what I'll do!"

The session should proceed in this fashion. After each sentence, have the student repeat the appropriate phrase in the manner indicated. The sequence of Easy or Difficult sentences has also shown to be very important. For Session 1, the entire sequence is as follows:

E E E D D D E E D E E E D D E E

Session 2

Begin this session with the tape recording again. Have the student again model the appropriate self-attributions out loud, in a whisper, and then silently. Review your goals and introduce the sentences as before. The sequence for this session should be:

E E D E E D D D E E E D D E E E

Session 3

You probably do not need the tape recorder anymore. Have the student review the appropriate attributions. The sequence of the sentences for this session should be:

E E D D D E E E D D E E D E E E

Session 4

Continue with the following sequence:
                    E E E D D D E E D E E D D E E

Session 5

Use this sequence:
                    E E D E E D D D E E E D D E E E

Session 6

End your training with this sequence:
                    E E D D D E E E D D E E D E E E

As training progresses, you need to make attempts to encourage generalization of appropriate "self-talk" in the student's classes. The following ways might be helpful:

1. Be sure to discuss the training process with all of the student's teachers. Ask them to encourage the student when they notice that he or she is using appropriate "self-talk" in the classroom situation.
2. If the student "forgets" to use the process, devise a nonverbal cue from teacher to student to do so.
3. Use a booster-training session about three weeks after the final training session is over.
4. Review progress periodically after that.

Finally, do not expect miracles from the program. Research shows that, while more appropriate "self-talk" and more effort results from the training, changes in self-esteem take longer and may require repeated boosters geared specifically to the subject area of difficulty.

Be patient—take one small step at a time.

Adapted from: Shelton, T., Anastopoulos, A., and Linden, J. 1985. An attribution training program with learning-disabled children. *Journal of Learning Disabilities* 18:5, pp. 261-265. Personal communication with Dr. Terri Shelton helped provide more details, particularly the sequence of the sentences for each session. Dr. Shelton can be contacted at Project Optimus, 77 Warren St., Brighton, Massachusetts.

Appendix 3-5

Relaxation Procedures for Teachers and Students

For Teachers

To begin this technique, find a comfortable chair to sit in. Let yourself settle in for a few minutes on each occasion before doing any of the exercises. The room the chair is in should be as quiet as possible, and you should try to do these exercises around the same time each day. You will probably require about half an hour to start with; but as you become more adept, you will likely need only fifteen to twenty minutes.

Put the instructions onto a cassette tape. This will allow you to keep your eyes closed as you go through the various tension-release items. Be sure to talk in a smooth, rather monotone voice while recording it.

Instructions

Imagine yourself carrying all your responsibilities in a big sack on your shoulders. With your eyes closed, imagine yourself putting down your load. For this time of relaxation, you don't have to worry about anything. You are responsible for nothing. You don't have to do anything but relax.

As you relax your various muscle groups, you may also wish to use the following image. Think of a marionette standing up straight, being held up by taught strings that make it move. If the puppeteer's hands let go of the strings, they will go loose and the marionette will crumple into a totally relaxed heap. Your brain is your puppeteer and it can let go whenever it wants. As you relax each muscle, imagine letting go of the marionette strings; and as it goes limp, you go limp.

1. Now tighten your right hand by making a fist and squeezing (5 seconds). Notice the tension. Now let it go. Imagine your limp puppet arm. Feel the difference (10 seconds). Now tighten your right arm again. Keep your eyes closed. Now let go. Feel the relaxation (10 seconds).

2. Now tighten your left arm (5 seconds). Now let it go. Imagine your limp puppet arm. It should be as limp as your right limp puppet arm. Now squeeze again (5 seconds). Now let go. Feel the difference. Feel how relaxed both arms are. As they relax, notice how your torso and shoulders also relax.

3. Keep your eyes closed. Bring your shoulders up as if to touch your ears with them (5 seconds). Notice the tension. Now let go and feel the difference (10 seconds). Feel yourself letting go, going limp and loose and relaxed. Put down your bag of responsibilities. Just take it easy (15 seconds). Now bring your shoulders up again (5 seconds). Feel the tension. Now let go and notice the difference (10 seconds). Just take it easy. Keep your eyes closed. Notice how good you feel.

4. Now press your lips tightly together (5 seconds). Now let go and enjoy the difference (10 seconds). Try it again and let go once more, feeling the tension leave your mouth and jaw as you relax deeper and deeper.

5. Press your head back against your shoulders. Feel the tension in your neck (5 seconds). Now let go. Feel the difference (10 seconds). Keep your arms and torso relaxed, like the limp puppet. Now bring your head back again. Notice the tension. Now let go. Feel how good the relaxation feels. Keep your eyes closed.

6. Now take a deep breath—so deep you feel it stretch your chest muscles. Hold it (5 seconds). Release it slowly. Feel yourself relax and go limp as the air leaves your lungs. It's good. It feels very good. Now take a deep breath again. Feel the tension.

Now relax and let the air out slowly. Now you feel your whole upper body is relaxed and limp and wonderful and that bag of cares seems so far away.

7. Now place your legs as far in front of you as you can. Now lift them slowly and hold (5 seconds). Feel the tension. Now let go and feel the difference (15 seconds). Feel the looseness that comes from letting go. Just hold it. Now lift your legs again and feel the tension. Now let go. Let your legs relax and become as loose and limp as your upper body. Feel the master puppeteer let go of more of the strings. Feel how good that feels.

8. Now point your toes back toward your chest. Feel the tension that creates in your calves. Now let go and experience the difference (10 seconds). Feel the relaxation. Now point your toes back again. See how tense your calves get. Now let go and see how good it feels to relax. To go limp and loose and easy.

9. Now curl your toes downward, like you're digging them into sand. Feel the tension in your arches. Now let go. See how your feet are becoming as relaxed as the rest of your body. Now curl them again and feel the difference. Now let go. See how good it feels.

10. Now your whole body is relaxed. Notice how you feel and how good it is. Check over your body to see if any tension remains. If any part still feels somewhat tense, tighten it and then let go. Now you are like a balloon with all the air out, like a puppet with no strings attached. Feel the relaxation, the easiness. Enjoy the feeling. Enjoy how good it feels to have a few minutes with no responsibilities, no cares, just an easy relaxed feeling. Just a soothing tingle all over. Just a few minutes of the kind of break you deserve.

You could tape five to ten minutes of easy-listening music at this point and let it play through you as you enjoy the state of relaxation you have created.

After you are through, begin to straighten up in your chair. Give your body a chance to come back to its normal state of readiness. Stretch, take it easy, then open your eyes.

As you become more expert, you'll need to rely on the tape or written instructions less and less. You'll find you can relax this way without going through every muscle exercise. You may even find the images you have selected will "trigger" a pleasant twenty minutes or half-hour of relaxation.

Teaching Children to Relax

After you have prepared your students for the usefulness of relaxation procedures, you will want to begin a systematic procedure for relaxing with them. This outside-in technique, adapted from an article in *Elementary School Guidance and Counseling* (October 1974) could be very useful to you. It follows the same sort of sequence as the adult technique . . . but has images children can identify with easily.

Your students should be comfortably seated in their desks although, if your room is suitable, they can sit against the wall. Their backs should have a means of support.

Tell your students they must follow some rules. They must do exactly as you say. They must try each of the exercises. They should pay careful attention to how their muscles feel when they are tense and when they are relaxed. Finally, they must practice as you direct them (usually no more than twice daily).

Give some preliminary instructions about getting comfortably seated. Let both feet be on the floor and let their arms hang loosely by their sides. Have them close their eyes and not open them until instructed to do so by you. As mentioned [elsewhere in the original text], if you have a student model the procedure, the process will go much more smoothly. You should now be ready to begin.

Hands and Arms

Pretend you have a whole lemon in your left hand. Squeeze it hard (5 seconds). Try to squeeze all the juice out. Feel how tight your hand and arm is as you squeeze. Now drop the lemon. Feel the difference (10 seconds). Take another lemon and squeeze it (5 seconds). Feel the tightness. Now drop the lemon and feel the relaxation.

Repeat the procedure for the right hand and arm.

Arms and Shoulders

Pretend you are a furry, lazy cat. You really want to stretch. Stretch your arms in front of you. Raise them high over your shoulders. Feel the pull in your shoulders. Stretch higher (hold for 10 to 15 seconds). Now let your arms drop by your sides (10 seconds). Feel the difference. Stretch again. Put your arms way out in front of you. Raise them over your head. Pull them way back. Now let them drop quickly. Keep your eyes closed. Remember, you are a lazy cat and you are just yawning. You don't really want to wake up and see anything. Feel how good and warm and lazy it is to be relaxed.

Shoulders and Neck

Pretend you are a turtle. You're sitting on a rock by a very peaceful pond, just relaxing in the warm sun (15 seconds). Oh oh! You sense danger. Pull your head into your house. Try to pull your shoulders up to your ears and push your head down into your shoulders. Hold in tight (10 seconds). It isn't easy to be a turtle in a shell. The danger is past now. You can come out into the warm sunshine again. Once more, relax and feel the warm sun. Keep your eyes closed (15 seconds). Here it comes again! Pull your head back into your house and hold it tight (10 seconds). Protect yourself. OK, you can come out again. Relax. Notice how much better it feels to be relaxed than to be all tightened up.

Face and Nose

Here comes a pesky fly. He has landed on your nose. Try to get him off without using your hands. Wrinkle up your nose. Make as many wrinkles in your nose as you can. Scrunch it up as hard as you can (10 seconds). Good. You chased him away. Now you can relax your nose. Feel how good it is without the fly (10 seconds). Oops, here he comes again. Right back in the middle of your nose. Shoo him away. Wrinkle up again. Hold it as tight as you can (10 seconds). OK, he flew away. You can relax your face. Notice that when you scrunch up your nose that your cheeks and your mouth and your forehead and your eyes all help you and they get tight as well. When you relax your nose, the rest of your face relaxes too, and that feels very good.

Stomach

Here comes a baby elephant. Oh oh. He's not watching where he's going. He doesn't see you sitting there in the grass and he's about to step on your stomach. Don't move. You don't have time to get out of the way. Just get ready for him. Make your stomach very hard. Tighten up your stomach muscles. Hold it (10 seconds). It looks like he's going the other way. You can relax now. Let your stomach relax and be as soft as it can be (15 seconds). Feel how good that is. Oh oh, he's coming back. Tighten up again. Real hard. If he steps on you it just won't hurt. Make your stomach like a rock. All right, he's moving away again. You can relax. Just get comfortable and feel relaxed in the warm sun in the open field.

At this point, you could let the students relax for a longer period of time, perhaps five minutes. It would be good to tape five minutes of music suitable for the purpose and let it play through at this point before you continue.

Legs and Feet

Pretend you are standing barefoot in a big mud puddle. Squish your toes down deep into the mud. Try to get your feet down to the bottom of the mud puddle. You'll probably need your legs to help you push. Push down, spread your toes apart, and feel the mud squish up between your toes. Now step up out of the mud puddle. Relax your feet (15 seconds). Let your toes go loose and feel how nice that is. Back into the mud puddle. Squish your toes down (10 seconds). Let your leg muscles help. Try to squeeze the puddle dry. OK. Come back out now. Relax your feet, relax your legs. Relax your toes. It feels good to be relaxed, with no tension anywhere. Just warm and tingly.

Finishing

Stay as relaxed as you can. Let your whole body go limp and feel all your muscles relax. In a while, I will ask you to open your eyes and that will be the end of the session. As you go through the day, it is important to remember how good it feels to be relaxed. Sometimes you have to make yourself tighter before you can be relaxed, just like in today's exercises. You can practice these exercises at home. A good time is at night, after you have gone to bed and the lights are out and you won't be disturbed. It will help you to get to sleep. When you become a good relaxer you can relax here at school. Just remember the elephant or the turtle or the mud puddle and you can do the exercises without anybody knowing.

Very slowly now, open your eyes and wiggle your muscles around a little. Very good. You've done a good job and will make super relaxers.

Reprinted from: Truch, S. 1980. *Teacher burnout and what to do about it*. Novato, California: Academic Therapy Publications.

Appendix 5-1

Word Banks and Word Sorts

Word Banks

Word banks are simply collections of words that the student places in some safe place such as a filing box. The words should be chosen primarily by the student, and should be based on his or her interests, experiences, and feelings. Each bank is therefore highly personalized. In fact, word banks will build confidence if the student sees them as personal. Word banks are associated with the language-experience approach, but can be extended in a number of ways useful to classrooms and remedial groups.

A number of teaching activities can be developed using the students' word banks. Here are some suggestions:

Exploring Self-Concept

1. Have the students write words describing their present feelings about school, family, and/or friends.
2. Select an exciting word, a frightening word, or a happy word from the word bank cards. Have the students share why the word evokes the feeling it does.
3. Write a word or find one from the bank that tells the names of pets, favorite toys, colors, TV programs, or movies.
4. Write names of places of interest, places recently visited, or exciting places to explore.
5. Choose a self-descriptive word for each letter in the student's name.
6. Write a word describing something fun to do.
7. Copy "best" words onto the chalkboard, or place the word cards in desk pocket charts and read them to other students in the group or class.
8. Write words that name special people, such as family members, friends, or teachers, and attach a picture of the person to accompany the name.
9. Select appropriate words from the bank and write an autobiography.
10. Select some self-descriptive words and write them in riddle form, ending with the words, "Who am I?" (e.g., "I like cats. I have a sister named Alita. I like to take ballet lessons. Who am I?").

Word Analysis Skills

These activities should of course be done within the context of the total language arts program to maximize transfer of learning.

1. Label items in the room with words from the word banks, then use the words in phrases.
2. Read a poem or listen to a song and find a word that rhymes with one of the words in the poem or song.
3. Select two words from the word bank to read to a partner or the class, then ask one of the following questions: Do they rhyme? Do they end the same? Do they begin the same? Use whatever questions are appropriate for the student or group.

4. Display a picture representing some object or activity. Have the student choose words with the same beginning sound as the object or activity, and attach the word to the picture.
5. Find as many words from a particular word family as you can. Illustrate them or use them in sentences.
6. Find more than one name for the same thing (e.g., lady, Mom, Mother, wife, aunt). Draw a picture to accompany the words.
7. Find a word for each letter of the alphabet.
8. Write one sentence using two words of opposite meaning (antonyms).
9. Cut out a picture from a magazine and write a title for it using word bank cards.
10. Find a word bank word to complete a sentence written on the chalkboard (e.g., This is a . . . dog).
11. Prepare a cloze passage omitting all nouns (or verbs or adjectives). Students select words from their word banks to fill in the blanks.
12. Select a word bank word to be Word for the Day. Use it wherever possible throughout the day.
13. Make a shopping list using word bank words.
14. Find words for things found in a kitchen, classroom, closet, etc.
15. Play Scavenger Hunt with words. The teacher gives each student a list of statements such as, "Find a color word," or, "Find the name of a farm animal," or, "Find all the food words." This activity also helps build categorization skills.
16. Sort out all the contractions in the word bank and write sentences using them.
17. Pick any word, then find another word that comes before it in alphabetical order.
18. Look for homophones, homonyms, antonyms, or synonyms. Write a sentence and draw a picture to show the meaning of each.

Written Language Activities

1. Write a poem or story using one or more word bank words.
2. After students participate in an activity such as popping corn, they choose words related to the activity to enter into their word banks.
3. Create sentences using word bank words. Add correct punctuation. Cards with punctuation marks may be added to the bank.
4. The teacher puts up a chart with a title such as "Special Words," or "Holiday Words," or "Three Bear Words," or "Lord of the Rings Words." Students can copy appropriate words from their banks onto the chart. They may also select words from the chart to add to their banks.

Social Studies Related Activities

1. Make a card to put in the bank, or find an existing card, that tells the name of a famous person or place.
2. Write the name of an occupation.
3. Write the name of a wild animal, article of clothing, or tool associated with a particular country or group of people.

4. Write a word from a foreign language.
5. Write a word describing most communities have, and tell why it is important.

Health-Related Activities

1. Make a menu for a meal using word bank words.
2. Write a word naming something important to good health, and make a poster using the word in a caption.
3. Write a word for something dangerous, and tell why it is dangerous.

Math and Science Related Activities

1. Write words for things in the shape of a triangle, rectangle, square, circle, etc. Make an "A Triangle Can Be . . ." book (e.g., "A triangle can be a tent").
2. Write a word that is a math or science term.
3. Write a word for an object made of a particular material (e.g., "A chair can be made of wood").
4. Write a word naming one of the sentences. Make a "Things I Can See" book or a "Things I Can Smell" book.
5. Pick any "naming word" (noun) and write a number of facts about the word.
6. Write a number and then write as many facts for that number as possible (e.g., *six*: 2 + 4 = 6; 3 + 3 = 6; 5 + 1 = 6; etc.).
7. Write a word for something from which many things can be made (e.g., trees, peanuts, corn), and tell what is made from it.

The word bank, as mentioned, is often associated with the language-experience approach, in which a group dictates a story out of their own experiences and the teacher writes it down. Dictation is followed by successive days of reading and underlining all words that the student knows. Using a card with a word-size window cut in it, the teacher evaluates each student's recognition of words in isolation. In addition to the words the student selects in the activities just listed (which can easily be adapted for older students or for those in special education classes), all underlined words in the chart story that are recognized two or three days after dictation should also be placed in the word bank. Desk pocket charts are ideal for helping the student to categorize his or her words. They can also be used for helping the student to use the cards in phrases and sentences. Many of the activities we have just outlined are well suited to a desk pocket chart format.

The suggestions made here help to integrate the language arts. The word bank should be used throughout the day—not just for reading.

Adapted from: Garton, S., Schoenfelder, P., and Skriba, P. 1979. Activities for young word bankers. *The Reading Teacher* (January) pp. 453-457.

Word Sorts

Word sorting is based on categorization of words in the students' vocabulary. Words from the word bank are appropriate, but the word can also be teacher-selected. The students learn to sort the words into groups based on either (1) feature analysis, or (2) induction (categorization).

When using feature analysis, the teacher can have the students sort their words (about 10 words at a time), finding features the words have in common, such as shared letters, similar sounds, same first or last letter or sound, similar structural elements, identical number of syllables, etc. Such a sort, guided by the teacher, with the criterion stated beforehand, is called a closed sort. It is a process which forces convergent thinking and deduction.

In an open sort, the teacher does not state the criterion. Rather, students select 10 words and sort them according to the categories they perceive. This forces divergent thinking and induction. This can also be turned into a small group game such as Guess My Sort, where other students try to figure out what criterion the student used for his or her sort. If students are nonreaders, pictures instead of cards can be used. If they are advanced readers, more advanced criteria can be used, such as meaning, etymology, parts of speech, etc.

Teachers can also modify the activity to suit the needs of a specific student. Here, for example, is Karen Clark's closed sort activity for a young student using only five words:

1. Prepare five word cards—one word on each card (e.g., thank-you, tree, with, bed, frog).
2. Place the cards in random order in front of the child. Read through the five words together.
3. The teacher reads questions on a card to the child. The child scans his cards for the one that answers the question. He points to it, and reads it.

Teacher's Card: Sample 1

1. Which word means something you sleep in?
2. Which word means a little animal that likes to sit on a lily pad?
3. What do we say when someone helps us?
4. What word begins with *w*?
5. Where would you expect to find a robin's nest?
6. Which word means an animal that likes to hop?
7. Which word means something that gives shade?
8. Which word ends with the letters *the*?
9. Where do you expect to find blankets and a pillow?
10. What do you think the little boy said when he received a birthday present?

The teacher collects the word cards and has the child read through them quickly.

Teacher's Card: Sample 2

The teacher reads a sentence, which has one word deleted, to the child. The child says the word and indicates the card. The child says the whole sentence:

1. The squirrel ran up the . . . .
2. Do you want to come . . . me?
3. Hop, hop, hop. Here comes a little green . . . .
4. When I am sick, I stay in . . . .
5. When you receive a gift, you should say . . . .
6. The dog came to school . . . the children.
7. When someone shares an apple with you, you should say . . . .
8. The . . . had a mosquito for lunch.

9. Mother said not to jump on the . . . .
10. The monkey climbed to the top of the . . . .

Note: Ten minutes is usually ample time to spend on this type of activity.

Adapted from: Gillet, J., and Kita, M. 1979. Words, kids, and categories. *The Reading Teacher* (February) pp. 538-542.

Word banks and word sorts obviously help students build their classifying and categorization skills. These are extremely important skills which underlie much of every student's learning. Gillet and Temple write:

> From the first weeks of life, children demonstrate their powerful, autonomous drive to explore, experience, and make sense of their world. They do this by developing cognitive categories of objects and events that are similar in some ways. These categories become apparent to adults when young children begin talking, for then they can provide labels for their categories and assign new experiences to the appropriate classes. Most parents have patiently explained over and over to a toddler, "No, that's not a doggy; that's a squirrel. No, that's not a horsie; that's a sheep." Children usually overgeneralize their categories, calling every four-legged animal *doggy* or, for a short time, calling every adult man *Dadda*, before they develop more numerous, sharply defined cognitive categories. Developing new cognitive categories and making old ones more specific are the bases for all cognitive growth and learning. Categorizing and classifying remain one of the most powerful learning processes we have throughout our lives.

From: Gillet, J. W., and Temple, C. 1982. *Understanding reading problems, assessment and instruction*, p. 137. Boston: Little, Brown. (This book is an excellent reference for the school psychologist interested in knowing more about the reading process and reading remediation.)

Appendix 5-2

Written Expression

A major focus of this book has been on relating the WISC-R to reading. In this appendix, I would like to make some links to writing. I believe the same language-immersion approach is as necessary for a writing program as it is for reading. As with reading, however, special education students generally require much more structure, direction, and skill-building than do regular class students.

Many similar top-down and bottom-up principles apply in the act of writing. As is the case for reading, writing requires that both processes act in concert. Frequently, special education students have great difficulty with many of the bottom-up skills such as rapid and automatic printing or writing (psychomotor speed). Therefore, there is need for many BUDs (bottom-up drills) in the act of writing.

I will begin by discussing written expression, as opposed to handwriting or spelling, which will be dealt with later.

The foundations of a good written expression program include:

1. Using the student's oral language to full advantage;
2. Using the student's background knowledge to full advantage;
3. Motivating the student by drawing out his own experiences and interests in the writing process;
4. Appropriately revising of one's writing; and
5. Publishing one's writing.

These principles apply in a special education classroom (with appropriate modifications) as much as in regular programs. A number of writers like Donald Graves from Australia and James Britton of England advocate this type of approach. I have seen it work very well even with severely learning-disabled students, provided that proper structure is used.

Students who do poorly on the Freedom from Distractibility triad on the WISC-R, or who do poorly on the Coding subtest alone, frequently have difficulty with writing. The difficulties may result from poor internal organizing, lack of planning, difficulties with the mechanics of writing (including spelling), or genuine difficulties with psychomotor speed. The integrated written expression approach I am advocating here considers many aspects of these problems.

This approach works best with a small group, usually no more than six students. It is on-going and long-term, and requires about 30 to 40 minutes per session.

Begin by building some group identity. Have students share some of their personal lives and experiences by talking about them. Tell them they are going to start a "writing file," where they will keep most of their ideas and written work. Show them their file folders. Tell them that the first step is just finding something to write about. It could be anything, but will likely be based on many of the experiences they have just discussed. Brainstorm with the group. Write some of their suggestions on the chalkboard or on a flipchart. Read these ideas over as a group. Then have the students list their own ideas on a sheet of paper from their file. As their teacher, you need not be concerned about any spelling errors they make at this point. The idea is simply to get them going. Ask them to try to list at least three ideas. Each time the writing group meets, they begin by listing more ideas on the same sheet. You will find by doing this that there will be a very long list indeed within a relatively short time. Students usually end up with many more topics than they can possibly write about in a school term. And the topics are of personal interest and concern to them.

The students then devote each writing period to writing and illustrating their stories. An important part of the process is sharing the stories with each other as much as possible. Let the students control some of the process, however, by asking questions from writing to audience and audience to writer. The following questions are very helpful for this purpose:

Questions writers can ask of their listeners:
1. What do you think my story was about?
2. What did you like about my story?
3. Were there any parts of my story which were unclear?
4. Was there any part of my story where I just told what happened without making it clear?
5. Were there any parts of my story which you would like to hear more about?
6. Were there any parts of my story which you found hard to believe even in a make-believe world?
7. Do you have any suggestions to help me with my story?

Questions listeners can ask of the writer:
1. What would you like me to listen and react to? (Ask this before the writer reads the piece aloud.)
2. What part do you like best?
3. What part gave you the most trouble?
4. What did you consider putting in and then decide against?
5. What would you like to change in your next draft?
6. What did you learn from writing this piece?

At this point, students are not going to do much editing. They are primarily listening and reacting to content. Peer editing should be introduced fairly soon in the process, however. Students can be assigned partners, and conferences can be held between writer and partner to help improve the story. Forms should be developed to help guide the conference process.

At some point, you will want to take the students' writing to a "publication" stage. Since the story is going to be "published," there will be a much larger audience (and, usually, greater student motivation); so, at this point, you can become more involved as the "editor" with the student. You will help each student come up with his best product, help with spelling errors, punctuation, etc. Tell the students you will also like to see to it that their stories are typed up (or you may introduce them to the word-processor on your computer, if you have one). They should illustrate their stories and spend time making the pictures colorful and pleasing.

When student and "editor" are satisfied that the product is a personal best, the story should be typed, laminated, and covered. A "library card" should be inserted on the inside back cover, so that other students can check the book out of the in-class library. An About the Author section should appear near the front. You may also include some space where whoever reads the story can make some written comment to the author. Students can share their books and stories with other classes or students as appropriate. They can also put them on display on the bulletin board for a time, or in the hallways of the school. Some teachers I know have gone to the trouble of actually publishing their students' work in printed anthologies.

This approach is highly motivating and works well at any age level (including first grade) and at almost every level of cognitive ability.

Handwriting

Often, students in remedial classes have poor handwriting. As such, a BUD such as this one, which incorporates a self-instructional procedure, can be helpful. These drills should be part of the overall written expression program within the special education classroom. Perhaps a "handwriting contract" such as the one that follows the self-instructional procedures could be used to more actively involve the student in the remedial process.

Self-Instruction Procedure to Improve Handwriting

This procedure is appropriate for students in fourth grade through ninth grade.

Procedure: Each day, the students perform two handwriting assignments. The first consists of 28 single words (within students' meaning and sight vocabulary), handwritten in cursive down two columns on lined paper. The student is to copy each word beside the respective stimulus word.

The second assignment consists of copying a paragraph (of about 125 words), also written in cursive, selected from suitable reading texts or books. The student writes below the paragraph.

Note: Students should do lists only for about five days before any paragraphs are used. When students first start, the word list is likely to be more accurate. As they progress, the paragraphs are likely to be better.

Method: The method consists of two separate procedures—self-instruction and self-correction. Each will be described in detail.

1. Self-Instruction. This consists of following the sequence, and is to be used for both lists and paragraphs:

    a. The student says aloud the word to be written.

    b. The student then says aloud the first syllable.

    c. The student names (aloud) each of the letters in that syllable three times.

    d. The student repeats aloud each letter as it is written down.

    e. The preceding steps are repeated for the remaining syllables.

   The steps can also be listed on a card which the student can tape to his desk or binder.

   At the beginning, the procedure should be explained by the teacher, and the cooperation of the student elicited. The teacher should spend five minutes or so explaining and modeling the sequence. Once the student begins, if he does not self-instruct or does so covertly (whispering or saying silently), the teacher should quickly review the steps and remind the student do do the work aloud. Such prompts should rarely be necessary. Of course, you should compliment the student's good work.

2. Self-Correction. This is really a simple addition which seems to improve the student's work even further. Once the student is used to the self-instruction method (after about a month), then ask him to circle the errors on the previous day's work immediately prior to copying that day's assignment.

   Keeping a progress chart showing percentage correct, as well as a separate chart for speed for both the word lists and paragraphs, is also strongly advised. Goal-setting with the student on a weekly basis can help sustain motivation, as well, and should be incorporated. A contract such as the one shown here can help:

Handwriting Contract

I, _____, need to improve

_____

for the next (# of days or weeks) _____.

I will _____

_____

to help me become a better writer.

Signature _____

Date _____

Duration: This procedure should be used until the student is able to print or write significantly better than when he started. When this point is reached, the procedure should be sufficiently automatic that the student could begin to internalize it without saying the words out loud. This will require a judgment from the teacher, since students should not be pushed to that point until the "out loud" method is thoroughly mastered and proven effective.

Students may require brief reminders to use the method, once it is mastered. If relapses are severe (as they may be over a long break during holidays or summer vacation), then go back to the first step and use the "out loud" method once more.

Adapted from: Kosiewicz, M. M., Hallahan, D.P., Lloyd, J., and Graves, W. 1982. Effects of self-instruction and self-correction procedures on handwriting performance. *Learning Disability Quarterly* (Winter) 5:1, pp. 71-78.

Compensation

Despite everyone's best efforts, students may still have real handwriting difficulties as they progress through school. This poses sometimes serious dilemmas for the classroom teacher and student alike. Often, a vicious circle develops, where the teacher interprets the student's disability as a "refusal" and "stubbornness" on his part. Of course, this is sometimes part of the problem, and flexibility is the key to its solution. For example, if the student can print, but not write, why force writing? If printing is the student's best functional means of communication, then it should be allowed. Karen Clark also suggests that experimentation is important. She says:

> Look at desk surfaces at different heights, or perhaps tilted slightly. Experiment with different textures of paper and with varying types of lines (e.g., color variations on the baseline, paper which has a middle dotted line, large- or small-spaced paper with raised lines). Try different writing instruments (e.g., pen, pencil, felt pen, fine-point versus medium-point widths, and pencil grips).

At the junior high school level especially, students sometimes require options. One of these is typewriting (preferably with an electric typewriter) and/or word processing. The student should receive instruction in proper fingering for the keyboard. For the student with serious handwriting problems, these technological options can be very helpful indeed. A tape recorder should also be considered if the student has difficulty keeping up with note-taking in class. The student can tape the lesson and write up notes for homework when there is more time.

In terms of the sheer volume of written assignments in junior and senior high school, I have found that options and choices given to the student work best. The student should not be excused from the assignment, but be given the choice, if the assignment is particularly lengthy, concerning which format the final product will take.

Of course, organizational skills are frequently lacking in such students. Many schools now offer courses on study skills and note-taking. These can be very helpful to the student, though some students still require much in the way of individual assistance. Things which appear obvious to the adult or even to other students, frequently have to be taught to the special education student.

Homework

Because of poor organizational skills, homework assignments are often not done. This is one area where teachers and students frequently have conflicts. One school psychologist and remedial teacher worked out the following homework organizer, which I have found very useful. It looks like this:

Homework Organizer

Student's Name or Initials	Hand Everything In	Hand Everything In on Time	Name and Date	Numbering	Neatness	Corrections	Preparation (books, pencils, etc.)

Adapted from: Schanzer, S., and Wohlman, J. K. 1979. Homework organizer for teachers and students. *Academic Therapy* (May) 14:5, p. 579.

This form is taped on the teacher's desk weekly, and the names of the students are listed. The first column is checked if the student hands in all required daily assignments. The second column is checked if the student does so without reminders. The "Name and Date" column refers to proper labeling. The rest of the columns are self-explanatory, and can be changed to suit your own needs.

At the end of each week, checks are tallied for each student. Those who earn 90 percent or more of the total possible checks receive certificates and/or free time. Lesser rewards are given to those who achieve a 75 percent level or more.

The authors of this procedure feel the advantages of the homework organizer are its clarity and specificity in identifying which components of assignments are being done to expectations. The homework organizer also places responsibility on the student—where it belongs. (I have found that a self-charting procedure, rather than a teacher-charting one, can also work very well. The authors say:[1]

> We have found that charting can usually be discontinued when the child has received 100 percent of his checks for three or four consecutive weeks. An occasional return to charting for about one week may be necessary for a particular child. Generally, however, the use of this charting system has been very effective in the establishment of good organizational and work habits.

The homework organizer serves several purposes.

First: It clarifies, in an objective manner, the exact components of the homework required of each child, and tells whether or not he has completed them. Thus, global statements about "good" or "bad" homework are eliminated, and help can be given in specific problem areas.

Second: It emphasizes the responsibility of each student for the total preparation of his work and materials.

Third: Finally, it serves as an incentive for the improvement of homework preparation in particular and work habits in general.

The homework organizer is certainly no panacea for this common problem. Students can still find many ways to "sabotage" the system. However, it does provide an important alternative worth trying, especially in the upper elementary grades.

A Word or Two on Spelling

Spelling should be a part of the integrated language arts approach. School psychologists need to be aware of the developmental nature of spelling. What does this imply: It means that:[2]

Learning to spell, like learning to speak, is best viewed as a complex cognitive activity that advances with qualitative changes in the child's state of knowledge. These changes in the state of the child's orthographic knowledge are apparent in the written productions of normally developing children, and, if the preliminary evidence holds up, in most learning-disabled children as well.

It is also important to have the proper perspective on spelling errors. This is because spelling is so "visible" in the writing of students. Sometimes what appear to be bizarre spellings (which lead to equally bizarre hypotheses regarding their causes) are indicative only of a lower level of developmental spelling maturity.

Gentry postulates five developmental stages in spelling which are useful for categorizing spelling errors. The five stages and some examples of each are:[3]

Precommunicative	*Semiphonetic*	*Phonetic*	*Transitional*	*Correct*
BTRSS	MTR	MOSTR	MONSTUR	MONSTER
OPSPS	E	EGL	EGUL	EAGLE
APPO	TP	TIP	TIPE	TYPE
RTAT	A	ATE	EIGHTEE	EIGHTY
BRSTA	UT	UNITID	YOUNIGHTED	UNITED

1. Precommunicative spelling—the student randomly strings together letters with no regard to sound-symbol relationships. RTAT, for example, was supposed to be *eighty*.

2. Semiphonetic spelling—the letters chosen by the student do represent sounds, but only a few sounds are represented. In the foregoing table, E was *eagle* and A was *eighty*.

3. Phonetic spelling—all the phonemes are represented by the student, but the spelling is unconventional. In the foregoing table, ATE for *eighty* is an example.

4. Transitional spelling—here the student comes much closer to mature spelling. Many English conventions and visual memory for a word are apparent. In the foregoing table, EGUL for *eagle* is an example.

5. Correct spelling.

Further, there is some evidence suggesting that students who have difficulty with spelling, particularly the learning-disabled group, are better seen as developmentally delayed rather than being a specific *type* of speller such as "visual," "dysphonetic," etc.[4] Older learning-disabled students, in other words, will likely make spelling errors similar to those of younger students of the same spelling ability.

How does the remedial teacher encourage more mature spelling? What recommendations should a school psychologist make? Recommendations are specific to the individual student, of course; but the following generalizations, which summarize numerous studies done on spelling acquisition in students with learning problems, provide a good starting point:[5]

1. Reduce the number of words to be learned in one week. Poor spellers seem to do better when they are given fewer numbers of words coupled with daily testing. For example, if the weekly list is 10 words, three words per day for three consecutive days is better than all 10 at the same time.

2. Corrective feedback and systematic spelling review are essential (see the following section on imitating children's errors for a good corrective feedback technique). Spelling practice should involve writing the words in isolation and in sentences.

3. Train for transfer by pointing out to the student how one word is spelled like another (e.g., *meat* is similar to *heat*, etc.); and by providing opportunities for words learned in isolation to be used in writing.

For the remedial teacher, the following facts about spelling are also important to know:[6]

1. Good readers can spell about 70 to 100 percent of the words they know by sight. Poor readers who know a word by sight in reading, however, typically can spell only about 50 percent of them correctly.

2. Where there are good sound-symbol relations between phoneme and grapheme, good readers will correctly spell 75 to 100 percent of them correctly. For poor readers, again, only about 50 percent will be spelled correctly.

Other researchers found that there is a sequence-related factor that discriminates good spellers from poor ones. They say:[7]

Good spellers, because they are able to benefit from the redundancies of written and spoken language by having internalized these sequential constraints, are more efficient memorizers. They use strategies . . . of reducing the memory load by means of "grouping" or "chunking."

And:[8]

The "sequential ability" of good spellers, according to the present study, may be defined as the internalization of the redundant stimuli that have been repeatedly associated sequentially . . . . Poor spellers have an inferior gross memory but do not show specific deficiency in the ability to correctly order their responses. In short, one cannot be expected to repeat five digits in correct sequence if one's gross memory extends only to four digits.

Overall, these studies suggest that chunking and grouping are useful strategies for spelling. Therefore, remedial activities which stress phoneme or syllable segmentation are likely to be helpful. Here is one such strategy, prepared by Karen Clark:

1. Pronounce each word carefully.

2. Look carefully at each part of the word as you pronounce it.

3. Chunk the word into two, three, or four parts; example: *Can-ada / Can-a-da / Ca-na-da*. Note: Chunking need not be by syllable. Chunk the word into groups of letters that will be easiest for you to remember.

4. Spell the word, pausing between chunks.

5. Attempt to recall how the word looks, then spell the word.

6. Check to see if you were right. (If not, begin at Step 1.)

7. Cover the word and write it.

8. Check to see if you were right. (If not, begin at Step 1.)

9. Write the word from memory four times.

10. Do not forget to rehearse. Keep practicing the words you know throughout the week.

The research I have just quoted also suggests that bringing the "internal sequence" of the letters in a word to the student's attention could be very useful. This might be accomplished in a number of ways.

One very interesting and quite simple approach that has proved to be very successful with both educable mentally handicapped and learning-disabled students in two separate studies, was simply imitating their errors, then providing the correct response, and then having the student rewrite the word. In doing so, the authors found that correctly spelled words rose to 95-percent accuracy for regularly spelled words, and 85-percent accuracy for irregularly spelled words. This is comparable to a level of normal spellers, as we have seen.

The procedure itself is very simple:[9]

1. On the weekly spelling test, praise the student for each correctly spelled word.

2. For incorrectly spelled words, say something like, "This one is wrong. Here's what you wrote [reproduce student error], and here is the correct spelling." Then have the student write out the correct spelling after you have done it.

3. If you wish, you can highlight or draw a box around the particular letters the student spelled incorrectly.

Notice how the procedure described is teacher-directed. It can be turned into a student-directed activity by having the student correct his own mistakes, putting a check mark next to each correct word. For every incorrect word, the student is to look at the misspelling and copy it. On their own, students can then look at the correct spelling on a card and say it, then turn the card over and write the word, then check it.

An additional cue of circling the incorrect part in red can be added. The student is to say to himself, "This is the part I need to remember." The student then points to the circled part and studies the difference between the correct and incorrect spelling. During practice, they are to point to the difficult parts they have circled on every trial.

This student-directed procedure, with the addition of the cues, produced the best results for students in one study.[10] Commenting on the results of their research, the authors say:[11]

> The results of both experiments show an advantage in imitating the child's error before presenting a correct model, especially in the case of words that are not spelled phonetically. In fact, the results of both experiments suggest that imitation may have a special value primarily in cases where regular phonetic rules do not apply and the child must therefore rely primarily on visual memory. The little time and effort required for such a technique in spelling instruction recommend it. This suggestion is all the more important in light of the folklore that teachers should never show a child the incorrect way of doing anything.

As to *why* the procedure is so effective, these authors propose that it may be due to the fact that it focuses the student's attention on the ways in which the correct spelling differs from the incorrect one. They also suggest it may result from the more general learning principle that, in teaching simple concepts, examples, followed by nonexamples of the concept, work best.

In summary, then, writing and spelling should be part of a meaning-based remedial program, with specific skill-building techniques incorporated within each.

Students with a weakness on the Digit Span subtest of the WISC-R, and/or on Coding, may have particular difficulty. The reasons are not always clear. Sometimes it is because the student does not spontaneously rehearse the digits. Perhaps the student also does not rehearse as he should when learning to spell. Or perhaps the student has weak visual memory, and has difficulty recalling the letter sequences in the words. Or perhaps the student has a weak auditory channel, and has difficulty remembering sound-symbol connections. Whatever the reason, the school psychologist has the task of making sensible recommendations for remediation. These should occur within the context of the total language-immersion environment.

REFERENCES

1. Schanzer, S., and Wohlman, J. 1979. Homework organizer for teachers and students. *Academic Therapy* 14:5, p. 578.
2. Gentry, J. R. 1984. Developmental aspects of learning to spell. *Academic Therapy* 20:1, p. 12.
3. Ibid., pp. 15-16.
4. Hall, R. J. 1984. Orthographic problem-solving. *Academic Therapy* 20:1, pp. 67-75.
5. Gettinger, M. 1984. Applying learning principles to remedial spelling instruction. *Academic Therapy* 20:1, pp. 41-47.
6. Whiting, S. A., and Jarrico, S. 1980. Spelling patterns of normal readers. *Journal of Learning Disabilities* 13:1, pp. 45-47.
7. McLeod, J., and Greenough, P. 1980. The importance of sequencing as an aspect of short-term memory in good and poor spellers. *Journal of Learning Disabilities* 13:5, p. 33.
8. Ibid.
9. Kaufman, J., Hallahan, D., Haas, K., Brame, T., and Boren, R. 1978. Imitating children's errors to improve their spelling performance. *Journal of Learning Disabilities* 11:4, pp. 33-38.
10. Gettinger, M. 1985. Effects of teacher-directed versus student-directed instruction and cues versus no cues for improving spelling performance. *Journal of Applied Behavior Analysis* 18:2, pp. 167-171.
11. Kaufman, J., et al., op. cit., p. 221.

Appendix 5-3

Self-Instructional Training for Arithmetic Operations

Self-instructional training is an attempt to influence and modify the problem-solving orientation of students with learning problems. This is done by guiding the students through the thinking process involved in the task. Usually, this is accomplished through four or five steps:

1. The teacher models the problem-solving process by "thinking out loud."
2. The student does the task, and the teacher prompts by "thinking out loud" as the student does it.
3. The student does the task while "thinking out loud."
4. The student does the task while subvocalizing the process.
5. The student does the task while silently rehearsing.

At the same time, some general problem-solving plan can be modeled.

For example, suppose a student has difficulty with multiplication. The five steps might go like this:

Step 1

Modeling by "thinking out loud." Problem:

$$\begin{array}{r} 63 \\ \times 24 \\ \hline \end{array}$$

"OK. What do I have here? The first thing is just to relax. I can take a deep breath or two to do that. (Pause.) There, that feels better. Now, what is the problem? Oh, I see I have to multiply. I looked carefully at the sign, and it's the multiplication one, so I know I have to do that. I'll keep my mind on multiplying. So, my plan is to work carefully and multiply the numbers in the right order.

"Now, where do I start? First, I multiply 4 x 3. That's 12. Now, I remember I just put the 2 down here and carry the 1. Now, 4 x 6 is 24, plus the 1 that I had to carry, so that's 25. So, my first row is 252. How am I doing? Is it right so far? I could double-check, just to be sure." (Do so, if necessary, "thinking out loud" the whole time.)

"Now, I start the next row. Let me see. 2 x 3 is 6. But where do I put the 6?; Oh yes, right here underneath the 5. I remembered. That's good. Now, 2 x 6 is 12, and I write out 12. So, my second row is 126. Now what? Now I have to add them up. So, first, a 2, now 6 + 5 is 11; but I write 1 and carry 1. Now, 2 + 3 is 5, so I write 5. Finally, 1 in the last column. So my answer is 1,512. I wonder, is that right? I could double-check before I hand it in to the teacher. (Double-check, if necessary.) Yes, I'm sure it's right. I did well. I followed my plan. I worked carefully and kept my mind on the problem."

Step 2

The student does the same problem, and the teacher "thinks out loud."

Step 3

The student does the problem while "thinking out loud" himself.

Step 4

The student does the problem while "whispering" (subvocalizing) the self-instructional statements.

Step 5

The student does the problem while silently rehearsing the statements.

The teacher's role is the "guide at the side" for Steps 2 through 5.

It's important to note that the self-instructional statements of Step 1 have to be modified to the student's level of performance. If the student does not know the multiplication tables, then the teacher has to drop to that level. Teaching the multiplication tables themselves can involve the five-step sequence, too, though not exclusively.

Adapted from: Davis, R. W., and Hajicek, J. O. 1985. Effects of self-instructional training on a mathematics task with severely behaviorally disordered students. *Behavioral Disorders* (August) pp. 275-282.

Appendix 6-1

Reciprocal Teaching: A Strategy for "Word-Callers"

There are many students who are able to decode word lists, but who have more difficulty comprehending reading passages. Reading comprehension depends in turn on at least these four things: (1) adequate decoding skills; (2) "reader-friendly" texts (i.e., the text itself is familiar in terms of syntax, style, clarity, etc.); (3) the student's background of knowledge (schemata) related to the passage; and (4) active *strategies* that enhance understanding and retention.

The technique of reciprocal teaching (which is similar to, but more elaborate than, the request-procedure) may be an important way to help readers start to activate the strategies so necessary in reading comprehension. The idea of reciprocal teaching is to have the student actively assume some teacher roles, though it is the teacher who acts as the "expert coach" on the side. Through modeling and prompting, the student learns eventually to internalize the strategies.

Research results have shown the excellent improvements in reading comprehension on both standardized and classroom-type tests in relatively short periods of time.

Time Required

Thirty minutes per day over four weeks.

Strategies Taught

1. Summarizing prose
2. Asking main ideas
3. Clarifying main ideas and evaluating a passage
4. Predicting

The foregoing strategies have been research-identified as those most important to enhancing the comprehension process.

The method works at any level, even first grade. It can be used in a regular classroom or resource room. It can be modified in that better students can be trained in the technique of reciprocal teaching, and be paired as tutors with weaker students.

Procedure

The authors of this technique write:

When reciprocal teaching is first introduced to the students, it is with some discussion regarding the many reasons why text may difficult to understand, why it is important to have a strategic approach to reading and studying, and how the reciprocal teaching procedure will assist the students to understand and monitor their understanding as they read.

The students are then given an overall description of the procedure, emphasizing that it takes the form of a dialogue or discussion about the text, and that everyone has a turn assuming the role of teacher in this discussion. The students are introduced to the four strategies with the explanation that they will use these strategies to help them lead the discussion. To illustrate, the person who is assuming the role of teacher will first ask a question that they think covers important information that has been read. The other members of the group answer that question and suggest others they may have thought of. The "teacher" then summarizes the information read, points out anything that may have been unclear, and leads the group in clarifying, and finally, predicts the upcoming content.

To ensure a minimal level of competency with the four strategies, the students receive practice at a very fundamental level with each of the strategies. For example, they summarize their favorite movie or television show. They then identify main idea information in brief and simple sentences, and graduate to more complex paragraphs that contain redundant and trivial information. Each strategy receives a day of introduction.

Beginning the Dialogue

After the students have been introduced to each of the strategies, the dialogue begins. For the initial days of instruction, the adult teacher is principally responsible for initiating and sustaining the dialogue. This provides the opportunity for the teacher to provide further instruction and to model the use of the strategies in reading for meaning. The adult teacher may wish to call upon more capable students who will serve as additional models, but it is important that every student participate at noting one fact that they acquired in their reading. This is a beginning. Over time, the teacher, through modeling and instruction, can guide the student toward a more complete summary.

As the students acquire more practice with the dialogue, the teacher consciously tries to impart responsibility for the dialogue to the students while he or she becomes a coach, providing the students with evaluative information regarding the job they are doing, and prompting more and higher levels of participation.

Example of Reciprocal Teaching

The following bit of transcript is taken from a reciprocal teaching lesson that was conducted with first-graders, and is provided for the purpose of illustrating the reciprocal teaching procedure:

Student 1:	My question is, what does the aquanaut need when he goes under water?
Student 2:	A watch.
Student 3:	Flippers.
Student 4:	A belt.
Student 1:	Those are all good answers.
Teacher:	Nice job! I have a question, too. Why does the aquanaut wear a belt; what is so special about it?
Student 3:	It's a heavy belt, and keeps him from floating up to the top again.
Teacher:	Good for you.
Student 1:	For my summary now . . . . This paragraph was about what the aquanauts need to take when they go under the water.
Student 5:	And also about why they need those things.
Student 3:	I think we need to clarify "gear."
Student 6:	That's the special things they need.
Teacher:	Another word for gear in this story might be equipment, the equipment that makes it easier for the aquanauts to do their job.
Student 1:	I don't think I have a prediction to make.

Teacher:	Well, in the story they tell us that there are "many strange and wonderful creatures" that the aquanauts see as they do their work. My prediction is that they will describe some of these creatures. What are some of the strange creatures that you already know about that live in the ocean?
Student 6:	Octopuses.
Student 3:	Whales?
Student 5:	Sharks!
Teacher:	Let's listen and find out. Who will be our teacher?

Another question that the teacher, as the "guide on the side," might ask in the reciprocal teaching context, is: "What questions do you think a teacher might ask?" Or the teacher might prompt, with something like: "Remember, a summary is a shortened version; it doesn't include detail." Or, "If you can't think of a question, you might summarize first."

The teacher should also provide *appropriate feedback*, such as: "Excellent prediction. Let's see if you're right."

The teacher can model by "thinking out loud," if necessary. If the student doesn't quite have it, the teacher could say: "I would summarize by saying . . . ."

The lessons should be continued for about 20 days' teaching time, with *different students taking the role of the teacher each day*.

You may also wish to pre- and posttest your students' reading comprehension scores, as research has shown *very significant* and *sustained* gains in reading comprehension in short periods of time using this method of reciprocal teaching, with emphasis on the four strategies of *summarizing, asking main ideas, clarifying main ideas,* and *predicting*.

Adapted from: Palincsar, A. S., and Brown, A. L. 1984. Reciprocal teaching of comprehension-fostering and comprehension-monitoring activities. *Cognition and Instruction* 1:2, pp. 117-175.

Index

Academic achievement,
    and intelligence, correlation of, 30, 101-102
ACID profile, 38, 145
Anxiety, 11, 58, 78, 129, 178
Arithmetic tasks, 128, 176-178, 257-258
Atmosphere, classroom, 60
Attention, 162
    developmental delay of, 125-127
Attention deficit disorder, 162
Attitudes,
    and reading improvement, 65-68
Attribute learning, 119-120
Attributions of low achievers, 180-181
Auditory Discrimination in Depth (ADD), 77-78, 132
Average range, 43, 223-227

Bannatyne, Alexander, 37, 38, 151
Basic Visual-Motor Association Test, 185
Berkeley Growth Study, 31
Bicognitive Inventory, 180
Bilateral Cooperative Reading Model, 82-88, 104, 163
    and the WISC-R, 83
Bimodal distribution, 15
Binet, Alfred, 9, 16, 21
Blissymbols, 104
Bottom-up and top-down information processing, 22-23, 29-30, 72-73, 75-76, 79, 97, 150
Brain damage, 17, 1098, 167
Burt, Sir Cyril, 21, 27, 97

California Achievement Test, 120
Categorization level of words, 113-114
Children's Embedded Figures Test, 151
Chunking, 131
CMLR (Chicago Mastery Learning Program), 28-29, 30
Conceptual tempo, 149, 160-163
Confidence band (error band), 11-12, 99
Cooper, Shawn, 41, 173, 174, 176, 178, 180, 182-186
Cultural differences, 16, 17
Culture-fair (bias), 9, 15-16
Culture-Free Self-Esteem Inventories, 178
Cylert, 12, 125

DAP (*Draw-A-Person*), 160
Deep relaxation, 60, 69-70, 78, 129, 237-240
Developmental delay in selective attention, 125-127
Deviation method of IQ calculation, 9
Diagnostic Achievement Battery, 178
Distar, 106-108
Distractibility, 39, 79, 125-126, 142
    remediation of, 217-219
Dreikurs, Rudolph, 58

Drug therapy, 125
Dyslexia, 18

Educable Mentally Handicapped Curriculum Guide, Alberta, 103-104
Effectiveness, teacher, 60, 107, 149
    self-rating scales of, 223-227
Embedded Figures Test, 151, 180
Emotional blocking, 59
Emotional disturbance, 17
ENIGMA Program, 115
Enrichment Triad Model, 133, 134
Error of measurement, 12, 18, 26
Expectations of students, 35, 67
Experience-based vocabulary development, 110-112

Facility with numbers, 37, 128, 176-178, 257-258
Factor analysis, 21, 34-36, 97
Factors of the WISC-R, calculation of, 34, 40
Feuerstein, Reuven, 28
Field dependent / independent, 149, 151-155, 180, 183
Field sensitive, 180-181
Frayer model, 79
Freedom from distractibility, 34, 37, 38, 42, 79, 97, 99, 123-132, 159, 176, 184
Frequency distribution, 39
Frost Self-Description Questionnaire, 129
Full Scale IQ score, interpretation of, 99-108
Fuller, Buckminster, 30

Gaussian (normal) distribution, 39
General Adaptation Syndrome, 57-58
Getting Along with Others, 179
Gifted students, 32, 132-143
    Enrichment Triad Model of delivery of service to, 133-134
Gifted underachievers, 135-142
Goddard, Henry, 9
Good Behavior Game Plus Merit, 63
Grade-equivalent scores, 40, 47-48
Group Embedded Figures Test, 151
Guilford, J. P., 22-23

Handwriting, 185, 248-250
Hayes-Binet Test, 15
Head Start Programs, 27
Hearing problems, 15
Hierarchical factor structure of the WISC-R, 97-99
High IQ profile analysis of the WISC-R, 142-143
Homework, 250-252
Human Figure Drawing Test, 138
Hyperactive, 125-126

IAR Scale, 173-179
IEPs, 26, 60, 88, 89-92
Imagery, 131
    and reading comprehension, 213

Impulsivity, 127, 186
Information processing, model of, 130-131
Instrumental Enrichment, 28, 30
Intelligence,
    and A, B, C, definitions of, 32
    and academic achievement, 30, 101-102
    g, 21-22, 97
    group tests of, 9, 15, 32
    heritability of, 24-25
    and occupational status, 100-101
    raising levels of, 25-32
Intervention Assistance Teams, 68

K-ABC Test, 7, 11, 24, 129, 156
Kaufman, Alan, 24, 34-35, 43, 97, 124, 129, 142, 146, 156, 158, 166, 168
Keyword approach to vocabulary development, 116-118
Kiddie QR, 70
Kinetic Family Drawing Test, 138

Labeling students, 18
Language development, 110-123
Language-immersion approach (whole-language), 30, 65, 76, 88, 104, 203-209
Learned helplessness, 180, 233-235
Learning disabilities, 25, 33, 41, 43, 46, 79, 86, 110, 128, 130, 135, 153
    diagnosis of, 48, 50
Learning styles and the WISC-R, 146-168
Letteri, Charles, learning style approach of, 149, 167-168
Level by level analysis of the WISC-R, 97
Lindamood Auditory Conceptualization Test, 132
Lindamood, Pat and Charles, 77
Luria, A. R., 156, 158-159

Matching Familiar Figures Test, 127, 160
McCarthy Scales, 11
Meeker, Mary, 22
Memory, 14, 41-42, 129, 130-132, 146, 162, 169-170, 185
Mental age, 9, 16
Metacomponent / performance component / knowledge component awareness, 28-29, 176-177
Meta-memory, 131-132
Method of loci, 119
Milwaukee Project, 27
Mnemonic strategies, 41, 116-121
Modality preference, 149-151
Multiple meanings of words, 121-123

Nature / nurture controversy, 24
Normal (Gaussian) distribution, 39

Occupational status, and intelligence, 100-101
Orton-Gillingham approach, 75

Parenting styles, 59
Peabody Individual Achievement Test (PIAT), 47-48, 140
Peabody Picture Vocabulary Test (PPVT), 160

Pegword approach to vocabulary development, 118-119
Percentiles, 18, 33, 39-40, 43, 46-48, 99-100, 120
    WISC-R scores, tables of, 51-56
Perceptual organization factor, 34-35, 124, 159
Philosophy for Children, 28-30
Phonemic analysis (manipulation), 37, 76-78, 88, 132
Piaget, Jean, 21, 128
Planning ability, 97, 160-163
Poor facility with numbers, 127-128
Potential, 17, 32-33, 46
Praise and encouragement distinction, 174
Prediction map, 163-166
Profile analysis of very high IQ students, 142-143
Psycholinguistic Model of Reading, 73-76, 104, 1096, 112
    and the WISC-R, 78-82
Psychomotor speed, 37, 85
Pyle, David, 21-22

Rapid naming ability, 181
Reciprocal teaching, 155, 259-261
Reading,
    and attitudes, 65-68
    beginning, 76-78
    Bilateral Cooperative Model of, 82-88
    concept of, 71-73
    imagery, 213
    Psycholinguistic Model of, 73-76
    purposes for, 63-65
    WISC-R patterns, 18-19, 71, 78-79, 83, 102-108, 110, Chapter 6
Rehearsal, 127, 130-131, 221-222
Reinforcement, 61-62, 229-230
Reliability,
    of intelligence scores, 32-33
Renzulli, Joseph, 132-135
    Enrichment Triad Model of, 133-134
Right / left brain, 149, 163-167
Ritalin, 12, 125
Rod and Frame Test, 151
Rogers, Carl, 57
Ross, A. O., 125-127

Sattler, Jerome, 97, 168-171
Self-attributions, 69, 233-235
Self-concept (-esteem), 11, 58, 135, 148,, 178
Self-control procedures, 184, 257-258
Self-efficacy, 68-69
Self-instruction, 127-128, 257-258
Selye, Hans, 57
Semantic-based vocabulary development, 112-116
Sequencing, 38, 170-186
    remediation of, in reading, 215-216
Short-term memory, 130-132
Sight-word acquisition, 221-222
Simultaneous / successive information processing, 37, 129-130, 149, 155-159

and Digit Span, 41
SOI Institute, 22
SQ3R method, 155
Spearman, 21
Spelling, 185, 252-254
Standard error of measurement, 46-47
Stanford-Binet Intelligence Scale, 9-10, 16-17, 26, 32
STEP (Systematic Training for Effective Parenting), 58
Sternberg, Robert, 28, 38
STET (Systematic Training for Effective Teaching), 58
Stress, 57-60, 69
Success in reading, 60-63

Teacher effectiveness, 60, 107, 149
    self-rating scales of, 223-227
Teaching Children Self-Control, 129
Temporal plotting of WISC-R subtests, 186-189
Think-out-loud procedure, 127, 163, 181, 183, 185
Think time, 174-175
Three-factor splits,
    calculation of, 34-36
    of WISC-R scores, 108-110, 123-132, 140, 187
Time and number concepts, 79
TM (Trancendental Meditation) technique, 70
Top-down and bottom-up information processing, 22-23, 29-30, 72-73, 75-76, 79, 97, 150
Trail Making Test, 160-161

VAKT approach, 150
Verbal Comprehension factor, 34, 98-99, 124
Verbal / Performance splits of WISC-R scores, 15, 108-123, 145
Vernon, Dr. Phillip, 21, 24-25, 32, 97
    hierarchical group factor theory, diagram of, 22
Visual handicap, 15
Visualization (imagery),
    and reading, 41, 213
Vitamin therapy, 125
Vocabulary development, 110-123, 178-179
    experience-based strategies of, 110-112
    keyword approach to, 116-118
    pegword approach to, 118-119
    semantic-based approach to, 112-116
Vygotsky, 33

Wait time, 174-175
Wechsler, David, 9, 16, 21, 24
Whole-language (language-immersion) approach, 30, 65, 76, 88, 104, 20--209
WISC-R,
    factors of, 34, 40
    Freedom from distractibility, factor of, 34, 37-38, 42, 79, 97, 99, 123-132, 159, 176, 184
    hierarchical factor structure of, 97-99
    high IQ profile analysis of, 142-143
    learning styles of, 146-168
    level by level analysis of, 97
    norming of, 40

psycholinguistic model of reading, 73-76, 78-82
reliability of, 11
subtests, interpretation of, 12-15
    Bannatyne's recategorization of, 37-38
    calculating relative strengths and weaknesses of, 42-43
temporal plotting of, 186-189
three-factor splits, 108-110, 123-132, 140, 187
    calculation of, 34-36
Verbal / Performance splits of, 108-123, 145

WISC-R Compilation, 26-27
Word banks, 78, 105, 176, 241-243
Words,
    categorization level of, 113-114
Word sorts, 176, 243-245
Writing output, 37, 185
    remediation of, 247-255

Zone of potential difference, 33, 37

The Author

Steve Truch, PhD, is a consulting psychologist who makes his home in Calgary, Alberta, with his wife and two daughters.

He obtained his doctorate in 1978 from the University of Calgary. Prior to that, he was a classroom teacher for several years. He has also had administrative experience in special education, serving as an Assistant Superintendent of Schools for the County of Mountain View. Today, he serves two school districts as their consulting psychologist.

Dr. Truch has extensive experience with administration and interpretation of the WISC-R, and has taught graduate-level courses on individual testing.

Dr. Truch's previous book, *Teacher Burnout and What to Do about It*, published by Academic Therapy Publications (Novato, California) became a national best-seller. His work on stress management is well known, and he continues to conduct many workshops for educators and business people on the topic. He also teaches an in-service course for practicing teachers on self-esteem, and has made many presentations to educators and parents on that topic.

He is active in his community and business and professional life, having served on a number of boards and organizations, including the Association for Children and Adults with Learning Disabilities.

The author enjoys a number of recreational activities, including swimming, tennis, and skiing. He particularly enjoys the family cottage in the summer months.